2011739

C000128821

The Europeanization of Po

In a broadly comparative, historical, and quantitative analysis, this study reveals the unity of European electorates and party systems. Investigating 30 countries in Western and Central-Eastern Europe over 150 years of electoral history, the author shows the existence of common alignments and parallel waves of electoral change across the continent. Europeanization appears through an array of indicators including cross-country deviation measures, uniform swings of votes, and correspondence between national arenas and the European Parliament, as well as in the ideological convergence among parties of the same families. Based on a painstaking analysis of a large wealth of data, the study identifies the supra-national, domestic, and diffusion factors at the origin of Europeanization. Building on previous work on the nationalization of politics, this new study makes the case for Europeanization in historical and electoral perspective and points to the role of left–right in structuring the European party system along ideological rather than territorial lines. In the classical tradition of electoral and party literature, this book sheds a new light on Europe's democracy.

Daniele Caramani is Professor of Comparative Politics at the University of Zurich. He is the author of *Elections in Western Europe since 1815* (2000), *The Nationalization of Politics* (2004), and *Introduction to the Comparative Method with Boolean Algebra* (2009). He edits the textbook *Comparative Politics* (2014, third edition) and regularly publishes in political science journals. He received UNESCO's Stein Rokkan Prize for Comparative Research in the Social Sciences in 2004 and the APSA Data Set Award in 2012.

The Europeanization of Politics

The Formation of a European Electorate
and Party System in Historical Perspective

DANIELE CARAMANI
University of Zurich

CAMBRIDGE
UNIVERSITY PRESS

32 Avenue of the Americas, New York, NY 10013-2473, USA

Cambridge University Press is part of the University of Cambridge.

It furthers the University's mission by disseminating knowledge in the pursuit of education, learning, and research at the highest international levels of excellence.

www.cambridge.org
Information on this title: www.cambridge.org/9781107544604

© Daniele Caramani 2015

This publication is in copyright. Subject to statutory exception and to the provisions of relevant collective licensing agreements, no reproduction of any part may take place without the written permission of Cambridge University Press.

First published 2015

Printed in the United Kingdom by Clays, St Ives plc

A catalogue record for this publication is available from the British Library.

Library of Congress Cataloging in Publication Data
Caramani, Daniele, 1968–
The Europeanization of politics : the formation of a European electorate and party system in historical perspective / Daniele Caramani, University of Zurich, Switzerland. – First [edition].
  pages   cm
Includes bibliographical references and index.
ISBN 978-1-107-11867-6 (hardback) – ISBN 978-1-107-54460-4 (pbk.)
1. Political culture – Europe – History – 19th century.   2. Political culture – Europe – History – 20th century.   3. Political culture – Europe – History – 21st century.   4. Political parties – Europe – History – 19th century.   5. Political parties – Europe – History – 20th century.   6. Political parties – Europe – History – 21st century.   7. Elections – Europe – History – 19th century.   8. Elections – Europe – History – 20th century.   9. Elections – Europe – History – 21st century.   I. Title.
JN10.C37   2015
324.2094–dc23   2015014840

ISBN 978-1-107-11867-6 Hardback
ISBN 978-1-107-54460-4 Paperback

Cambridge University Press has no responsibility for the persistence or accuracy of URLs for external or third-party Internet Web sites referred to in this publication and does not guarantee that any content on such Web sites is, or will remain, accurate or appropriate.

Contents

APPENDICES

Figures

Tables

Preface and Acknowledgements

In 2004 *The Nationalization of Politics* was published, a book on the formation of national electorates and party systems from the 19th century until the present time. In concluding that study I hinted at one possible, natural continuation of that line of work – namely, the analysis of the incipient supra-national integration and formation in Europe of electorates and party systems; their "Europeanization" as it were.

The present volume is a step in that direction. One of the lessons, perhaps the main one, from the nationalization study was that – within the boundaries of the nation-state, the most important political unit over the past two centuries – politics transformed from territorial to functional, with non-territorial dimensions of contestation (first and foremost the left–right class cleavage) overwhelming and replacing territorial ones. With the blurring of national boundaries through European integration, the question is whether today "nationalization at the European level" is taking place along the same lines of nation-states at an earlier stage of political development. Research for this volume, however, soon showed that, rather than "incipient", electorates and party systems have long been "Europeanized".

This study thus investigates in a *long-term and historical perspective* the extent to which electoral politics (voting behaviour, party systems, ideological families) transforms from national, that is centred on national-territorial specificities, to European, with alignments cutting across national units. Similarly to the work on the nationalization of politics, it is an analysis of democratic integration. Europeanization is operationalized as homogeneity among nation-states in Europe and uniform, simultaneous electoral shifts. Further, it is defined in terms of ideological cohesion among parties of the same family across Europe and of vertical correspondence between national and European electoral arenas. Also similarly to the work on nationalization, this study challenges the conventional view that such integration began after

World War II. It shows, on the contrary, that the Europeanization of electoral politics is a much longer process, starting in the 19th century, and that a European electorate has long existed and manifested itself through common and simultaneous "waves" of change across the continent – both Western and Central-Eastern Europe.

Research has been supported by the Swiss National Science Foundation (NCCR programme "Challenges to Democracy in the 21st Century"). Parts of the framework in Chapters 3, 4, and 5 have been presented in Caramani (2012, 2011a, and 2006). An earlier version of Chapter 6 has been published as Camia and Caramani (2012). To finalize the manuscript I have profited from a sabbatical leave from the University of St. Gallen which I spent at the European University Institute, Florence. I am very thankful to both institutions for making it possible. I am very grateful to Ken Kollman, Hanspeter Kriesi, and Gary Marks, as well as the anonymous reviewers, whose comments on the draft manuscript have greatly contributed to improve it. The usual disclaimer about responsibility for omissions and mistakes applies.

Abbreviations

Acronyms for political parties are not listed.

CMP	Comparative Manifesto Project
CV	Coefficient of variability
DN	Dynamic nationalization
EB	Eurobarometers
EMU	European Monetary Union
ENEP	Effective number of electoral parties
ENPP	Effective number of parliamentary parties
EP	European Parliament
ESS	European Social Survey
EU	European Union
F	Fractionalization index
GINI	Gini coefficient (Gini2 controlling for number of units, Gini2W weighted)
IPR	Index adjusted for party size and number of regions
LSQ	Least squared index of disproportionality
MC	Minority coalition
MWC	Minimum winning coalition
OC	Oversized coalition
PR	Proportional representation
P(S)NS	Party (system) nationalization score
QCA	Qualitative comparative analysis
S/DN	Static/distributional nationalization
SPMA	Single-party majority cabinet
SPMI	Single-party minority cabinet
STV	Single transferable vote system
V	Volatility (DV differential volatility, EV European volatility, MV mixed volatility, NV national volatility)

Abbreviations

Introduction

Electoral Integration in Europe

At the turn of the 20th century politics in Bulgaria was dominated by a large liberal party representing the democratically oriented bourgeoisie and independent entrepreneurs who favoured constitutionalism, parliamentarism, and social policies while the main opposition was constituted by conservatives of the richer upper classes and clergy.[1] These elitarian parties ruled until World War I when the challenge coming from the parties of the "masses" – the socialist BRSDP and the agrarian BZNS – became majoritarian among the enfranchised male electorate, only to be in turn overtaken as soon as 1920 by the Bulgarian Communist Party. An unstable party system consisting of socialists, agrarians, and communists on the left and liberals and conservatives on the right managed to survive until 1931 – the last democratic election until the fall of the Berlin Wall in 1989.

Such early party system development is typical of Europe and appears in classical accounts of political parties from Ostrogorski (1902), to Michels (1911), Duverger (1954), and Rokkan (1970), among many others.[2] In fact, it is the story of most European party systems whether of Britain and its early parliamentarism; of Germany, Italy, and Switzerland as they formed from the struggle for national unification; of Austria and Hungary and the other nations emerging from the break-up of multi-national empires in Central and Eastern

---

[1] The liberals eventually split over the "national question", namely whether military action was needed to face the Russian Balkan policy, into various parties among which was the National Party willing to collaborate with the conservatives who favoured negotiations.

[2] The exhaustive 1999 compilation of Stein Rokkan's work is used throughout this volume unless specified otherwise. The date 1970 refers to the seminal collection of previous work *Citizens, Elections, Parties* (Bergen: Universitetforlaget). Ostrogorski's detailed analysis in the first volume focuses on the United Kingdom, long seen as a model of party system development. See also classical volumes by Neumann (1956), Epstein (1961), Dahl (1966), LaPalombara and Weiner (1966), and Sartori (1976).

Europe; or of the Nordic countries. Indeed, a contemporary commentator simply described the Bulgarian party system as "European".[3] The early opposition between liberals and conservatives during the periods of restricted suffrage, the rise of parties of mass mobilization with the extension of franchise to workers and peasants, the division of the left into socialists and communists after the Soviet Revolution of 1917, and even the breakdown of democracy under totalitarian ideologies in the 1930s are common features of electoral history during the constituent phases of European party systems. Such commonality persists in later phases of electoral development after World War II with the rise of Christian democracy and the welfare state,[4] the new politics of emancipatory values eventually leading to green parties, and the radical-right politics of anti-globalization and anti-immigration which have recently manifested in populist parties throughout the continent.[5]

These common patterns stand in stark contrast to the diversity of Europe – a territorially fragmented continent with a variety of institutional orders; separate and conflictual historical trajectories; a complex mosaic of languages, religions, ethnicities, and political cultures; as well as social and economic conditions ranging from modern and open urban centres to backward and secluded rural or mountain regions. Not only have some of these territories dominated others for centuries as in the case of the Habsburg, Ottoman, and Russian Empires or in the British Isles and Scandinavia, some of them achieved statehood centuries before others could reach independence or unification.[6] Which commonality exists between regions geographically, economically, and culturally as far apart as latifundia-dominated southern Italy and the old Hanseatic trading cities and the early industrializing North? How can the politics of a small, inward-looking, Alpine republic like Switzerland be based on similar state–church and left–right divisions as neighbouring colonial and maritime world power France? What makes, as it were, the party system of a "peripheral" south-eastern Balkan country like Bulgaria look so "European"?[7]

---

[3] See Konstantin Irechek in his *Knyazhestvo Balgaria* (1899) quoted in Todorov (2010).

[4] After World War II the acceptance on the part of the Catholic Church of liberal institutions led to a general transformation of former conservative Catholic parties into broader Christian democratic parties (the label stressing the compatibility between Christian values and democratic institutions), often based on the Church's social doctrine. On Christian democracy see Irving (1979) and Kalyvas (1996).

[5] Social movements (feminism, environmentalism, civil rights) and populism can be seen as issued from the post-industrial revolution and the post-national phase. On the former see Inglehart (1977) and on the latter see Betz (1994), Kitschelt (1995), and Kriesi et al. (2008 and 2012).

[6] The different patterns of state formation in Europe are captured by Rokkan's conceptual map (1999). See also Tilly (1975), which includes Rokkan's chapter on state formation and nation-building, although most of it is confined to Western Europe.

[7] The terms *left* and *right* are defined later in this book. For the moment, suffice it to say that under restricted suffrage such terms were used to designate ideological differences between liberals/radicals and conservatives (as in *sinistra* and *destra* in the Italian liberal galaxy before World War I) or

The diversity of Europe's nations in terms of their geopolitics, cultures, and economies can hardly be overstated whether one contrasts the first Atlantic nation-states of the West to land-locked empires of the East, or early civilized Mediterranean peninsulas and their Middle Eastern and North African connections to the civilizations that emerged in the North. The first available literacy statistics show an abyss between Catholic and Protestant areas. Up to the present, radically different juridical traditions and political cultures persist among European countries, as do differences in citizens' attitudes – be it in regard to women's position in society or citizens' relationship to state authority. Past agrarian structures were based on different arrangements of land holding in North-Western Europe and Central-Eastern Europe, and the transformation from agrarian into industrial societies took place at different moments and paces, and with diverging forms. Not only have various European territories had different historical trajectories, but to a large extent they unfolded independent from one another and often in isolation.

Yet something unites this remarkable diversity. In spite of the cultural and socio-economic diversity, and in spite of the variety of historical paths, the democratic electoral struggle is astonishingly similar across Europe. The quest for equality and freedom, and for political and judicial institutions guaranteeing fundamental civil, political, and socio-economic equality and participation is strikingly alike – and parallel. More precisely, the *social divisions* and *cultural conflicts* over the degree of civil, political, and socio-economic equality and freedom are similar: Which civil rights, what degree of inclusion for political rights, how deep the correction of socio-economic inequalities and privileges through state intervention?[8] And what balance between equality and freedom? The fundamental conflicts over which societies divide since the philosophical and technological Enlightenment take forms that are surprisingly common in the most different possible contexts. Since the emergence of a free public sphere (Habermas, 1989) and the "invention" of representative government (Manin, 1997), socio-economic and cultural divisions structure in comparable ways European party systems with similar electoral behaviour on the part of European voters over a century and a half of competitive elections. A story of similarity, rather than diversity.

In spite of this common development, after the early contributions from pioneering political scientists pointing to a deterministic converging path towards mass democracy following the Anglo-Saxon model, often through the lens of the systemic-functionalist paradigm, scholarship turned to the analysis of divergence – first in the outcome of political regimes, second in the type of democracy after the inclusion in the analytical comparison of small countries.[9] Most

---

specific parties (as in the case of the Scandinavian *venstre* and *højre* or *høire*). With mass suffrage and industrialization, *left* becomes synonymous with socialism and republicanism.

[8] This follows Marshall's sequence of civil, political, and social rights (Marshall, 1964).

[9] On the first point see the analysis by Moore (1966) followed by Skocpol (1979) and work in the same line by Rogowski (1989), Luebbert (1991), and Acemoglu and Robinson (2006).

current comparative electoral studies seem to have lost interest in such general and long-term perspectives in favour of an often myopic focus on recent periods. As is argued later in this Introduction, this tendency magnifies "deviations" and "change", which, in a larger perspective, disappear as marginal detail.

However, even a cursory and superficial look at the broad trends of European political history reveals a great amount of commonality and simultaneity, starting with the revolutionary "waves" that wiped across Europe in 1789, 1830, 1848, and after World War I when general representation replaced estates, and parliamentary control was definitively imposed on the ruling elites of the past. This continues with the transformation of electoral politics from an exclusive liberal-conservative elitarian game to "mass and class politics" – with the struggle for universal suffrage and socialism – between the end of the 19th century and the aftermath of World War I, with social policies after World War II and the transformation of left–right in the wake of post-industrialism. No doubt there is variation across countries, as there is with the almost general breakdown of democracy in the 1920s–30s and the imposition of communist rule in Central and Eastern Europe after World War II.[10] Nonetheless, the scope of variation is not such as to dent – let alone discard – the commonality and simultaneity of trends which deserve more careful consideration.[11]

How homogeneous is the development of cleavages, party politics, and electoral behaviour across European countries? How parallel are the electoral waves? To what degree do political ideologies converge over time across different nations? What pattern of increasing similarity emerges across space between East and West and between North and South? And which countries make exception in this landscape? The present investigation paints the broad traits of the European party system, and the main commonalities and deviations from it – historically, comparatively, and quantitatively.

This is less of concern in the present study, which focuses on electoral politics and thus democratic regimes. On the second point see the analyses of Norway by Rokkan (1966), Austria by Lehmbruch (1967), Switzerland by Steiner (1974), Belgium by Lorwin (1966), and the Netherlands by Daalder (1966) and Lijphart (1968) – most of which were published in Dahl's volume *Political Oppositions in Western Democracies* (1966) and systematized in Lijphart's typology between Westminster and consociational democracies (1984).

[10] The divergence represented by the extreme-right challenge to democracy in inter-war Europe (Linz and Stepan, 1978 and Capoccia, 2005) appears only to a limited extend in electoral figures. As Capoccia shows (2005: 10), the peak of anti-system politics in terms of votes (including communists) is reached in Germany and Italy (above 60 per cent), Czechoslovakia and Finland (30 per cent), Belgium and France (20 per cent), while in the remaining countries it remained below 10 per cent.

[11] The Europe-wide nature of these patterns appears in the historical sequence of civil, political, and social rights in Marshall (1964), as well as in the sequence of thresholds of democratization in Rokkan (1999: 244–60). Similarly, Dahl (1971) distinguishes the liberalization and incorporation dimensions. Palmer (1959) speaks forcefully of the "age of democratic revolution", Hobsbawm (1973) of the "age of revolution", and Huntington (1991), Kurzman (1998) and Weyland (2014) of a "wave" of democratization. Indeed, the National Revolution in Rokkan's model is a juncture stressing similarity and simultaneity.

Commonality and simultaneity are the themes of this book. However, the question marks used in the previous paragraph illustrate immediately that a "theme" is not a research question, and that the study presented in this book is an *empirical* research whose goal is to *assess* the degree of commonality and simultaneity and – possibly – its increase over time in a process of convergence, or "Europeanization". Assessing whether Bulgaria and other countries have always been Europeanized (the term *always* meaning since the beginning of competitive parliamentary politics) or if they have become so over a temporal process is an empirical matter. Investigating such questions empirically – that is not simply formulating a "thesis", an "interpretation", or a "reading" of European electoral history – must be done quantitatively. The claim is not that such research questions have never been asked.[12] The claim is that a quantitative investigation of aspects that so far have been left to interpretation, qualitative typologies, and historical accounts has been missing.

This book is not an account of common parallel patterns. It is an analysis based on a range of different operational indicators tailored to quantify dimensions of "Europeanization" – both across space and over time. While many aspects look familiar in the following quantitative analysis – the "internal" nature of party systems under restricted suffrage, the entry of "external" mass parties with enfranchisement, the "freezing" of party systems with full enfranchisement and PR after World War I – a quantitative measurement of commonality versus "deviation" from the European pattern has never been carried out systematically. This is one of the contributions this book intends to make. Europeanization, in other words, is a variable.

These questions are impellent in our time with growing debates around a truly Europe-wide democracy at the level of the European Union (EU). Europe-wide party alignments, analogous attitudes and preferences among voters from different countries over common issues and problems, and uniform, simultaneous electoral change in different places (in favour or against given policies) provide an extraordinarily strong case for the possibility of supra-national representation. There is still a mismatch between national democratic control and supra-national decision making with a directly elected European Parliament (EP) whose powers and role – especially the control of the executive – remain limited. Responsiveness and accountability are diminished if voters are divided territorially along segmented electorates and reacting to "local", or even national, issues only. As is argued in the Conclusion, the Europe-wide nature of partisan alignments is a precondition for the enhancement of democratic representation in Europe.[13]

---

[12] For one, Stein Rokkan's model of party systems development is probably entirely devoted to this question.

[13] From Burke onwards writings on representation pointed to the negative effects on representation of institutions and socio-economic structures that territorially fragment electorates, including, among other things, small constituencies, majoritarian electoral systems, and territorial cleavages.

Methodologically, the analysis of Europeanization should therefore not be limited to recent periods, nor to the start of European integration proper in the 1950s. One of the claims this book makes is that Europe was "Europeanized" long before the EU. This claim can only be validated by an *empirical analysis starting roughly 150 years back*, that is (and allowing for differences between countries) since the transition to representative democracy, competitive elections, and the structuration of modern party systems – which often took place in concomitance with state formation and nation-building.[14] Temporally, the analysis covers the crucial steps of European electoral development, be it the introduction of universal suffrage and proportional representation (PR) or the technological transformation of communication and media systems. The analysis covers the whole of Europe (Western and Central-Eastern Europe, as well as Southern Europe and the Mediterranean islands), leaving aside only the most problematic cases of longitudinal data availability, namely Yugoslavia and most of its successor states.[15]

Theoretically, the investigation is based on the blueprint provided by the *theory of the "nationalization of politics"* and by the large amount of research carried out in the wake of macro-historical and comparative work.[16] This theory provides the main indicators on which the measurement of Europeanization is based (Chapters 3 and 4) and prepares the ground to develop complementary ones (Chapters 5, 6, and 7) in Part II. In particular, work on European nation-states in a historical perspective has shown that processes of homogenization of party support between different territorial units within countries – regions, provinces, constituencies – resulted in nationally integrated electorates. The decisive push for nationalization from the mid-19th century until the 1920s consisted of the territorial homogenization of electoral politics leading to the transition from territorial to functional politics in Europe's nation-states. This process – albeit to different degrees in different countries – characterizes all European countries. What the present investigation attempts is the transfer of *"nationalization"* to *"Europeanization"* and treating Europe as one large, possibly integrating (or already integrated), electorate and party system – in short,

[14] These aspects are combined in Rokkan's concept of National Revolution (see Chapter 2), referring to the formation of a national citizenship with horizontal cross-local ties enhanced by linguistic homogenization (nation-building); parliamentarism; individual civil and voting rights as well as social rights (democratization); and the construction of a centralized and secular state (state formation).

[15] The analysis excludes Russia and Turkey on grounds of both the difficulty of carrying out long-term quantitative analysis and the internal contention of being part of Europe. Such exclusion does not imply that commonalities with these countries are absent, but in both cases one main dimension of contestation is the relationship to the "West".

[16] The literature on nationalization has taken off following two books: Caramani (2004) and Chhibber and Kollman (2004). None of the subsequent papers or books, however, takes a historical perspective. For references on nationalization work see Chapters 1 and 3. First adaptations of nationalization to Europeanization are provided in Caramani (2006; 2011a; 2012) and Camia and Caramani (2012).

"nationalization at the European level". This study on Europeanization may therefore be labelled a study of *nationalization processes at the Europe-wide level* or a *"European nationalization"*. The exact transfer of the theory, its conceptual categories and operationalization – as well as the development of new indicators – are described in Chapter 1.

The shift from nationalization to Europeanization is a logical step to take in the light of the formation of a new political system, something that recent interpretations have likened to phases of state formation and democratic structuration at the national level. Indeed, as reviewed in Chapter 1, a growing quantity of work on European integration takes a comparative politics approach.[17] The adaptation of nationalization to Europeanization follows this same model. Furthermore, the shift from nationalization to Europeanization is a logical step in the light of work on post-national and de-nationalizing politics. Too often this phrase has meant re-territorialization of politics at the national level. In fact, institutional and economic regionalization did not lead to significant regionalism in electoral politics. De-nationalization through the removal and unbundling of national boundaries must instead be interpreted as a process of "re-territorialization" at the European level. The question thus becomes whether supra-national integration leads to *territorial politics at a higher level*, namely over diverging national interests and identities within a new polity in Europe, and *whether such "territoriality" will be or has been removed in a process of Europeanization*. How strong is the territorial dimension at the European level? Has it become weaker (or stronger) in recent decades as a consequence of European integration, or does it follow previously initiated long-term processes of Europe-wide convergence?[18]

The adaptation of nationalization to the question of Europeanization faces the issue that, while the study of the former could be carried out on several political units – and thus allows for truly comparative analysis – the study of the latter relies on an "N = 1". There is only one such case. Nationalization varies across countries as well as over time. Europeanization, on the other hand, varies over time and the cross-country comparison must be addressed in terms of deviations from a general pattern. The Conclusion provides a macro-comparison between levels of Europeanization and levels

---

[17] This work adapts concepts and models from the work of Deutsch (1953), Hirschman (1970), and Rokkan mostly (see Chapter 1 in Caramani, 2004). The first attempt is Hix (1994) on the EP. Schmitter (2000) mentions the impact of cleavages of the past on new Europe-wide alignments, as do Marks and Wilson (2000) and Marks and Steenbergen (2002) on "cleavage residues". For a systematization of concepts and dimensions of the EU as a new integrating political system, see Bartolini (2005). Jérôme, Jérôme, and Lewis-Beck (2006) provide an analysis of Europe as "one nation".

[18] De-nationalization is here understood as globalization and post-nationalization (Zürn, 1998). One of the first formulations about the reappearance of the territorial dimension in Europe is Kohler-Koch (1998). For approaches based on territorial diversity caused by the enlargement to Central and East Europe, see Zielonka (2002).

of nationalization in nation-states (European ones but also the United States and India). Yet the perspective adopted in this work privileges commonality and simultaneity over differences across space and in timing. As mentioned, especially after Rokkan's powerful macro-sociological "fresco" of Europe, the focus has been on variation and deviation. The unity of European political development, its similarity, and parallel trends were moved, at best, to the background and, in most cases, disappeared totally. Every country became an exception until only exceptions were left and the picture became so cluttered that the broad traits of party systems disappeared.[19] Even the most general electoral phenomena – class politics and workers' mobilization through unions and parties after the Industrial Revolution – was analyzed in terms of variation.[20] Unlike classical sociologists and historians analyzing the general transformation of society in the 19th century, more recent scholars dropped generality and simultaneity from the picture.[21]

The present study intends to re-establish the balance between commonality and variation, between generality and deviation. Indeed, the main results of the various analyses that follow in this volume complement the ones stressed in past work by pointing to *commonality and simultaneity, similarity across space and convergence over time*. This sheds a different light on the development of party systems in Europe – a light indeed other than the one we are so used to. In this light, European electorates and party systems are homogeneous and have been so for a long time – namely since the very first decades after the democratic transition in the mid-19th century.

The argument of this book is that *Europe is Europeanized* and has been *Europeanized for a long time*, namely since the very beginning of parliamentary representative democracy and the birth of competitive elections. National party systems are similar in their format and convergence over time (*dimension of homogeneity*). They change simultaneously at critical junctures through Europe-wide swings (*dimension of uniformity*). They are homogenous horizontally but also vertically across the different levels of national and supra-national electoral arenas (*dimension of correspondence*). There is a great deal of similarity in the content of the programmes and policies among parties of the same family across different countries (*dimension of cohesion*). Finally, cabinet composition and their policy programmes are increasingly similar (*dimension of closure*).

---

[19] The cleavage model on which this is based is best found in Rokkan (1999: 284–92 and 320–39, which includes the famous essay by Lipset and Rokkan, 1967) and Flora (1999: 40–9). For a summary of Rokkan's work see also Caramani (2011b; 2014).

[20] This is the case of Bartolini's encompassing study of the class cleavage and the rise of socialism in Europe (2000).

[21] Besides the mentioned work on the revolutionary age of the 19th century, the very birth of sociology can be linked to that general transition: from agrarian to industrial economy, from rural community to urban society, from local to national identity and communication networks, from caste- to class-based social structures, and from autocratic to democratic political systems.

As will become clear, the picture is more nuanced than this. Yet the core finding is that Europe is Europeanized and that national electorates and party systems have surprisingly a great deal in common. Further, electorates and party systems were "Europeanized" long before the process of European integration started in the 1950s. The Europeanization of national electorates and party systems can also be placed before the technological revolution of communication and media after World War II. Hence the title of this Introduction: integration in Europe, not European integration, signalling that there was Europeanization *before* the EU even if this process did not come to a halt after 1945.

The research design on which this conclusion is based includes 30 countries over a period of time starting in the mid-19th century for those countries that were democratic at the time. This wealth of data assembled in a new data set allows for the quantitative measurement of Europeanization based on indicators relating to the *format of party systems* (and cabinet composition). The focus on morphology is justified by the necessity to look before and after major thresholds of democratization in the 19th century up to World War I. Analyzing periods since World War II, however, offers the possibility to use indicators relating to the *contents of party systems* and the ideological placement of parties and voters, preferences and attitudes, and policy programmes. The data set has therefore been complemented by different types of data in a multi-pronged strategy (sources are given in the single chapters and in Appendix 6):

- *Electoral data*: These data include the collection of *national elections* with a classification of each party into 25 families, and European elections from 1979, or later depending on the data of EU accession. These data are used for the indicators of *homogeneity* in Chapter 3, *uniformity* in Chapter 4, and *correspondence* in Chapter 5.[22]
- *Party manifesto data*: These data include the Comparative Manifesto Project (CMP) collection that has been linked to electoral data starting in 1945 and ending with the most recent data available in the online update of the CMP (at the moment of analysis). These data are used for the indicators of *cohesion* among party programmes within the same family ("elite" level) in Chapter 6 and of *closure* among cabinet partners in Chapter 7.
- *Survey data*: These data include various rounds of Eurobarometers for the period 1973–2000/2 and European Social Surveys for the period after 2002. These data are used for the indicator of *cohesion* among electorates of parties belonging to the same party family in different countries ("mass" level) in Chapter 6.
- *Cabinet composition data*: These data include the ParlGov data on the executives and coalitions from 1945 until 2010 for all countries on the

---

[22] The collection starts with the first competitive election for each country up to the most recent one by 2012 and includes for each election all parties receiving at least 1 per cent of the votes nationwide.

basis of which *cabinet composition* and *type of coalition* have been calculated. These data are used for the indicator of *closure* among executives in
Chapter 7.

This book distinguishes three groups of factors to explain electoral
Europeanization. First, *supra-national factors* (such as the outcomes of World
War II and the Cold War or European integration) that have a common and
similar impact on all national party systems and cause their convergence.
Second, *within-national factors* (such as democratization and the Industrial
Revolution or the rise of emancipative values), that is socio-economic and
political change taking place in most countries in a similar way and thus having a similar impact on party systems. Third, *trans-national factors* (such as the
spread of fascism, the Soviet Revolution, the adoption of Western programmes
in Central and Eastern Europe after 1989, or the populist wave) whereby convergence is caused by diffusion. Chapter 8 assesses the impact of each group
of factors on the different dimensions of Europeanization in a historical and
mass-electoral perspective.

As becomes clear in the chapters in Part II of this book, *left–right* and the
party families that make up most of this dimension (socialists, liberals, and
conservatives, as well as Christian democrats) play a crucial role in explaining Europeanization. If one asks what creates the homogeneity of party systems and the uniformity of shifts over time, or if one wonders which traits
account for the correspondence between national and EP electoral levels, or if
one examines in what respect cabinet composition is similar, evidence invari-
ably points to *left–right as a feature of commonality in Europe*. This central
dimension of major social divisions and cultural conflicts over civil, political,
and socio-economic rights is the most important dimension across all national
systems as well as in the EP. At the same time, it is the most homogenous
dimension across countries and the one along which the largest simultaneous
waves of electoral change take place historically.

Brought about by supra-, within-, or trans-national factors, the conflict
over the (re-) distribution of resources and the nature of and participation
in the national polity quickly imposes itself in all European systems, making
them very similar. Left–right overwhelms and, soon after democratization, dis-
cards cultural factors such as ethnicity, language, and even religion, as well
as pre-industrial factors such as agrarian politics – precisely the factors that
genetic models based on cleavage structures identified as sources of diversity
in Europe. This study shows the irrelevance of these factors and points to left–
right as the dominant dimension everywhere, and thus as a *factor of similarity
and commonality*. Cultural and pre-industrial dimensions of party mobilization are indeed factors of diversification in Europe. Quantitative measurement,
however, shows how marginal this differentiation turns out to be. None of
the "deviations" are quantitatively strong enough to alter the fundamental
similarity of Europe given by left–right. And even the deviations that can be

observed originate primarily from variations on left–right itself rather than from ethno-linguistic, religious, or agrarian factors.

Left–right is a formidable factor of integration, at both the national and European levels, because of the functional nature of this alignment.[23] The division over left–right (issues, interests, and values) is not a territorial division but, on the contrary, a division between social groups *cutting-across territorial units*, be it regions, localities, or nation-states. As the findings in this book suggest, European citizens are not opposed along national fronts (Germans vs. French vs. British, etc.) but rather along partisan and ideological ones, based on their positions in the economy and their values. Party ideologies are very similar across countries, as is the strength of these parties across borders. Using the famous phrase by Marquant, the *Europe des partis*, rather than the *Europe des patries*, is already a reality.[24] Contrary to what is often thought, it has been like that since the 19th century.

The two bloodiest wars in history were fought between European nations. This has left an almost indelible image of disunity. And yet alternative images exist and have been framed in terms of "European civil war" – not *between* but *within*.[25] Such a division is between groups of a same nation, not simply among nations. Italians fought Italians in 1930s Spain (as did Germans), and Frenchmen fought Frenchmen during the Vichy regime – as happened in most European countries during the period of the resistance. These conflicts were ideological. They cut across national borders. Further back in time oppositions in Europe included various forms of cultural clashes between state and Church and other *Kulturkämpfe*, during and after the Enlightenment, and between what was generally referred to as *progress* versus *reaction*. In 19th-century Europe the cross-country international contacts between nationalist elites from different countries were frequent, as were those between leaders of the international workers' movement later on.[26] With industrialization, with the national, liberal, and secular state, with welfare redistribution policies, and with the rise of the "electoral age", this role has been played by the left–right cleavage and the political parties that emerged from it. This is not to say that national differences and specificities do not exist or matter. Simply, it is worthwhile also

---

[23] The study on the nationalization of politics had already stressed the role of left–right in integrating national electorates and party systems by replacing highly territorial cleavages based on ethno-linguistic, religious, and agrarian factors through a functional cleavage cutting across localities. In a way, therefore, nationalization can be seen as the precondition for Europe-wide integration, insofar as national processes imposed left–right everywhere in a similar way.

[24] This conclusion is supported by findings of party cohesion among MEPs (Hix, Noury, and Roland, 2007) who vote increasingly along party lines rather than according to their nationalities. This approach is here applied at the level of mass electorates and party systems.

[25] See Hobsbawm (1994) and, even more generally, Schumpeter (1962) on the opposition between totalitarianism and liberalism.

[26] As an example take the contacts between "Mazzinian" nationalists discussed in LaPalombara and Weiner (1966: 13).

investigating aspects of unity in Europe, a unity that *does not mean absence of conflict but rather conflict common to all parts of Europe*, which opposes similar social and ideological groups and whose fault lines are not defined territorially. This is the theme of Chapter 8 in Part III.

This book is structured in three parts. Part I includes the theoretical framework (Chapter 1) and methodological design with data trends in Europe since the transition to representative democracy in the 19th century (Chapter 2). Given the variety of indicators and methods, only the general features of the research design are mentioned, with more details in the various chapters (and the Appendix). Part II includes the analysis of the dimensions and indicators of Europeanization: homogeneity, uniformity, correspondence, cohesion, and closure (Chapters 3–7). In Part III the sources of Europeanization are investigated in terms of three main mechanisms: supra-, within-, and trans-national factors (Chapter 8). The Conclusion provides a comparison between Europeanization and nationalization in Europe, the United States, and India, together with a discussion on the normative implications of the findings for representation and democracy in Europe.

PART I

FRAMEWORK

I

Theoretical Framework

Europeanization in Historical Perspective

Introduction

The task of this chapter is to identify the dimensions of Europeanization from a broad comparative and historical perspective. Concepts from various integration theories are relevant for an encompassing view of Europeanization. This chapter attempts to bring them together to derive indicators for assessing the degree to which Europeanization processes have taken place over the past 150 years. As "Europeanization" is analyzed historically and intended as referring to "nationalization" processes on a vaster scale, the definition given in this book as *long-term convergence between national electorates and party systems in Europe* is unavoidably broader as well as focussed differently than most definitions.[1]

This definition is broader first of all in temporal terms as it views Europeanization as a process not necessarily linked to European integration. Convergence between national electorates and party systems may be independent of the constitution of a supra-national level of governance (institutions and policies) and therefore may have taken place *before* European integration since the 1960s. This definition is broader also insofar as convergence is not necessarily related to EU issues or to a cleavage on European integration. It is therefore distinct from "EU-ization". The long-term convergence of electorates and party systems may be detected in *issues other than EU integration*, for example in how environmental issues structure publics in European countries, or in similar anti-immigrant reactions to globalization. This definition is broader, finally, because the *causes of Europeanization are identified in*

---

[1] *Europeanization* is a term usually related to a specific research field of the EU on the impact of European integration on member-states and "third countries". The top-down perspective on the consequences of integration for member-states follows the initial focus on the process of integration through neo-functionalism and inter-governmentalism mainly.

factors other than EU integration only. While centralization of competences and coordination of policies at the European level clearly have an impact on the degree to which electorates and party systems homogenize over time, this book includes other factors as well.[2]

Additionally, this definition of Europeanization has a different focus. The focus of this study is on the *structuring of mass politics* and views Europeanization from an *electoral perspective*. It is therefore different from work on the impact of EU governance on national policies and administrative structures. While there is work on electorates and party systems in a "European integration perspective", it is usually a literature limited to the European question, that is favourable versus unfavourable views of integration as expressed by voters either in referenda or through anti-Europe parties, or in the position established parties take on Europe (i.e. Europeanization as politicization of the cleavage on European integration). Finally, the definition of Europeanization as a long-term process takes into account not only *top-down vertical processes* (for example, the impact of integrated monetary policies on party programmes) or *bottom-up vertical processes* (the formation of party groups in the EP and European party federations), but also *horizontal processes* in the form of factors leading to convergence located at the national level but that are similar in the various countries, or through diffusion.

The theoretical framework in this chapter tackles the Europeanization of *electorates and party systems as caused by a variety of factors through both vertical and horizontal processes.* The framework must also account for periods of convergence prior to European integration. In this sense, it should guide an analysis of Europeanization *beyond and before* EU integration. The simplicity of a definition in terms of convergence is justified – as will be argued later in this chapter – as it is a valid indicator of a variety of dimensions.

Approaches to Europeanization

Work on Europeanization has focussed on the vertical dimension of integration, either top-down or bottom-up. What follows in this section discusses four main approaches: (1) policies, regulations, and administrative structures; (2) the EU as a dimension of contestation; (3) cross-national policy transfers; (4) European party federations and parliamentary groups in the EP. The goal is to extract from each the elements to build a framework for the analysis of the Europeanization of electoral politics. The horizontal dimension is discussed in the next section.

---

[2] To take a recent example, the breakdown of communist regimes in Central and Eastern Europe has had a huge impact on the degree to which countries have been affected similarly and, consequently, converged towards similar structures.

The EU's Impact on National Policies and Administrative Structures

The typical definition of Europeanization – one that rarely applies to studies on elections and party systems – is that of the change in national policies and administrative structures under the impact of European integration, that is the formation of a supra-national level of governance, the centralization and integration of policies in various fields, and the transfer of legislative competences to the EU. This "EU studies" definition in terms of the impact of the EU on countries applies to member-states as well as to "third countries" in its more or less direct neighbourhood, but also to systems, such as China, in search of legitimate and cost-effective regulatory standards.[3]

This type of Europeanization takes the form of spread of standards and regulations from the European centre. While geographically such spread emanates from "Brussels" (as the locus of EU institutions) towards member-states and their peripheries, these are vertical, top-down processes whereby countries adopt or adapt to standards set by a supra-national level of governance.[4] There exists a variety of mechanisms through which Europeanization exerts its influence, with general distinctions between a "logic of consequences" (sanctions and rewards) and "logic of appropriateness" (social learning) or more specific ones between modes of regulatory policies such as compliance, competition, and communication.[5] A particularly useful distinction applicable to the Europeanization of electorates and party systems is the one proposed by Diez, Stetter, and Albert (2006) between two types of impact. First, *EU-driven and specific impact (direct impact)*. The impact is driven by clear goals and supported by sanction-and-reward mechanisms. The role of agency is present through concrete measures (financial and legislative). Second, *non-driven and generic impact (indirect impact)*. The impact is not specifically intended, is not supported by sanction-and-reward mechanisms, and does not necessarily require the role of agency.

The specificity of the Europeanization of electorates and party systems appears in applying this distinction: the EU has much more an indirect than a direct impact. This does not mean that a direct impact of the EU on national electorates and party systems cannot exist. As the literature on "conditionality" shows, a direct impact is conceivable in the sphere of party politics even if, so far, political conditionality has rather been applied since the early 1990s to

---

[3] While most research has dealt with Europeanization of member-states (Knill, 2001), a great deal of work has appeared on "Europeanization beyond the EU" (Schimmelfennig, 2007), for example in Eastern Europe (Bauer, Knill, and Pitschel, 2007; Knill and Lenschow, 2005; Lavenex, 2004; Schimmelfennig and Sedelmeier, 2005), in the Mediterranean area (Joffé, 2001), or in a non-member-state such as Switzerland (Sciarini, Fischer, and Nicolet, 2004).

[4] This definition of Europeanization is not very different from the one given to the adoption in African post-colonial states of constitutions inspired to or imposed by European powers (Gagnon, 2012).

[5] The two logics of consequences and appropriateness were initially formulated by March and Olsen (1989). Similar mechanisms apply also to processes of supra-national integration outside Europe.

broader issues of democracy, human rights, rule of law (as essential elements of agreements with the EU), and, later, good governance. Other examples of a direct impact include rather different strategies on the part of the EU such as civil society support and socialization, both oriented at strengthening political organizations, NGOs, and the media.[6]

Yet the scope for direct impact on electorates and party systems is limited. First, it applies foremost to "third countries" (Turkey and Yugoslavia's successor states) aiming at membership and on whom conditionality provides more leverage. Second, political conditionality has never included formal or content elements: (1) formally, such effects could imply the adoption of standards of political rights (franchise), rules for campaigns, party finances, communication through public and private media, or the creation of political parties; (2) content-wise, the impact of the EU has never gone beyond condemnations and there are no EU regulations against the formation of parties with, say, fascist or anti-Semitic ideologies. Third, and more important, this is very far away from having an impact on electoral competition, altering it, or even constraining it. There is no direct impact to speak of in the sphere of electorates and party systems significantly determining alignments and oppositions, or limiting the room for manoeuvre in the strategies of single parties.[7]

When it comes to the Europeanization of electorates and party systems the type of impact one must consider is therefore clearly the indirect/generic one. In addition, this allows one to include the impact of factors such as – to stay with the EU case – the constraints coming from the European Monetary Union (EMU) or – if one goes beyond the EU case as this book intends to – the breakdown of communist regimes in Central and Eastern Europe in 1989. The example of the EMU is illustrative of how European integration may have a general impact on national structures and how this leads to cross-national convergence. It is an example of literature on Europeanization that provides a systematic *evaluation of the ways European integration affects states*. The literature on Europeanization generally – and that on the EMU in particular – is not only able to account for the generic impact on nation-states but is also concerned with *cross-national convergence in Europe* resulting from the narrowing of the policy alternatives for national actors (be it parties or governments) caused, on one hand, by economic and monetary integration and the loss of various policy instruments and, on the other hand, by the "internalization" of external economic imperatives.[8]

---

[6] On political conditionality specifically, see Schimmelfennig (2005), Schimmelfennig and Sedelmeier (2004), and Youngs (2001).

[7] An interesting case is the pressure exercised by the EU on the Austrian coalition government between the Austrian People's Party and the extreme right-wing FPÖ in 2000. The discrimination of ethnic minorities (such as Rom communities) in Eastern Europe belongs more to the sphere of human rights than electoral competition.

[8] On convergence see in particular Bennett (1991), Börzel (1999), and Knill (2005). See also Featherstone and Radaelli (2003), Green-Cowles, Caporaso, and Risse (2001), and Radaelli (2000). More specifically on the EMU see the introduction to the volume edited by Dyson (2002).

This broader set of consequences of European integration links up directly with the next approach.

Europe as a Dimension of Contestation

An approach broadening the top-down impact of the formation of the EU supra-national level of governance is the one looking at national cleavage systems. This approach is not limited to direct and specific impacts. In addition, it looks at influences beyond policies and administrative structures. Finally, it tackles the question of change at the level of electorates and party systems and allows for a historical perspective.

The main contribution from this approach is to consider the impact of the formation of a supra-national level of governance on national patterns of contestation.[9] First, such an impact is visible at the level of party systems, with a new dimension of contestation imposing itself at the national level – namely, a pro/anti-European integration sovereignty dimension. Second, the impact is visible in direct votes on EU accession and treaty reforms in referenda. In both national party arenas and direct democracy, the push towards the widening and deepening of integration has generated new oppositions and one main cleavage alongside established ones (as described by national cleavage models), and in particular the left–right dimension.

The impact of the EU on national party systems is part of a broader background of changing alignments in European countries analyzed since the 1980s.[10] The impact of the EU manifests itself in two ways: first in the emergence of new parties; second in the position on the pro/anti-Europe issue of established parties. While there seems to be agreement that one of the main new actors since the 1980s (alongside the greens) is the populist right, it is still debated whether these parties are primarily anti-European parties or if Euro-scepticism is part of their opposition to more general threats coming from globalizing labour markets and the blurring of economic boundaries.[11] The usefulness of such a line of research is that, ultimately, it points to the EU as a supra-national factor of change overarching national party systems and thus possibly yielding to cross-national convergence. As will appear in Chapters 3 and 4, the sceptical response to European integration from such parties represents a factor of homogeneity of European party systems and of

---

[9] Note that, unlike the distinction sketched earlier, Bartolini defines such an impact as "direct" rather than indirect (2005: 359).

[10] New cleavages and the transformation of old ones were first the object of the analysis of the politicization of post-materialism as a new dimension since the pioneering work of Inglehart (1977). Comparative and long-term analyses of the (in)stability of cleavage structures have been produced by Bartolini and Mair (1990), Crewe and Denver (1985), Dalton, Flanagan, and Beck (1984), and Franklin, Mackie, and Valen (1992), among others.

[11] On this point see Mair (2000). On the early rise of extreme-right populist parties see Betz (1994), Ignazi (2003), and Kitschelt (1995). On Euro-scepticism as an ideological component of a variety of parties see Taggart (1998).

common shifts of the electorate in a broad historical context – albeit a weak one in comparison to others.

Where cleavage theory appears more neatly is in the positioning on the EU integration issue by established parties. A group of authors has put forward the hypothesis that the process of European integration has given rise to a new cleavage within national party systems, and that such a cleavage has modified both the meaning of historical ones (left–right in particular) and parties' ideologies. Furthermore, this research has addressed the relationship between cleavages, with the hypothesis that the left–right placement of parties explains views on European integration.[12] These studies confirm that while left parties (labour, socialists, social democrats) have notoriously opposed further economic integration because of the fear it would undermine welfare and Keynesian economic policies, as well as the possibility to conduct monetary policy, at the same time they came to favour political integration as a solution to the loss of policy instruments at the national level. The position of social democrats in this regard is particularly important as European integration is viewed as a neo-liberal and, in part, a Christian democratic project.[13]

The general impact of European integration on national party systems is thus one of modification of the ideological space in which a predominant left–right dimension is complemented by a sovereignty dimension of contestation between "nationalism" and "supra-nationalism". While initially empirical results pointed to a high degree of overlap between the two dimensions (the left side of the axis being more anti-European while the liberal right was more pro-European), with the ideological change of social democrats, who saw Europe as the possibility to conduct economic policy once integration had progressed enough, the two dimensions became "orthogonal" with the extremes of the left–right axis opposed to integration for either economic or cultural reasons, but in both cases through claims from the "losers of integration". Chapters 6 and 7 follow this line of analysis and test the hypothesis that not only has the European issue modified national ideological spaces, but also that it has made them more similar. It does so by covering the whole 1945–2010 period.[14]

The merit of this top-down approach to the impact of the EU on national political systems is that it provides a framework for an indirect and generic impact, beyond the sphere of policies and administrative structures, and can address transformations at the level of mass politics. Yet it is an approach that

[12] The seminal article by Marks and Wilson (2000) on "The Past in the Present" has been accompanied by a number of highly valuable contributions in part based on expert surveys (see Chapter 5): Hooghe and Marks (2001, in particular chapters 8 and 10), Marks and Steenbergen (2002), and Marks, Wilson, and Ray (2002).

[13] The position of socialist parties on Europe was first analyzed by Ladrech (1993). See also Holmes and Lightfoot (2011), Poguntke et al. (2007), and van dem Berge and Poguntke (2013).

[14] One of the shortcomings of expert surveys is the short period of time covered by the data. For this reason the analyses in Chapters 6 and 7 are based on party manifestos.

limits itself to the impact of the EU uniquely.[15] Europeanization as defined in this book – that is as increasingly similar electorates and party systems – is affected *not only by one single supra-national issue*, albeit an important one, but by a *variety of supra-national factors*, some of which can be placed temporally before the period of European integration since the 1960s. It is in this sense that the analysis in this book considers Europeanization *before and beyond* European integration.

In addition, while the "sovereignty" dimension has a high salience during the first phases of European integration and has modified national cleavage constellations, with the general acceptance of the EU by mainstream parties, the issue has transformed from a question of "how much" to one of "which" integration. The focus of such a dimension of contestation is more specific in that it addresses how parties construct and promote different images of Europe. The dimension of contestation that emerges shifts from the pro versus contra aspect to one of "polity-ideas", or "images" of Europe.[16] These contributions, however, lack the link to party competition. Ideas of Europe are instruments of mobilization. This appears most clearly in the literature on populist parties, which are not simply Euro-sceptical but put forward an alternative conception of Europe based on ethnic and religious identity (rather than civic citizenship), with subsidiarity and federalism in place of centralization and cultural standardization, and are critical of bureaucracies and lobbies at the EU level. These visions of Europe are culturally distinct – from both Islamization and Americanization – and economically protectionist.[17]

This leads to a related research programme on the top-down impact of supra-national factors that has analyzed the transformation of national party systems under the impact of globalization more generally.[18] For the purpose of this book, such an approach is particularly significant as it stresses the need to consider factors other than only the EU issue on the transformation of national party systems – namely migrations and the integration of financial markets, among others. Although these authors do not address the issue of convergence between national systems, they offer an analysis of the impact of supra-national factors on national party systems, a top-down process.[19]

---

[15] This would be the same as saying that European party systems are "Americanized" because pro- versus anti-Americanism is present as a cleavage. See Lijphart (1984) and Sartori (1982) on foreign policy as a political alignment before the end of the Cold War.

[16] For one of the first formulations along these lines see Jachtenfuchs, Diez, and Jung (1998). The authors distinguish four polity ideas in relation to the EU: (1) inter-governmental cooperation; (2) federal state; (3) economic community; (4) network.

[17] For an empirical study see Caramani and Mény (2005).

[18] Among the many social scientific contributions by this group of researchers, the main references are Kriesi et al. (2008 and 2012). For a shorter publication pointing in the same direction see Kriesi et al. (2006).

[19] The possibility that globalization generates the convergence of national political spaces is mentioned as a hypothesis in the conclusion of Kriesi et al. (2008: 325).

By linking globalization with European integration this approach expands the one mentioned earlier on new dimensions of contestation by *taking into consideration multiple supra-national factors that may alter national cleavage structures*.

The empirical analysis presented by Kriesi et al. (2008 and 2012) confirms the existence of a "sovereignty" cleavage translating in the rise of new parties and in the new positioning of established parties in the ideological space. The emergence of a new cleavage in national party systems is not simply a reflection of changing socio-economic and cultural structures – with the usual distinction between "losing and winning" social groups in the globalized world – but is articulated by parties' mobilizing strategies.[20] It is through this process of mobilization of new issues and themes that parties operating on pre-existing socio-economic and cultural dimensions "embed" the sovereignty cleavage with mainstream parties taking up the function of articulating new preferences. This analysis thus also confirms that anti-European stances are present in "peripheral" parties mostly (i.e. the extremes of the left–right axis) and that the relationship between position on European integration and left–right is that of an "inverted U curve".[21]

For the purpose of this book, this approach is important as the top-down process of transformation of national cleavage structures and party systems initiated by globalization or European integration leads to a *convergence of the national spaces*. It is, however, an approach that very much remains focussed on recent changes – namely the process of European integration since the 1990s and the current globalization. Historical sources of Europeanization, such as the outcome of wars or the end of the Cold War, which may have a strong influence on the process of Europe-wide convergence of national electorates and party systems, are not considered. As mentioned earlier, the goal of this book is to *go beyond European integration* as a factor at the origin of Europeanization, as well as to look at periods of time during which Europeanization took place before globalization. Furthermore, the neglect of other supra-national factors such as the end of communism leads to overlooking the extent to which the re-alignment within Western electorates is caused by the disappearance of the option of extreme left representation brought by the end of communism.

Finally, transformations of cleavage structures leading to convergence can be observed also in the *absence* of one over-arching supra-national factor such as European integration or the end of communism. The literature on "new

---

[20] Tellingly Kriesi et al. (2008) speak of *demarcation versus an integration* divide, a wording closer to "nationalism vs. supra-nationalism" (used by Marks and collaborators) than "losers vs. winners". In the same vein Bartolini (2005) speaks of "independence vs. integration".

[21] Taggart (1998) speaks about "peripheral parties" in regard to Euro-scepticism. For the inverted U curve see Hooghe, Marks, and Wilson (2002) and Van der Eijk and Franklin (2004). While some have initially highlighted primarily the economic aspects of left–right (neo-liberal policies, state intervention, etc.), others have stressed the role of the cultural dimension (nationalism, traditional values, immigration, etc.).

politics", especially when focussing on green parties, has described the parallel and simultaneous shift of electorates in the wake of cultural or value change that took place in most European countries almost simultaneously.[22] Structural socio-economic change has made possible the emergence of new values and concerns among Western publics. Cross-country convergence, then, originates not so much from supra-national factors leading to increasingly similar national cleavage structures, but rather from *similar developments in the various national systems*. Such "horizontal" processes are due not only to change resulting from cultural shifts, but also to structural changes in the labour market or immigration policy. Other processes than top-down are therefore at work in bringing about Europeanization.

Policy Transfer and Political Parties

Policy transfer (and policy learning) between European countries increases the homogeneity between countries horizontally. The notion that transfers of policies take place between countries has long been present in a vast literature on policy making, especially when looking at executive politics.[23] Most of the literature on policy transfer is not preoccupied with the electoral level. In the past years, however, more specific research has looked at *trans-national transfer among political parties*, especially parties belonging to the same ideological family.[24] These studies can also show the relevance of policy transfer from an electoral perspective. In addition, they discuss concepts and mechanisms relevant for the study of Europeanization.

The first concept is *diffusion*. Since the first formulation of the so-called Galton's problem, diffusion has haunted comparative politics and its methodological assumption of independence of cases. It is through public policy analysis that this important issue has received the attention it deserves also at the empirical level.[25] While diffusion has been analyzed mainly in relation to

---

[22] New politics has been described primarily outside the sphere of conventional party politics and, in particular, in the rise of new social movements, such as the civil rights movement in the 1960s, the feminist and Third World movements in the 1970s, the ecological movement since the 1980s, and the anti-globalization movement since the 2000s (Della Porta and Caiani, 2009; Koopmans, 1992; Tarrow, 1994). As far as green parties are concerned, see Müller-Rommel (1989). The broad culture shift has been the object of the analysis by Inglehart (1977, 1990) and Inglehart and Welzel (2005).

[23] The first major contribution to this area is Rose (1993). For a review of the early literature see Dolowitz and Marsh (1996, 2000). Although this literature distinguishes terminologically between concepts of policy transfer, diffusion, learning, and lesson drawing, it fundamentally points to mechanisms by which experiences in policies, administrative arrangements, and ideas from other settings are used for policy making.

[24] See Paterson and Sloam (2005) as one of the most significant analyses of social democracy in Eastern Europe, and Sloam (2005a) and Zaborowski (2005). On socialists see also Holmes and Lightfoot (2011). More generally, see Enyedi and Lewis (2006), Ladrech (2008, 2009), Poguntke et al. (2007), Pridham (1996), and van dem Berge and Poguntke (2013).

[25] See Braun and Gilardi (2006).

governance models (regulatory agencies) and policy innovation, among major studies of spatial diffusion are analyses of welfare provisions and social security, a topic studied in the following decades in the literature on comparative political economy.[26] These models can be used to *interpret the "waves" of change* that wipe across Europe mentioned earlier, such as the development of welfare states after World War II. However, these models are also relevant to the research question of this study insofar as *diffusion narrows down the spectrum of policy alternatives and programme variation* as the work on the diffusion of market ideology and economic liberalism demonstrates.[27]

The second concept is *convergence*. Cross-national convergence is a consequence of policy transfer and diffusion, and of mechanisms of emulation and lesson drawing. This is directly relevant for the definition of Europeanization in terms of cross-country convergence and spatial homogenization.[28] If, on one hand, it is difficult to disentangle diffusion and transfer effects as one of the possible causes, among others, of cross-country convergence (see Chapter 8), on the other hand it appears from this literature that convergence can be used as an *indicator of Europeanization*. In addition, it appears that diffusion and cross-national convergence are not limited to the decades since the beginning of European integration proper, but that they are indicators with historical value making it possible to be used for Europeanization beyond EU-ization.

The Formation of a Supra-national Competitive Arena

Finally, one must consider the bottom-up elements of Europeanization: first, the integration of national parties as European federations in the EP and the formation of a multi-level party system; second, how the European level increasingly acquires the character of an arena distinct from national ones. Both perspectives are relevant for the analysis of Europeanization from an electoral mass-politics perspective. However, while the first process leads to cross-country convergence through trans-national coordination, a distinctive EP arena (with different dimensions, issues, and platforms from national ones) does not have such an effect.

The party system at the European level – in elections to the EP – has been most fruitfully analyzed through the transposition of categories of comparative politics initially devised for the analysis of national systems, in particular Stein Rokkan's concept of cleavage.[29] The dimensionality of the party system in the

---

[26] The major work encompassing all these fields is Wilensky (2002).

[27] On the diffusion of market and democracy see various contributions in the influential volume by Simmons, Dobbin, and Garrett (2008).

[28] As Radaelli has noted, Europeanization is not synonymous with convergence, but convergence is a *consequence* of Europeanization (defined as a top-down process in this case; see Radaelli, 2000: 6).

[29] On this important contribution viewing the EU as a political system rather than an inter-governmental organization, and in particular on its forming party system, see first and foremost Hix (1994) and the subsequent volume on *Political Parties in the European Union* by Hix and Lord (1997), but also Hix (1999 and 2005) and Kreppel (2002).

EP and its elections has been treated similarly to that of any other political system. This analysis sides research on the organization of European parties pointing to the formation of trans-national federations in European elections and party groups in the EP (the so-called Europarties).[30] Since the first direct election to the EP in 1979, groups and federations have become more integrated and organized. From the perspective of the voting behaviour of the members of the EP, party groups have become more cohesive along the left–right cleavage with the competition between the two main groups: the European Socialist Party and the European People's Party.[31]

Even if this research focuses on elites (members of the EP in roll-call votes and party organizations) rather than electorates, it is relevant for the question of Europeanization as addressed in this book. First, this level of the forming multi-level party system in Europe implies the same type of *cross-national alliances, coordination across borders, and "linkage" between different territorial units* similar to what the literature on the nationalization of politics has described as taking place at the national level during earlier periods of political development. This element of coordination has a direct impact on the degree of cross-national *convergence among parties of the same ideological family* (Chapters 6 and 7). The theoretical implications are addressed in the next section.[32] Second, the linkage between national parties of the same family has in turn a more general *impact on the level of territorial segmentation of the European electorate and party system* (Chapters 3 and 4). The analysis presented in this book points to a pattern of transformation of the Europe-wide cleavage structure *from territorial to functional*. This aspect, too, is discussed further in a subsequent section of this chapter. What is important at this stage is to link it to the literature on parliamentary groups in the EP and party federations in terms of cross-national alliances and coordination with a similar meaning to that of nationalization.

Alongside this bottom-up process of Europeanization of parties, a second aspect is the degree to which, within the European multi-party system, *the upper EU layer becomes increasingly distinct from national party systems*, in terms of issues, platforms, and dimensions. It is one thing to say that a new EU arena is forming with party groups in the EP and party federations becoming increasingly interlinked and cohesive. It is another thing to examine whether

---

[30] For early analyses including data see in particular Bardi (1992, 1994, and 1996) and Pedersen (1996). See also the volume edited by Gaffney (1996), which includes Hix (1996).

[31] The most encompassing analysis of the cohesiveness of voting behaviour within party groups can be found in Hix, Noury, and Roland (2007). See also Hix (2001), Hix and Kreppel (2003), and Hix, Kreppel, and Noury (2003 and 2005).

[32] Bartolini (2005: 327–8) has already noted the similarity between processes of nationalization and Europeanization from a territorial perspective in his four developmental considerations on the multi-level party system of the EU. In the theoretical chapter in Caramani (2004) it had previously been pointed out how exit–voice models, nationalization theories, and the dichotomy between functionality and territoriality could be applied to any forming political space, not just national ones.

this new arena simply mirrors national politics or, conversely, is based on its *own distinct logics of contestation*, with different cleavages, programmes, and issues from national politics.

The guiding hypothesis in this regard is that the acceleration of integration since the 1980s has created new dimensions of contestation at the EU level that were not present previously in national arenas, and that may come to the fore more prominently in European elections.[33] If this is the case, such dimensions should translate into a different political "offer" – either in terms of different parties in the EP or through the same parties but campaigning on different platforms or entering different alliances in elections to the EP as compared to national elections (for example, parties or alliances forming around anti-European themes). Eventually, the distinctive character of EU politics translates to a different "response" on the part of electorates who vote differently in elections to the EP than in national elections.

Such a hypothesis claims that the impact of bottom-up Europeanization on the multi-level party system is one of *differentiation between the national and EU levels* and increase of the *divergence between the two competitive arenas*. On this question, however, research has so far emphasized "overlap" rather than "distinctiveness" between national and EU layers. First, research on second-order elections has found little support for the hypothesis of differentiated electoral behaviour in European elections as compared to national elections.[34] Second, indicators based on measures of electoral volatility have shown that both political offer and electoral response do not differ significantly between European and national elections.[35] Both strands of research point therefore to two sets of elections fought on similar policy issues and to European elections fought on issues overlapping national ones.[36]

While the literature on party groups in the EP and party federations analyzes the Europeanization of electoral politics from the point of view of elites, the literature on second-order elections and distinctive multi-level competitive arenas approaches the question from a mass-electoral angle. While the former leads to the hypothesis of cross-country convergence as supra-national

---

[33] This concerns the process of the EU's "constitutionalization", transfer of competences to the EU, the direct election of the EU since 1979 giving rise to competition between Europarties as seen earlier, and debates and referenda mobilizing ever larger segments of the European electorate on crucial questions of national sovereignty and identity.

[34] The variables usually considered at the origin of a diverging pattern between European and national elections can all be traced back to the perceived lack of salience of the EP leading to more protest voting, punishment effects of incumbents in national governments and major parties, and more "sincere", less "tactical" voting (Marsh and Franklin, 1996; Schmitt, 1990). On second-order elections see the seminal article by Reif and Schmitt (1980), as well as Kuechler (1991), Marsh (1998), Reif (1985a,b, 1997), and Van der Eijk and Franklin (1991).

[35] On the analysis of European elections from 1979 until 2004 in comparison with national elections since the 1970s see Caramani (2006).

[36] Following Thomassen, Noury, and Voeten (2004) and Thomassen and Schmitt (1997), Bartolini (2005: 349) labels them "normal" issues, as opposed to constitutive ones.

integration of party structures and ideologies, the latter leads to the hypothesis that if the EU level of the multi-party system is a mirror of national politics, then it will not have consequences on the convergence between national party systems. Chapter 5 carries out the analysis of the "correspondence" between the national and EU levels by means of volatility indicators.[37]

Summing up, in this section we have seen how different approaches and theories contribute to the conceptualization of the Europeanization of electoral politics in a historical and mass-electoral perspective. However, it has also been highlighted how each is too limited for the definition of Europeanization:

- Europeanization involves not only the top-down impact of European integration on national structures but also of *other supra-national factors* "beyond and before" European integration. For this reason a historical perspective is crucial.
- Europeanization is not limited to the direct impact of supra-national factors on national policies and administration, but has an *indirect* impact on dimensions of contestation. This is relevant for Europeanization applied to electorates and party systems.
- Europeanization should not be confined to convergence uniquely on the "sovereignty" dimension. A broad definition of Europeanization must allow for the *convergence of other dimensions* as well. The simultaneous emergence of cleavages takes place on a variety of issues.
- Europeanization is not only top-down but also *bottom-up* with *the formation of an additional competitive arena* above (more or less distinct from) national ones.
- Europeanization also involves a *horizontally driven process of convergence* and cannot be conceptualized exclusively on the vertical dimension. Convergence can be caused by similar factors in different national systems and through diffusion, not necessarily in the presence of overarching supra-national factors.

The next section is therefore devoted to depicting a broader scheme of the dimensions of Europeanization as a historical process of cross-country convergence in Europe.

From Nationalization to Europeanization

Nationalization from the mid-19th century until the 1920s consisted of the territorial homogenization of electoral politics and of cross-regional convergence that led to the transition from territorial to functional politics in Europe's nation-states. The fundamental integration of national electorates and party systems was consolidated in the period since World War II, when tendencies

---

[37] As direct elections to the EP have taken place since 1979, this part of the analysis will have a shorter historical scope and will cover, roughly, the past 30 years of electoral history in Europe.

towards institutional and economic regionalization did not lead to significant re-territorialization of electoral politics.[38] But if the re-territorialization of electorates and party systems did not happen through the re-instatement of *internal boundaries* (regionalization), some have argued that it is happening by the removal of *external boundaries* (globalization).

This seems to be the thesis put forward by authors addressing issues of *de-nationalization*,[39] as well as by authors claiming that supra-national integration leads to *territorial politics at a higher level*, namely through the integration of nation-states with diverging interests and identity within a new polity in Europe.[40] This is the dependent variable in the present work. *How strong is the territorial dimension at the European level? Has it become weaker or stronger as a consequence of European integration, or are these decades following previously initiated long-term processes?* This study on Europeanization may then simply be labelled a study of *nationalization at the Europe-wide level* – a sort of *"Europe-wide nationalization"*.

Because the approach taken in this book strongly relies on theories and methods developed within the framework of the nation-state (state formation, nation-building, political structuring) this section starts by discussing the approach that has based the study of European integration on such theories before moving on to the specific field of "Europeanization" from an electoral politics perspective, its indicators, and its operational definitions.

The Structuring of Political Space: A Comparative Political Sociology Approach

Theorists of state formation, nation-building, and mass democratization have been concerned with the structuring of the political space at the national level during the crucial phases of the 19th and 20th centuries, with Stein Rokkan in particular attempting to systematize processes towards the liberal nation-state in Europe.[41] This framework – constructed in the context of the nation-state – is

---

[38] Such "new" regionalisms are often more institutional and economic than electoral and, in fact, usually have old roots, that is going back to phases of state formation and nation-building. On new regionalism see Keating (1988, 1998) and Keating and Loughlin (1997).

[39] De-nationalization is here understood as synonymous with globalization or post-nationalization. See Beisheim et al. (1999), Zürn (1998, 2001), Zürn et al. (2000), and Zürn and Walter (2005). The lowering of national boundaries does not, however, imply an automatic convergence between the components, and therefore de-nationalization does not necessarily mean Europeanization.

[40] For one of the first formulations of the hypothesis about the reappearance of the territorial dimension in Europe see Kohler-Koch (1998). For a similar formulation based on the growing territorial diversity coming from EU enlargement to Central and Eastern European countries see Mair and Zielonka (2002) and Zielonka (2002).

[41] The term *liberal* summarizes elements of parliamentarization, democratization, and secularization of the state based on the national ideal of social citizenship (see Bendix, 1964; Dahrendorf, 1959; Deutsch, 1953; Gellner, 1983; Poggi, 1990; and Smith, 1986 among others) as it emerged from the transition to industrial society and later led to social rights alongside civil and political

abstract enough to allow for its application to other forming political spaces, such as Europe. While it was impossible to foresee the evolution the EU would take after the Maastricht Treaty in 1992 when these models were devised, the concepts of centre formation, peripheral integration, and administrative standardization shed new light on European integration, as well as on the consequences this has for the re-aggregation of interests and identities in new alignments and Europe-wide cleavages.

A number of influential writings have transposed comparative political sociology approaches of the structuring of political spaces at the national level to European integration. These attempts are important insofar as they use a rich conceptual and theoretical corpus from Hirschman's twin concepts "exit" and "voice" and Rokkan's concept of political structuring.[42] Theories of state formation and nation-building, cleavage structures, and centralization constitute in this view promising models for interpreting European integration. Indeed, some of the most innovative work done in this area moves from these concepts, starting with Joseph H. H. Weiler, who first saw their potential applied to the legal sphere with the reduction of "selective exits" through the jurisprudence of the European Court of Justice.[43] An important step towards a systematic application to the EU was done by Peter Flora, Stefano Bartolini, and others with applications in a variety of fields.[44] Also the aforementioned research on new cleavages can implicitly be ranged within this approach. If European unification is comparable to previous processes of state formation and mass democratization in nation-states, then the "sovereignty dimension" represents an instance of territorial, "peripheral" resistance to centre formation. The European party system depends strongly on the interaction between the territorial "sovereignty" dimension and other cleavages such as left–right.[45]

---

ones (Marshall, 1964). On Rokkan's oeuvre see Caramani (2011b) and Flora (1999). For a comparison between European integration and state building see the volume by Klausen and Tilly (1997), in particular the chapter by Marks (1997).

[42] See Hirschman (1970) and the subsequent elaboration by Rokkan (1974a, 1974b). For a rather detailed account see Caramani (2004: 17–18).

[43] See the essay on "The Transformation of Europe" re-printed in Weiler (1999: 10–101). Lodge (1975) provides the first application of "exit" and "voice" concepts to Britain's stance on European integration. On the use of these terms see also Brack (2012).

[44] See Flora's introduction to Rokkan's work (Flora 1999, in particular pp. 88–91), as well as Bartolini (2004, 2005), Flora (2000), Karvonen and Kuhnle (2000), and Olsen (2007). On the re-structuring of the "space of solidarity" (welfare) see Ferrera (2005).

[45] On these points see Bartolini (2002: 130–55). Also, according to Marks and Steenbergen (2002), the interaction between cleavage "residues" from the 19th and 20th centuries and the pro/anti-EU dimension determines the shape of the European party system. As an alternative to the left–right dimension Schmitter (2000: 68) points to agriculture – a cleavage that has disappeared in national constellations but that has re-emerged at the EU level. On the contrary, the religious cleavage has moved "outside" Europe, with Christianity as a common element of European identity demarcating it from other cultures.

Within this broad approach of comparative political sociology, the *theory of the nationalization of politics* occupies a special place as it is directly concerned with the *territoriality of cleavages* and with the process of replacement of territorial cleavages by functional ones – in particular the left–right cleavage. As the whole approach, this theory, too – initially devised to understand the integration of national electorates – is a powerful tool for the analysis of integration of electorates at the European level. Nationalization theory can be fruitfully transposed to Europeanization.

Since Weber we think of two-dimensional political spaces as broadly composed of a territorial and a functional dimension, but other elements of the political system such as social boundaries (territorial or membership), representation channels (constituencies or corporations), and cleavages (weak or strong territorial segmentation of groups) also follow this distinction.[46] According to the "exit–voice" model, the structuring of political spaces involves inversely related external and internal dimensions. The *reduction of exit options through external boundary building* (both physical borders and membership delimitations) enhances the *internal expression of voice*: (1) the development of institutional channels of representation (be it through territorial, electoral constituencies or functional and "pillarized" interest representation); (2) the opposition among groups and individuals along cleavages (either functional cleavages such as left–right or cleavages with a high degree of territoriality such as centre–periphery). During processes of "system building", the internal territorial dimension of cleavages becomes less significant compared to the functional dimension. The *strengthening of external boundaries* is therefore paralleled by the *weakening of internal (territorial) boundaries*. The replacement of territorial cleavages by cleavages cutting across territory means empirically *territorial homogenization and convergence between parts of the territory undergoing structuration*.[47]

While homogenization has been analyzed empirically for the structuring of national political spaces ("nationalization"),[48] it can be fruitfully applied

---

[46] See Weber's definition of a political group: "We say of a group of domination that it is a *political group [politischer Verband]* insofar as its existence and the validity of the norms are assured in a permanent way within a *territory [Gebiet]*. What characterises the political group ... is the fact that it claims the domination of its administrative leadership and of its norms upon a territory" (Weber, 1978: part I, chapter 1, 17.1). After Weber "[f]ew sociologists have gone as far as Rokkan in making the *territoriality* of political systems one of the pillars of his comparative analysis" (Flora, 1999: 63).

[47] For details on these models see the theoretical work done in the volume on nationalization (Caramani 2004: 15–32).

[48] For major comparative work see Caramani (2004) on Western Europe and Chhibber and Kolman (2004) on Britain, India, Canada, and the United States. A number of more specific studies have followed. On Latin America see Alemán and Kellam (2008), Harbers (2010), and Jones and Mainwaring (2003). On South-East Asia see Croissant and Schächter (2008) and Hicken (2009). On Central and Eastern Europe see Bochsler (2010a). Further work is quoted later in this chapter and in Chapter 3 in regard to measures and indices, as well as in the

to the structuring of Europe as a new political space (what this work labels "Europeanization"). At the European level, too, the formation of a European party system depends on *whether the functional dimension of cleavages prevails over the territorial one.* This is a matter of empirical investigation, and not simply of theoretical elaboration. It is such an empirical investigation that this book intends to carry out in a historical and mass-politics perspective.

Convergence as an Indicator of Europeanization

Territoriality is therefore used as the main indicator of the Europeanization of electorates and party systems. Convergence and homogenization reveal the loss of territoriality of alignments and the replacement of territorial oppositions with functional ones as determined by the various processes described by the literature on Europeanization reviewed in the previous section, the top-down impact on national cleavage systems of European integration and of the trans-national coordination resulting from party federations, as well as the homogenizing impact from similar socio-economic and cultural transformations. Before proceeding to systematize these dimensions, however, it is necessary to address the indicator of convergence more precisely.

The first point concerns the *level of analysis.*

The analysis focuses on convergence between European *nation-states.* As Europeanization is analyzed before and beyond European integration, it includes countries that have not always or have never been EU member-states. The analysis covers 30 countries even though, because of different democratization (Southern and Eastern Europe most notably) and independence/unification patterns, not all countries are included since the beginning of the time period considered, approximately 1848. The main reason for using countries as opposed to other territorial units is that nation-states are, over the period considered, the most important sovereign political units.[49]

The second point concerns *units of analysis.*

The analysis concentrates on the convergence of three different units: (1) national *party systems* taken as a whole (converging over, say, similar cleavage structures) but also individual parties in each country (for example, socialist parties converging towards de-radicalized positions); (2) dimensions of contestation as analyzed through *party families* (when all countries display similar structures); and (3) *executives and governmental coalitions* converging over policy preferences. Each of these units of analysis may or may not converge to some degree across European countries.

Conclusion on the comparison between Europeanization and nationalization in Europe, the United States, and India.

[49] Data availability and the reliability of sources also play a role in the time coverage for various countries. In addition, as documented in the chapters that follow, over time a number of important border changes have taken place, in particular in Germany before and after the wars, but also with re-unification in 1990.

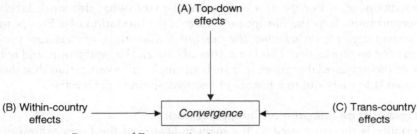

FIGURE I.I. Processes of Europeanization.

The third point concerns *properties*.

The analysis concentrates on the convergence over *electorates and party systems' formats and contents*. Europeanization is analyzed over voters' preferences, parties' ideological and programmatic positions, party systems' morphology, and electoral alignments (cleavages). Europeanization is analyzed *statically/distributionally and dynamically*.[50] In the first case convergence means that the homogeneity of properties (say, the vote for populist parties) across countries is measured in a sequence of points in time, for example years $(t, t+1, \ldots t+n)$. In the second case convergence means that there is uniformity and simultaneity across countries in the *change* between two elections (say, populist parties increase votes everywhere between t and $t+1$).

The diverse dimensions of the Europeanization process defined in terms of convergence and territorial homogeneity, as well as the related literatures reviewed in the previous section can be summarized as in Figure I.I. Under (A) *top-down effects* one finds the homogenizing impact on national electorates and party systems across Europe of *overarching supra-national factors* such as, to take some examples, the Soviet Revolution in 1917 leading in all European countries to the division of the workers' movement in the immediate aftermath, or the breakdown of communism in 1989 with the effect of de-radicalizing the left. Under this mechanism one finds the top-down impact of the transfer of policy competences to the EU as well as the effects of the formation of supra-national party federations in the EP. Under (B) *within-country effects* one finds the homogenizing impact on national electorates and party systems across Europe of *factors in single countries that are similar* such as industrialization with similar effects on the rise of mass and class politics, growth and economic security with generation-based socialization effects on political culture (post-materialism) leading to new politics movements, population ageing with pressure effects on parties' positions regarding the welfare

---

[50] These terms are taken from Morgenstern, Swindle, and Castagnola (2009), who speak of *static/distributional nationalization* (S/DN) and *dynamic nationalization* (DN) following the distinction present in the classical literature on nationalization since Schattschneider (1960).

state and social security provisions. Under (C) *trans-country effects* one finds the homogenizing impact on national electorates and party systems across Europe of "diffusion factors" that spread from country to country such as policy transfer and policy learning from Western to Eastern European social democratic parties in the aftermath of democratic transition, emulation effects such as the organization of green parties or anti-system populist protest. Figure 1.2 depicts each process of Europe-wide convergence.

As far as *top-down processes* are concerned, the convergence indicator must identify critical junctures – that is events or factors which all countries confront and to which a response is given. As the literature on nationalization has stressed (more on this later), if the *electoral "response" to a common "stimuli" is uniform*, then this is clearly a sign of an integrated system. In the present case it would point to Europeanization as it would be a sign that electorates react to a common issue. However, a non-uniform response from electorates (i.e. different electorates responding differently) may also be a reaction to a common issue. It is, however, only with uniform responses that one can be sure – unless uniformity is caused by coincidence.[51] In Chapter 4 this effect is captured through the analysis of electoral swings.

Figure 1.1 does not depict *bottom-up processes* as top-down effects subsume bottom-up processes such as policy convergence, transfer of competences to the supra-national level, trans-national coordination (for example international party organizations), and so forth. Bottom-up processes *in turn affect convergence* in the top-down process. Once in place, supra-national factors have an effect on cross-country convergence. Convergence as an indicator, therefore, also captures the effect of bottom-up integration, such as the reduction of policy options for parties caused by coordination within the same family or through common policies. This effect is captured by ideological convergence as analyzed in Chapters 6 and 7.

Convergence and territorial homogenization provide a parsimonious indicator of this variety of processes and of the multi-faceted nature of Europeanization, from coordination and collaboration (Third International, party groups in the EP) to the narrowing of ideological alternatives (Washington consensus, EMU), the similar responses to supra-national events (Soviet Revolution, financial crises of the 1930s and 2000s) or diffusion effects (social democratic Westernization of Eastern European post-communist parties). The scheme depicted in Figure 1.1 could be filled with many more examples. What matters is that *convergence and territorial homogenization provide an indicator able to capture a variety of Europeanization processes*, to address Europeanization from a *mass-politics*

---

[51] In the earliest writings on nationalization both Schattschneider (1960: 79–93) and Stokes (1965) consider the uniformity of responses across territorial units an indicator of the presence of common factors "above" territorial units. For a critique, in particular of *non*-uniformity as a possible response to common factors, see Claggett, Flanigan, and Zingale (1984). The whole discussion is summarized in Caramani (2004: 32–43).

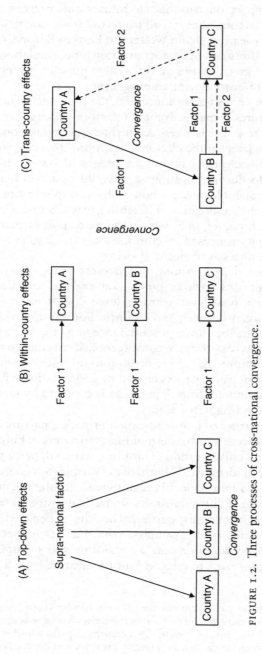

FIGURE 1.2. Three processes of cross-national convergence.
Note: Convergence under the assumption that the same factors have the same impact in different countries.

perspective with a focus on electorates and party systems, in a *historical perspective* since the 19th century. Convergence and homogenization are, therefore, tools to analyze Europeanization before and beyond EU-ization. In Part II specific hypotheses are formulated about convergence as engendered by top-down, within-country, or trans-country effects. The goal of Chapter 8 in Part III is to identify which of the three processes (A, B, or C) is at work.

Operationalization

How the integration of electorates and party systems can be addressed empirically has been the focus of two theories: one can be labelled "the theory of the nationalization of politics" and the other "cross-district coordination theory". Both address *national-level integration* and focus on the main electoral units within countries, that is constituencies (districts). Both can be applied to European-level integration.[52]

1. **The theory of nationalization of politics.** – The theory describes the reduction of the territoriality of cleavages. In its broader formulation in comparative political sociology applied to long-term historical development, this process involves two dimensions:

- First, a *horizontal* process of territorial homogenization of political attitudes and behaviour. At the national level, this is a process of *penetration and standardization* during phases of state formation and nation-building since the 19th century.
- Second, a process of *vertical* dislocation of issues, organizations, competences, and identities from the lower to the upper level of governance. At the national level this is the process of *centre formation*.

These two dimensions appear in the very early writings on nationalization. On one hand, nationalization means *homogenous* voting behaviour throughout a territory. On the other hand, nationalization refers to the *shift* of factors affecting voting behaviour from the local to the national level. The first dimension includes both *static and dynamic* aspects: in the first case we have a territorially *homogenous support for parties*; in the second case we have a *uniform change across regions* from one election to the next. In addition, but receiving less attention, one finds the dimension of *correspondence* between a more or less large number of party systems at the local level, and the party system at the national level.[53]

---

[52] Two books are broadly representative of these two theories: Caramani (2004) and Chhibber and Kollman (2004).

[53] The theory was first developed in the US setting. Schattschneider (1960: 79–93) describes the shift between 1896 and 1932 from "sectional" to "national" politics during the Depression and the New Deal and, later, during the Cold War. Stokes (1965, 1967) compares US and British politics and focuses on the "location" of factors that influence voters' behaviour (local versus national) and on the correspondence of party systems between the two levels. For a detailed

Subsequent literature has addressed the problematic issue of determining empirically the "location" of the factors that determine voters' electoral choice. Several attempts have been made to derive the location from the uniformity of responses with the argument that if all parts of the country were "swinging" uniformly towards (or away from) one of the parties, factors at the upper level must be at work (only coincidence could produce uniform swings if local factors were at work).[54] This is an attempt to link horizontal and vertical dimensions of nationalization by saying that if the "level of influence" is national, then the "type of response" from the electorate is one of uniform swings. Nationalization theory shows that both territorial homogeneity (static measure) and swings' uniformity (dynamic measure) capture the impact of national factors on voting behaviour such as centralization of policy competences, standardization of the administration, strong national/federal institutions such as a presidency, and nationwide issues such as wars, economic crises, and so forth.[55]

These three dimensions of *"homogeneity"*, *"uniformity"*, and *"correspondence"* between *units* (constituencies) and *levels* (local and national) can be transferred from nationalization to Europeanization with *units* being nation-states and *levels* being the national and European ones. It is also easy to see how the literature reviewed earlier in this chapter on the various processes of Europeanization and convergence fits in well with these dimensions of "Europe-wide nationalization". If supra-national factors have an impact (top down), then one would expect to see increasing homogeneity between countries (static measure) as well as uniform swings away or towards a specific party family (dynamic measure). Chapters 3 and 4 therefore apply the indicators of "homogeneity" and "uniformity" to Europeanization. The third indicator is that of "correspondence" between the local (in the present case, national) party systems and the party system of the upper level (i.e. that of the EP). Chapter 5 links this dimension to the literature on second-order elections and investigates the degree of correspondence between electoral behaviour in national and European elections through the measure of volatility between the two levels in the European multi-party system.

Nationalization theory has used indicators relating to the *format of the party system*. The focus on the format is justified by the necessity to look at

---

theoretical reconstruction and for the evolution of the literature see Caramani (2004: 32–43). For the term *correspondence* (Stokes used a different term) see Hearl, Budge, and Pearson (1996) and Lee (1988).

[54] The critique formulated by Claggett et al. (1984) and Katz (1973) is that national factors not only produce uniform swings across all regions but also non-uniform swings (when regions respond differently to national factors). As discussed in Caramani (2004: 38), however, uniform swings can be safely assumed to detect national factors if one excludes the unlikely possibility of coincidence of local factors producing nationwide swings.

[55] For example, Chhibber and Kollman (2004: 101–60), Harbers (2010), Lago-Peñas and Lago-Peñas (2011), and Morgenstern et al. (2009).

the early phases of formation of national electorates and party systems before and after major transitions to democratization in the 19th century up to World War I. Format needs not be limited to party systems and can be applied to cabinet coalitions as well, as is done in Chapter 7. Analyzing periods since World War II, however, also offers the possibility to use indicators relating to the *contents of both party systems and cabinet coalitions*: that is increasing homogeneity between units and levels in regard to ideological placement, preferences and attitudes, policy programmes, and relevant issues. Accordingly, Chapters 6 and 7 also address "contents".

2. Cross-district coordination: linkage theory. – One of the empirical findings of the nationalization theory is the role of competition in the formation of national electorates and party systems. Nationalization resulted from parties' competitive strategy to spread through territory (through lists and candidates) to maximize electoral returns, competing in the *territorial space* before competing in the *ideological space* as described by Downs and the subsequent "spatial" analyses.[56] This competition perspective follows closely the more formal pioneering work done on cross-district coordination and linkage.[57] This literature has a different starting point, namely the conditions under which the effect of majoritarian electoral laws on two-party systems at the district level extends to the national level. Following Sartori's argument that majoritarian laws have a reductive effect on the number of parties *at the national level* only if parties are "nationalized", this literature stresses that only when there is cross-district linkage and coordination between candidates of the same party can one observe the effect of majoritarian laws on the structuring of two-party systems at the national level.[58]

The question thus becomes why candidates and parties link across districts. While nationalization theory stresses that parties spread across districts in search of new electoral support bases and, in doing so, overcome cultural (ethno-linguistic, religious) and economic barriers (urban–rural), linkage theory stresses elements such as pursuing a presidency or premiership, campaign finances, upper-tier seats, and so forth to explain why parties "aggregate" nationally. Even though linkage theory views parties' aggregation as passively mirroring the centralization of the political system (federal-level policies acquiring more prominence), it is clear how such a perspective is relevant to understand the *"aggregation" of – or linkage between – national parties at the European level* in terms of federations, coordination of policy programmes, common parliamentary groups in the EP, and so forth. Such aggregation can be viewed as

---

[56] For the analysis of party competition and "catch-allover" parties see Caramani (2004: 230–46, and 2003).

[57] See first and foremost *Making Votes Count* (Cox, 1997: especially chapter 10 on "Putting the Constituencies Together"; see also Cox, 1999).

[58] See Sartori (1986). As Cox noted, such arguments were already present, although in a more discursive form, in Duverger (1954).

the result of the *bottom-up transfer of policy competences from the national to the supra-national level and of the coordination between national governments.*

3. **Measures and indices.** – Both approaches reviewed earlier produce a number of indices and measures. Most measures address the operationalization of the dimension of *"homogeneity" or static/distributional nationalization* (S/DN) seen earlier. Such measures include standard deviation (S^2), coefficient of variation (CV), cumulative regional inequality index (CRII), party (system) nationalization score (P(S)NS), various versions of the Gini coefficient, and different types of inflation and aggregation measures.[59]

Much less attention has been devoted to *"uniformity", or dynamic nationalization* (DN) measures looking at the degree of similar change across territorial units between two time points. This indicator has received less attention in part for the mentioned reason that it is unable to detect the "location of forces" that affect individual behaviour as some had hoped. In Chapter 4 this indicator is nonetheless used in its own right, that is as an indicator of the commonality of change across European countries, for which uniform swings are the appropriate measure and on which some literature is available.[60] In its simplest form the operational definition of uniformity is the percentage of territorial units (in the present case countries) swinging in the same direction (away from or towards a specific party family) simultaneously – which implies a problematic definition of simultaneity when national elections do not take place in the same year in different countries.

The indicator of *"correspondence" or vertical homogeneity* is more heterogeneous as it has been employed in different ways with different goals. First, it has been addressed by the literature on nationalization in terms of similarity between a number of regional party systems and the national party system. Second, it has been addressed by the literature on second-order elections aiming to identify the degree of overlap versus deviance between levels of electoral competition – mainly between national and European levels – as well as to identify the causes of such deviation when present. Third, it has been addressed by the literature using volatility indices applied to subsequent elections taking place at different levels, in particular through measures of "mixed volatility" between national and European elections capturing the degree to which voting behaviour changes between the two "orders" of elections.[61]

---

[59] On these measures see Bochsler (2010b), Caramani (2004), Chhibber and Kollman (1998, 2004), Jones and Mainwaring (2003), Kasuya and Moenius (2008), Moenius and Kasuya (2004), and Nikolenyi (2009), among many others. See also Chapter 3.

[60] After the initial insights and analyses in the 1960s and 1970s, this indicator has been revisited by Brady, D'Onofrio, and Fiorina (2000). See also Carrubba and Timpone (2005), Lyons and Linek (2010), and Morgenstern and Potthoff (2005). On electoral swings applied at the European level see Caramani (2011a).

[61] On the first strand of literature see Lee (1988) and Hearl et al. (1996). On the second see the literature on second-order elections quoted earlier, mainly Reif and Schmitt (1980) and Reif (1985a, 1985b, 1997). On mixed volatility see Caramani (2006).

TABLE 1.1. *The Operationalization of Convergence*

Units of Analysis	Dimensions of Convergence		
	Horizontal Static	Horizontal Dynamic	Vertical Static
Party system	Convergence of cleavage constellations and party systems across countries. – Historical analysis, electoral data. (Chapter 3)	Simultaneous swings of party systems either left or right across countries. – Historical analysis, electoral data. (Chapter 4)	Volatility between national party systems and party systems of EP. – Since 1970s, electoral data. (Chapter 5)
Electorate	Ideological convergence of voters across countries. – Since 1970s, survey data. (Chapter 6)	Not covered by the analysis.	*Not applicable*: European and national electorates are the same.
Party family	Ideological convergence of parties of the same family across countries. – Since 1945, CMP, survey data. (Chapter 6)	Simultaneous gains/losses of party family across countries. – Historical analysis, electoral data. (Chapter 4)	Not covered by the analysis.
Executives	Cross-country ideological convergence of cabinets and governmental coalitions. – Since 1945, cabinet composition, CMP. (Chapter 7)	Not covered by the analysis	*Not applicable*: No political cabinet at the European level.
Indicators	"Homogenization", "Cohesion", "Closure"	"Uniformity"	"Correspondence"
Operationalization	Standard deviation, IPR, various weighted measures	Trends, spread, swings	Mixed/differential volatility

39

The details of the various measures – given their variety as well as the variety of the data to which they are applied – are discussed in the relevant chapters in Part II of this volume. What should be stressed at this stage is that, not only other measures than those of the nationalization literature are used (e.g. volatility measures), but also that these measures are *applied to units of analysis other than parties and party systems alone*, in particular to *party families and cabinet coalitions*. The structure of the following chapters appears accordingly in Table 1.1. The analysis is based on a variety of data covering different time periods:

- *Electoral results*: National parliamentary elections to the lower houses (in the earliest cases since the mid-19th century) and elections to the EP since 1979: analysis of homogenization, uniformity, and correspondence (Chapters 3, 4, and 5).
- *Text data*: CMP data on party manifestos (in the earliest case since 1945): analysis of ideological convergence within party families and among national cabinets (Chapters 6 and 7).
- *Survey data*: Eurobarometers and European Social Survey mostly since the mid-1970s: analysis of the cross-national convergence of electorates' attitudes (Chapter 6).
- *Cabinet composition*: Data on the composition of governmental parties or coalitions of parties in the executive (in the earliest case since 1945): analysis of cross-national convergence among cabinets' policy programmes (Chapter 7).

A Europeanized electorate and party system is one becoming *increasingly similar*, with similar cleavage and party systems across countries, and in which voters "move" in the *same direction simultaneously* reacting to *common issues* and in which there is a high degree of multi-level *correspondence between lower (national) and upper (European) levels (format)*. A Europeanized electorate and party system is furthermore one in which parties of the same family are *ideologically similar (contents)*across countries and cabinets' policy programmes and national electorates' priorities.

Evidence on the various dimensions of convergence that follows in Part II of this book is meant to be used as an indicator of Europeanization processes taking place according to top-down, within-country, or trans-country mechanisms. Each of them may be at the origin of convergence. Distinguishing which of these three mechanisms is at work is the task of Chapter 8 in Part III.

2

Research Design

European Party Families and Party Systems

Introduction

The analysis that follows in the five chapters in Part II of this book is based on a data collection covering 713 national and seven EP elections spread across 30 countries over roughly 150 years of electoral history in Europe. This chapter addresses general issues of cross-sectional and cross-temporal comparability that such a broad comparative and longitudinal analysis entails. This chapter further addresses other general methodological issues to clear the way as much as possible for the analysis in the rest of this book.[1]

As seen, the analysis of Europeanization of electoral politics is multi-pronged in the type of data it relies on. Yet – whether analyzing electoral results, party manifestos, cabinet data, or surveys – the basic units of analysis are political parties and party families. The homogeneity of electoral support across countries is based on a definition of party families. Similarly, the uniformity of electoral swings in Europe is based on simultaneous gains or losses of equivalent parties in different countries. The level of ideological cohesiveness and convergence among European parties of the same family (based on manifestos and voters' preferences) also requires a classification of national parties into Europe-wide families. Finally, the analysis of similarity of cabinet composition across countries has party families as its basic unit. In all cases party classification is crucial for the analysis in this book.

The first task of this chapter is, therefore, to build *party families* and a classification useful for diverse countries and over a period of more than a century (first section of this chapter). To do this, what henceforth is referred to as "the cleavage model" is used, and various aggregations of families are proposed. This section also addresses aspects relating to the data file, codes, and overall

---

[1] More details on specific methodological issues relevant to each dimension of Europeanization are given at the beginning of the five chapters in Part II and in the Appendix.

indices as the number of parties, fractionalization, volatility, and disproportionality. Second, this chapter provides an overall picture of the "European" *party system* (second section of this chapter). This serves as a reference for the analysis of "deviation" of single countries or areas in Europe. It is the overall "model" against which variation of national systems is measured in Part II. Time periods covered for each country and issues relating to different electoral years are also addressed in this section.

European Party Families

The Origins of Party Families: The Cleavage Model

The largest parties and party families originated from the socio-economic and political changes between the mid-19th century and the first decades of the 20th. This transformation is among the most radical in human history: from agrarian to industrial economy, from rural community to urban society, from local to national identity and communication networks, from caste- to class-based social structures, and from autocratic to democratic polities. These are major and unprecedented processes of social and political mobilization.

In his cleavage model, Rokkan (1999) distinguishes two aspects of this transformation (see also Bendix, 1964, Lipset and Rokkan, 1967; and Mann, 1993):

- The *National Revolution* refers to the formation of national democratic citizenships with vertical mass–elite ties and horizontal cross-local ties enhanced by linguistic homogenization (nation-building), as well as to parliamentarization, individual civil and voting rights, social rights, and secular institutions (democratization and liberalization); it further refers to the construction of the state with the centralization of administrative structures (state formation).
- The *Industrial Revolution* refers to industrialization and urbanization, the emergence of class society, the commodification of labour, and the disruption of local communities and their identities, as well as the development of nationwide networks of communication.

These radical changes produced socio-economic and cultural divisions opposing different groups, values, and interests – generally labelled *cleavages*.[2] Political parties represent the *politicization* of cleavages during phases of parliamentarization and suffrage extension, mirroring the socio-economic and cultural divisions created by the two "revolutions".[3] The original model distinguishes

---

[2] According to Bartolini and Mair's definition (1990: 216–19), a cleavage is a persistent division in society entailing three dimensions: (1) *social base*: classes, religious groups, ethnicities, age cohorts, gender; (2) *group identity*: values and beliefs, sources of solidarity and trust, norms; and (3) *organization*: trade unions, churches, parties, interest groups. Social divisions become cleavages when they are organized for political action.

[3] In these models there is no automatic translation or deterministic reflection of social divisions into party organizations, which is why cleavage structures are distinguished from party systems.

four main cleavages produced by the National and Industrial Revolutions. Subsequent transformations – the International Revolution and what can be labelled the Post-Industrial Revolution – have produced additional cleavages (see Table 2.1).

The National Revolution produced two cleavages. First, the *centre–periphery* cleavage between the central state administration and nation-building culture on one hand, and ethnically/linguistically distinct and economically dependent peripheral populations on the other, which led to the formation of ethno-linguistic, autonomist parties against the (mainly) liberal state builders. Second, the *state–church cleavage* between the emerging individual and secular citizenship (moulded through socialization processes such as compulsory schooling and conscription into the army), as well as democratic parliamentary systems on one hand, and the privilege of the clergy in matters of land, estate representation, and education, as well as the strong role of the monarchy on the other, which led to the formation of conservative, Catholic, and later Christian democratic parties against the liberal elite and its reforms.[4]

The Industrial Revolution created two further cleavages. First, the *rural–urban cleavage* between agricultural, landed interests in protectionist tariffs and traditional rural cultures on one hand, and the free trade liberalizing policies of the rising industrial entrepreneurs on the other, which led to the formation of agrarian and peasants' parties against the liberal-industrial elite. Second, the *employers–workers (class) cleavage* between employers and owners of the means of production on one hand, and the emerging class of industrial workers, tenants, and labourers over job security, pensions, social protection, degree of state intervention in the economy, and correction of market- and privilege-generated inequalities on the other, which led to the formation of workers' or labour parties, that is socialists and social democrats.

In a further transformation, the International Revolution produced two more party families. First, the rise of communism in the Soviet Union in 1917 produced a division within the workers' movement, the *communism–socialism divide*. In all countries communist parties formed as splinters from the socialist

---

Not all cleavages are politicized in every country. According to the model, which cleavages are politicized is a matter of complex interactions between actors, elites, and agents in their strategies and alliances.

[4] Liberal and conservative parties were the first to form under parliamentarism and to create organizational infrastructures under restricted suffrage (Kirchner, 1988). Both are parties of "internal origin" in Duverger's words. Even before the extension of suffrage, their ideological positions were referred to in terms of "left" and "right" in many countries – where the former term identified the propensity to reform (constitutionalism, parliamentarism, and equal political rights) and the latter the propensity to maintain the status quo of the old order (for a historical reconstruction see Noël and Thérien, 2008). The term *conservative* that replaced *Tory* in England after the 1830s originates from Chateaubriand's ultra-royalist publication *Le Conservateur*. In Scandinavia the label "right" was maintained. The term *liberal* that replaced *Whig* in England, referring to the principles of the 1688 revolution, originates from the *liberales* supporting the constitution in the Córtes of Cádiz in 1812.

parties over the acceptance of the lead of the Soviet Communist Party in the international revolutionary movement and also ideological differences, namely whether a revolution would be necessary to take the proletariat to power, or if electoral means could achieve this goal. Second, in part as a reaction against the radicalization of the working class, and its powerful action through the mass-party organization, fascist parties emerged in a number of European countries and, more or less directly, dominated during the 1930s. These parties favoured the nation over class and "internationalism" and private property over communism.[5]

What can be labelled the Post-Industrial Revolution (Bell, 1976) created two further and more recent cleavages. The first one is the *materialism–post-materialism cleavage* between generations over sets of values that emerged in the 1960s and 1970s as a consequence of the protracted period of international peace, economic wealth, and domestic security since World War II (Inglehart, 1977). The younger cohort developed "post-materialist values" of tolerance, equality, participation, expression, emancipation, environment, fair trade, peace, and Third World solidarity, as opposed to the "materialist" values of the war generation centred around priorities of national security, law and order, full employment, protection of private property, tradition, and authority (within the family and the state).[6] In terms of new party organizations, however, there are only a handful of examples of a significant impact of these "new left" movements, the main one being green parties.

The second pervasive impact of the Post-Industrial Revolution is on the "new right" through the *globalization cleavage* between sectors of the economy that profit from the blurring of national boundaries, and sectors that suffer the competition from new markets and cheap labour in the East and Asia. "Losers" of globalization and integration have reinforced support for populist protest parties that favour trade barriers to protect local manufacture and "locals-first" policies in the labour market. These groups are the small

---

[5] The fascist totalitarian form of mobilization – with communism one of the two alternative forms of mass politics to liberal democracy – represented the product of the radicalization of the industrial bourgeoisie threatened by socialist policies, and of the aristocracy threatened by redistribution through land reforms. In terms of the impact of class alliances on the regimes' outcomes, see Luebbert (1991), Moore (1966), and Rogowksi (1989). The interaction between processes of state formation and cleavage structuration is crucial for understanding the rise of fascism. National cases are characterized by either decline in post-colonial phases (France, Portugal, Spain) or other forms of national frustration after World War I, and/or a problematic definition of statehood with late national unification and Catholic influence – leading to strong centre–periphery and state–church cleavages (Germany, Italy).

[6] Post-materialist values were initially expressed primarily in social movements: the civil rights movement in the United States in the 1950s, pacifism against the Vietnam War in the 1960s, feminism in the 1970s claiming equality in the labour market and the family, and environmentalism in the 1980s. In the 1990s, new anti-globalization movements developed against the globalization of the economy and the Americanization of culture (for an overview see Snow, Soule, and Kriesi, 2004).

TABLE 2.1. *Cleavages and Their First Politicization*

"Revolution"	Timing	Cleavage	Divisive Issue(S)	Party Families
National	Early 19th century (restricted electorates)	Centre–periphery	Degree of state administrative centralization and cultural standardization	Ethnic, regionalist, linguistic parties versus liberal-nationalist elite of state builders
		State–church	Secularization, democratization of participation in representative institutions	Conservatives, Catholics, and other denominational parties, Christian democrats
Industrial	Late 19th century (suffrage extension)	Rural–urban	Degree of liberalization of industrial trade, maintenance of agricultural tariffs	Agrarian and peasants' parties versus liberal elite of the rising industrial bourgeoisie
		Employers–workers	Degree of state intervention in market economy and extension of social rights	Workers' parties, socialists, social democrats, labour parties
International	Early 20th century (mass electorates)	Communism–socialism	Centrality of Soviet international leadership and reformist versus revolutionary strategy	Communist parties
Post-industrial	Second half of the 20th century (de-mobilized electorates)	Materialist–post-materialist values	Policy priorities over civil rights, pacifism, feminism, and the environment	New left parties, social liberals, greens, feminist parties
		Open–closed societies	Openness of labour markets, international trade, immigration, economic integration	Protest parties, extreme right-wing parties, populists

and medium firms, unskilled workers, craftsmen, and agricultural producers. The economically defensive attitude of these groups is reinforced by cultural, anti-immigration, and xenophobic stances stressing religious and national values against multi-ethnic society and communitarianism. Where such opposition to the opening up of national borders from both a cultural-immigration and an economic-trade perspective is directed against the EU, the EMU, and the process of European integration in general, such parties take the more specific form of anti-Europe parties.[7]

The cleavage model is a starting point and fulfils a number of functions for the classification of parties and the construction of party families:

• Although not fully exhaustive, the model covers all of the *most important party families*, leaving out only less relevant party families such as pensioners, animalists, personal parties, and various "niche" or "issue" parties (for example anti-tax or pro-alcohol parties). As specified later, the classification used in the analysis also includes social liberals and nationalists which require additional specifications.
• The model is *comparatively* and *longitudinally* effective as it applies to all European countries and can cover the whole period since the beginning of competitive parliamentary life, as well as *cross-levels* because it covers EP elections too.[8]
• The model allows a classification of parties based on their ideologies, programme positions, and policy preferences *compatible* with various sources of data, in particular party manifestos, as well as with parties' self-descriptions (most importantly through their names), facilitating categorization.

Spatial Variation in Europe

The most important function that the model fulfils, however, is that it provides the basis from which *variation* in the format and ideological contents across European party systems can be measured quantitatively. Party families are the basic units allowing the assessment of similarities and differences between national party systems, their parallel growth or decline over time, and their ideological cohesiveness. Europeanization as a "variable" is measured through the degree to which party families are distributed homogenously (across countries and levels of governance), swing uniformly, and are ideologically cohesive.

---

[7] Populism is also a reaction to changing security conditions since the end of the Cold War which have created a resurgence of law-and-order values. The literature on the globalization cleavage and populism, as well as the pro/anti-Europe dimension of contestation is quoted in Chapter 1.
[8] The model has been criticized for its static nature coming in part from the formulation of the "freezing hypothesis", namely that party systems formed up to the 1920s crystallized and remained stable in the subsequent decades through (1) barriers to representation; (2) PR and universal suffrage; and (3) saturation of the electoral market. This thesis has been supported by empirical analysis based on aggregate data (Bartolini and Mair, 1990) although rejected by work at the individual level (Franklin, Mackie, and Valen, 1992) and by the de-alignment thesis (Dalton et al., 1984).

The more variation among national party systems, the less Europeanization. The comparative analysis in Part II has precisely the goal of assessing *empirically and quantitatively the degree of cross-country variation of national party systems* as composed of these families, of identifying the *features of variation and diversity* (party families responsible for "deviations") and *features of similarity and commonality* (party families responsible for similarity), as well as measuring the *degree of the families' internal ideological cohesion*.

From the abstract grid just summarized, the cleavage model does indeed proceed to analyze deviations and spatial variations. Primarily, the sources of variation between countries are identified in the survival of cultural and pre-industrial factors resulting in varying strength of *agrarian parties, ethno-regionalist parties, and linguistic parties*, as well as religious and *denominational parties*. Such factors are important not only because they survive and politicize in some countries but not in others, but also because they affect to a varying degree (across countries) the *unity and strength of parties on the left–right dimension* such as socialists, conservatives, and liberals. In the model, the explanation of cross-country variation in the development of a party system is articulated at two levels: (1) a *structural-historical level* whereby variation is explained through the impact of the type of state formation, class composition, linguistic, and religious structure on whether certain party families exist; much of the structural differences are derived from Rokkan's famous "conceptual map of Europe" highlighting territorial differences along a cultural North–South dimension and an economic West–East dimension[9]; (2) an *agent-strategic* level whereby variation is explained through the impact of the costs and pay-offs of alliances between actors, the institutional opportunity structures, and choices made at critical junctures on the politicization of cleavages in political parties in certain countries but not in others.[10]

Before looking for models explaining variation in Europe and country deviations, however, empirical analysis must *first assess the scope of such variation*. The richness of such theoretical models rests on thin ice if it is not supported by quantitative evidence about *how much diversity* and about *how much each party family contributes* to this diversity. So far models have relied on accounts

---

[9] The cultural dimension is largely based on the outcome of the Reformation in the North-West (Protestantism, where Christian parties did not develop but where agrarian parties appeared), the city-belt (mixed religious structures, where Catholic parties mobilized the rural population), and South (Counter-Reformation, where the interaction of the class cleavage with the state–church cleavage contributed to dividing the left). The economic dimension is largely operationalized by urban structures and regimes of land tenure.

[10] In this case it is the analysis of the costs and pay-offs of specific alliances between actors (the state apparatus, the Roman Catholic Church, national churches, landowners, industrial entrepreneurs, peripheries, etc.) and their coalitions to predict which cleavages are politicized and which are not. The politicization is shaped by opportunity structures (including institutions such as electoral systems) in sequences of choices at various critical junctures when they are confronted with alternative alliances, path dependence, and restrictions due to previous choices (Rokkan, 1999: 314; on critical junctures see Capoccia and Kelemen, 2011).

of the diversity of national party systems. But just how sure are we that, say, regionalism varies so much as to account for a fundamental diversity of some systems? Or, to take another example, that agrarian politics is concentrated in some areas and absent in others? Or that green parties have appeared everywhere and are a source of a uniform wave in Europe? Or that in the past decade there has been a Europe-wide growth of right-wing, populist parties?

As far as this work is concerned, the answers to these questions need to be addressed quantitatively. The factors that these models have been identifying as sources of variation across countries are treated in this analysis as *hypotheses* to be tested empirically. Only if agrarian politics is a source of variation, explanations must be put forward as to why in some countries agrarian parties are strong and in others they are weak. Similarly, only if there are strong swings towards regionalist parties in a given part of Europe but not in another, explanations of this non-uniformity are needed. What is claimed here is that the *impact* of these cultural and pre-industrial factors, as well as all other factors such as the divided or unified nature of the left, needs to be *tested quantitatively* before concluding that they are sources of diversity in Europe.

Central and Eastern Europe

In most of what follows, the analysis covers the whole of Europe. In a number of cases, however, evidence is presented in a disaggregated way for Western and Central-Eastern Europe. Assessing differences between the two "halves" of Europe is an empirical matter and it remains to be seen how distinct they are. Yet caution is necessary from the outset given their radically divergent historical paths – mainly but not limited to the post–World War II period until 1989 – as this divergence involves socio-economic structures, ethnic and religious composition, institutions, and state administration. Not many attempts to extend the cleavage model to Central and Eastern Europe have been made,[11] but a number of critical junctures can be distinguished that have an impact on the politicization and structuration of party systems. Each juncture established specific "legacies" (Wittenberg, 2013) separating the development of party systems in the two parts of Europe. They can be summarized in five points.

1. **State formation and nation-building.** – While with Atlantic trade the expansion of the seaward empires of the West (Portugal, Spain, and, later, England, the Low Countries, and France) was directed outside Europe, the expansion of the landward empires in Central and Eastern Europe was directed towards the weaker surrounding territories (Habsburg, Ottoman, and Tsarist Empires). Consequently, in the West political

---

[11] The fact that the cleavage model has been developed for Western Europe requires a specific discussion of its applicability to Central and Eastern Europe. This should incorporate elements highlighted by work such as Urwin (1980) and Moore (1966). A recent large-scale attempt at applying the model to Central and Eastern Europe is Kommisrud (2009). On the divergent paths see Caramani (2003b).

structures were integrated through the formation of national centres, whereas in Central and Eastern Europe states remained fragmented and heterogeneous. With the breakdown of the three empires after World War I the new states faced an accumulation of challenges. With late sovereign independence they had a short time to build up new institutions, and at the same time faced the double challenge of international pressure from established states and internal pressures from mass mobilization (franchise, war de-mobilization, industrialization). The absence of a national "container", institutional instability, frequent border shifts, and ethnic migrations until World War II hindered the consolidation of institutions and the organization of political representation (party alignments) in the context of an uncontested national citizenship.

2. **Reformation versus Counter-Reformation.** – Furthermore, the outcome of the Reformation contributed to hinder processes of nation-building in Central and Eastern Europe similarly to Southern Europe.[12] The Reformation in large parts of Western Europe strengthened the division with Central and Eastern Europe – both the Orthodox territories and the areas of the Counter-Reformation (Austro-Hungarian Empire and Poland). Under the Reformation national languages developed in parallel to national religions through the "alliance" between state and church and the creation of national churches and state religions. The integrated state administrations and national identities (based on national religions and vernaculars) developed primarily in the Protestant North-West after 1648 with the Peace of Westphalia. In Central-Eastern Europe the cross-territorial church hindered the process of nation-building and conflicted with national institutions and identities, with an impact on the strength of the state–church cleavage.

3. **Napoleonic reforms.** – The spread of the French Revolution and Napoleonic administrative reforms stopped at the borders of Central Europe. The national idea could not directly be imported as happened in Germany, Italy, the Low Countries, Portugal, and Spain. Even in the most culturally fragmented territories, such as Switzerland, the idea of the nation and popular sovereignty imposed itself. Reforms included constitutions, centralization and rationalization of the state, the republican ideal, parliamentary representation, and the abolition of aristocratic and clerical privilege. Both administratively and ideologically the impact of these reforms was enormous in shaping the modern state, whereas the Habsburg territories and beyond were not confronted directly with such pressures.

4. **Industrial revolution.** – While in Western Europe at the elite level industrial entrepreneurs emerged from the commercialization of agriculture, at the mass level the industrial working class emerged from new

---

[12] Religion has directed the West and the East on two different trajectories since the Schism of 1054, reinforcing the earlier division after the collapse of the Western Empire.

production systems and urbanization. This produced the class cleavage. In Central and Eastern Europe agrarian politics remained dominant because of the delay of industrialization until after World War II.[13] The delayed industrialization in Central and Eastern Europe thus did not produce a working class in territories that were mostly agrarian economies in which serfdom persisted.

5. **Socialist rule.** – After World War I there was a period of national politics in the newly independent and democratic states in Central and Eastern Europe. But democracy was short-lived under the attacks of communist and fascist ideologies. The democratic experience was then definitely put to end when Central and Eastern Europe became dominated by the Soviet Union until 1989. In the new democracies during the 1990s electorates had little sense of party attachment or identification. Because of one-party regimes, cleavages were not politicized. Further, the ideology and policy that had sought to transcend class, ethnicity, and religion eradicated social stratifications. Not only was politicization difficult, but the very social divisions were missing. This hindered the emergence of cleavage structures and new parties were weakly anchored in society and unstructured, and the electorate was volatile.[14]

The contrast between Western and Central-Eastern Europe is not perfect, and many variations exist within both areas. Rather, the divergence comes from the fact that Central and Eastern Europe had a different trajectory on all junctures. This matters greatly because what follows presents a broad, quantitative description of the whole European party system over a century and a half and an attempt to measure the variations around the overall model of development. A presentation along this fault line will therefore be necessary.

Data File and Party Codes
In the basic data file information has been collected for each national and European election.[15] This information includes the basic electoral figures (absolute and percentage):

- Number of persons entitled to vote, actual voters (turnout), valid votes.
- Votes for single parties above the threshold of 1 per cent of votes nationwide.
- Total seats for lower houses and distribution of seats across parties.

[13] The lack of commercialization of agricultural production has geo-economic origins: the remote location with respect to the city-belt's economic network first, and the Atlantic trade routes later. The weakness of the city network strengthened the gap, as agriculture was not confronted with the need to produce a large surplus for urban populations as in the West.

[14] On the early development of cleavages and party systems in Central and Eastern Europe after the fall of the Berlin Wall see Berglund and Dellenbrant (1994), Klingemann, Mochmann, and Newton (2000), and Lewis (1996).

[15] Only lower houses have been considered. Also for elections to the EP results are considered at the national level.

Each party has been given a code consisting of two digits "country", two digits "family", and two digits of continuous numbering. For example, the main Bulgarian agrarian party (BZNS) has been given the code 094001 (09 = Bulgaria, 40 = agrarians, 01 = continuous). Further agrarian parties have been given the codes 094002, 094003, and so forth. These codes are kept unchanged when parties change names. This is crucial for giving continuity to the analysis (for example in the computation of volatility levels or swings between two subsequent elections). It has been attempted *to keep as much continuity as possible*, which is sometimes problematic because of *splits* of and *mergers* between parties.[16] Only in very exceptional cases has the code of a party been changed on the basis of *ideological change*, for example from communist to socialist or from agrarian to liberal or conservative. Such cases are documented in the various chapters.

Based on electoral figures a number of systemic indicators (i.e. for the whole party system rather than for single parties or families) have been computed. These include the fractionalization index for votes and seats (Rae, 1971), the effective number of parties measures ENEP and ENPP (Laasko and Taagepera, 1979), the index of electoral volatility for votes and seats (Pedersen, 1979), and the least squared index of disproportionality between votes and seats (Gallagher, 1991).[17]

More important, the data file includes *indicators of the Europeanization of electoral politics* mentioned in the previous chapter and described in detail in the corresponding chapters in Part II of this book: (1) indicators of *homogeneity* (standard deviation, various versions of the Gini index, IPR, etc.) used in Chapter 3; (2) indicators of *uniformity* of swings used in Chapter 4; and (3) "mixed" and "differential" volatility used in Chapter 5 to measure *correspondence*. The data file also includes the necessary data to calculate (4) the indicators of the ideological convergence among party manifestos and the voters' preferences for parties in the same family used in Chapter 6 and Chapter 7 (*cohesion*). Finally, it includes (5) cabinet composition data and the ideological position of each coalition partner to calculate homogeneity and convergence patterns among executives used in Chapter 7 (*closure*).

In many countries and for several party families, there is more than one party per family (for example two agrarian parties). In the basic data file votes and seats are therefore available at *party level* and at *family level*. Family-level figures have been created by adding the figures for parties belonging to the same family. Accordingly, all indicators are available at both levels (in addition to being available for votes and seats): ENPP, ENEP, Gallagher's LSQ,

---

[16] In the case of mergers, the code of the new party is that of the largest of the two or more parties that merged. In the case of splits, the code of the old party is transferred to the largest of the splinter parties.

[17] See Chapter 3 for a detailed description of these indicators and Appendix 3 for formulas.

TABLE 2.2. *Party Families*

Code	Shortcut	Families
11	Socialists	Socialists, social democrats, labour, and workers' parties
12	Communists	Communists and other radical left
13	New left	Other small and new left parties
20	Conservatives	Conservatives (includes hunters)
25	Nationalists	Nationalist parties, independence movements
30	Liberals	Liberals and radicals
35	Social liberals	Socially but not economically permissive parties (includes pirate parties and pacifists)
40	Agrarians	Agrarians, peasants, and "centre" parties
50	Greens	Greens, ecologists, and environmentalist parties
51	Animalists	Parties for the protection of animals
55	Anti-Europe	Anti-Europe, anti-EU integration parties
60	Regionalists	Parties for regional autonomy
65	Ethnic	Ethnic parties
70	Extreme right	Radical right and populists; includes monarchists, fascist-Nazi parties, and royalists
75	Feminists	Women's lists
78	Pro-alcohol	Parties for the promotion and consumption of beer
80	Orthodox	Orthodox parties
81	Catholics	Catholic parties in religiously mixed countries
82	Protestants	Protestant parties
83	Inter-confessionals	Inter-confessional parties in religiously mixed countries
84	People's parties	Christian democrats and Catholic parties in Catholic countries
85	Pensioners	Pensioners' lists
86	Personal	Personal parties
91	Europeans	Pro-EU alliances and parties specific to EP elections
92	Others	Other parties and independent candidates (below 1 per cent of votes)
00	Unknown	Unknown parties/candidates

volatility, F, and so forth, as well as swing figures. In the following chapters analyses are presented at one or the other level, or both.

The basic *time units* of the analysis are election years in each country. For comparison, however, election years cannot be used because single countries vote for national parliaments in different years. For a number of analyses five-year periods have been used instead as the comparable time unit. If, in a given country, two or more elections took place within a five-year period, averages have been used. This choice has also the advantage of reducing erratic movements that may occur if considering single elections. In several graphs, evidence is presented according to five-year periods as time units whereby the date of, say, 1970 refers to the five-year period 1970–4. Only for the last period the number of years is not five insofar as the data collection ends with the last election in 2012 (2010–12).[18]

The Classification of Parties into Families

Analyzing whether party families exist everywhere and measuring the extent to which they are distributed homogeneously across Europe presupposes a classification of single parties into party families. Also, studying whether parties of the same family converge ideologically towards similar ideological positions (for example, on the left–right scale) requires a prior definition of which parties belong to a specific family.[19]

The various analyses that follow in the subsequent chapters rely on a classification of parties in a number of families larger and more detailed than those of other studies. Table 2.2 lists the 24 families into which parties have been categorized, plus the two categories of "others" (i.e. parties that in a specific election received less than 1 per cent) and "unknown" (i.e. parties for which it was not possible to establish their ideological or programmatic nature).[20] As can be seen from the list of party families in Table 2.2 they are of very different natures, some being large, ideological parties offering societal and cultural *Weltanschauungen* (socialists, people's parties, liberals, conservatives) and others being specific "single-issue" families (animalists, pensioners, feminists, pro-alcohol parties). Furthermore, the list of families is quite detailed, and includes the category of personal parties, which is defined strictly in terms of groups supporting a specific candidate whose name is the name of the list.[21]

---

[18] This does not apply to the same extent to elections to the EP, except for countries that joined the EU after an election had already taken place and voted years later. Details on such delayed votes of new EU member-states are given in Table 5.1. For the analysis of cabinets in Chapter 7 calendar years are used as basic time units.

[19] The full classification appears in Table A.1.1 in Appendix 1 (see Table A.1.2 for parties contesting EP elections exclusively).

[20] Contrary to other comparative projects *all parties* with at least 1 per cent of national votes have been coded and classified into families. For contributions relying on family classifications see Bornschier (2010), Ennser (2012), Mair and Mudde (1998), Thomas (2006), and Volkens and Klingemann (2002). For an analysis of the literature on parties classified by family see Caramani and Hug (1998).

[21] Differently than some recent definitions, political parties clearly dominated by a charismatic leader are not classified as "personal" if the programme and label of the party are not exclusively intended to promote a candidate. The category includes parties supporting the return of a given monarch.

The choice has been made to have more detailed families in the initial classification which can be aggregated into broader categories. The case of religious parties goes clearly in this direction with the distinction between large, religiously inspired parties (inter-confessional Christian democratic people's parties) on one hand, and smaller denominational parties (Protestants, Catholics, Orthodox) on the other.[22] Also ethnic and regionalist parties (those with a territorial claim) have been initially coded separately, as parties that are on the far right of the spectrum (extreme-right parties; nationalist, anti-European parties). On the left the classification is more differentiated than usual with – besides the distinction between socialists and communists – families of the "new left" (non-communist far left) and "social liberals" that include socially liberal and culturally tolerant parties but that do not espouse state intervention in the economy. This family includes early republican and "libertarian" parties with strong emphasis on individual rights (for example "pirate" parties).

Several criteria have been employed to allocate parties to families:

- *Common knowledge and name*: This is the criterion used for most of the large, socialist, conservative, liberal, agrarian, green, extreme-right, communist, and people's parties for which there is consensus in the literature. The name of the party is also a useful indication of the nature of the party when it is unambiguous (for example, for ethnic parties, the Jewish Coalition in Latvia, Ukrainians in Poland, etc. or, for religious parties, the Orthodox Rally in Greece).
- *Primary sources*: These sources include the description of parties by themselves in their manifestos and on their Web sites. This has mainly been necessary for small, marginal parties on which the existing academic literature is lacking.
- *Secondary sources*: First, the various sources used to compile and refine the data collection include discussions on the nature of parties (Caramani, 2000; Nohlen and Stöver, 2010) and the large corpus of academic literature available on the main parties in Europe. Second, the classification has been cross-checked with other similar efforts such as the CMP (Budge et al., 2001; Klingemann et al., 2006) and available data from expert surveys.[23] Deviations from such classifications are discussed in the text later (for example the SVP in Switzerland has been classified as conservative rather than extreme right). The CMP and expert surveys do not classify all parties but only major ones.[24]

---

[22] Jewish parties between the two world wars that existed in several Central and Eastern European countries have been classified as ethnic parties.

[23] Among major expert survey projects see Benoit, Hunt, and Laver (Benoit and Laver, 2006 and 2007; Laver and Hunt, 1992; Mikhaylov, Laver, and Benoit, 2008) and the Chapel Hill projects (Marks et al., 2006; Ray, 1999; Steenbergen and Marks, 2007).

[24] To avoid misunderstandings, it is important to stress that parties have not been classified into party families based on their ideological positions on scales constructed on the basis of text data

TABLE 2.3. *The Aggregation of Party Families*

Code	Shortcut	Families	Code	Shortcut	Families
01	Far left	Communists (12) New left (13)	07	Far right	Nationalists (25) Anti-Europe (55)
02	Left	Socialists (11) Communists (12) New left (13)	08	Religious	Extreme right (79) Orthodox (80) Catholics (81)
03	Liberals	Liberals (30) Social liberals (35)			Protestants (82) Inter-confessionals (83)
04	Right	Liberals (30) Conservatives (20)	09	Great right	People's parties (84) Right (04)
06	Minorities	Regionalists (60) Ethnic (65)			Religious (08)

Special seats reserved for ethnic minorities (such as for Hungarian and Italian representation in Slovenia) have been treated as votes for ethnic parties. Among other major classification decisions worth mentioning at this stage, the various German parties in Czechoslovakia after World War I have been added together in one single "party",[25] and in Italy the "Destra" and "Sinistra" (meaning *right* and *left*) within the liberal constellation that dominated Italian politics between unification and World War I have been classified as conservative and liberal, respectively.

For a number of purposes these detailed party families have been aggregated into broader categories as shown in Table 2.3. The two broader categories of "far left" (communists and new left parties) and "left" (which includes socialists) are not particularly problematic even if one could add social liberals to them (which, for some countries, includes republican and radical parties). Also fairly straightforward is the aggregation of ethnic and regionalist parties into a "minority parties" category (as regionalists are often characterized by ethnic distinctiveness, although the opposite is not always the case), of liberals and social liberals together, and of extreme-right parties, anti-Europe parties, and nationalists. More problematic is the category of religious parties for two reasons. First, as mentioned, this category includes both broad inter-confessional Christian democratic people's parties and more specific denominational parties. Second, in several countries these parties are the functional equivalent of

or surveys. A socialist party is classified as socialist if it defines itself in those terms and if the description of its ideology and societal vision fits that label, even if the quantitative measurement in the scales would position it on the extreme left.

[25] German parties made up about 22 per cent of the electorate in Czechoslovakia. They were divided ideologically into Christian democratic, socialist, and agrarian parties. To treat them uniformly as "ethnic parties" clearly has an impact on the analysis of this period.

conservative parties. For this reason a broad category of "great right" has been created and employed in some of the analyses – which, however, also includes the liberals (on the ground of a similar economic-policy dimension), as well as the small denominational parties.[26]

The variable classification into narrower or broader party families is important for the analysis that follows in Part II, insofar as *the way parties are classified has a major direct impact on measures of Europeanization of electoral politics*. The broader the categories, the more homogenous the European landscape. For example, if one would apply the categories of "left", "right", "greens", "ethno-regionalists", and "others", the European countries would look very similar as all countries have parties that correspond to these categories (even if levels of support may vary). If, on the other hand, one would consider categories so specific as to correspond to the names of the parties, then countries would look extremely different. This is an artificial impact of the aggregation of parties into families which is dealt with, first, by presenting results according to various possible classifications, and, second, by avoiding extreme aggregation or fragmentation and by excluding party families such as animalists and pro-alcohol parties which are very small and make only sporadic appearances in European party systems.[27]

European Party Systems

Countries and Time Periods

The 30 Western and Central-Eastern European countries covered by this study – the current 27 EU member-states plus Iceland, Norway, and Switzerland – as well as the periods of time for each are shown in Table 2.4.

Time periods vary according to the type of data used for the different indicators. In regard to national elections, periods covered for each country are determined by the timing of *state formation and democratization* (i.e. independence or unification, and competitive parliamentary elections), as well as by *data availability*, which concerns not only the availability of electoral results, but also the information about candidates' party affiliations and names of lists. Concerning elections to the EP, all member-states at the moment of the election are included since the first direct election in 1979 plus those countries

---

[26] As far as nationalists are concerned, these are parties within the countries of their claims, such as Sinn Féin in Ireland, GVP in Germany, or PUNR in Romania. Irish parties in the United Kingdom and German parties in Poland or Czechoslovakia, and so forth are classified as ethnic or regionalist parties. Nationalists, therefore, include parties making claims for territorial expansion (irredentists) or defence of populations abroad but active in their "home" lands. The aggregation with extreme-right parties makes sense as the latter often include fascist parties making such claims as in the case of the Italian and German parties between the two world wars.

[27] As will be seen later, the analysis of executive politics and cabinets relies on a slightly different classification based on left, centre-left, centre, centre-right, right, and "other" (i.e. great and oversized coalitions). For details see Table 7.3.

TABLE 2.4. *Countries and Time Periods Covered (National Elections)*

Countries	19th Century–World War I	Inter-War Period	Since World War II
Austria	–	1919–30	1945–2008
Belgium	1848–1912	1919–39	1946–2010
Bulgaria	1899–1914	1919–31	1991–2009
Cyprus	–	–	1960–2011
Czech Republic[a]	–	1920–35	1946, 1990–2010
Denmark	1849–1918	1920–43	1945–2011
Estonia	–	1919–32	1992–2011
Finland	1907–17	1919–39	1945–2011
France	1876–1914	1919–36	1945–2012
Germany[b]	1871–1912	1919–33	1949–2009
Greece	–	1926–46	1946–64, 1974–2012
Hungary	–	–	1990–2010
Iceland	1916	1919–42	1946–2009
Ireland	–	1922–44	1948–2011
Italy	1876–80, 1895–1913	1919–21	1946–2008
Latvia	–	1920–31	1993–2010
Lithuania	–	1920–26	1992–2008
Luxembourg	–	1919–37	1945–2009
Malta	–	1921–39	1945–2008
Netherlands	1888–1918	1922–37	1946–2010
Norway	1882–1918	1921–36	1945–2009
Poland	–	1919–22	1991–2011
Portugal	–	–	1975–2009
Romania	–	1926–37	1946, 1990–2008
Slovakia	–	–	1990–2010
Slovenia	–	–	1996–2011
Spain	–	1933–6	1977–2011
Sweden	1911–17	1920–44	1948–2010
Switzerland	1848–1914	1917–43	1947–2011
United Kingdom[c]	1832–1918	1922–35	1945–2010

Notes: Dates indicate election years.

[a] As Czechoslovakia in 1920–46.

[b] Boundary changes over time (in particular during losses after the two world wars and during the division with the German Democratic Republic from World War II until 1990).

[c] Includes Ireland until 1918 and Northern Ireland since 1922.

that joined later and voted with delays of one or two years (see Table 5.1). The number of countries, therefore, increases until we see 30 for the past decades (and 27 at the most recent EP elections considered at the moment of analysis, namely the election of 2009). The time period of the analysis in Chapter 5 starts, therefore, later than the analysis in Chapters 3 and 4. Chapters 6 and 7 do not cover the same period of 150 years as they rely on party manifesto data, cabinet composition data, and survey data available since 1945 (or the 1970s with survey data). Details are given in the respective chapters.

The long-term historical analysis based on aggregate data (homogeneity in Chapter 3 and uniformity in Chapter 4) also faces several issues of democratic interruption, inconsistent electoral results, and border changes (transfer of regions in particular after the two world wars). This is not the place to provide a thorough list of these issues. In general terms, suffice it to give some reference points. Overseas territories and colonies are never included in the analysis (for example for France, the Netherlands, or Portugal), and also for Denmark the Farø are excluded. Until 1918, however, the United Kingdom includes what in 1922 became the Irish Free State and later the Irish Republic. Furthermore, only lower house election results are considered and no by-elections are included.[28] Finally, no elections to parliaments based on estate representation have been included, but only since the transition to general and individual representation.

Electoral systems pose a number of issues which have – as far as possible – been dealt with in a consistent manner (unless stated otherwise). In case of two-or-more-ballot formulas, election results of the first round have been used, as well as first preferences for countries like Ireland and Malta voting with single transferable vote (STV). In mixed systems combining PR list systems and some form of majoritarian elections in single-member constituencies, PR votes have been used (in Germany since 1949 *Zweitstimmen* have been taken). In periods of plural and multiple voting (i.e. where voters had different amounts of votes according to wealth and status, and as many votes as seats to fill in a constituency, the computation of national totals is problematic.[29] While for some countries such as Switzerland estimates based on "fictitious voter" figures are available, or excellent sources such as F. W. S. Craig's series on the United Kingdom have been published (see also Rallings and Thrasher, 2007), for countries like Denmark estimates have been calculated for the period 1849–98 when election results exist at the constituency level only.[30]

---

[28] In Belgium until the aftermath of World War I both general elections and partial elections (when half of the lower house was renewed in a staggered process) were held. From 1848 until 1912 only general elections have been considered. In Luxembourg, on the contrary, until World War II partial elections have been considered as otherwise there would not have been enough time points.

[29] More details can be found in the country chapters in Caramani (2000; for a summary see also Caramani, 2004: 44–8). On sources see Appendix 6 at the end of this volume.

[30] In Denmark country totals are not available because of the high number of unopposed seats, open voting (by show of hands), and the practice of asking for the count of "*nej*" (no) votes when candidates were unopposed (for details see Caramani 2000: 199–200 and 2003a). For these reasons also "voters" figures are not available as in many constituencies actual voting did not take place. Estimates have been produced by attributing a total of 1,000 votes to uncontested candidates. Percentage distribution of votes is similar to percentage distribution of seats. "*Nej*" votes have been added to the "other parties" category.

With few exceptions, the longer time series are those for Western European countries. As far as the early established states are concerned (before the Congress of Vienna, 1815), electoral official returns in the United Kingdom have been recorded since the 1832 reform. In France, results at the national level are available roughly since the Third Republic. Establishing candidates' party affiliations in France is particularly problematic because of the fluid nature of the party system and systematic official data on elections do not appear until after World War II. Previous periods are based on secondary sources. In Denmark, the period from 1849 to 1895 relies on J. P. Nordengård's work (*Valgene til Rigsdagen i 100 aar*). Since 1895 data also appear in statistical yearbooks. For Sweden, data are available since 1866, when the bicameral Riksdag replaced the estate system. Party affiliations, however, are available only since the introduction of PR in 1911. For the Netherlands data are available by parties since 1888. For Portugal and Spain data are not available until after the end of the long authoritarian period in the mid-1970s, although for Spain election results are available for the Second Republic until the Civil War of 1936.

As far as newly independent countries are concerned, for Ireland 1922 is the starting point after the Anglo-Irish Treaty gave dominion status to the 26 counties of the Irish Free State. Independence from the United Kingdom also gives the start of the time series for Cyprus and Malta. For Finland, election results are published regularly since 1907 when the first election took place before the country's secession from the Russian Empire (1917). For other Nordic countries too, independence cannot be considered the relevant starting point. Iceland became an independent republic in 1945, but elections are registered since 1874. Only since 1916, however, are party affiliations available. Sweden recognized Norway as independent in 1905, but elections to the Storthing had been held and registered since 1815. Periodical series have been published since 1882. In Belgium elections were held since independence from the Netherlands in 1830, but statistics by parties are available since 1848. For Greece, which gained independence progressively from the Ottoman Empire, data are not available until 1926. A special mention concerns Austria for which, similarly to Central and Eastern European countries, the period of time covered by the analysis starts with the break-up of the Habsburg Empire (although elections were held since 1873 in the estate parliament).

For other countries state unification determines the starting point of the time series. This is the case for Switzerland with the creation of the federal state in 1848, as well as for Germany in 1871 and Italy (in the latter case slightly later because of the non-partisan nature of elections). The Italian election of 1922, furthermore, is usually not considered a democratic election and has been excluded from the analysis.

What characterizes Central and Eastern Europe is, first, state formation with the break-ups of the Habsburg, Ottoman, and Russian Empires after World War I and, second, the long democratic interruption from World War II until 1989. The earliest data is available for Bulgaria since 1899.[31] For a number of countries election data are available between the two world wars starting in 1919 as in Estonia and Poland and in 1920 as in Czechoslovakia, Latvia, and Lithuania or later as in the case of Romania (1926). For the latter, the 1919 and 1920 election results are unfortunately not available and are excluded as are the Polish elections since 1928 which cannot be considered democratic. For Poland the 1947 election is a manipulated election and has been excluded. For two countries – Czechoslovakia and Romania – one election after World War II is available and has been included in the analysis (1946 in both cases).

For Hungary, Slovakia, and Slovenia, finally, no data are available before the democratic transitions after the breakdown of communism in 1989. For Hungary elections from 1919 until 1939 were formally competitive but took place in an authoritarian context after the republican revolution, with extensive territorial border changes, the Soviet republic, and the fall of the regime through invasion by Romanian and Czech troops, after which the army took de facto power. Furthermore, data are incomplete because of a mixture of open and secret voting, and a high number of uncontested constituencies. These elections are also excluded.

The "European" Party System

As seen at the beginning of this chapter, from the work of classical authors on the origin and evolution of party systems – from Ostrogowski and Michels through Duverger until Rokkan and Sartori – a typical account of the European party families emerges. Rarely, however, has such an account gone beyond a qualitative analysis and included a systematic quantitative picture. Furthermore, rarely does one "see" the European party system and its families. It is, therefore, useful to start with a picture of what the European party system looks like from the broadest perspective. The graph depicted in Figure 2.1 makes use of the longitudinal and cross-national data collection for 30 countries and over roughly 150 years.

The graph visualizes the account of European electoral history. It portrays the European party system as one single entity, as well as the party families that compose this system as they emerged from the National and Industrial Revolutions in the course of the 19th century. The figure shows the period of liberalism in Europe and the dominance of the families of "internal" origin under restricted suffrage and majoritarian elections, and the challenge that came from families of "external" origin under the impact of mass and class politics. At the same time, the famous dilemma of the left also appears neatly with class politics never becoming majoritarian against the hopes of the proponents

---

[31] For this country the 1911 election has been considered rather than the election of the constitutional assembly in the same year. Furthermore, the 1938 election is missing, and for the elections of 1939 and 1945 data are inconsistent. These elections are excluded.

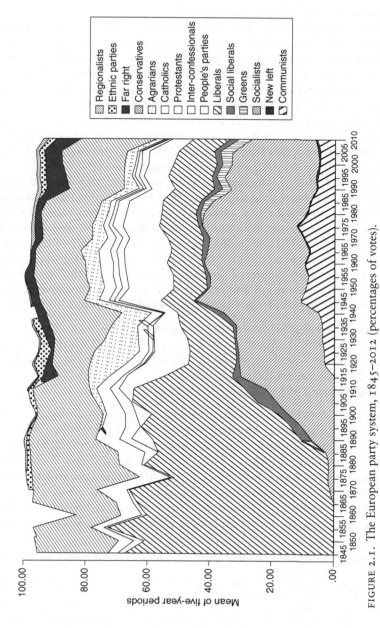

FIGURE 2.1. The European party system, 1845–2012 (percentages of votes).

Notes: The period 1830–44 has been removed from the graph because of only one country concerned (see Figure 2.2 for this period). The time point 2010 does not cover a five-year period but 2010–12. The number of countries included varies over time (see Table 3.1).

of electoral socialism.[32] It shows the division of the left, the decline of the liberal family when universal suffrage was introduced after World War I, and the rise of Christian democracy after World War II.

The figure also shows the fate of pre-industrial factors such as territorial politics, denominational politics, and agrarian politics that become marginal in a landscape dominated by left–right as it emerged from the National Revolution and the class cleavage. In the most recent periods, the figure reveals the rise of right-wing, extreme populism and the weak effect of post-materialism in terms of party organizations. The "freezing hypothesis" about the stability of party systems after the introduction of PR in most European countries and of the extension of franchise to all adult men (and later women) appears visually and convincingly. Remarkably, this whole typically "Western" account applies to a figure that includes both Western and Central-Eastern Europe.[33]

As the legend in Figure 2.1 indicates, a mixture of more specific and more aggregated families has been used to produce the graph. On one hand, most of the detailed classification of Table 2.1 has been applied as in the case of the various religious parties, socialists, communists, agrarians, liberals, social liberals, conservatives, and ethnic and regionalist parties. In the case of far-right parties, on the other hand, extreme-right parties, nationalists, and anti-Europe parties have been taken together.[34] In spite of the level of detail, the graph does not suffer from excessive fragmentation and is clear in its patterns. The same applies to Figure 2.2 where the period since 1845 has been divided into four periods:

1. The period of restricted and majoritarian elections.
2. The inter-war period after the introduction of PR and universal suffrage.
3. The post–World War II period before the 1989 transition to democracy in Central and Eastern Europe.
4. The period since 1989 including 30 countries.

Breaking down the entire period reveals visually the high level of stability in the configuration of the European party system since World War I – as maintained by the "freezing hypothesis" and confirmed by long-term data on electoral volatility (Bartolini and Mair, 1990). The most radical transformations in the European party system take place in the first period of structuration between the mid-19th century and World War I.

When looking broadly at the European party system it becomes evident that there is a fundamental opposition between left and right, where the left is

---

[32] The classical analysis of electoral socialism is the one provided by Przeworski and Sprague (1986). See also Kitschelt (1994: 8–39).

[33] From a party organization perspective the passage from elite to mass parties is described by Panebianco (1988) and Katz and Mair (1992, 1994).

[34] Smaller and occasional families such as animalists and feminists do not appear in the graph. The graph includes results of national elections only and no data from elections to the EP since 1979. For this reason the families (such as pro-Europeans) that receive a larger amount of votes in EP elections do not appear.

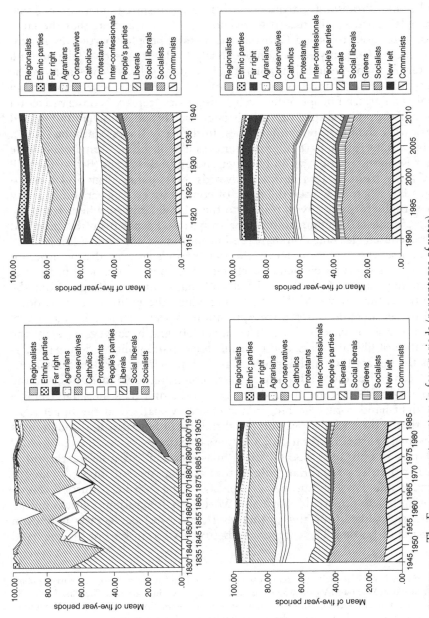

FIGURE 2.2. The European party system in four periods (percentages of votes).

Notes: The time point 2010 does not cover a five-year period but 2010–12. The number of countries included varies over time (see Table 3.1).

dominated by socialists or social democrats and workers' labour parties, and the right by liberals, conservatives, and religious parties – either denominational Catholic and Protestant parties, or Christianity-inspired inter-confessional and people's parties.[35] In regard to religious parties, it is clear that the large bulk of votes goes to broad Christian democratic people's parties (as in religiously mixed Germany or in homogenously Catholic Austria, Belgium, and Italy) rather than specific denominational parties such as Protestants in the Netherlands and in Scandinavian countries or Catholics in Switzerland and in Central and Eastern Europe. Where religious parties "replace" conservatives on the right of the political spectrum it is through such broad, Christianity-inspired parties rather than denominational ones. In the early stages, Catholics play a more important role in particular in countries like Belgium, Germany until the Weimar Republic (1919–33), and Switzerland up to the 1970s (before the SVP moved away from its agrarian base towards Swiss nationalism and a populist agenda), where they take the place of conservatives. The remaining party families are by far minor with respect to these large families, whether it is the ethno-regionalists, communist, or agrarian parties. Parties from the class and the state–church cleavage dominate the European party system.

Of course, the evolution across the four periods of time distinguished in Figure 2.2 also reveals elements of change. The most dramatic difference is between the long period of restricted and majoritarian suffrage (from the mid-19th century to World War I), during which the political space is dominated by the liberal–conservative opposition as seen in the cleavage model before the rise of class politics. The upper-left graph conveys visually the importance of liberal parties and their ideological and political dominance, as well as the impact they had during this period in shaping parliamentary institutions, centralization of administrative structures, national identities, and the secularization of the state. Towards the end of the time axis the small triangle in the right-hand corner harbingers the change visualized in the upper-right graph, that is the socialist rise and the shrinking of liberal vote through mass politics, mass party organizations, and mass electorates.[36]

But this is only one aspect of the "massification" of politics, the other one being the rise of agrarian politics that accompanies so forcefully labour in Central and Eastern Europe, as well as in the Nordic countries and in Switzerland. Between World War I and World War II agrarian politics appears with the short-lived (not always that short, however) democratic politics in those parts of Europe. The comparison between Western Europe on one hand

---

[35] As mentioned, Jewish parties (present in several Central and Eastern European party systems between World War I and World War II) have been coded as ethnic parties. The classification in Figures 2.1 and 2.2 does not allow for more specific denominations of Protestants. Because of their small and sporadic nature Orthodox parties have not been included.

[36] The Italian republicans, the French radicals, the Belgian liberal-socialist cartel, and the Danish Radikale Venstre, among others, are examples of parties classified as social liberals in the present study.

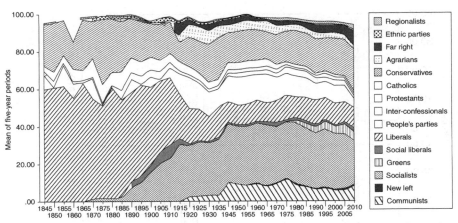

FIGURE 2.3. The Western European party system, 1845–2012 (percentages of votes).

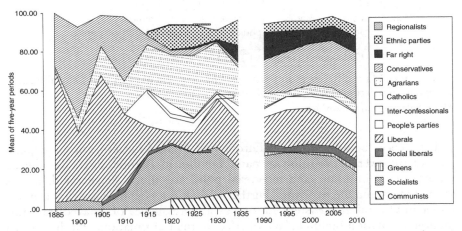

FIGURE 2.4. The Central-Eastern European party system, 1885–2012 (percentages of votes).

and Central-Eastern Europe on the other appears in Figures 2.3 and 2.4. Also in the light of the divergence on junctures between the two halves of Europe seen earlier, the most important difference is certainly the size of agrarian electoral support. With the "massification" of politics after World War I in Central and Eastern Europe, liberals and conservatives are reduced to small shares of the electorate. In the overall picture, after World War II agrarian parties decline in correspondence to the exclusion of Central and Eastern Europe from the figures. During the more recent period since 1989 agrarian politics has basically disappeared from the European landscape.[37]

---

[37] In Western Europe agrarian interests were channelled through large and electorally significant parties only in Scandinavia and in some Protestant cantons in Switzerland, while in the

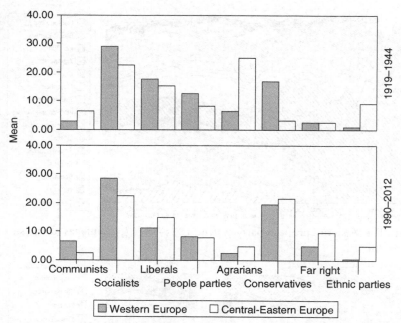

FIGURE 2.5. Main differences in party systems between Western and Central-Eastern Europe in two periods (percentages of votes).
Note: Selected party families.

Differences between Western Europe and Central-Eastern Europe explain part of the overall evolution of party families in Europe. First, the alleged recent revival in ethnic and territorial politics is much exaggerated. It was stronger between the two wars. Furthermore, it is a phenomenon that is much larger in Central and Eastern Europe as a consequence of delayed state formation and nation-building, lack of effect of the Reformation, and the uneven spread of Napoleonic influence previously discussed. As one can see from the juxtaposition of the graphs for the two parts of Europe (Figure 2.5), ethnic parties have indeed a much stronger electoral support in Central-Eastern Europe, where nation-building was not in the position of achieving the same degree of cultural integration as in Western European nation-states. The social fragmentation of Central-Eastern Europe, as well as its ethnic and religious variety, is unmatched in any part of Western Europe, and includes a variety of minorities – Ukrainians, Poles, Russians, Hungarians, Jews, and so on.

remaining countries agrarian support was spread across short-lived, small parties. In Central and Eastern Europe, on the contrary, agrarian politics was much more pervasive and linked to patterns of land tenure (see, in particular, Linz, 1976 and Urwin, 1980). The classical analysis of the role of the peasant world is that of Moore (1966). On the distribution of land see data presented by Russett (1964), Taylor and Jodice (1983), and Vanhanen (2000).

Second, in the most recent period since 1989 the overall graphs show an increase of votes of far-right parties. This is clearly an effect of the inclusion in the sample of countries of Central and Eastern Europe revealing a stronger presence of these parties, in particular extreme-right parties and populist parties since 1989, but also nationalists. Historically, the graph for the period between the two wars indicates a growth of the far right. As already mentioned, however, the extent of this overall "wave" is grossly underestimated by electoral data because most of the elections in which extreme-right parties (fascists in particular) succeeded have been excluded from the analysis as their democratic credentials are doubtful. The figures for the period between the two wars, in many cases, reflect patterns of nationalism (irredentism, as in Ireland), and independence in countries in which elections took place before full sovereignty was achieved (cases such as Finland and Iceland).

Third, in the overall evolution of party systems in Europe one notes the relative rise of communist parties with peaks of about 10 per cent across Western Europe (for the period 1945–89) – a figure strongly influenced by countries with a "divided left" such as Finland, France, and Italy. It is also the phase of large Christian democratic parties again in countries like France and Italy, but also Austria, Belgium, and Germany. During this third period, socialist parties establish themselves firmly as the largest electoral force throughout Europe. Overall, vote shares decline mainly for Christian democratic and religious parties in general. Shares decrease also for communists, while liberal parties make gains especially in Central and Eastern Europe. Mostly, however, it is the far right – more particularly in the form of populist parties – making gains since 1990. This is true for both Western and Central-Eastern Europe. The growth of parties out of the value cleavage (be it left or green parties or, more recently, pirate parties) does not alter the format of the European party system.

The most important differences between Western European party systems on one hand, and those of Central and Eastern Europe on the other, are captured by the histograms in Figure 2.5 for the two periods (between the two wars, and since 1989) for which a comparison is possible. The two main differences noted earlier appear clearly: first, agrarian politics between the two wars and, second, ethnic politics. The socialist party family is about 5.0 percentage points weaker in Central and Eastern Europe compared to Western Europe and, today, also communist parties are much weaker. In the period 1919–44, however, communism was stronger in Central and Eastern Europe. Finally, for the most recent period of time, right-wing populist parties and nationalists are stronger in Central and Eastern Europe.

Conclusion: Framing the Research Question

This broad picture gives the "model" of development of the European party system from an empirical and quantitative point of view. The basic question of the subsequent analysis is to establish the degree of "deviation" around it, how much difference there is between countries in terms of format and content, and the evolution over time. Part II turns to the central focus of the analysis in this study, namely (1) to what extent are party families homogeneously distributed across Europe in terms of support; (2) how uniformly does change in favour of or against specific party families take place simultaneously; (3) how overlapping are the two main levels of elections in the multi-level European party system (national and EP); (4) to what extent are the parties belonging to the same families "comparable" in terms of actual ideological positions; and, finally, (5) how similar is the cabinet composition across Europe and the policy position of cabinets? These five questions give the structure to Chapters 3–7 in Part II.

PART II

ANALYSIS

3

Homogeneity

Convergence and Deviation in European Electoral Development, 1848–2012

Introduction

Toward the middle of the 19th century parliamentary representative institutions began replacing absolute regimes throughout Europe in the wake of the democratic revolutions that spread across the continent in successive waves. Albeit at different moments and paces – and often with reversals – competitive elections became the means by which representation in newly created parliaments was organized, executive power held accountable, and increasingly large segments of society incorporated in the political sphere through the right to vote.[1]

Classical accounts of the formation of political parties as the main organizations and actors in the new "invention" of representative democracy (Manin, 1997), and party systems, that is sets of cooperating and competing parties, have described their rapid development across Europe in the 19th and early 20th centuries. Duverger's analysis (1954) pointed to the difference between parties of "internal" and "external" origin; the former, liberals and conservatives, based on the mobilization of elites within parliaments under conditions of restricted suffrage and majoritarian elections; the latter, socialists and agrarians, based on the mobilization of the masses incorporated later through the extension of the franchise. The cleavage model presented in Chapter 2 pointed to the socio-economic and cultural origin of party families as they emerged from fundamental conflicts created by the disruption of the old political and social order through the National and Industrial Revolutions.

---

[1] On the process of democratization and the cross-country variation in Europe see Bendix (1964), Dahl (1966), and Rokkan (1999). On the development of representative democracy see Manin (1997). On later waves of democratization, especially in Central and Eastern Europe but also in Southern Europe, see Huntington (1991), Kurzman (1998) and Weyland (2014). For data see Braunias (1932), Caramani (2000, 2004), Nohlen and Stöver (2010), Rokkan and Meyriat (1969), and Sternberger and Vogel (1969).

Long-term historical analyses of democratic and electoral development in Europe – be it democratization and enfranchisement, the birth of party competition and partisan oppositions, or systemic properties such as volatility and nationalization – are characterized by two, in part contrasting, features. On one hand, these accounts point to *commonalities, similarities, and simultaneous patterns of change* over time. On the other hand, they point to *variations and differences across European countries and to country-specific deviations* from the general pattern. The analysis in Part II of this volume addresses the question of the balance between these two tendencies from an empirical and quantitative perspective using a variety of indicators tailored to capture the multi-dimensionality of the concept of Europeanization as specified in Chapter 1.

This chapter starts by defining the precise measurement and operationalization of Europeanization in terms of *homogeneity* (the first of the five dimensions) and then moves to the presentation of evidence of Europeanization levels since 1850. In the second section on "mapping party families" various indices are used to compare the degree of homogeneity of different families to investigate the origins of diversity in Europe and which party families account for deviation. The measurement of homogeneity of the vote does not only include the electoral support for parties but also turnout. In the third section on "mapping party systems" the analysis concentrates on the deviations of specific countries or areas from overall patterns of development. Again the focus is on the electoral support of parties, but the discussion also includes deviation in terms of the structuration of party systems with indicators of volatility, effective number of parties, and fragmentation.[2]

Methodological Issues

Countries, Time Points, and Families

One of the difficulties in a comprehensive study of European party systems is the varying number of countries over time in which competitive elections take place. Only for the most recent decades – that is since democratization in Central and Eastern Europe – are data available for all 30 countries. From the 1830s until World War I the number of countries included in the analysis increases with democratization, state formation, and data availability.[3] Between 1830 and 1848 only the United Kingdom is included, which does not allow for any measure of homogeneity. Since the five-year period of 1845–9 Belgium, Denmark, and Switzerland are added, and progressively Germany, France, Italy, Norway, Bulgaria, Finland, and Sweden are included when these countries form as independent and/or unified states and democratize their institutions.

---

[2] The analysis includes vote and seat figures when it includes indicators of disproportionality of electoral systems and their effect on homogeneity. Party systems that look similar based on votes may look different considering seats through the distortive impact of electoral systems.

[3] Crucially, data availability concerns the distribution of votes across parties.

After World War I the number of countries included is 22 but this number decreases with the breakdown of democracy in many countries. Particularly affected is the five-year period of 1940–4 for which only five countries have elections. After World War II Central and Eastern European countries are concerned with a long period of discontinued democratic life, as are Portugal and Spain, and to some extent Greece. Finally, for the very last five-year period (2010–present) at the moment of completion of the analysis (January 2013) not all countries had had an election. Details are provided in Table 3.1. In the following graphs a line indicating the number of countries in the analysis is added whenever possible to facilitate the interpretation of the results.[4]

Measures of homogeneity are calculated for each family across countries. As countries hold elections in different years, the basic data points are *five-year periods* to create simultaneity. In several countries more than one election takes place during such periods. Average party votes between elections within a period have been used.

As in Chapter 2, the classification using families from the cleavage model provides units of analysis covering the whole of Europe. For the sake of a more comprehensive and comparative analysis party votes have, therefore, been *added together between parties of the same family in a given election*. Obviously, if in a given election there is only one, say, agrarian party, then party and family votes are identical.

A crucial point for the analysis of homogeneity is how to treat cases in which given families do not exist. Indicators of homogeneity can be computed on two different sets of cases:

- Countries *in which a given party family exists* (i.e. receives more than 1 per cent of the votes at a given election). The number of cases may, therefore, be less than the number of countries in which there are democratic elections. For example, out of 20 countries in 1980–4 with democratic elections, only seven had a green party. In such a case, indicators are computed on seven countries only.
- Countries *in which democratic elections take place* (disregarding whether the family exists). The number of cases is, therefore, equal to the number of countries with democratic elections. For example, the indicator of homogeneity for green parties would include 20 countries in 1980–4. The votes for the greens in countries in which the family does not exist would be 0.0 per cent and this figure would enter the computations.

---

[4] It does not follow, however, that these countries after their first appearance have elections in all five-year periods. This concerns Belgium, which held general elections rarely and for which partial elections (renewal of one half of parliamentary seats only) have not been included in the analysis. Also in Britain there is no election between 1860 and 1864, and between 1875 and 1879. The same applies to other countries but, more important, it concerns the period between World Wars I and II when democracy was discontinued in many countries and after World War II mostly in Central and Eastern Europe.

TABLE 3.1. *Countries Included in the Analysis*

Five-Year or Multiple Five-Year Periods	Number of Countries	Additional Countries (from Period Onwards)	Excluded Countries (for Specific Period)
1830–44	1	United Kingdom	
1845–9	4	Belgium, Denmark, Switzerland	
1850–4	3		Belgium
1855–9	4		
1860–4	3		United Kingdom
1865–9	3		Belgium
1870–4	5	Germany	
1875–9	5	France, Italy	Belgium, United Kingdom
1880–4	7	Norway	Belgium
1885–9	8	Bulgaria, Netherlands	Belgium, Italy
1890–4	8		Bulgaria, Italy
1895–9	8		Belgium, Bulgaria
1900–4	10		
1905–9	10	Finland	Belgium
1910–14	12	Sweden	
1915–19	17	Austria, Estonia, Iceland, Luxembourg, Poland	
1920–4	22	Czechoslovakia, Ireland, Latvia, Lithuania, Malta	
1925–9	22	Greece, Romania	Italy, Poland
1930–4	22	Spain	Czechoslovakia, Italy, Lithuania
1935–9	17		Austria, Bulgaria, Estonia, Germany, Italy, Latvia, Lithuania, Poland
1940–4	5	Elections in Denmark, Iceland, Ireland, Sweden, Switzerland	All other countries excluded.
1945–9	19		Bulgaria, Estonia, Latvia, Lithuania, Poland, Spain
1950–9	17		Bulgaria, Czechoslovakia, Estonia, Latvia, Lithuania, Poland, Romania, Spain

Five-Year or Multiple Five-Year Periods	Number of Countries	Additional Countries (from Period Onwards)	Excluded Countries (for Specific Period)
1960–4	18	Cyprus	Bulgaria, Czechoslovakia, Estonia, Latvia, Lithuania, Poland, Romania, Spain
1965–9	16		Bulgaria, Cyprus, Czechoslovakia, Estonia, Greece, Latvia, Lithuania, Poland, Romania, Spain
1970–4	18		Bulgaria, Czechoslovakia, Estonia, Latvia, Lithuania, Poland, Romania, Spain
1975–89	20	Portugal	Bulgaria, Czechoslovakia, Estonia, Latvia, Lithuania, Poland, Romania
1990–4	29	Hungary, Slovakia	
1995–2009	30	Slovenia	
2010–12	19		Austria, Bulgaria, Germany, Iceland, Italy, Lithuania, Luxembourg, Norway, Portugal, Romania

Notes: Czechoslovakia appears as the Czech Republic after 1992. Countries excluded for specific periods because of no democratic elections held or because no data available. Belgium includes general elections only whereas Luxembourg includes also partial elections. Slovenia not included earlier because of data reliability issues.

What is the rationale of these two options? In the former, homogeneity is computed only for countries in which a given party family exists. In the latter, homogeneity is computed among all countries, and where a family does not exist it is viewed as receiving no votes. In most tables and figures in what follows both figures are included.

The Choice of Measures
Nationalization literature has produced a number of more or less sophisticated indices to measure the homogeneity of party distributions across territory, that is static/distributional nationalization (S/DN). These measures are now applied to measuring party distributions across Europe with countries as territorial units. To assess the homogeneity and convergence of voting behaviour among European party systems one looks at the level of similarity of share of votes, measured over time, among parties of the same family across countries.

This section discusses how suitable these measures are when applied at the Europe-wide level (formulas are given in Appendix 3).

The first indicator is "presence": In how many units (countries) does a party "exist" as a percentage of the total number of countries? For example, a family that is present in 20 out of 30 countries has a score of 66.6 per cent. The measure is called *territorial coverage* or *spread*.[5] The higher the coverage of a given party family, the higher the level of homogeneity according to this indicator. This measure is not weighted as regards (1) the size of units in which the family is present (whether it is large Germany or small Estonia) and (2) the size of the family (whether it is the large socialists or small greens). The remaining measures are indices of *homogeneity and convergence* of electoral support for parties across countries. Much of the discussion about indices at the national level is also relevant at the European level as it addresses three difficulties: (1) the varying number and size of territorial units on which indices are computed; (2) the varying size of parties for which indices are computed; and (3) the aggregation of party scores into scores for the entire party system. On all three points the various measures have advantages and disadvantages.[6]

Similarly to territorial coverage, indicators based on variance across territorial units do not take into account the varying size of the units across which they are computed. Such measures include variance (S), mean absolute deviation (MAD) or index of variation, mean standard deviation (MSD), standard deviation (S^2), coefficient of variation (CV), and the Lee index.[7] The index adjusted for party size and number of regions (IPR) is similar to the Lee index. It takes into account the number of territorial units but does not weight the varying size of units (i.e. it is "adjusted" to discard size effects).

Most of these measures face the problem of party size (also sometimes referred to as "scale invariance"). When comparing the level of homogeneity for two or more party families one must make sure that the families' sizes do not affect the measure. IPR and CV, as well as Gini-based indices (for example, party nationalization score or PNS, which is the inverted Gini), allow for such

---

[5] What is meant by being "present" or "existing" is that a party receives at least 1 per cent of the vote nationwide. This measure belongs to the family of competition or frequency measures including the proportion of uncontested districts and safe seats (Cornford, 1970, Rose and Urwin, 1975). These measures do not apply to the European level. For an analysis at the national level see Caramani (2003a and 2004: 230–46).

[6] The best discussion of advantages and disadvantages of nationalization measures is Bochsler (2010b). So-called inflation measures are not included in this chapter as they are devised for entire party systems but not for single parties or families. See Chhibber and Kollman (1998), Cox (1999), Kasuya and Moenius (2008), and Moenius and Kasuya (2004).

[7] See Ersson, Janda, and Lane (1985), Hearl, Budge, and Pearson (1996), Jones and Mainwaring (2003), Lee (1988), and Rose and Urwin (1975). For an overview and assessment see Caramani (2004: 58–70).

a comparison whereas the standard deviation is affected by the mean size of party families across units. However, when aggregating scores of homogeneity for different parties into an overall measure for the entire party system it is necessary to take into account the size of party families and therefore use *weighted measures*, such as the standard deviation, or the Gini (or PNS) but weighted by the mean size of a given party family. Such is the principle on which the party system nationalization score (PSNS) is based.[8] In the party system average, homogeneity scores of large parties should have more weight than those of small parties.

Whereas some indices have upper limits (such as the IPR or Gini that vary between 0 and 1), others do not. How standardized indices vary between the two extreme values is, however, problematic. Gini-based coefficients have been transferred from inequality studies and the scores are highest (1.00) when all votes are concentrated in one unit (100 per cent) and none in the other units. The same applies to the IPR. Both are indices of *concentration* of votes as they measure the *distribution* of a pool of votes across units. On the contrary, scores of the standard deviation are highest when half the units have the highest level of votes and the other half the lowest (namely, 0 per cent) and the fewer the units, the higher the values. In the case of only four countries with a family receiving 100 per cent of votes in two and 0 per cent in the other two (again mean of 50 per cent), the standard deviation is 57.73. Of course, the smaller the size of the family, the lower the upper limit. The standard deviation is an index of *division, segmentation, and sectionalism* of votes as it measures the *variance* of votes across units. "Distributional" and "variational" measures are not, therefore, perfectly interchangeable.[9]

Empirical evidence is presented by making use of a variety of these indicators depending on whether the analysis needs to take into account the size of party families (with homogeneity scores weighting more for large families than for small ones), for example when presenting aggregated levels of homogeneity for all families, or whether the analysis needs scores not influenced by party family size, for example when comparing homogeneity scores between families. On one hand, it appears in Table 3.2 that correlations among the indicators controlling for party size are strong. Gini2 correlates positively with IPR (0.968 and 0.780 depending on whether countries in which families do not

---

[8] Insofar as for the indices used in the following analysis high scores of variability mean low Europeanization, the Gini is not used in its inverted version (PNS) as it would show low scores for low Europeanization going in the opposite direction.

[9] What follows does not use the weighted and standardized measure that Bochsler (2010b) proposed, which gives more weight to large territorial units (and corrects for the number of units). When comparing national party systems the territorial or demographic size of countries should not come into account. The version of the Gini (Gini2) used in the following analysis simply controls for the number of units across which distribution scores are calculated (countries) as their number varies over time.

TABLE 3.2. *Correlation Matrix between Indicators*

Indicators of Homogeneity	Coverage	Gini	Gini2	Standard Deviation	CV	IPR	Lee	Gini2W
				Computed on all countries with elections (upper half)				
Coverage	–	−0.330**	−0.954**	0.618**	−0.914**	−0.962**	0.538**	0.691**
Gini	0.513**	–	0.447**	−0.356**	0.373	0.298**	0.146*	−0.349*
Gini2	−0.035	0.396**	–	−0.606**	0.904**	0.968**	−0.412**	−0.666**
Standard deviation	0.545**	0.271**	0.266**	–	−0.639**	−0.541**	0.656**	0.982**
CV	−0.212**	0.233**	0.948**	0.175**	–	0.878**	−0.522**	−0.705**
IPR	−0.383	0.027	0.780	0.081	0.895	–	−0.475**	−0.618**
Lee	0.686	0.796	0.262	0.646	0.069	−0.094	–	0.730**
Gini2W	0.617	0.356	0.273	0.979	0.133*	0.017	0.750	–
				Computed on countries where families are present only (lower half)				

Notes: Computed for the following families: socialists, communists, new left, conservatives, liberals, social liberals, agrarians, greens, minority parties, far-right, and religious parties. Period 1830–44 excluded.
Statistical significance ** (p < 0.01), * (p < 0.05) in two-tailed test.

TABLE 3.3. *Correlations with Number of Countries and Party Size*

Indicators of Homogeneity	Number of Countries		Party Family Size	
	All Countries with Elections	Countries in which Families are Present Only	All Countries with Elections	Countries in which Families are Present Only
Coverage	−0.026		0.808**	0.681**
Gini	0.872**	0.631**	−0.443**	0.035
Gini2	0.178**	0.498**	−0.905**	−0.385**
Standard deviation	−0.204**	−0.069	0.647**	0.677**
CV	0.097	0.369**	−0.739**	−0.458**
IPR	0.001	0.185**	−0.873**	−0.516**
Lee	0.465**	0.415**	0.343**	0.408**
Gini2W	−0.140*	0.018	0.671**	0.668**

Notes: Computed for the following families: socialists, communists, new left, conservatives, liberals, social liberals, agrarians, greens, minority parties, far-right, and religious parties. Period 1830–44 excluded.
Statistical significance ** ($p < 0.01$), * ($p < 0.05$) in two-tailed test.

exist are included in the computation) and with CV (0.904 and 0.948). As one would expect, the correlations with the standard deviation and other indicators not controlling for family size (standard deviation, Lee index, and Gini2W, which has been weighted to incorporate family size) are negative. On the other hand, correlations between coefficients in which party size is not controlled for are significant and high, in particular between Gini2W and the standard deviation (0.982 and 0.979). Finally, coverage correlates positively with Gini2W, the Lee index, and standard deviation (larger party families are present in more European countries) and negatively with Gini, IPR, and CV.

Table 3.3 informs about the impact on indicators of the number of units and the size of party families. In regard to the *number of units*, the number of countries included in the analysis has a strong impact on the Gini index.[10] This is the case for values of distributions of votes across countries calculated, including countries where a family does not exist (share of votes of 0.0), and without such countries (meaning that the number of countries is lower). The same applies, although to a lesser extent, to the Lee index. Gini2, which adjusts for the number of units included in the computations, does, on the contrary, not correlate with the number of units as expected. The same applies to the IPR. However, while Gini2 correlates with the number of countries when only countries in which families exist are considered, the IPR is never affected by the

---

[10] As often noted this is a major source of bias in the PNS index, which is simply the inverted Gini (PNS = 1−Gini).

varying number of countries on which it is calculated. The indicators in which the size of the party matters (standard deviation, CV, and Gini2W) are negatively correlated with the number of units, meaning that larger parties tend to be present in a higher number of countries. On the whole, apart from Gini (or PNS) and Lee, none seems influenced strongly and positively (higher heterogeneity) by the larger number of countries, and only the standard deviation is to some extent influenced negatively (lower heterogeneity).

In regard to the *size of parties*, as expected, the indicators not controlling for the size of party families are correlated with higher mean percentages across countries. The larger a party family's mean votes, the larger the standard deviation, and the Gini2W, as well as the Lee index. On the contrary, the indicators which control for the size of party families (such as Gini2, CV, and IPR) are correlated negatively, meaning that the larger a party family's mean votes, the smaller the scores of these indicators. Finally, coverage correlates highly and positively with family size, indicating that the larger families are present in a larger number of countries.

A final issue of homogenization measures concerns the passage *from party to party system scores*. At the national level the literature has stressed the need for measures weighting party scores of homogeneity by the size of parties (in terms of mean votes across constituencies), so as to have large parties weighting more than small ones. At the European level, the equivalent to a party is a family and the equivalent to a systemic measure is when all families are aggregated together. For indicators which do not control for the size of parties the aggregation through the average is straightforward.[11] For indicators which do control for the size of parties, such as the Gini, a weighted measure (Gini2W) must be used.

Mapping Party Families: The Europeanization of Electoral Politics

Empirical evidence on which the analysis is based is presented in two steps. This section includes the analysis of the spread and homogenization of party families across national party systems in Europe. Has there been a process of Europeanization of electoral politics over the past 150 years? Are some party families more "Europeanized" than others? How similar is the vote for parties of the same family across national party systems? The next section analyzes the "deviations" and "distinctiveness" of national systems. The focus of this section is party families. The focus of the next is party systems.

---

[11] In this aggregation one problematic aspect is to decide which party families to include in the average (apart from "others" and "unknown", small and rare party families such as the animalists or women's lists can be excluded while for others such as new left, anti-EU, or nationalists the exclusion is less obvious). Furthermore, the level of aggregation of families themselves has an influence on systemic scores (whether, for example, the various Orthodox, Catholic, Protestant, etc. families are considered together as "religious" or separately). This point is discussed later in the presentation of the overall results.

TABLE 3.4. *Overall Figures by Period*

Period	All Countries with Elections				Only Countries where Families are Present		
	Coverage	Standard Deviation	Gini2W	(N)	Standard Deviation	Gini2W	(N)
1850–1914	54.38	11.64	0.54	72.0	10.04	0.46	62.0
1915–44	55.21	10.82	0.52	52.0	10.61	0.54	51.0
1945–89	49.74	8.91	0.45	91.0	8.65	0.47	47.0
1990–2012	54.63	8.43	0.42	55.0	8.62	0.44	54.0
Entire period	53.03	9.91	0.48	270.0	9.37	0.47	255.0

Notes: Number of cases refers to five-year periods for each family. Families included: socialists, communists, new left, conservatives, liberals, social liberals, agrarians, greens, minority parties (regionalists and ethnic parties), far-right, and religious parties.

Overall Figures

Looking broadly at the electoral history of Europe – both Western and Central-Eastern Europe – the impression is one of very similar compositions of party system. Liberals and conservatives (in some cases Catholics) dominate during phases of restrictive but democratizing suffrage, with "mass and class" politics making its forceful entry towards the end of the 19th century in the form of social democratic and agrarian parties. The division of the left into socialist and communist, albeit to different degrees, occurs everywhere in Europe as did, in more recent times, new politics both on the left with post-materialism (green parties) and on the right with populist parties. The overall picture, in spite of deviations from these patterns in the form of regional, ethnic, and religious politics, is one of similarity. But just how true are these impressions historically and empirically? And what has been the trend of diversity versus similarity between European party systems?

Table 3.4 and Figures 3.1 and 3.2 provide aggregate points of reference, starting with the indicator of territorial coverage (expressed as the average percentage of countries in which party families are present).[12] Coverage is about half the countries in which there are democratic elections. This average level of territorial coverage in Europe does not change significantly across the four periods distinguished in Table 3.4: a period of restricted suffrage and mostly majoritarian electoral systems; a period between the two world wars of mass suffrage and mostly PR electoral systems; a period during which Central and East European countries are not democratic and therefore

---

[12] Besides the "other parties" category (i.e. those receiving less than 1 per cent nationally) and the "unknown" category, figures in tables and graphs in this chapter are computed excluding animalists, women's parties, pensioners' parties, personal, anti-tax, and European parties.

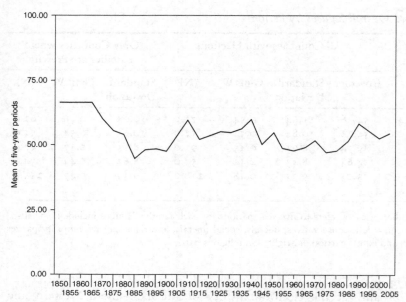

FIGURE 3.1. Territorial coverage in Europe (families' average), 1850–2009.

Notes: Families included: socialists, communists, new left, conservatives, liberals, social liberals, agrarians, greens, minority parties (regionalists and ethnic parties), far-right, and religious parties. Periods 1830–49 and 2010–12 excluded.

excluded from figures; a period after the third wave of democratization in Central and Eastern Europe.

Because the measure of territorial coverage does not take into account the weight of small and large families in the average, this measure is more useful for the comparison of party families (see later in this chapter). What appears nonetheless is the *absence of trend*, with levels of coverage remaining the same over 150 years. While waiting to look at the disaggregated results, for the moment the information resulting from this indicator is that a process of Europeanization measured through coverage cannot be observed for the period since the mid-19th century.[13] Yet this indicator gives equal weight to large and small families. Furthermore, the fact that party families exist in an increasing number of countries does not imply that their levels of support converge over time. What one needs to address, therefore, is whether differences across Europe in *electoral support* for parties of the same family

---

[13] In Figure 3.1, in fact, there is a trend of declining coverage between 1850 and 1885 when the addition of newly democratic countries to the computation brings new families which, contrary to conservatives and liberals, are present in some countries only, such as religious parties (which are considered distinct from conservatives), regionalist and ethnic parties (Irish parties in the United Kingdom), and even the first social democrats (as in Denmark).

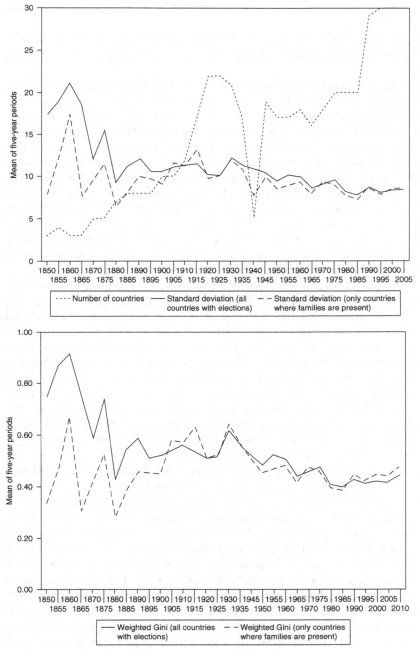

FIGURE 3.2. Homogenization in Europe, 1850–2009.

Notes: Families included: socialists, communists, new left, conservatives, liberals, social liberals, agrarians, greens, minority parties (regionalists and ethnic parties), far-right, and religious parties. Periods 1830–49 and 2010–12 excluded.

decrease over time. Is there, from 1850 to the present day, a process of convergence or homogenization of support for party families across European countries?

Using measures taking into account the size of party families into the overall cross-family average leads to a different picture. Figure 3.2 presents two curves for the standard deviation and Gini2W each (computed for all countries with elections and for only countries where families are present). These indicators weighting scores of homogeneity by the size of party families show that *the period from 1850 to 1885 is one of fundamental homogenization of electoral politics*. This result appears quite consistently with both sets of indicators: there is a decline of diversity in electoral behaviour in the first three decades since the period of democratic revolutions and parliamentarization of political life around 1848–55. The 1850s–70s are years of convergence between national party systems in Europe. This result is made more robust by the fact that homogenization takes place in spite of an increasing number of countries included in the Europe-wide average.[14]

What happens after the three decades 1850s–70s? Since the 1880s the temporal pattern is one of *slight and almost continuous Europeanization*. There is a revival of divergence between the two world wars when many Central and Eastern European countries are added to the Europe-wide aggregation and (lower graph) since democratization after 1989. As Table 3.1 shows the overall number of countries increases with many Western European countries also forming and/or democratizing (Austria, Ireland, and Greece, among others). After World War II, when Central and Eastern European countries cease to be democratic and do not enter the European average, as well as the period after 1989 when these countries recover their electoral history, *trends do not reveal major changes* in a process that appears as one of *stabilization of the homogeneity* between national party systems in Europe.

Importantly, the most dramatic convergence towards similarity in the format of national party systems in Europe takes place "early" – meaning soon after the almost general transition to parliamentary democracy and nation-states in Europe. This process of convergence occurs before, and is not disrupted by, World Wars I and II and by the breakdown of democracy between them. Nor is it a process that parallels European integration since the 1960s or the "wave" of new politics in the wake of the post-materialist transformation in the 1970s–80s. Nor, finally, is it a process triggered by economic globalization since 1990 and by the increasing interdependence and coordination of national policies. Europeanization rather seems the result of the *similar and simultaneous basic transformation of politics in Europe leading to similar cleavage constellations and party organization mobilizing the newly enfranchised European citizens*.

---

[14] The robustness of this finding is further strengthened by the fact that this period would look even more homogeneous if conservatives, Catholics, and people's parties would have been considered as one single family.

These are processes typical of the 19th century. It is during these phases that what looks like a European electorate and party system forms.

The dashed curves display aggregate figures on the homogeneity of party families across Europe computed only for countries in which these families exist.[15] As is visible in the graphs, homogeneity is larger if only the countries where party families exist are taken into account. For example, in the 1850s conservatives existed in Denmark and the United Kingdom, but elections also took place in Belgium and Switzerland. In these two countries conservatives did not "exist", as Catholics were coded separately. It is, therefore, logical that homogeneity between Denmark and the United Kingdom (where conservatives scored around 35 per cent) is higher than between these two countries and Belgium and Switzerland, in which they are attributed the equivalent of 0.0 per cent.

As seen earlier, the standard deviation correlates negatively with the number of countries included in the analysis: the more countries included, the lower the standard deviation. To a lesser extent this is also the case for Gini2W.[16] This explains the higher levels in the period up to 1880 when the number of countries in the analysis is low. However, the increase in the number of countries does not produce further homogenization during the inter-war period nor, after World War II, does the reduced number of countries increase diversity. Overall, levels of homogeneity are high. For the standard deviation, the highest possible score is when in half the units a family gets 100.0 per cent of the votes and in the other half 0.0 per cent. With only four countries in the early decades, the maximum level of standard deviation is 57.73. With 30 countries the maximum is 50.85. Yet levels of standard deviation are hardly above 10.00 since the end of the 19th century. This points to a high level of homogeneity in party distribution across Europe since early periods of electoral development.

Spread and Homogenization of Party Families

While some party families exist in all countries, and thus account for a basic similarity in Europe, a number of families exist only in some countries or areas and thus are factors of dissimilarity in Europe. This section starts with the simple but fundamental question of presence and spread of party families before turning to the homogeneity of their electoral support. The left half of Table 3.5 and Figure 3.3 include the relevant information for this first part of the discussion.[17]

---

[15] If a country had democratic elections but a given family (say, Catholic parties in the United Kingdom) did not exist, the country is not included in the average. In the solid line, on the contrary, the United Kingdom would appear in the average with the mean votes for Catholic parties being 0.0 per cent.

[16] See Table 3.3. The correlation coefficients are −0.204 and −0.069 for the standard deviation, and −0.140 and 0.018 for Gini2W.

[17] To avoid overwhelming readers with graphs and data, figures in this section are limited to those computed on all countries in which there are elections (i.e. including countries in which some families do not exist).

TABLE 3.5. *Spread and Homogeneity of European Party Families, 1850–2012*

Families	Spread (Territorial Coverage)				Homogeneity (Gini2)			
	1850–1914	1915–44	1945–89	1990–2012	1850–1914	1915–44	1945–89	1990–2012
Left	67.62	99.24	99.42	98.95	0.55	0.24	0.16	0.22
Socialists	67.62	98.26	98.86	98.26	0.55	0.25	0.23	0.24
Communists	–	53.78	77.58	54.90	–	0.65	0.57	0.68
New left	–	–	12.15	14.48	–	–	0.90	0.89
Greens	–	–	31.67	57.41	–	–	0.77	0.61
Great right[a]	100.00	99.02	99.38	99.33	0.05	0.22	0.16	0.17
Right[b]	100.00	91.91	90.37	94.92	0.13	0.32	0.39	0.29
Liberals[c]	100.00	76.09	76.19	79.59	0.14	0.48	0.49	0.53
Liberals	100.00	76.09	74.46	75.21	0.14	0.47	0.49	0.53
Social liberals	30.33	17.13	24.80	26.80	0.77	0.86	0.82	0.87
Conservatives	71.86	57.93	61.07	76.35	0.44	0.58	0.58	0.43
Agrarians	24.17	68.11	28.97	30.87	0.84	0.59	0.79	0.80
Religious parties	44.78	54.48	70.51	65.33	0.64	0.61	0.52	0.61
Orthodox	–	4.62	–	3.97	–	0.95	–	0.96
Catholics	34.78	21.93	16.69	8.45	0.68	0.84	0.88	0.94
Protestants	22.39	9.38	24.04	20.35	0.80	0.94	0.85	0.85
Inter-confession	–	7.21	7.15	9.76	–	0.94	0.93	0.93
People's parties	18.02	35.05	42.09	35.90	0.85	0.73	0.68	0.76
Far right	11.50	30.77	30.59	65.48	0.89	0.81	0.76	0.61
Extreme right	11.50	23.17	21.95	56.02	0.89	0.85	0.83	0.66
Anti-Europe	–	7.95	5.45	11.93	–	0.92	0.94	0.92
Nationalists	–	14.08	10.07	8.50	–	0.89	0.92	0.94
Regionalists	31.51	14.20	10.65	15.29	0.86	0.88	0.92	0.90
Ethnic parties	15.38	23.86	5.49	20.63	0.86	0.84	0.94	0.87
All families	60.69	47.64	45.85	45.23	0.54	0.67	0.68	0.69

Notes: Figures computed on all countries in which elections took place. Italics used for aggregations of party families in the rows underneath in round characters. Agrarians, regionalists and ethnic parties are not part of aggregations. Animalists, women's parties, pensioners, personal, anti-tax, and pro-Europe parties not included.

[a] "Great right" aggregates conservative, liberals, and all religious parties.
[b] "Right" aggregates conservatives and liberals.
[c] "Liberals" aggregates liberals and social liberals.

Looking at the presence of party families across countries over a long period of time shows clearly how party systems in Europe structured in a similar way. The second half of the 19th century is initially characterized by the general presence of the *liberal* party family (100.0 per cent of the countries, even if at this stage the "N" is very small, that is four to five countries) persisting roughly until World War I, opposed to a "right" which includes either *conservatives* (Denmark, France, United Kingdom) or a religious equivalent in the form of *Catholics or people's parties* such as in Belgium, Germany, and Switzerland, among others. If taken together, the coverage is also 100.0 per cent until World War I. This is the fundamental opposition between party families of "internal origin" during the early phase of competitive parliamentary life. As it appears from the table and graph, the liberals lose ground after World War I but still exist in a majority of countries (about 75–80 per cent of them).

One of the reasons for the liberals' loss of presence is the rise towards the end of the 19th century of *socialists, social democrats, and labour*. Restrictive suffrage and majoritarian electoral systems are replaced under the impact of the Industrial Revolution by mass and class politics. Quickly between the 1880s and 1900s workers' parties appear in all countries (coverage of nearly 100.0 per cent by World War I). This is up to now the only party family that is almost always present in all countries with very few exceptions.[18] No other party family is present in basically all countries at any point during the period since the introduction of universal suffrage. Also notable about socialists is that in all countries they are present with a major party plus a number of smaller ones with more or less sporadic existence over time.

The second important party family from the "massification" phase of politics includes *agrarian, farmers', and peasants' parties*. This party family increases its presence throughout Europe dramatically and reaches its highest coverage between World Wars I and II when many Central and Eastern European countries are included in the analysis following independence and democratization. Agrarians had already a presence in Northern Europe. However, their number and size in Central and Eastern Europe are more impressive. With the dominance of Soviet regimes after World War II and the exclusion of these countries from the computations, the curve on agrarian coverage in Figure 3.3 declines with, again, a revival of agrarians' presence after the breakdown of communism in the aftermath of 1989.

Historically, the various *religious parties* display a more complex pattern. Catholics have a strong incidence in the territorial coverage during the early phases of competitive elections in the mid-19th century when they had the role of "conservatives" in countries like Belgium (a Catholic country), Germany, and Switzerland (multi-religious countries). Towards the end of the century such parties also had a role in other multi-religious countries

---

[18] Exceptions are Romania and Greece between the two world wars, Greece in the first election after World War II, and then Cyprus in the 1970s and Latvia in the 1990s.

such as the Netherlands.[19] Protestant parties are to be found towards the end of the 19th century mainly in the Netherlands and Switzerland, as well as in Scandinavian countries. Finally, Orthodox parties are small parties existing in Latvia between the two world wars (Russian minority) and Greece since the 2000s. Taken separately these denominational parties account for great diversity among national party systems in Europe. If aggregated one sees that, on the contrary, religion is a factor of commonality with levels of coverage around 70 per cent since World War II. However, the crucial point, which has already been mentioned, is that in many countries such parties have the function of the main right-wing party in place of conservatives. If taken together with other right-wing parties their level of coverage is equivalent to that of the socialists.

Overall, a glance at the upper graph in Figure 3.3 reveals a high level of territorial coverage across Europe for socialists, conservatives, religious parties, and liberals (all around 75 per cent). The exception among these historical party families is that of agrarian parties present in roughly only a fourth of countries today. This picture of homogeneity contrasts with that of heterogeneity in the lower graph in Figure 3.3 where – with a few exceptions – most party families are present in a small number of countries (around 25 per cent). In this case, too, there are some striking patterns over time.

After the end of World War I *communist* parties appear in many countries in a general split from socialist parties. These parties are present in just more than half the countries, increasing to roughly 75 per cent of Western European countries after World War II. There is a clear decline of coverage since the breakdown of communist regimes in Central and Eastern Europe which had a general impact on the radical left in all European countries. On average since 1990 communist parties are present in 54.9 per cent of the 30 countries considered, roughly half. *Regionalist and ethnic parties* are present in about a fourth of the countries but this proportion is larger in concomitance with the inclusion in the computations of Central and Eastern Europe, roughly between the two wars and since 1990, where ethnic diversity and border tensions are much larger than in Western Europe.

In the last decades, on the contrary, two party families have been characterized by a sudden spread across countries. On one hand, *greens* have been "conquering" territory dramatically since the five-year period 1975–9 when they existed only in France. Since 2010 they exist in 60 per cent of the countries (18 out of 30). On the other hand, *far-right parties* had a first peak between the two world wars and then more recently since the 1990s. However, the information needs to be disaggregated (see Table 3.5 above). First, extreme-right parties

---

[19] In Belgium and Switzerland these parties have been coded Catholic (rather than people's parties) because of the strong religious cleavage with liberalism (which in Switzerland overlapped with Protestantism). The same applies to the Zentrum Party in Germany. After World War II, when this opposition lost intensity, such parties are coded as people's parties (for example, the Austrian ÖVP). The German CDU and Dutch CDA are coded as inter-confessionals. The Bavarian CSU is coded as Catholic.

(a) Main historical party families

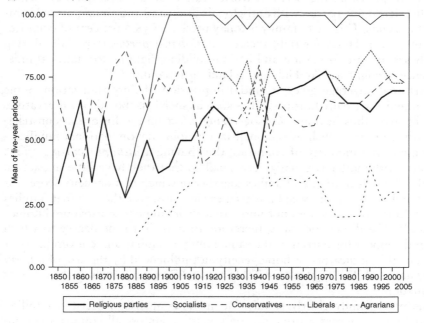

(b) Minor and recent party families

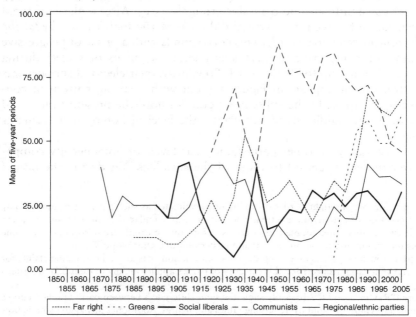

FIGURE 3.3. Territorial coverage by party families, 1850–2009.

include the *fascist parties* between World Wars I and II.[20] Second, they include populist right-wing parties with anti-globalization and anti-immigration claims since the 1990s. This party family is today present in 56.6 per cent of countries (17 out of 30). Third, far right includes *nationalist parties* (especially during the phases of state formation and nation-building) fighting for national independence in countries like Finland, Iceland, or Ireland.[21]

Territorial coverage gives an initial impression of Europeanization. Some party families are truly Europe-wide – such as socialists, but also conservatives and liberals – thus having a *homogenizing effect* on the European constellation, while others – such as regionalists and some denominational families – are present in a minority of countries, thus having a *dishomogenizing effect*. The size of the latter is usually very small so that they have little impact on overall measures putting all families together in which homogeneity scores for large families have more weight as seen earlier. However, the fact that families exist in most countries does not imply that their support is distributed homogeneously. The discussion must, therefore, turn again to the degree to which electoral support for parties of the same family is similar and converging over time. For this, indicators of homogeneity not influenced by the size of a party family are used. The right side of Table 3.5 and Figure 3.4 include the relevant information.[22]

One party family clearly stands out in the comparison between families. *Socialist parties* across Europe not only exist in almost all countries continuously, but also receive a level of support that is very similar with a Gini2 coefficient constantly around 0.25 since roughly 1915. After a phase of rapid homogenization between the 1870s and the 1910s, *the socialists are by far the most Europeanized party family*. This corresponds with a phase of progressive but rapid enfranchisement of increasingly larger segments of society during the decades leading up to World War I. Previously, their electoral support was rather diverse as it appears in Figure 3.5 but with a strong pattern of convergence up to 1919. In the subsequent decades until the present time – and in spite of further additions of countries – the level of homogeneity remains unchanged.

Taken separately no other party family has levels of homogeneity comparable over the entire period to those of the socialists. Yet during the period

[20] The figure for extreme-right parties is heavily underestimated as such parties are counted only on the occasion of democratic elections and not once they replaced them with authoritarian rule. They are, therefore, counted in elections before they created fascist regimes. The same applies for communist parties in Central and Eastern Europe after World War II.

[21] Such parties include parties defending the interest of nationalists abroad or making claims for territorial annexation. Since 1990 this category of parties applies mainly to Central and Eastern Europe.

[22] Because IPR, Gini2, and CV basically show the same differences between party families, figures are limited to Gini2 to avoid overcharging tables and figures. Additional (dis)aggregated figures are given in Figure 3.6.

(a) Main historical party families

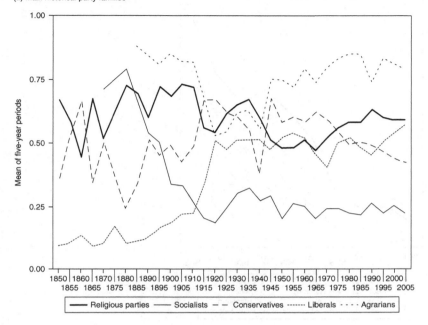

(b) Minor and recent party families

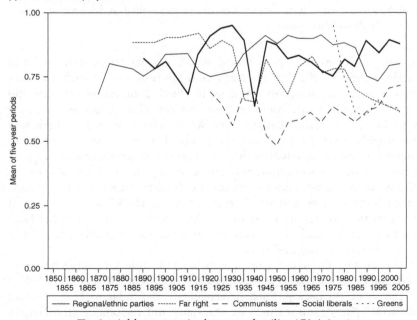

FIGURE 3.4. Territorial homogeneity by party families (Gini2), 1850–2009.

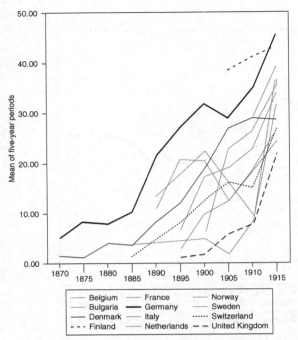

FIGURE 3.5. Vote for socialist parties in European countries, 1870–1919 (percentages). *Notes*: Line patterns used only for selected countries mentioned in the text; the others appear in grey without distinctions.

from the mid-19th century up to World War I – a period of restricted and majoritarian politics – *the liberal electoral support is also distributed very homogeneously* across European countries in which competitive elections did take place (the overall Gini2 coefficient for this period is as low as 0.14 as it appears in Table 3.5). This changes after World War I when the coefficient jumps to roughly 0.50. As discussed, the levels of *homogeneity of conservatives* depend very much on whether they are aggregated with Catholics or people's parties. For this reason different coefficients appear for different possible aggregations and the same is done in Figure 3.6. If taken together with religious parties, their level of homogeneity is around 0.35 on the Gini2 coefficient. If the right is further aggregated together (which makes more sense for later periods when liberals and conservatives converge ideologically), the Gini2 coefficient is between 0.29 and 0.39.

Figure 3.6, as well as disaggregated coefficients in Table 3.5, shows how heterogeneous the religious vote is in Europe. The Gini2 coefficient is never below 0.52 for the 1945–89 period. Such heterogeneity is similar to that of other "pre-industrial" party families such as agrarians and regionalist/ethnic party families. As far as agrarians are concerned, again an indicator of homogeneity

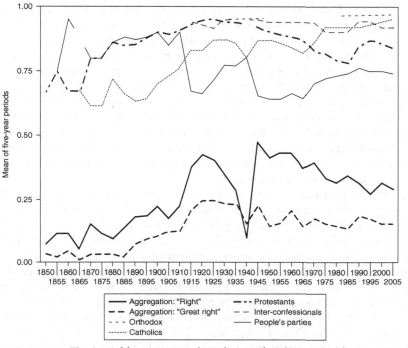

FIGURE 3.6. Territorial homogeneity by religious families and right-wing aggregations (Gini2), 1850–2009.

such as Gini2 confirms the analysis based on territorial coverage. This is a factor of heterogeneity in Europe with levels around 0.80 with the exception of the period between World Wars I and II when many Central and Eastern European countries had high and comparable levels of electoral support of these parties, similar to the Nordic countries. As far as regionalist/ethnic parties are concerned, the levels of heterogeneity in support across national party systems in Europe are even larger, indicating that only in a few countries do such parties have high levels of support.[23] As it appears in the lower graph of Figure 3.4, the curve for regionalist/ethnic parties is quite stable above the 0.75 mark even if in the last two decades a slight homogenization seems to take place. This has more to do with ethnic parties in Central and Eastern Europe than with regionalists in Western Europe.

[23] Ethnic parties are mostly present in Central and Eastern Europe. In Western Europe the major case of an ethnic party is the Swedish People's Party in Finland. The most important regional parties exist in Belgium, Italy, Spain, and the United Kingdom. The Wallon and Flemish wings of the Belgian Catholics, socialists, liberals, greens, and communists have not been coded as ethnic or regionalist, but rather according to their ideology.

The lower graph in Figure 3.4 also points to the heterogeneous nature of electoral support for party families which emerged relatively recently such as greens and right-wing populists. Yet for both party families the last two or three decades have meant not only increase of support, but also a more homogeneous support across Europe, even if their scores on the Gini2 coefficient remain relatively high, around 0.60 for both. Finally, communists represent one of the major cases of dishomogenizing trends with electoral support for this party family diverging across European national party systems, the other being the liberals after World War I (agrarians had a strong homogenizing moment between the two wars). For communists the levels of heterogeneity since 1990 return to those of post–World War I Europe after a period of a more homogenous support after World War II.

The most Europeanized party families – in terms of both presence and homogeneity of their support across countries – are *the typical party families of the left–right dimension* as they emerged from the cleavages triggered by the National and Industrial Revolutions in the 19th century. It is first and foremost *socialists, liberals, and conservatives* who are present homogeneously and continuously throughout the long period of electoral history covered by this study. Conservatives and liberals are the two party families of the phase of restricted and majoritarian elections, present in all countries (with conservatives replaced by Catholics in some countries). The pattern of Europeanization of conservatives is smooth and progressive. The pattern of liberals is, on the contrary, one of de-Europeanization when, towards the end of the century, they are challenged by the rise of mass and class politics. Socialists spread across countries and homogenize rapidly. These families taken together make Europe's similarity, are responsible for the cross-country convergence, and are factors of Europeanization.

The least Europeanized party families are, on the contrary, those stemming from other historical cleavages – which one may term "pre-industrial": *centre–periphery, ethno-linguistic and ethnic factors, and farmers and peasants' party families, as well as religious ones have a fragmented presence across European national party systems and rely on levels of electoral support that are very different from country to country.* These are not Europe-wide families, confined to few countries and therefore creating diversity among party systems. Such families are factors of differentiation in the European landscape. However, for the most part, such party families are (in the European average) small. While territorial coverage considers small and large families at equal weight when the European average is taken, the weighted indicators of homogeneity such as the standard deviation and Gini2W show that *the impact of these small families on the overall levels of Europeanization is very limited*. The families of the left–right dimension are not only the most Europeanized but also the larger ones so that their weight in the Europe-wide average is larger and ultimately the cause of the overall levels of Europeanization.

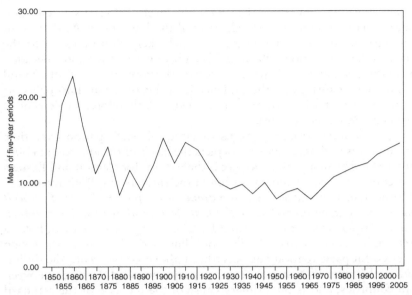

FIGURE 3.7. Homogeneity of turnout levels in Europe, 1850–2009 (standard deviation).

Turnout

One other major element of electoral behaviour beside party votes is *electoral participation*. While the homogeneity of party supports measures the strength of the territoriality of political cleavages, high territorial disparities in turnout indicate differences in the extent to which mass electorates participate, are integrated, and make use of representative institutions. Disparities between countries reflect differences of styles in political participation and political cultures, but also institutional differences as, for example, in the presence of direct democracy or compulsory voting. Finally, trends towards divergence may indicate different degrees of disaffection towards representative institutions across European countries. Overall, it is a measure of Europe-wide similarity of participation in representative democracy.

Figure 3.7 shows the level of diversity in electoral participation between European countries over a century and a half measured through the standard deviation (in this case there is no need to use measures controlling for size or number of units as for party support). The peak of diversity between 1855 and 1864 is difficult to interpret.[24] But what is certain is that with the addition

---

[24] There is a strong variability especially between Belgium on one hand (turnout rates around 80 per cent) and Denmark on the other (around 40 per cent), with the United Kingdom (about 55–60 per cent) and Switzerland (about 50 per cent) in between. In subsequent decades turnout rates of the two latter countries converge while data for Denmark are partly missing and for Belgium not applicable because of partial elections.

of new democratic systems since the 1870s the level of diversity in electoral participation between countries stabilizes until the late 1960s. At that point countries start diverging in the extent to which their electorates go to the polls. The standard deviation, which had been below 10.00 for some decades, starts increasing steadily until the most recent elections at a level of around 15.00.[25] Looking at this graph the evidence is of divergence in Europe as far as this form of electoral behaviour is concerned and, therefore, an element of de-Europeanization of electorates.

Looking at country-specific patterns of electoral participation over time helps interpret this finding. Figure 3.8 depicts the levels of turnout for 30 countries since 1965. The first striking aspect is the pattern for Central and Eastern European countries since democratization in the early 1990s. With the exception of Slovenia, in all countries there is a *dramatic drop in the levels of turnout* (of about 20 percentage points) *since the first election after democratic transition until the present time in Central and Eastern Europe.*[26] The case of Poland is different only insofar as (see the flat solid line at the bottom of the group of lines) electoral participation has never been above 50 per cent. The declining trend in this part of Europe accentuates the overall differences between European countries, and is the primary cause of the increase of the standard deviation.

Considering turnout rather than party families thus reveals a different picture, pointing to the existence of *"two Europes": European electorates, in this sense, are not Europeanized as the European party systems.* The pattern of electoral participation is, on the contrary, clearly one of *divergence* where one half of Europe is increasingly distinct when it comes to an indicator of inclusion and participation in representative democracy. Central and Eastern European turnout figures, however, have an impact only since the early 1990s and cannot account for increasing disparities between 1965 and 1990. A similar *declining – and diverging – trend can be observed for a number of Western European countries* as well (see thick dashed lines). These countries are Finland, France, Ireland, Portugal, and the United Kingdom. The decline is not quite so strong as for Central and Eastern European countries (about 15 percentage points less) and takes place over a longer period of time (50 years as opposed to 20). To this group of countries one needs to add Switzerland, which, historically, always had low levels of turnout. Again, as the decrease of turnout in these countries is stronger than in the other Western European countries, it is *a cause of divergence among national European electorates* reflected in the increasing standard deviation in Figure 3.7.

[25] From both graphs in Figures 3.7 and 3.8 the last time point (2010–12) has been removed as at the moment of the analysis not all 30 countries had voted (see Table 2.1).
[26] In Slovenia turnout levels also decrease but less dramatically, that is from about 70 per cent to about 65 per cent between 1996 and 2011.

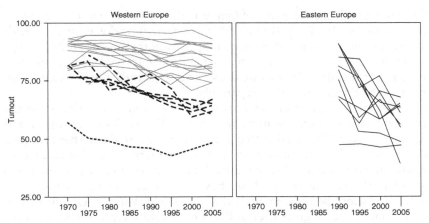

FIGURE 3.8. Turnout levels in 30 European countries, 1965–2009 (percentages).
Notes: For Western Europe line patterns are used only for selected countries; the others appear in grey without distinction. Thick dashed lines: Finland, France, Ireland, Portugal, United Kingdom. Dotted line at bottom of graph: Switzerland.

To some extent this trend is present also among the countries that in Figure 3.8 are not highlighted. Among these remaining 15 countries a divergence in the levels of electoral participation appears since 1965 which points more to a general process of declining turnout affecting the whole of Europe with the exception of some countries. In many ways, therefore, the divergence between countries reflects primarily different degrees to which a general Europe-wide process of declining participation takes place and, thus, a Europe-wide element of de-structuring of electoral politics. Whether this conclusion is supported by other indicators such as volatility and fragmentation is dealt with later in the chapter.

Mapping Party Systems: The European Party System and Its Variations

A Left–Right European Party System

In this section the discussion turns to the deviations of single national party systems from the overall pattern seen in Chapter 2. Before doing so let us combine the evidence gathered in Chapter 2 and Chapter 3 so far.

The overall picture that emerged from the latter part of Chapter 2 on the European party system is quite clear and without major transformations since the beginning of the 20th century. The main parties of the left–right dimension dominate. What one can now add, in the light of what has been seen in this chapter, is that *the largest families*, that is the families who dominate the European party systems *are also the most homogenous and "Europeanized" families*. These are mostly left–right parties such as socialists, conservatives, and liberals. Combined, these three families make up more than half the votes in Europe since World War I. If one adds the extremes of this dimension with extreme right-wing parties and communists, and another increasingly homogenous family (i.e. the greens), the total votes for "Europeanized" families is above 70 per cent today. The picture does not change radically if Western and Central-Eastern Europe are taken separately.

One can, therefore, start the analysis of deviations in this section from the premise that most of the European party system is aligned along a Europeanized left–right dimension. The families that are less Europeanized and that therefore are at the origin of fragmentation in Europe are marginal in this landscape. Agrarians and ethno-regionalists combined make up less than 5 per cent nowadays and in the past never reached above 10 per cent of the Europe-wide electorate (for short periods between the two world wars).[27] As seen earlier, religious families vary a great deal in Europe, therefore representing a source of fragmentation. At the same time this is mainly an effect of classification. If taken together the picture looks more homogenous, in particular if one considers inter-confessionals and people's parties as functional equivalents of conservatives in many countries.

A number of further qualifications are necessary at this stage. First, the homogeneity seen so far concerns the format of the party system and not the contents, namely what left–right stands for and how new actors, such as the greens, have changed its meaning. This is a matter of programmes and ideology investigated in Chapter 6. Second, change over time points to different phases, "waves" of parallel shifts sweeping across Europe. Uniform swings are analyzed in Chapter 4. Third, the previous discussion does all the same point to a number of differences, leading us to address "deviations" of specific countries in the remainder of this chapter. In a first step, the analysis introduces a measure of "country specificity". This allows for comparative analysis of countries' "fit" with the European party system. In a second step, other indicators of systemic structuration of electoral politics (beside turnout) are analyzed, more particularly volatility, effective number of parties, and fragmentation.

Deviations, Specificities, and "Uniqueness"

The set of questions asked in this section concerns the extent to which single countries deviate from the overall picture presented so far. From the cleavage model of the formation of party systems hypotheses are derived about the origin of the differences between European party systems and the extent to which cultural and socio-economic factors account for the presence of ethno-regionalist parties, agrarian parties, and religious parties of various type and denomination. Such models stress variety across Europe. However, these models do not

---

[27] As noted in Chapter 2, agrarian politics, together with the presence of ethnic parties, is one of the main features distinguishing Central and Eastern Europe, especially between the two world wars.

take a quantitative perspective and the presence of ethno-regionalists, confessionals, and agrarians is not weighted by their actual electoral size.[28] What this part of the analysis does is to *quantify national party systems' deviations* rather than only look at the simple existence of specific families.

To this end an "index of country distinctiveness" has been calculated based on the degree to which votes for party families deviate from the overall Europe-wide average. For each five-year period since 1830 the European average of votes for each family has been calculated (say, regionalist parties in the period 1970–4). For each party family in each country at each five-year period the *difference between family share of votes and European average* is computed, revealing how different the vote for that family in a specific country and period is, compared to the Europe-wide average in the same period.[29] For each country the mean of all family differences is taken, giving an overall average of deviation across families for a country. The formula (see Appendix 3) gives the average deviation for a country's families in percentage points.[30]

Table 3.6 presents the results for all countries divided into four periods, as well as for the entire period since the beginning of democratic elections. How should the figures be read? For example, the figure of 10.22 for Malta during the period 1990–2012 means that, on average, the share of the vote for Malta's parties departs ±10.22 percentage points from the European share of votes. For the last period, Malta clearly appears as the most differentiated country with respect to "the" European party system. At the other extreme, Sweden is the country – during the period 1990–2012 – that is the least distinct with an average deviation between the share of votes of its families and the European average of only 3.70 percentage points. The share of votes of party families in Sweden, and the share of votes for party families in the European average (where they exist) are, therefore, almost identical. Sweden appears as "typically" European. Taken together, *the overall level of distinctiveness of all countries has decreased over time, which is another indication of a process of*

[28] For example, Spain appears as a deviating country in terms of presence of regionalist parties. Once their size is taken into account, however, the party system appears as dominated by two left–right parties with regionalist totalling weak national support.

[29] Countries in which elections do not take place are excluded. In countries with elections, cases in which specific families do not exist are included (with 0.00 per cent as votes), but only since the first appearance of the family (say, greens in 1975–9). Absolute deviations are used rather than + and – in case a family in a country receives more or less votes compared to the Europe-wide average (see later in this chapter for the distinction between positive and negative deviations from the European average).

[30] A formula computing percentages can be obtained by dividing the share of votes for a family in a country by the overall share of votes for a family Europe-wide (and multiplied by 100). This, however, treats small and large parties equally and thus defeats the purpose. A small party with 2 per cent divided by the European average of 1 per cent would be 100.00 per cent more (a deviation, in fact, of only 1 percentage point) while a large party receiving 45 per cent divided by the European average of 30 per cent would be 50.00 per cent more (but, in fact, a deviation of 15 percentage points).

TABLE 3.6. *Country Distinctiveness by Period, 1830–2012 (Absolute Percentage Points)*

Countries	1830–1914		1915–44		1945–89		1990–2012		Entire Period	
	Mean	(N)	Mean	(N)	Mean	(N)	Mean	(N)	Mean	(N)
Iceland	–	–	12.12	(52)	10.13	(91)	7.51	(44)	10.06	(187)
Malta	–	–	11.57	(36)	8.65	(91)	10.22	(44)	9.67	(171)
Romania	–	–	11.56	(27)	10.53	(9)	8.18	(44)	9.58	(80)
Cyprus	–	–	–	–	9.96	(53)	8.64	(55)	9.29	(108)
Greece	–	–	10.16	(27)	9.80	(81)	7.29	(55)	9.02	(163)
Latvia	–	–	8.08	(27)	–	–	8.89	(55)	8.63	(82)
Austria	–	–	9.90	(35)	8.34	(91)	8.01	(44)	8.58	(170)
Ireland	–	–	10.21	(44)	8.85	(91)	6.80	(55)	8.57	(190)
Slovakia	–	–	–	–	–	–	8.06	(55)	8.06	(55)
Belgium	13.49	(37)	7.20	(44)	6.31	(91)	7.12	(55)	7.85	(227)
United Kingdom	8.48	(68)	9.34	(44)	7.68	(91)	5.67	(55)	7.75	(258)
Bulgaria	7.77	(30)	8.80	(35)	–	–	6.71	(44)	7.67	(109)
Netherlands	10.36	(45)	8.78	(44)	6.35	(91)	6.39	(55)	7.58	(235)
All countries	8.53	(560)	8.60	(914)	7.24	(1,674)	6.57	(1,518)	7.44	(4,666)
Poland	–	–	10.66	(17)	–	–	6.32	(55)	7.35	(72)
Germany	7.76	(60)	7.82	(35)	6.86	(91)	6.97	(44)	7.26	(230)
Finland	10.56	(15)	7.93	(44)	7.12	(91)	5.85	(55)	7.21	(205)
Portugal	–	–	–	–	6.34	(33)	7.76	(44)	7.15	(77)

Denmark	7.57	(76)	7.76	(52)	6.47	(91)	6.81	(55)	7.09	(274)
Spain	–	–	10.16	(18)	5.50	(33)	7.01	(55)	7.07	(106)
Italy	6.77	(41)	6.01	(17)	8.35	(91)	4.05	(44)	6.83	(193)
Switzerland	10.41	(76)	5.84	(52)	5.76	(91)	4.40	(55)	6.79	(274)
Estonia	–	–	6.14	(35)	–	–	7.02	(55)	6.68	(90)
Luxembourg	–	–	8.70	(44)	5.44	(91)	6.87	(44)	6.59	(179)
Lithuania	–	–	7.20	(18)	–	–	6.25	(44)	6.53	(62)
France	6.38	(55)	10.13	(44)	6.03	(91)	4.60	(91)	6.52	(245)
Czech Republic[a]	–	–	8.24	(27)	6.78	(9)	5.04	(55)	6.16	(91)
Hungary	–	–	–	–	–	–	6.05	(55)	6.05	(55)
Sweden	7.46	(7)	6.41	(52)	6.03	(91)	3.70	(55)	5.55	(205)
Slovenia	–	–	–	–	–	–	5.34	(44)	5.34	(44)
Norway	6.56	(50)	6.00	(44)	4.27	(91)	4.39	(44)	5.13	(229)

Notes: Countries are ordered by greatest distinctiveness over the entire period (last column). N refers to the number of families whose mean deviation of votes from the European mean of votes has been calculated at each five-year period (in which the family is present) for each country.

[a] As Czechoslovakia until 1992.

FIGURE 3.9. Party systems' distinctiveness over time (percentage points).

Europeanization of electoral politics (see the overall average in the middle of the table for "all countries"). While the average country distinctiveness was 8.53 percentage points in the period up to 1914, it is 6.57 in the most recent 20 years.

Figure 3.9 visualizes over time *the average distinctiveness of all national party systems from the "European party system" declines.* The average deviation from the European mean passes from about 9.0 percentage points to about 5.0. This means that over a century and a half *national party systems have converged towards one another.* Also there are no signs of reversal. All this points clearly to a *pattern of Europeanization* defined as *declining distinctiveness of single national party systems.*[31]

Differences in the degree to which countries are distinct from the European landscape exist, especially for the earliest period. During this period, countries like Belgium, Finland, the Netherlands, and Switzerland have deviations from the European average of 10 percentage points or more. And even the more "typical" European party systems such as those of Bulgaria, France, Germany, Italy, and Norway display differentiation levels around 7 per cent

---

[31] The Pearson's correlation coefficient between the variable "five-year period" and party systems' distinctiveness is $r = -0.497$ (sig. $= 0.01$), meaning that the more time passes (1830, 1835, 1840, etc.), the smaller the distinctiveness of national party systems from the European average.

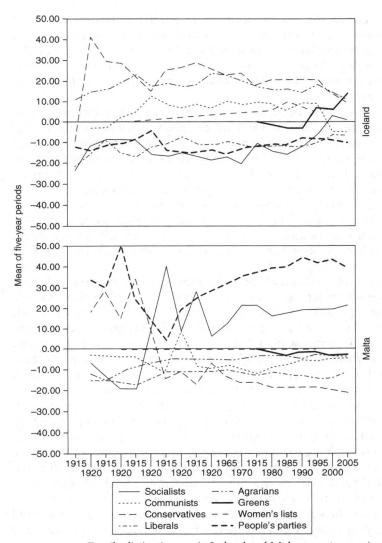

FIGURE 3.10. Family distinctiveness in Iceland and Malta, 1916–2009 (percentage points).

or higher.[32] Between the two world wars the levels of differentiation remain, on average across countries, at the levels of the previous period, but then decline after World War II. The period starting in 1990 is the one with the

[32] Italy during this period is usually considered very atypical because of the liberal dominance of the party system. It should be remembered, however, that votes have been classified as liberal and conservatives according to *sinistra* and *destra*, making it more similar to the pattern in other countries.

least differentiation *in spite of the addition of Central and Eastern European countries*. Overall, no country seems to stand out with the exception of Iceland between World Wars I and II and then again after World War II,[33] and Malta since 1990. In general, Table 3.7 *does not point to any really atypical or deviating country from the European average, supporting the thesis of fundamental similarity*.

Figure 3.10 shows for Iceland and Malta where the distinctiveness of these two countries originates, that is from which specific "deviation" the overall distinctiveness is generated. On one hand, in Iceland conservatives and agrarians receive many more votes (almost 20 percentage points more) than the European average. This is the case also for communists and the women's party (and, more recently, the greens). On the other hand, socialists and liberals (as well as the people's party that does not exist) receive overall votes below the European average. In Malta, families above the European average are very clearly the people's party and the socialists (between 20 and 40 percentage points more), while all other families receive fewer votes than the European average.[34]

To gain a more solid ground about which families are at the origin of country deviations, multivariate analysis is necessary. The question that the next correlation and regression analyses try to answer is which particular family deviations from the overall European mean votes contribute more (or less) to the deviation of entire party systems (countries). The dependent variable is the degree to which national party systems are distinct from the European average (at each time point). Independent variables are the degree to which single national families are distinct from the European average.[35] As is evident from a quick glimpse at Table 3.7 it is the large party families of the left–right dimension whose deviations from the European mean correlate higher with the overall national party systems' deviations. Even if there are differences between the four time periods, it is clear that it is mainly the cross-country deviations of socialists, conservatives, and liberals that are at the origin of the overall deviations of national party systems from the European mean. These correlations are significant and strong (mostly r between 0.40 and 0.60). On the contrary, the correlations for the small families are for the most part not significant and weak as in the case of social liberals, new left parties, agrarians, greens, and so forth.

---

[33] Romania during this period also displays high differentiation, but it concerns only one election after World War II.

[34] As one can see, if conservatives and people's parties would be considered together as one family the overall distinctiveness of these countries, and in Europe overall, would be even lower.

[35] For each country and five-year period, correlations are calculated between the mean deviation of national family votes from the European average and the overall deviation of all national families from the European average. Absolute deviations are used (not considering + and − of national deviations from the European average).

TABLE 3.7. *Correlations between National Family Deviations and National Party System Deviations (Pearson's r)*

Party Families	National Party Systems' Deviations				
	1830–1914	1915–44	1945–89	1990–2012	Entire period
Socialists	0.519**	0.439**	0.630**	0.465**	0.432**
	(73)	(104)	(165)	(138)	(480)
Liberals	0.417**	0.578**	0.347**	0.375**	0.405**
	(90)	(104)	(165)	(138)	(497)
Conservatives	0.402**	0.208*	0.553**	0.380**	0.395**
	(90)	(104)	(165)	(138)	(497)
Communists	–	0.220*	0.425**	0.201*	0.278**
		(87)	(165)	(138)	(390)
Far right	–0.078	0.498**	0.109	0.302**	0.161**
	(44)	(104)	(165)	(138)	(451)
Agrarians	0.182	0.157	0.008	0.014	0.103*
	(48)	(104)	(165)	(138)	(455)
Social liberals	–0.018	0.015	–0.100	0.219*	0.101*
	(48)	(104)	(165)	(138)	(455)
Ethno-regionalists	0.309**	0.022	–.085	0.208*	0.036
	(77)	(99)	(165)	(138)	(479)
New left	–	–	–0.100	–0.082	–0.124
			(129)	(138)	(267)
Greens	–	–	–0.213	–0.038	–0.129
			(60)	(138)	(198)
Religious parties:	0.519**	0.294**	0.279**	0.488**	0.398**
	(90)	(104)	(165)	(138)	(497)
People's parties	0.547**	0.270**	0.207**	.430**	0.268**
	(84)	(104)	(165)	(138)	(491)
Catholics	0.050	0.031	0.030	–0.081	0.196**
	(90)	(104)	(165)	(138)	(497)
Protestants	0.243*	0.142	–0.060	–0.281**	0.160**
	(90)	(99)	(165)	(138)	(492)
Orthodox	–	0.227	–	0.000	0.089
		(65)		(79)	(144)
Inter-confessionals	–	–0.066	0.022	0.051	–0.003
		(82)	(165)	(138)	(385)

Notes: Cases (N) refer to five-year periods for each country and family. Party families are ordered by strongest correlation on the entire period of time, except for religious parties. Statistical significance ** (p < 0.01) * (p < 0.05) in two-tailed test.

Single-party families are characterized by changes over time in the extent to which they cause national party systems' deviations. Interestingly, the ethno-regionalist parties' deviations correlate with overall party systems' deviation in the period of the 19th century and then again – to some extent

(r = 0.208*) – in the most recent period since 1990. This is an indication of the growth of this family in some countries, but not in others, rendering entire party systems different. A similar case is that of far-right parties for which a period in which they caused differentiation is the one between the two wars (r = 0.498**), and also presently with the growth of populist parties since the 1990s in many countries. A third family for which change over time can be observed is that of the communists for whom there is an effect on the differentiation of national party systems after World War II (until 1989) when this party family was strong in some countries but not in all.

Once again a more nuanced discussion is needed for religious parties. The result for the aggregation of all types of religious parties together shows that this family is responsible for a large part of the deviations among national party systems from the European mean (with r = 0.398** for the entire period but higher in the early and latest periods). The reason for this high correlation is that the aggregation includes very different parties such as, on one hand, large people's parties equivalent to conservatives in other countries and, on the other hand, small "denominational" parties such as Catholics and Protestants. Taken separately, these small denominational party families have only a weak effect on the distinctiveness of national party systems, while the degree of deviation of people's parties does have an effect on the overall distinctiveness of national party systems.

The indication from these correlations is, therefore, that *the distinctiveness of national party systems from the European average originates primarily from deviations for the large left–right families* such as socialists, conservatives, and liberals, and *much less or not at all from the "pre-industrial" families* that classical studies of party systems' development have identified as factors of differentiation – namely agrarians, ethno-regionalists, and religious (denominational) party families. Table 3.7 is quite explicit in showing how some family deviations contribute more than others to the country differentiation across Europe. Such an effect is captured also by the descriptive evidence in Table 3.8 and by the regression models presented in Table 3.9. Table 3.9 includes two different sets of independent variables in the form of different party families whose deviation may cause the overall distinctiveness of national party systems. One "model" includes the main left–right families; the other includes "pre/post-industrial" families. The comparison of the two models confirms what was seen earlier, namely that variation in family strength among left–right families explains much more than variation in the strength of other families the extent to which party systems diverge in Europe. The R-squares are 0.54 and 0.61 for the two "left–right" models (with and without people's parties), whereas they are 0.09 and 0.29 for the "pre/post-industrial" models (depending on the aggregation of religious parties).[36] In the first model all regression

---

[36] The labels "pre" and "post" refer to families that cannot be classified along the economic left–right dimension that issued from the National and Industrial Revolutions. The greens stemmed

TABLE 3.8. *Family Distinctiveness by Period, 1830–2012 (Percentage Points)*

Party Families	1830–1914		1915–44		1945–89		1990–2012		Entire Period	
	Mean	(N)	Mean	(N)	Mean	(N)	Mean	(N)	Mean	(N)
Religious parties	14.86	(90)	16.42	(104)	17.42	(165)	11.73	(138)	15.17	(497)
Conservatives	15.48	(90)	14.46	(104)	14.80	(165)	13.42	(138)	14.47	(497)
Socialists	6.00	(73)	10.59	(104)	11.12	(165)	9.53	(138)	9.77	(480)
Liberals	10.89	(90)	11.22	(104)	8.16	(165)	10.16	(138)	9.85	(497)
All families	8.53	(560)	8.60	(914)	7.24	(1,674)	6.57	(1,518)	7.44	(4,666)
Communists	–		3.67	(87)	8.39	(165)	5.37	(138)	6.27	(390)
Agrarians	2.02	(48)	9.91	(104)	6.30	(165)	4.76	(138)	6.21	(455)
Far right	0.83	(44)	3.96	(104)	2.80	(165)	6.33	(138)	3.95	(451)
Minority parties	2.32	(77)	4.25	(99)	1.71	(165)	3.98	(138)	2.99	(479)
Social liberals	6.52	(48)	1.87	(104)	1.87	(165)	2.99	(138)	2.70	(455)
Greens	–		–		1.32	(60)	3.23	(138)	2.65	(198)
New left	–		–		0.50	(129)	0.83	(138)	0.67	(267)

Notes: The order of families is based on the largest distinctiveness from the Europe-wide mean for the entire period (last column). N refers to the number of families whose mean deviation of votes from the European mean of votes has been calculated at each five-year period.

TABLE 3.9. *Two Regression Models of Party Systems' Differentiation*

Deviations for Party Families	"Left–Right" Models		Deviations for Party Families	"Pre/Post-Industrial" Models	
	(1)	(2)		(1)	(2)
Socialists	0.083*** (0.009)	0.077*** (0.008)	Agrarians	−0.005 (0.022)	0.004 (0.019)
Conservatives	0.075*** (0.007)	0.067*** (0.007)	Ethno-regionalists	0.045 (0.029)	0.103*** (0.026)
Liberals	0.083*** (0.008)	0.085*** (0.008)	Greens	0.110* (0.049)	−0.110 (0.043)
Communists	0.060*** (0.011)	0.063*** (0.010)	Catholics	−0.010 (0.032)	
Far right	0.015 (0.014)	0.025 (0.013)	Protestants	−0.220*** (0.054)	
People's parties		0.051*** (0.007)	Inter-confessionals	0.024 (0.015)	
			All religious		0.102*** (0.012)
Constant	2.836	2.236		5.900	3.995
Adj. R²	0.54	0.61		0.09	0.29
N	(389)	(389)		(197)	(197)

Notes: Regression coefficients shown with standard errors in parentheses. The dependent variable is the distinctiveness of national party systems from the European average for each five-year period. Independent variables is the distinctiveness for each party family from the European average in each country/five-year period. Absolute deviations over the entire period have been used. Estimation: OLS.

Statistical significance *** ($p < 0.001$), ** ($p < 0.01$), * ($p < 0.05$) in two-tailed test.

coefficients are significant with the exception of the far-right family. The variation in their electoral strength does not seem to have an impact on the degree of party systems' distinctiveness in Europe. On the contrary, most coefficients in the second models are not significant except for religious parties when aggregated and ethno-regionalists for the periods up to World War I and since 1990.

This evidence shows the limited impact on distinctiveness of pre- and post-industrial families. This is an effect of their small size while, in fact, these are the families previously identified as the most heterogeneous.[37] Their *small size hinders their heterogeneity across party systems to disrupt the general homogeneity* of European party systems. In fact, distinctiveness rather than

from the materialist versus post-materialist dimension after World War II. Agrarian, religious, and linguistic groups existed before the transition of the 19th century. Social liberals and new left parties have not been included in the regression.

[37] See the levels of the standard errors in Table 3.9 as well as the level of the intercept.

being caused by what the qualitative literature has identified as "deviations" originates from variations in the otherwise homogeneous left–right party families – mainly as an effect of their large size.

Structuration: Volatility and Fragmentation

The last section reverts to indicators about systemic features of party systems. As seen for electoral participation, while indicators of the homogenization of party families support the thesis of Europeanized and Europeanizing party systems, the use of a general indicator such as turnout points to an opposite trend, with countries moving away from one another. The question this section addresses is if other general indicators support this finding.

The following analysis relies on two types of indicators of the structuring of electoral politics: the *volatility* within party systems and their degree of *fragmentation*. Both types of indicators – the propensity to change vote and the propensity to diffuse it – represent dimensions of structuration and distinguish structured from unstructured party systems. Like turnout, these are systemic measures that do not distinguish across party families and, therefore, add an important element to the analysis insofar as they indicate convergence or divergence on systemic features other than vote for parties. For each of the two dimensions of structuration indicators have been computed at two levels (formulas are given in Appendix 3):

- Indicators computed on the basis of *party votes* for each election (even when there is more than one party per family in an election).
- Indicators computed on the basis of *family aggregations* for each election (when there are two or more parties of a same family in an election).[38]

While this is not the place to reproduce important comparative and long-term studies, it is useful to start with the general trends. Figure 3.11 displays the evolution of volatility between subsequent national elections for all countries in which competitive elections took place since 1830. While the curve is continuous for Western Europe (where some countries always had elections, even during the wars), for Central and Eastern Europe the curves are interrupted for periods of authoritarian rule. For Central and Eastern Europe the curve is also shorter starting with Bulgaria in the 1890s. What also appears from both graphs in Figure 3.11 is that the curves calculated for parties and for family

---

[38] The indices are the ones commonly used in electoral research. The formula for volatility is the "Pedersen index" (1979), or "total volatility" used in Bartolini and Mair (1990). The formula of the effective number of parties (ENP) is the one devised by Laakso and Taagepera (1979) and gives the number of parties in a system without upper limit. The formula calculates the number of parliamentary parties (ENPP) or electoral parties (ENEP) based on either seats or votes figures. Rae's fractionalization index is also available but evidence based on this indicator is not presented in this chapter because of space constraints. By and large it reproduces the results of the effective number of parties.

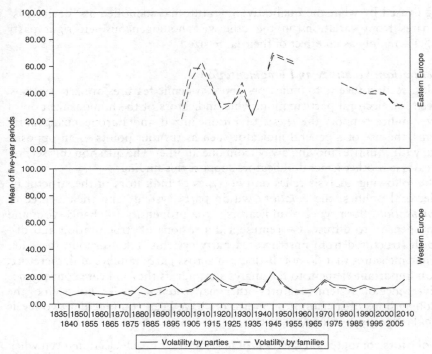

FIGURE 3.11. National volatility in Europe, 1830–2012.

aggregations are basically overlapping, indicating that volatility between single parties is not higher than volatility between families.[39]

Volatility patterns in Western Europe are quite clear. With the exception of the war periods and their aftermaths when average volatility "peaks" to almost 20 per cent, scores are stable around the level of 10–15 per cent. After 1975, when in Western Europe additional countries such as Cyprus, Greece, Portugal, and Spain are included, the curve increases slightly and only progressively declines in the two subsequent decades. Finally, it is also possible to note an increase of volatility in the most recent period, especially since 2000. Quite remarkably, volatility levels are very low for most of the 19th century with a smooth and marginal increase when more countries are added and in concomitance of new parties entering the electoral arena. Volatility patterns in Central and Eastern Europe look, on the contrary, much more "volatile",

---

[39] The overlap between the two curves shows that for most families there is one party per election. Volatility calculated on families resembles to some extent that of "bloc" volatility between left and right (Bartolini and Mair, 1990) but more detailed.

as it were, and erratic over time.[40] Volatility, in spite of dramatic changes over time, is at least double, sometimes triple, that of Western Europe, again with the highest peaks reached in the aftermath of the two world wars. Also after 1989, volatility remains at least double that of Western Europe.

While the discrepancy between Western and Central-Eastern Europe points to very distinct levels of party system structuration in the two parties of Europe, one remarkable piece of information in Figure 3.11 is *the declining trend of cross-election volatility in Central and Eastern Europe,* from levels around 50 per cent to around 30 per cent, in the period since 1989. Such a trend points to convergence, in the levels of party system structuration, towards those of Western Europe.

The pattern of the evolution of the effective number of parties is similar. There is a recent increase in the number of parties in Western European party systems and a decrease in Central and Eastern European ones (Figure 3.12). In Western Europe the 19th century is characterized by a two-party system (conservatives or Catholics versus liberals) as long as suffrage was restricted in the countries concerned (Belgium, Denmark, Switzerland, and the United Kingdom). During this period there is also no difference between ENEP and ENPP (based either on single parties or on family aggregations). With enfranchisement and the inclusion of Germany, France, and Italy the number of parties increases (especially the party figures, less the family ones). The number then stabilizes around 3.0 and increases towards 4.0 since the 1980s. The most recent figures point to an average ENEP of about 5.0 for Western Europe. In Central and Eastern Europe the trend is again very erratic until the end of World War II. Since 1989, however, the number of parties in Central and Eastern European party systems is quite similar to that of Western Europe. For this part of Europe the past 20 years represent a period of structuration of party and electoral politics as already seen with volatility figures. While this points to convergence in Europe according to the indicator of the number of parties, it appears nonetheless that *the trends in the two parts of Europe are in contrast to one another.* While the number of parties decreases in Central-Eastern Europe it increases in Western Europe.

One of the *institutional commonalities* that characterize Europe until roughly World War I is majoritarian electoral systems based on either plurality or repeated-ballot absolute majority systems. And one of the major *institutional changes* occurring almost simultaneously is, in those countries in which representative systems did not break down, the shift from majoritarian to PR

---

[40] Clearly, overall levels for Central and Eastern Europe are influenced by which countries are included and many Central-Eastern European countries had short-lived democratic experiences after World War I with one or two elections held. In the 1930s only Romania had elections. The same applies to the late 1940s and early 1950s when elections were held only in Czechoslovakia and Romania (see Table 3.1).

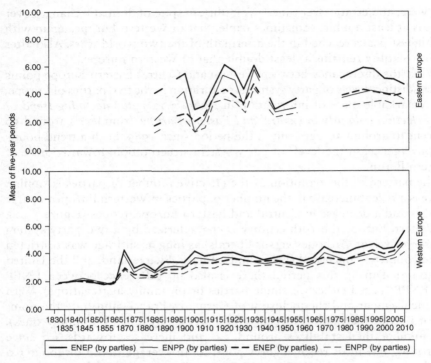

FIGURE 3.12. Effective number of parties in Europe, 1830–2012.

systems.[41] Majoritarian systems helped shaping the two-party system appearing in Figure 3.12. If one looks at the levels of "disproportionality" of electoral systems in this period – that is the over- and under-representation of parties when votes are translated into parliamentary seats – it is clear that the period up to World War I is dominated by systems favouring the dominant conservatives and liberals.

In Figure 3.13 the levels of disproportionality of electoral systems basically halve around World War I. The index of (dis)proportionality is very low for the first decade (only the United Kingdom is included) when neither conservatives nor liberals were under- or over-represented, and third parties did not yet challenge the two dominant parties (with the exception of the Repealers). The index then increases with the addition of both new parties and countries to reach levels around 10.00.[42] Between 1905 and 1924 levels of disproportionality drop

[41] The first country is Belgium in 1899, then Finland and Sweden in 1907 and 1911, respectively; eventually most others followed after World War I. On this change see Boix (1999), Cusack, Iversen, and Soskice (2007 and 2010), and Kreuzer (2010).

[42] To calculate the (dis)proportionality between votes and seats the Least Square index of disproportionality or LSQ (Gallagher, 1991; Gallagher and Mitchell, 2005: appendix B) has been used (the formula is given in Appendix 3). Zero indicates full proportionality.

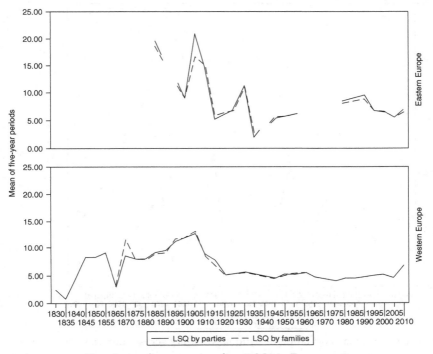

FIGURE 3.13. Votes/seats disproportionality (LSQ) in Europe, 1830–2012.

to about 5.00, remaining constant under predominantly PR systems throughout Western Europe (with the major exception of the United Kingdom and
partly France) until the most recent period since 2010.[43] Such a Europe-wide
institutional pattern, while not the focus of the present study, is nonetheless a
clear indication of commonality and simultaneity in Europe.

The main question of this section, however, is to what extent European
countries become more similar over time in terms of the indicators of volatility and fragmentation. To this end among all the countries in a given
five-year period the standard deviation across their levels of national volatility
and ENP has been calculated. The levels of cross-country diversity appear in
Figures 3.14 and 3.15. At first sight there is no cross-country convergence since
the 19th century in either the levels of volatility or the levels of party system
fragmentation. This result thus seems to confirm once more a trend towards

---

[43] As already noted, the (self-)selection of countries included in Central and Eastern Europe is
problematic for the period up to World War II. Since 1989 most Central and Eastern European
countries have adopted mixed systems, translating into slightly higher levels of disproportionality than for Western Europe.

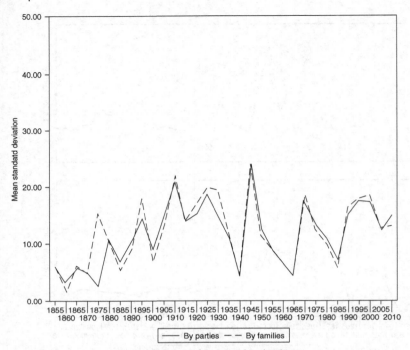

FIGURE 3.14. Standard deviation of national volatility across countries, 1855–2012.

de-Europeanization when it comes to the degree of structuration of national party systems in Europe as for turnout.[44]

A closer look at the data, however, leads to a more nuanced conclusion. In Figure 3.14 there is an increase in the cross-country levels of diversity in volatility until World War I which has something to do with additional countries included in the calculation of the standard deviation. One then observes three peaks (disregarding the 1940–4 drop during which only five countries held elections): first, right after World War II when party systems in many countries underwent fundamental change; second, in the mid-1970s under the effect of new democracies in Southern Europe; third, since 1990 under the effect of higher volatility levels in Central and Eastern Europe. Based on the volatility indicator, therefore, the diversity in the levels of party system structuration across Europe seems closely linked to the *inclusion of newly democratic systems*. In fact, *after each of these peaks the levels of homogeneity increase* (shown by a decreasing standard deviation), meaning that *the initial diversity of party systems caused by the inclusion of new democracies is "absorbed"*

---

[44] Disaggregated figures show higher levels of standard deviation for Central and Eastern Europe than for Western Europe. This means that countries in Central-Eastern Europe are more diverse among each other than countries in Western Europe.

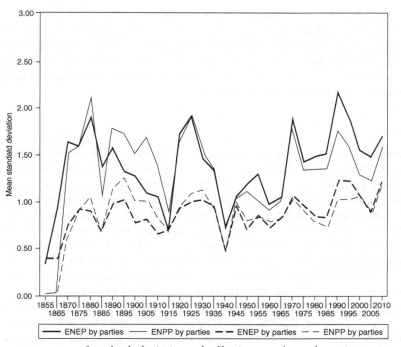

FIGURE 3.15. Standard deviation of effective number of parties across countries, 1855–2012.

through a process of structuration of party systems. Such repeated patterns, rather than simply pointing to diversity in Europe as one could have concluded at first sight, support the thesis of Europeanizing party systems with similar levels of electoral volatility across elections soon after democratization in the various waves of inclusion of new democracies.

Figure 3.15 on the effective number of parties allows addressing a different part of the story. First, the observation of the curves does not reveal major differences between figures calculated on votes (ENEP) and seats (ENPP). Second, however, there is a systematic difference between figures calculated for single parties (effective number of parties) and families (in which parties of the same family in an election have been aggregated). This latter figure really is one of "effective number of families", and is systematically lower than the figure for parties. The different levels of standard deviation across countries for the two figures reveals, therefore, that *cross-country differences are due to less-varying families than to varying parties* within these families. Over time, cross-country differences based on families increase only slightly in the most recent period.

Where differences between countries are high is in *the number of actual parties*. The levels of the standard deviation are higher and show that, especially for the period since the 1970s, there is a pattern of *de-structuration*. This process, however, takes place *within the family blocs*.[45] To a large extent this is related to the high changeability of party organizations in Central and Western Europe, a feature that involves many mergers and splinters, changes of names of parties, and, overall, short-lived parties suddenly appearing, running in one or two elections, and then disappearing again.

Conclusion

Asking about the balance between commonality and deviation in European's party systems, this chapter reaches conclusions that complement classical studies of electoral and partisan development. The quantitative approach points to an early and fundamental *process of Europe-wide homogenization soon after the major democratic transition of the mid-19th century*, in particular in the period 1850–85. This is very similar to nationalization, which also took place in the period of structuring of party politics in Europe when basic alternatives around functional cleavages imposed themselves on pre-industrial cultural factors. Until the end of the 19th century Europeanization is fast. Then, in the period up to the present, the process continues but smoothly. Not only is there a process of Europe-wide territorial homogenization in the levels of support for party families, but the overall levels of diversity are quite low and decrease in spite of the varying composition of the "sample" of countries based on whether democratic elections take place.

The dimension around which commonality in Europe structures is the *left–right dimension* composed of the largest and dominant party families, in particular socialists, liberals, and conservatives. These party families have a *homogenizing effect in Europe* as they exist almost everywhere and receive similar levels of support across the countries. While for the parties of "internal origin" in periods of restricted suffrage (liberals and conservatives) the process of homogenization is continuous and smooth since the beginning of competitive elections, for the party families of "external origin" which emerged with the extension of suffrage to the masses (socialists), the process of homogenization is steep between 1870 and World War I.[46] This points to a "wave" – the topic of the next chapter. The analysis further reveals that cultural and *pre-industrial factors have a dishomogenizing effect* on politics in Europe. Cultural party families, but also the party family resulting from the urban–rural cleavage, are

---

[45] Disaggregated results (not depicted in the graphs) show that in Central and Eastern Europe countries are becoming more similar to each other in terms of number of parties. In Western Europe the trend is flat: the levels of the standard deviation do not vary over time even if countries are slightly more dissimilar since the 1970s.

[46] Liberals are characterized by a process of de-Europeanization parallel to their decline after World War I as a consequence of enfranchisement and the rise of class politics.

not distributed homogenously across national party systems, thus differentiating Europe.

Yet in contrast with classical studies which have identified these factors as sources of diversity, this chapter shows the *marginal effect of these party families on the overall measures of distinctiveness*. Cultural and pre-industrial factors are too small to affect significantly the overall levels of similarity in Europe. Regionalists, ethno-linguistic parties, denominational parties, and agrarians are just too weak for their heterogeneity to disrupt the fundamental commonality in European party systems. On the contrary, where distinctiveness persists it is a result of variation in the levels of support of the main left–right party, reiterating once more the important role of this dimension. Re-interpreting quantitatively the cleavage model of development and deviations reveals that the focus has been on families that do not play a significant role in differentiating national party systems.

With systemic indicators of turnout, electoral volatility, and effective number of parties, the convergence between national party systems in Europe must be interpreted differently. First, *turnout levels are clearly de-homogenizing*. This effect is due to the inclusion since the early 1990s of Central and Eastern European countries in the computations for which turnout levels are dramatically low, but also to the trends in some countries such as Finland, Ireland, and the United Kingdom in which turnout levels decline much more than elsewhere (plus Switzerland, where they have always been low). Second, indicators of *volatility and fragmentation reveal a different pattern of convergence*. Rather than displaying a continuous decline of cross-country differences, with the addition of new countries in the sample (most notably after periods of democratization such as the mid-1970s or 1990s) heterogeneity in Europe increases as an effect of high volatility, number of parties, and fragmentation in the new democracies. With the structuring of electoral behaviour in the new democracies, however, volatility and fragmentation decline soon after, bringing the levels on a par with the more established party systems.

4

Uniformity

Electoral Waves and Electoral Swings across Europe, 1848–2012

Introduction

Since the first pioneering electoral analyses carried out in the United States and Europe at the beginning of the 20th century, the commonality and simultaneity of electoral change has been considered an important indicator of the degree to which a political system is integrated. Common shifts of votes occurring between elections in all territorial areas of a political system mean that the system's parts move together and that everywhere its electorates respond similarly to common factors and issues. Such general simultaneous change of votes towards or away from party families points to an advanced degree of integration of political systems. This classical indicator of vote shifts allows assessing the presence of "waves" or "tides" of electoral change across Europe.

While in the past uniform change has been investigated across constituencies at the national level, this chapter uses this conceptual tool to analyze the formation of a Europe-wide electorate. The detection of waves can be interpreted as an indicator of a "Europeanized" electorate that refers to common supra-national issues, is affected by similar vote determinants, or undergoes similar structural change. When used at the level of national electorates and party systems, shifts of votes are considered an important indicator of the degree of "nationalization" of electoral politics. This chapter extends the use of this indicator to assess the degree of "Europeanization" of electoral politics. Insofar as one can detect common waves of change that take place simultaneously everywhere in Europe – or, at least, in most European political systems – we can speak of a Europeanized or integrated dimension of electoral politics.

To what extent is – in a long-term perspective – electoral change common and simultaneous in Europe? To what extent do national electorates move together in waves of change over the past century and a half? What are the most important waves in the past and how do recent waves compare to those fundamental transformations? Are the waves of the past mostly along the left–right axis while since the de- and re-alignment in the 1970s such waves take place along other dimensions of contestation?[1] This chapter addresses these questions and aims to assess the degree to which waves of change that wipe across Europe at the same time indicate the development early on, that is soon after first democratization, of an incipient Europe-wide party system. This chapter departs from much of the recent literature's tendency to focus on short-term dynamics and considers different types of broad shifts.[2] It also aims to look systematically at the useful but mostly impressionistic attempt among observers to identify continent-wide shifts in electorates' "moods" following major electoral or cabinet changes in a few large countries. The goal of this chapter is thus broader, both cross-sectionally and historically.

The first section starts with a theoretical discussion of different types of "waves" and defines what characterizes uniform swings apart from other types of waves and what they measure. The chapter then moves to the methodology of the analysis based on the indicator of uniform swings. The main sections are devoted to the presentation of broad cross-country and longitudinal evidence of electoral waves.

Analyzing Temporal Change: Swings, Trends, and Spread

This chapter uses the concept and indicator of "uniform swings" as its main tool for analysis. Because this concept is closely related to other types of temporal processes, namely "trends" and "spread", it is important to start by disentangling them and distinguishing the purposes for which they can be employed in the analysis of Europeanizing electorates and party systems. All three refer to a "dynamic" – or cross-temporal – definition of Europeanization (Table 1.3).

Uniform swings of votes across territorial units can be considered a classical indicator of electoral studies going back to periods of time when individual investigation techniques based on surveys did not exist and when analyses relied on aggregate, that is territorial data. The golden age of electoral geography includes the earliest electoral studies as those of M. Hansen (*Norsk Folkepsikologi*, 1898), A. Siegfried (*Tableau Politique de la France de l'Ouest*, 1913), and H. Tingsten (*Political Behavior*, 1937). More recently, two further

---

[1] As seen in Chapter 1, the three main recent waves of change that the literature has identified are the green wave of the 1980s, the parallel institutionalization of "new politics" especially through environmental parties as the main partisan translation of the generational materialist versus post-materialist cleavage; the regionalist wave of the 1990s, the emergence of ethno-regionalism in the spaces left void by the alleged weakening of the normative and identity role of the nation-state; the populist wave of the 2000s, the emergence of extreme-right parties from the cleavages between "winners" and "losers" of integration and globalization and the threats to identities and labour markets with the opening up of national barriers.

[2] This is in particular the literature concerned with economic voting. See Lewis-Beck and Paldam (2000) and Powell and Whitten (1993). For an overview see Lewis-Beck and Stegmaier (2007).

seminal books have used this indicator, namely E. E. Schattschneider's *The Semisovereign People* (1960) and D. Butler and D. Stokes' *Political Change in Britain* (1974), both path-breaking and inspiring electoral analyses. The indicator has been largely forgotten, which is unfortunate as it can be fruitfully applied to Europeanization.

In the literature on the nationalization of electoral politics, uniform swings are one among a variety of dimensions. While "nationalization" refers to a process of transformation from local to national, processes of "Europeanization" – by transposition – refer to the transformation from national to European. Such processes of electoral integration, whether at the national or European level, entail distinct dimensions (for a full account see Caramani, 2004: especially 32–43). As seen in Chapter 1 there is, first, a *horizontal dimension* of territorial homogenization of electoral behaviour in the units composing a system (a process of standardization). Second, there is a *vertical dimension* of dislocation of issues, organizations, and competences from the sub-systemic to the systemic level (a process of centralization).[3] The horizontal dimension includes both (1) the *homogenization* of support for different parties across territorial units and (2) the *uniformity of change between two elections* (that is, swings). Both measure territorial similarity of electoral behaviour: the first (Chapter 3) is static whereas the second is dynamic (this chapter).[4]

Since Schattschneider's work, swings have been used in a further, but ultimately unsuccessful, attempt, namely to operationalize the *vertical dimension* and the location of the "forces" influencing voters' behaviour and electoral choices. In particular Stokes' analyses have been aimed at measuring "where" voters' stimuli are located – whether at the local, regional, or national level.[5] These studies attempt to establish the location of issues and factors relevant in the voters' choices through variance component models based on the degree of uniformity of swings across regions or constituencies. However, as Claggett, Flanigan, and Zingale demonstrated, "there is no means in analysis of variance-based techniques to distinguish among the *types* of forces which may cause the nonuniform response by the local units" (Claggett et al., 1984: 83). Whereas it is plausible that uniform swings in a country are caused by national influences (if one excludes the possibility of coincidences), in cases

---

[3] Schattschneider observed these two dimensions in the US party system noting that, on one hand, the two main parties spread in all states and receive increasingly homogeneous shares of votes with uniform swings across states from one election to the next and, on the other hand, that national issues started to dominate the political agenda, replacing local ones (Schattschneider, 1960: 79–93).

[4] The homogenization of voting behaviour has been referred to as static/distributional nationalization (S/DN) by Morgenstern, Swindle, and Castagnola (2009), while the uniformity of change has been referred to as dynamic nationalization (DN). The terms *homogeneity* (Chapter 3) and *uniformity* (this chapter) correspond to these two types of nationalization.

[5] See Stokes (1965 and 1967) and later publications by Butler and Stokes (1974), Katz (1973), and Sundquist (1973).

of non-uniform swings it is impossible to determine at what level the stimulus is located. Since then attempts at measuring the location of forces through swings have been abandoned.[6]

In this chapter no attempt is made to operationalize the location of forces influencing voters' choices: whether European, national, or regional. As mentioned, the measurement of this dimension presupposes survey data.[7] What uniform swings do allow saying, nonetheless, is that *parallel waves that take place simultaneously all over Europe indicate similar concerns and issues* across national electorates. In Schattschneider's words, "we ought to suspect that something has happened to the political system when we observe that the Republican party gained ground in *every* state in 1952 and lost ground in forty-five states in 1954, gained ground throughout the country in 1956 and lost ground in nearly every state in 1958" (Schattschneider, 1960: 93).

The indicator used here to operationalize uniform swings aims to assess precisely the level of *generality* throughout "states", that is European countries, of simultaneous change (gaining and losing ground) as in Schattschneider's study. The indicator must assess *the generality and simultaneity of similar change* in voting behaviour. Swings entail a change that covers all or almost all territorial units of a political system (constituencies or regions at the national level; countries at the European one). Three elements are thus important:

- A *similar* change: It is not just measuring "change", but change in the same direction.[8]
- A *general* change: Similar change must take place everywhere or almost everywhere (a spatial dimension).
- A *simultaneous* change: Similar and general change must take place at the same time point in all territorial units (a temporal dimension).

In addition, however, when one speaks of the similarity of change, two different aspects are included. First, the uniformity of the *direction of change* in the vote for a party (or a party family) from one election to the next, that is whether it increases or decreases its share of votes. This refers to the signs + and –. The more similar the various territorial units, the more uniform change.

---

[6] It is generally considered that determining the location of forces must rely on survey data. Techniques based on aggregate data underestimate national influences as non-uniform swings, too, can be produced by common national factors to which local units give a differentiated response (Katz, 1973). In their analysis of British elections Butler and Stokes find results attesting to the presence of local factors modifying the effects of national influences (on the so-called Butler-Stokes hypothesis see Butler and Stokes, 1974: 143ff).

[7] Unfortunately, the absence of a suitable question on this dimension in existing cross-national surveys in Europe (consistent over time) prevents a chapter on the historical dislocation of "forces" from national to European in this volume even only as far back as the 1970s.

[8] This refers to "gaining and losing ground", that is, increasing or decreasing shares of votes for each party. In this sense it is different from measures of volatility (for example, the Pedersen index) which are aggregates for all parties and are based on absolute change between elections measured disregarding + and – signs.

Second, the uniformity in the *amount or size of change* in the vote for a party (or party family) from one election to the next. One has to establish whether a party increases/decreases its support everywhere (in each territorial unit) with equivalent percentages. This aspect presupposes a similar direction of change.

What about "trends" and "spread" in this context? General (everywhere), simultaneous (at the same time), similar change (same direction and size) must be distinguished from *trends* of Europe-wide increase or decrease of votes. First, upward and downward trends can be due to one or a few territorial units (countries) only and not necessarily to all or most. Trends are, therefore, not necessarily general. Second, trends may be general but not taking place at the same time. Trends are, therefore, not necessarily simultaneous. What swings measure, instead, is the degree to which a *similar and general* change takes place *at the same time*. As is discussed later in this chapter, this is expressed as the share of territorial units in which the similar and simultaneous change takes place. If a party family increases its electoral support in the same year in all countries but one or two (about 90 per cent), one may speak of a uniform swing. The higher the percentage, the more general the swing. Furthermore, the higher the percentage of votes, towards or against a given family, the stronger the swing (its size).

In the past, swings have been analyzed exclusively in the context of two-party systems (Britain and the United States). Swings take, therefore, a "back-and-forth" form between the two existing parties. The concept of *spread*, however, adds an important feature as it refers to the appearance of new party families. This is crucial in a historical study over a century and a half. From a territorial perspective new party families appear first in one country and then progressively in more. The classical use of swings, therefore, needs to be complemented by patterns of *appearance or new parties*, what here is called *spread*, and *disappearance* of old ones (or *shrinking*). As will be seen, this is closely related to measures of uniform swings. If in all or most countries parties of the same family appear simultaneously, this must be considered a swing from 0.0 to a given percentage of votes (positive swing). Similarly, the disappearance is considered a negative swing if it takes place simultaneously in many countries.

Data and Indicators

Time Periods and Party Families

The analysis in this chapter covers the same countries and time period as in Chapters 2 and 3. As for the analysis of homogeneity, the analysis of uniformity relies on a varying number of countries depending on patterns of democratization, structuration of the party systems, and data availability. The time periods are, therefore, the same as those documented in Table 3.1.

One crucial difference with the data covered in the analysis of homogenization is that, because uniformity refers to a cross-election temporal change, *pairs of subsequent elections* are needed to compute swings. For this reason, for *the first election in each country the value of swing cannot be calculated* because there is no election before.[9] In addition, it makes little sense to calculate swings between two subsequent elections if these are *very far apart in history* as, for example, in Central and Eastern Europe, where many countries voted in democratic elections before World War II for the last time and then again only after 1989 with the end of communist rule. For a number of countries, therefore, the first election of the new period has not been considered, as the election "before" is too far back in history.[10] Not only is the interruption very long, but the party systems changed completely.

As mentioned, the indicator of swing uniformity across territorial units has been applied in research at the national level to detect nationwide "tides" of change. Compared to swings across (sub-national) constituencies in national elections, however, the analysis of the uniformity of swings across countries faces two additional problems. Both have been mentioned in relation to the analysis of homogeneity, too.

First, parties across countries are different organizations, whereas across constituencies in one country the parties are the same.[11] It is a matter of "sameness". In Europe there is no such thing as a pan-European party. For this reason the analysis that follows is based on *party families* rather than single parties. The use of party families is necessary if one wishes to aggregate party votes at the supra-national level to see whether there is a swing in Europe. The party families used in this chapter are those discussed in Chapter 2 and on which the analysis of homogeneity in Chapter 3 is based. There are 24 basic families which are quite detailed, plus a number of aggregations of party families into larger categories such as religious parties or right parties (liberals and conservatives), minority parties (ethnic and regionalists), and so on (see Tables 2.2 and 2.3 for details). The degree to which parties from different countries but belonging (from the point of view of the classification) to the same family are ideologically similar is analyzed in Chapter 6.

A related problem is the presence of two or more parties of the same family in a country (say, several regionalist parties in Spain). In this case again the *votes for parties of the same family have been added together at each election in each country*. It would make little sense in a comparative perspective to

---

[9] The same applies to volatility measures (see Chapters 3 and 5).

[10] This choice has been made for seven countries with long democratic interruption: Bulgaria (1931/1991), Czechoslovakia (1946/1990), Estonia (1932/1992), Latvia (1931/1993), Lithuania (1926/1992), Poland (1922/1991), Romania (1946/1990), and Spain (1936/1977). Dates refer to election years. For the latter of the two figures (the first election of the new period), no swing has been computed.

[11] At the national level this means that they run under the same label and symbol, and are part of the same organization, but it is not necessarily true for territorially decentralized (non-nationalized) party systems such as India, Switzerland, and the United States (especially in earlier periods of time), where candidates of the same party may enter different alliances and adopt varying labels and symbols across constituencies.

calculate swings for each individual party. Party families are included in the analysis since their first appearance. This issue very much relates to what has been said about territorial spread. A party family may initially exist only in one country and then subsequently appear in other countries until, eventually, it exists everywhere.[12] While initially two party families (liberals and conservatives) exist "everywhere" in the (few) countries with competitive elections, most other party families appeared later, last the greens in the second half of the 1970s. Insofar as before the appearance of these party families, swings towards/against them would be systematically zero, for the periods *prior to their first appearance* they are not included in the analysis.

Second, while in national elections all constituencies vote at the same time, at the European level there is *no common time point*.[13] It is a matter of "simultaneity". In Europe there is no such thing as a general election. When considering electorates from a Europe-wide perspective, election points are not simultaneous insofar as national elections take place in different years according to the countries. Because countries hold elections in different years, the "election year" cannot be used as a time unit for comparative purposes. Periods of time of five years have been used instead as in the previous chapters. Again, this not only allows one to create simultaneity across national elections but also to include more than one election (and there are cases of two or more elections within the same calendar year) within each five-year period, mitigating the effect on indices of outlying elections. Concretely, this means that when two elections in a country take place during the same five-year period the average swing (between the two or more elections) towards/against each family is taken. This solution also diminishes short-term changes between two elections for a family and, on the contrary, shifts the focus to broad patterns.

Indicators of Uniform Swings

Indicators of swing are calculated on votes (rather than seats) as percentage points. As seen earlier, swings basically refer to a party or family either winning or losing votes in an election with respect to the previous one. In the case of gains of votes the swing is positive (+), while in the case of loss of votes the swing is negative (−). A family in a country losing 3 per cent of the votes from election t to election $t+1$ will have a swing of −3.0 at election $t+1$. While all this is straightforward, a number of issues arise from the computation of the uniformity of swings.

---

[12] The measure used to calculate such a territorial presence is that of "coverage". In this chapter it refers to the concept of "spread".

[13] At the national level this is not entirely true as the existence of staggered elections proves. This applies to Belgium and Luxembourg in particular, where until World War II parliament was renewed not simultaneously but through alternating elections in half the constituencies only. How these two countries are treated in the present study is documented in Chapter 3.

1. **Direction.** – The first issue relates to the direction of the swing. If between *t* and *t+1* a party family (say, the greens) increases its votes in all 30 countries (that is, in 100 per cent of them), one would say that the swing for the greens in *t+1* is *uniformly positive*. Conversely, if this family loses votes in *t+2* in all 30 countries (again 100 per cent), one would say that the swing in *t+2* is *uniformly negative*. Both cases would be taken as evidence of Europe-wide "waves" of change between these time periods but, as one can imagine, such high levels of uniformity are rare.

A much more likely scenario would be that 25 out of 30 countries swing in a direction (say, positive), while the remaining five swing in the opposite direction (negative). The question thus becomes from what threshold it is possible to consider swings as uniform across Europe. A way to approach this question is to take the middle point between perfect uniformity and perfect non-uniformity. A *perfectly uniform swing* is one in which *100 per cent* of the countries (30 out of 30) swing in the same direction (either positive or negative). On the contrary, a *perfectly non-uniform swing* is one in which half the countries swing in one direction and the other half in the opposite direction, that is a swing of *50 per cent*. The middle point is *75 per cent*: above this threshold in the following analysis a swing is considered uniform (that is about 22–3 countries out of 30 swing in the same direction).

This, however, entails a "denominator problem" in the calculation of percentages of countries swinging in the same or opposite directions. First, as discussed earlier, only for the most recent period of time does the data set include 30 democratic countries.[14] Especially in the early period the number of countries is much fewer. The denominator thus needs to be *adjusted to the number of democratic countries*. Second, percentages can be calculated in two different ways according to the existence of party families. There are two possibilities:

- The number of countries in which a swing is positive or negative (i.e. in which the family wins or loses) *as a percentage of the number of countries in which this family exists*. The denominator in this case is not necessarily the total number of democratic countries with competitive elections. This is the case when a given family does not exist in some countries.
- The number of countries in which a swing is positive or negative *as a percentage of all countries in which democratic elections take place*. In this second case a family that does not exist and does not appear in the subsequent election is considered "zero swing" (from nothing to nothing). Obviously in such a case there is no upper and lower limit of perfect (non-)uniformity.

In the evidence presented later this distinction is made whenever necessary.

Finally, the issue of *appearance (spread) and disappearance (shrinking)* of party families needs to be addressed. In a given country a party family that did

---

[14] See Table 3.1 for the list of countries included according to each five-year period. As in the previous chapter, in calculating percentages countries have not been weighted by size or population.

not exist in election *t* and then appears in *t+1* is considered a positive swing (from 0.0 to some votes). Conversely, a party family that in a given country existed in election *t* and then disappears in *t+1* is considered a negative swing (from some votes to 0.0).[15]

2. Size. – Besides direction, the second issue relating to the uniformity of swings is their size. The concept of size refers in the first place to that of the amount of the shift of votes. In the analysis of Europeanization of electoral politics it is of course of primary importance whether uniform swings have a meaningful size in sheer terms of votes. Size in this sense refers to large and small swings across countries. If the uniformity of direction is an indicator of Europeanization it is even more so if this uniformity concerns vast proportions of the electorate swinging in the same direction across countries. In this chapter, this aspect is referred to as *strength* of a given swing.

In the second place, however, size also plays a role in the evaluation of the degree of uniformity. One may very well observe a highly uniform swing in terms of direction (say, 28 countries out of 30 swinging towards the same party family), but the size of these swings may be very different from country to country with the same family increasing by a mere +0.5 per cent in a country and +20.0 per cent in another. In such a case one would not conclude that it is a uniform swing in terms of size. To assess such a uniformity measures of spread such as range and standard deviation are used later in the empirical analysis.[16]

Uniformity in Europe

Time: "Trends"
The term *trend* denotes the general temporal patterns of increase or decrease of votes for given party families. Contrary to uniform swings, trends need not be patterns that take place simultaneously in European countries, yet represent a form of wave and help identifying possible patterns of spread and swing. The first step of the examination of commonalities of change in electoral behaviour

---

[15] Operationally, in the data set appearance/disappearance means reaching the 1 per cent of votes necessary to be included in the computations. All parties below this threshold are grouped in the category "other parties". In such cases appearance and disappearance are "caused" by electoral behaviour.

[16] The *strength* of swing (average swing between two time points across countries) is calculated only among countries swinging in the same direction (either positively towards a family or negatively against it). The *uniformity of size* (range and standard deviation) is calculated for all countries irrespective of the direction of swing. A difficulty is caused by the relationship between amount of change and size of party (or party family) in the different territorial units (countries). If the size of the party family is different across countries, the amount of change tends to be proportional to the family's share of votes. The uniformity of amount, therefore manifests itself through a non-uniformity of values (see Butler and Stokes, 1974: 142–3). This links uniform swings to homogeneity across countries.

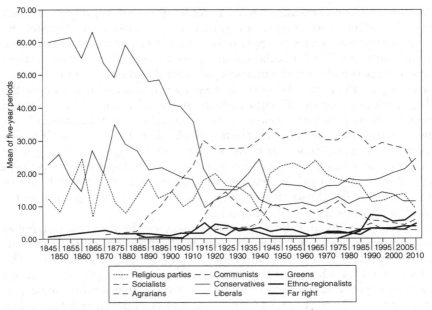

FIGURE 4.1. Trends in Europe, 1848–2012 (percentages of votes).

across Europe is to look closer at the main trends over the past 150 years of elections.

Looking broadly at the trends since the mid-19th century reveals the main phases of change in electoral behaviour that wipe across Europe. As mentioned earlier, patterns of electoral behaviour parallel the main institutional passage from absolutism and estate representation to general representative democracy, enfranchisement, and lowering of thresholds allowing for the formation of class and mass parties challenging established elite parties such as liberals and conservatives. In Figure 4.1 the rise of parties of "external origin" appears clearly in the curves for socialists and agrarian parties.[17] The socialist trend is obviously the steepest with percentages of electoral support increasing from nothing to roughly 30 per cent in the period from the end of the 1880s to World War I.[18]

This trend crosses that for liberals and conservatives, the two main established families from the period of restricted suffrage.[19] There is a sharp decline during the very same period. As for socialist vote, the levels of electoral support

[17] In both cases dashed lines have been used. Dashed lines have also been used for communist parties, for whom there is a sharp increase of votes after World War II.

[18] Percentages are Europe-wide averages. In countries in which a family does not exist the vote is considered 0.0 per cent.

[19] Liberals and conservatives are depicted by solid lines. The upper one is the liberal trend.

for liberals and conservatives somewhat settle after that period and remain more or less stable until the present time. For these three party families the "freezing hypothesis" seems to apply fully even if the most recent decade since 2000 indicates a decline for socialists and a rise for liberals and conservatives (mostly as a consequence of the inclusion of Central and Eastern Europe in the analysis). Up to the period between the two wars it is interesting to note the stable pattern of confessional parties which are the substitute of conservatives in countries such as Belgium, Germany, the Netherlands, and Switzerland. For religious parties there is an increase after World War II – a sort of Christian democratic "moment" when, after the fascist period in Europe, the Catholic Church fully accepted liberal democracy and entered the electoral competition instead of opposing it from an anti-system position. Since the 1970s, however, electoral support for Christian democrats and people's parties (as well as for the smaller denominational parties) declines.

In Figure 4.1 bold solid lines have been used for the three party families which the most recent literature has identified as sources of re-alignment: (1) ethno-regionalists; (2) environmentalists; and (3) right-wing populists. The long-term trend for ethnic and regionalist patterns is very stable at low levels of electoral support. Only since 1990 is there a very slight increase mainly as a consequence of the inclusion of Central and Eastern Europe in the data. The trend of the greens is one of weak increase since 1975, while the trend for right-wing populists is of steep increase to about 8 per cent of the Europe-wide vote.[20] In the wider continental and century-long picture such trends appear as marginal.

Space: "Spread"
While trends tell us that some families increase or decrease their support and help identify crucial "moments" of change, they do not tell us whether this happened everywhere and/or simultaneously, which is the information we need for the form of Europeanization which is the object of the analysis in this chapter. Figure 4.2 does not inform about the variations in the electoral strength of party families over time, but about variations in their spatial spread across countries. This information disregards whether families are large or small in terms of votes.[21]

"Spread" denotes the appearance across countries of a specific party family. Spread must be distinguished from trends as the latter may be caused by the increase of votes in one or few national parties only, without the appearance of parties in other countries and without any spread. First, spread indicates the rise of *new party families*. Historically, all families can be considered new at

---

[20] For the cross-country variation of these patterns and for the analysis of the impact of such variations on the overall homogeneity of Europe see Chapter 3.

[21] This part of the discussion very much relates to that of territorial coverage in Chapter 3. Here more attention is devoted to "spread" (temporally) than "coverage" (purely in spatial terms).

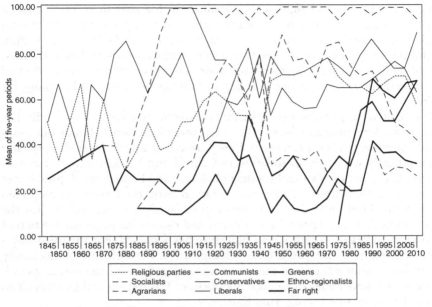

FIGURE 4.2. Spread in Europe, 1848–2012: Territorial coverage.

some point with the exception of the two families of internal origin (liberals and conservatives). Socialists are probably the major case of a new party family, but agrarians and communists, among others, have to be considered new at the moment of their first appearance. Since the "freezing" of party systems there are few new party families, the greens being the clearest case, alongside the very minor families such as feminists, parties for the protection of animal rights, pro- or anti-European parties, and pensioners' parties. Second, spread also involves the *appearance across countries of party families that were confined to one or few political systems* in the past. In both cases there is a spatial diffusion of party families in political systems in which they previously did not exist. As for trends, this need not be a simultaneous process across countries.

For a number of party families the information that territorial spread provides is similar to that of trends: increasing electoral support is parallel to increasing territorial presence across Europe. This already points to swings. Such is the case of the socialist and Christian democratic (to a lesser extent also agrarian) increase, as well as of the liberal decrease. There are very clear patterns of spread and, in the liberal case, of shrinking across the European territory.[22] On the contrary, for a number of party families territorial spread is much stronger than the increase of votes. This is particularly true for two

[22] Another case of shrinking is that of communists since 1989.

families: the greens and right-wing populists. In the past three decades such parties have started appearing in many countries (as a percentage of the total number of countries with democratic elections). As seen in Figure 4.1 it does not follow that these are parties with large electoral support. But their existence becomes a feature in more and more countries (about 60 per cent of the countries up from 30 per cent for right-wing populists and nothing for greens).[23]

For right-wing populists the picture is different insofar as this family has existed for a long time and, before the recent spread, it existed already in a number of countries.[24] Their presence in European countries increases sharply after 1990 not only with democratization in Central and Eastern Europe but also because of the rise of National Fronts in Belgium and France, the Republikaner in Germany, the National Bewegong in Luxemburg, the Centrumdemocraten in the Netherlands, and the Ny Demokrati in Sweden, among others (for the list see Table A.1.1 in Appendix 1). Greens and right-wing populists are two of the three families on which recent literature has focussed. For the third one – ethno-regionalists – the spread is not as impressive. The diffusion of this family is only from about a fourth of the countries to about a third and – even including the new democracies of Central and Eastern Europe – it is thus difficult to speak of a regionalist wave across Europe.[25]

For both trends and spread, information is aggregated at the European level. And both do not provide information about the simultaneity of spread of similar change between elections (increase or decrease of votes). There are, however, clear links. The spread of party families in "new" countries, that is in which they previously did not exist, is a form of increase of votes from 0.0 While spread does not give information on the level of simultaneity of this change, it is part of what the next section defines and analyzes as uniform swings.

Time and Space: "Swings"
The focus of this chapter is on the more specific acceptance of Europe-wide temporal processes of change that stresses similarity, simultaneity, and generality of change. Uniform swings indicate similar change (either towards or

---

[23] In the five-year period 1975–9 there is only the French green party, but soon the number of countries in which a green party exists increases. In some countries they have recently "disappeared" as in Denmark and Luxemburg after 2005 (not counted for their small size below 1 per cent).

[24] In the 1970s such parties include the Austrian FPÖ, the Danish Fremskridspartiet, the Finnish Unity Party (which soon disappears), the Greek National Alignment, the Italian Movimento Sociale, the Norwegian Fremskrittspartiet, and the Swiss Schweizer Demokraten (the Swiss People's Party – often considered a populist party in comparative research – is classified as conservative in the present study).

[25] Whereas regionalists existed in Belgium, Iceland (sporadically), Spain, Sweden (an ethnic party), and the United Kingdom, one sees such parties appear also in Switzerland and, most notably, in Italy with the Lega Nord.

against specific party families) that takes place simultaneously in a more or less large number of territorial units – in the case of the present investigation, countries.

As mentioned, both uniformity of direction and size matter, as well as the strength of swing, namely how large (in terms of votes) swings are. This information, furthermore, can be computed for all democratic countries or, alternatively, only for countries in which a specific party family actually exists. To produce Table 4.1 swings are aggregated for five-year periods. The table lists 24 swings singled out from all swings as the most important ones according to four criteria:

- The swing must take place in *at least 50 per cent* of countries in which competitive democratic elections take place during the five-year period.
- The overall number of democratic countries must be *at least four* within the five-year period (this excludes the period 1830–44).
- The swing among only the countries in which the specific family exists must be *at least 75 per cent*.[26]
- The strength of the swing must be *at least ±3.0 per cent* of votes.

The operational definition of swings based on these four criteria is quite reasonable and even conservative. One would not speak of a swing if it takes place in fewer than half the countries with elections (and a minimum of four democratic countries is a very low threshold that allows including periods in which not many countries were democratic). Furthermore, the choice of the middle way between perfectly uniform and non-uniform swing is not very stringent. Finally, a swing of less than ±3.0 per cent would not really be worth considering given its weakness in terms of shift of votes.

Table 4.1 is divided into two parts: the list of 10 positive swings and the list of 14 negative swings that fulfil the four criteria listed earlier. The table indicates for each swing which party family is concerned by it (either positively or negatively) and when (i.e. during which five-year period). The first two columns indicate how many democratic countries there are during this period, and in how many of them the party family exists (i.e. receives more than 1 per cent of votes).[27] The table then includes the information about swings. First, the percentage of countries swinging in the same direction (both on all democratic countries and on countries in which the family exists only). Second, the strength of the swings in terms of votes shifted towards (in case of positive swing) or against (in case of negative swing) the party family. Third, the uniformity of size is indicated (standard deviation, minimum and maximum swing among the countries concerned).

---

[26] As seen earlier, 75 per cent is exactly midway between perfectly uniform swing (100 per cent of countries in the same direction) and perfectly non-uniform swing (50 per cent of countries in one direction and 50 per cent in the other).

[27] These two figures are used to compute the column "coverage", which is the figure on which the discussion of spread is based.

TABLE 4.1. *Uniform Swings in Europe, 1845–2012*

Five-Year Periods	Party Family	Number of Countries with Elections	Number of Countries in which Family Exists	Uniformity of Direction (% of Countries With Elections)	Uniformity of Direction (% of Countries where Family Exists)	Coverage (% Family Presence on Countries with Elections)	Strength of Swing (Mean Across Countries)	Uniformity of Size (Standard Deviation)	Minimum Swing	Maximum Swing
Positive swings										
1900	Socialists	10	10	90.0	90.0	100.0	4.5	3.2	-0.4	9.3
1895	Socialists	8	7	87.5	100.0	87.5	4.1	3.2	1.2	10.1
1910	Socialists	12	12	83.3	83.3	100.0	3.0	5.2	-13.3	5.9
1880	Liberals	7	6	71.4	83.3	85.7	11.3	13.5	-0.2	32.2
1945	Communists	19	15	63.2	80.0	79.0	6.3	7.2	-6.6	20.9
1890	Socialists	8	5	62.5	100.0	62.5	7.1	4.8	2.3	13.2
1885	Conservatives	8	5	62.5	100.0	62.5	3.5	1.8	0.8	5.3
1870	Religious parties	5	3	60.0	100.0	60.0	8.1	3.1	4.5	10.1
1915	Socialists	17	12	58.8	83.3	70.6	11.0	8.5	-1.7	27.3
1920	Agrarians	22	14	54.6	85.7	63.6	4.2	5.0	-9.7	11.1
Negative swings										
1900	Liberals	10	10	100.0	100.0	100.0	-5.7	6.9	-0.1	-21.4
1870	Liberals	5	5	80.0	80.0	100.0	-7.7	4.4	1.3	-9.3
1985	Left[a]	20	20	75.0	75.0	100.0	-3.8	3.3	1.7	-8.8
1885	Liberals	8	6	75.0	75.0	75.0	-3.4	3.6	-0.1	-9.8

1890	Liberals	8	8	75.0	75.0	100.0	-3.9	4.4	5.1	-8.3
1880	Conservatives	7	5	71.4	100.0	71.4	-11.9	13.7	-1.8	-32.3
1895	Conservatives	8	6	62.5	83.3	75.0	-6.1	6.0	2.1	-16.1
1905	Conservatives	10	8	60.0	75.0	80.0	-8.9	13.8	15.1	-34.1
1920	Liberals	22	16	59.1	81.3	72.7	-3.3	4.1	7.3	-5.9
2010	Religious parties	19	13	57.9	84.6	68.4	-4.3	5.4	8.8	-13.5
1945	Agrarians	19	11	57.9	100.0	57.9	-3.3	4.0	-0.4	-14.3
1915	Liberals	17	12	52.9	75.0	70.6	-13.9	13.3	6.1	-41.9
1945	Far right	19	10	52.6	100.0	52.6	-8.9	12.9	-2.0	-43.9
1890	Conservatives	8	5	50.0	80.0	62.5	-7.2	9.4	5.3	-20.1

Notes: Swings are listed by uniformity calculated for all countries with democratic elections from largest to smallest. Swings in fewer than four countries, below an average of 3 per cent, and in fewer than half the democratic countries are excluded. Dates refer to five-year periods (for example, 1900 = 1900–4).

[a] Left includes socialists, communists, and new left parties.

At this stage of the analysis, these swings are still quite disaggregated. The first aspect to note is that most of the swings singled out by the operational definition are quite old. Only five (one positive and four negative) swings take place after World War II. In fact, three of them take place exactly after World War II in the five-year period 1945–9: the positive swing towards communist parties (12 out of 19 democratic countries, with a strength of +6.3), the negative swings against agrarians (11 out of 19, with a strength of –3.3) and against far-right parties (10 out of 19, with a strength of –8.9). In the case of agrarians and far-right parties, they lost ground in all the countries in which they existed at the time (100.0 per cent). The communists made progress in 80 per cent of the countries where they existed during 1945–9. Obviously, the cases of the communists' gain and the far right's loss can be interpreted through the outcome of the fight against fascism.[28] The other two swings after World War II are more recent and both negative. First, the 1985–9 swing against the left in 15 countries (on average a loss of votes across countries of –3.8). Second, the 2010–12 swing against religious parties in 11 out of 19 countries (57.9 per cent) with an average loss of –4.3.

The remaining 19 swings all belong to older periods. This is quite remarkable and points to the fundamental socio-economic and institutional transformations that have had an impact everywhere in Europe. What is also striking is that these swings concern three party families: *socialists, conservatives, and liberals* (and exceptionally religious parties and agrarians). Again we find three swings in the aftermath of a war. The five-year period 1915–19 is mostly composed of elections that took place in 1919 at the end of World War I. One swing is the agrarian positive swing in 1920–4 in 12 out of 22 democratic countries (slightly more than half). Agrarian parties made progress in particular in Austria, Bulgaria, Estonia, Lithuania, Norway, Sweden, and Switzerland. As far as the positive socialist and negative liberal swings are concerned, however, these should not be discussed as such but in *conjunction with a series of successive swings* that characterize these two party families and whose swings after World War I simply represent the end of a longer process.

To get a broader picture, therefore, it is necessary to put some of these five-year periods together as they are temporally adjacent. Two "long uniform swings" emerge from this:

- The "long positive socialist swing" between *1890 and 1919*: This includes the swings according to the operational definition given earlier of 1890,

---

[28] For a number of countries the temporal "jump" from the election(s) in 1945–9 is quite long as in the cases of Austria (1930/1945), Czechoslovakia (1935/1946), Italy (1921/1946), and Germany (1933/1949) It is, therefore, quite surprising not to see more swings in this five-year period. The maximum gain in communist progress (+20.9 percentage points) is that of Czechoslovakia, while the maximum loss in far right decrease (–43.9 percentage points) is the figure for Germany.

1895, 1900, 1910, and 1915 (see Table 4.1).[29] Of all the countries with democratic elections, this swing covers between 58.8 per cent of the countries (1915) and 80–90 per cent (1895, 1900, 1910). Among countries in which socialists exist, in more than 80 per cent they increase their vote in this period. In the five-year period 1915–19 the average increase in vote is +11.0 percentage points.

- *The "long negative liberal swing" between 1885 and 1924*: This includes the swings of 1885, 1890, 1900, 1915, and 1920. Of all the countries with democratic elections, this swing covers between 52.9 per cent (1915) and 100.0 per cent (1900). In the countries in which liberals exist, in more than 75 per cent of them they decrease their vote in this period. In the five-year period 1915–19 the average decrease in vote is −13.9 percentage points.

These two "long swings" are the *two single largest Europe-wide swings in the electoral history of the continent since the beginning of parliamentary life and competitive elections* in the middle of the 19th century, and they represent the rise of class politics and the decline of the liberal party family. In the broadest terms liberal decline and socialist rise symbolize the transition from elite to mass politics, from the party family of "internal origin" which as such represents the elite party organization in times of restricted suffrage to the mass bureaucratic party of "external origin" that so much classical literature has described. The rise of class and decline of liberal politics wipes across Europe for various subsequent five-year periods, but it is clear from the figures on the strength of swings that the decisive moment is the aftermath of World War I when the rise of socialism increases from swings between +4.0 and +7.0 percentage points to a swing of +11.3. Also for the liberals, the negative swings increase from between −3.0 and −5.0 percentage points to −13.9 after World War I.

Figures 4.3 and 4.4 convey visually the strength of these two sets of subsequent swings. The graph in Figure 4.3 on the socialist family indicates also the number of countries in which this family is not present. Since after 1900 this party family exists in all countries (with few exceptions in short periods of time),[30] the oscillations around the 50 per cent reference line are quite symmetrical and easy to interpret. The percentage of countries with positive swings is high during the entire period from the last decade of the 19th century to 1919. There is then a negative swing in 1920–4 which can be explained by the loss of votes due to the creation of communist parties as splinters from the socialists, and then again a positive swing (even if a lesser one).

What appears very clearly in Figure 4.3 is also that *in comparison to the period 1890–1919, positive and negative swings after World War II are much weaker*. There are two moments when socialists experience a negative swing

[29] It may be helpful to remind readers that these dates imply five-year periods, thus 1890 meaning 1890–4, 1895 meaning 1895–9, and so on.

[30] For example, in Estonia, Iceland, Luxembourg, and Poland before 1919 and Czechoslovakia in 1920–4, Cyprus in the 1960s, and Estonia and Lithuania at the beginning of the 1990s.

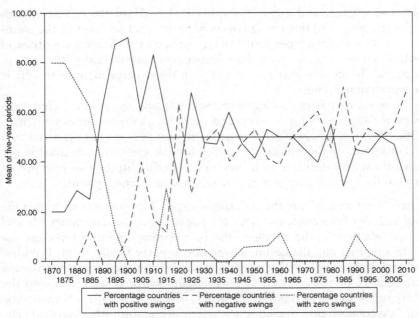

FIGURE 4.3. Uniform swings for socialists, 1848–2012 (percentages of all democratic countries).

(1985–9 and the most recent period since 2010), but – as their absence from Table 4.1 proves – they are not general and strong enough according to the operational definition given earlier to appear in the table. Similarly, general and simultaneous change in class politics takes place earlier in European electoral history. Even more clearly these "waves" appear in the upper graph in Figure 4.5, where only countries in which socialists exist are considered. Only for the period before 1920 are peaks above the threshold of 75 per cent of countries observed.[31]

Socialist and liberal swings from 1885 to 1919 are a first very clear indication of Europeanization according to this indicator during the crucial periods of the structuration of party systems. It also appears that these two swings are particularly important as – with this aggregation into "long swings" – the number of positive and negative swings is reduced to five and nine, respectively. Yet a number of other swings remain to be noted. In particular, a second major indicator of Europeanization according to the operationalization in terms of uniform swings comes from *the alternation that can be observed between conservatives and liberals during the 1885–1919 period*. A closer look at the liberal pattern shows that the story is more complex than one of simple decline.

---

[31] In Figure 4.5 the lower graph depicts visually the long negative swing for the liberals.

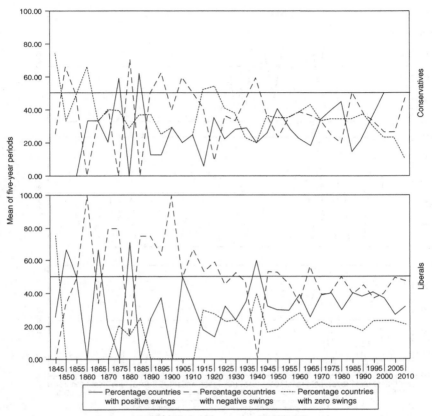

FIGURE 4.4. Uniform swings for conservatives and liberals, 1848–2012 (percentages of all democratic countries).

Looking again at Table 4.1 the alternation of negative swings between liberals and conservatives is quite striking:

- 1870–4: *liberal* negative swing (–7.7 percentage points in 80.0 per cent of countries).
- (1875–9: no swings according to operational definition.)
- 1880–4: *conservative* negative swing (–11.9 in 71.4 per cent of countries) with simultaneously a liberal positive swing (+11.3).
- 1885–94: *liberal* negative swing (–3.4 and –3.9 in 75 per cent of countries).
- 1895–9: *conservative* negative swing (–6.1 in 62.5 per cent of countries).
- 1900–4: *liberal* negative swing (–5.7 in 100 per cent of countries).
- 1905–9: *conservative* negative swing (–8.9 in 60 per cent of countries).[32]

---

[32] Only negative swings are listed. The fact that one of the two party families – liberals and conservatives – is characterized by negative swings does not necessarily mean that the other one

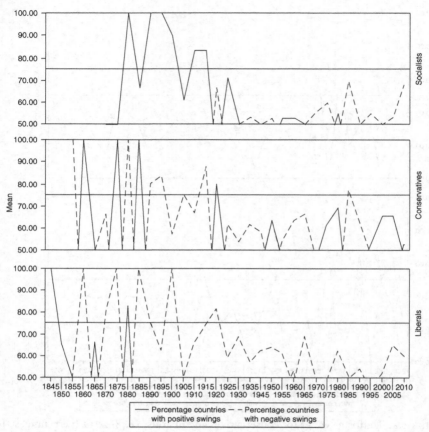

FIGURE 4.5. Uniform swings for socialists, conservatives, and liberals, 1848–2012 (percentages of countries in which families are present).

This simultaneous alternation in Europe is reminiscent of Schattschneider's quotation of the United States on parties gaining ground in all states in one election and losing ground in all or most states in the next election. Until World War I this alternation appears visually in the two graphs in Figure 4.4 on conservatives and liberals. Because the percentages of countries swinging in the same direction are computed on all democratic countries the reference line is positioned on the 50 per cent mark. One sees that in correspondence of the two positive peaks for conservatives (solid lines above the reference mark) there are two negative peaks for liberals in 1875 and 1885, and vice versa between

experiences a positive swing. In terms of positive swings there is the strong (+11.3 percentage points) liberal positive swing of 1880 in 71.4 per cent of countries and the weak (+3.5) conservative positive swing of 1885 in 62.5 per cent of countries.

these two periods in 1880. As for the socialists the pattern of Europeanization in terms of uniform swings (similar, general, and simultaneous change) appears more clearly when only countries in which the party families are present are considered (see the graphs for conservatives and liberals in Figure 4.5). Also similar to the socialist pattern, no evidence of uniform swings for liberals and conservatives can be observed after World War II. The largest occurrences of swings for the three main party families in European party systems take place between 1885 and World War I.

To gain a more precise picture of these important swings before World War I one needs to take into account that, overall during the 19th century, there were fewer democratic countries than today.[33] There are few instances of countries going against the socialist tide during this period. In 1900–4 it is France only and in 1910–14 it is Bulgaria and Switzerland. A period during which no positive socialist swing appears in Table 4.1 is 1905–9, during which many countries have negative swings: Bulgaria, France, Germany, and Italy. Also 1920–4, as noted, does not indicate a positive socialist swing as in many countries these parties suffer from the communist breakaway and the consequences in losses of votes.

Concerning liberals there is almost no instance of countries going against the various negative waves that hit this party family in various moments during the period 1870 until 1924. In 1870–4 this is the case only for Denmark (where liberals make a gain of 1.3 percentage points) and in 1890–4 in Switzerland (+1.7). In the period 1915–19, as mentioned, liberals suffer from a strong negative swing and they make very small gains in only three countries (Belgium, Denmark, and Sweden). In all others they suffer massive losses, in particular in Bulgaria (–41.8), Italy (–22.5), the Netherlands (–12.2), Switzerland (–15.8), and the United Kingdom (–18.0). Of all the conservative uniform swings identified through the operational definition employed in Table 4.1 only Norway and the United Kingdom go against the 1890 and 1895 uniform negative swings (with +5.3 and +2.1 percentage points, respectively), and in 1905–9 only France albeit with a massive +15.1 percentage points. For both socialists and the liberals/conservatives couple, the party families with the most uniform and strongest swings (positive and negative, respectively), the deviations from the overall Europe-wide tide are fundamentally sporadic and small.

The period since World War II and, in particular, the most recent period since the 1970s, needs a closer look. Already at this stage, however, it is possible to stress the absence of major uniform swings and of major similar, general, and simultaneous electoral shifts in Europe after World War II. Even for the periods during which Central and Eastern Europe are absent from the computation – that is a more homogenous group of Western European countries – uniform swings are for most of the time absent. The indicator of uniform

[33] The countries during this period are Belgium, Bulgaria, Denmark, France, Germany, Italy, the Netherlands, Norway, Switzerland, and the United Kingdom. At the beginning of the 20th century Finland and Sweden are added.

swings and the operational definition according to which the threshold of uniformity is defined (percentage of countries and minimum strength of swing) tell us that *Europe's electorates were shifting in a "Europeanized" way until World War I*. The fact that after World War II there are no large continental swings, however, does not mean that the various European countries move in a more independent way from one another, that is not simultaneously in their electoral shifts and that European party systems were more Europeanized then than now. The absence of swings seems to reveal an *absence of major change in European party systems* in the latest periods considered in this study and, by the same token, that *large Europe-wide swings are connected to periods of formation of party systems*. Also, the absence of swings today does not mean that electoral shifts in the single countries follow their own logics (i.e. a pattern of de-Europeanization), but rather that shifts are too small to be captured by the definition given earlier.

To conclude, this section turns to the past four decades with the less stringent criteria of "strength" and "generality". According to a large amount of literature, changes in European party systems took place along new cleavages such as centre–periphery, materialism/post-materialism, and winners versus losers of integration and globalization, that is smaller party families. According to this literature, ethno-regionalist parties, greens, and anti-European right-wing populist parties have gained ground in Europe at the expense of the traditional left–right alignment. This issue has already been addressed. Here the question rather concerns the existence of uniform swings along these lines, that is similar, general, and simultaneous changes towards these three party families in particular.

Already in Table 4.1 the absence of major populist, regionalist, and green temporal trends has been noted. In Table 4.2 the threshold of a uniform swing in at least half the democratic countries has been lowered to a third (a "generality" of 33.3 per cent) and the threshold of "strength" of at least ±3.0 percentage points has been removed. Both the table and Figure 4.6 show that the picture is still one of absence of major uniform swings, not only for these three party families but also more generally. In the graphs in Figure 4.6 the dotted curves (zero swings) show the pattern of spread for greens and right-wing populists, meaning that they do not exist in fewer and fewer countries (which is not the case for ethno-regionalists). However, one also sees that these patterns of spread do not produce uniform swings (i.e. simultaneous growth across countries) with very few exceptions. The clearest is the green case of 1985–9 when greens make gains in 50 per cent of democratic countries and in 90.9 per cent of countries in which greens exist (see Table 4.2). The strength of this swing, however, is not very impressive (+2.6). In 2005–9 there is another green swing but only in 46.7 per cent of democratic countries and concerning only 77.8 of countries in which greens exist. The level of uniformity of this swing is similar to that of right-wing populists in 1985–9 (however, this family existed in only 9 out of 20 democratic countries in that period). Based on regionalists,

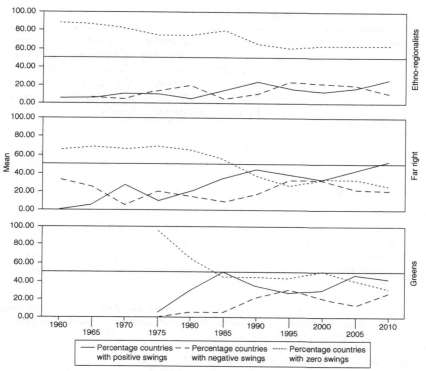

FIGURE 4.6. Uniform swings for ethno-regionalists, far-right parties, and greens, 1960–2012 (percentages of all democratic countries).

greens, and populists, therefore, it is difficult to say that Europe "moves together" with uniform and simultaneous changes of votes since the 1970s. These results would rather point to the fact that in most cases it is national specificities that predominate.

The absence of left–right swings also appears. Based on a large amount of literature one would have imagined swings in the early 1980s towards the right in the wake of landmark elections in Germany and the United Kingdom and what the field of political economy has labelled the neo-liberal, anti-Keynesian decade. This does not appear in the evidence even with the lowered thresholds to qualify for uniform swing. On the contrary there is a negative swing against conservatives in 1985–9 when these parties lose ground in half the countries and in 76.9 per cent of the countries in which they exist.[34] In two periods, 1990–4 and since 2010, there is a backlash against religious parties (at their most aggregate level,

[34] Uniform swings do not appear using different types of aggregation either, for example "right wing" (liberals and conservatives together).

TABLE 4.2. *Uniform Swings in Europe, 1970–2012*

Five-Year Periods	Party Family	Number of Countries with Elections	Number of Countries in which Family Exists	*Uniformity of Direction* (% of Countries with Elections)	*Uniformity of Direction* (% of Countries where Family Exists)	*Strength of Swing* (Mean across Countries)
Positive swings						
1975	Far left[a]	20	17	65.0	76.5	3.8
1985	Greens	20	11	50.0	90.9	2.6
2005	Greens	30	18	46.7	77.8	2.3
1985	Extreme right	20	9	35.0	77.8	3.1
Negative swings						
1975	Left[b]	20	20	75.0	75.0	−2.5
1985	Left[b]	20	20	75.0	75.0	−3.8
2010	Religious	19	13	57.9	84.6	−4.3
1985	Conservatives	20	13	50.0	76.9	−1.7
1990	Religious	29	17	44.8	76.5	−3.9

Notes: Swings are listed by uniformity calculated for all countries with democratic elections from largest to smallest. Swings in less than a third of the democratic countries excluded. Dates refer to five-year periods (for example, 1990 = 1990–4).
[a] Far left includes communists and new left parties.
[b] Left includes socialists, communists, and new left parties.

that is including people's parties and denominational ones). This is particularly true for the 2010–present period because in the previous one it concerns a minority of countries throughout Europe. Also in these cases, however, the swings are quite weak, between −3.9 and −4.3 percentage points. Finally, similar figures can be observed for the left at its most general level of aggregation in 1975–9 and 1985–9.

Uniform Swings and the Spread of Party Families

It was seen earlier that countries in which a party family "appears" where, up to that point, it was non-existent must be considered a positive swing, from 0.0 per cent of the votes to some level of support. This concerns party families that spread across countries and are present with candidates and lists in a growing number of them. Conversely, countries in which a party family "disappears" must be considered a negative swing from some level of support to 0.0 per cent in the next election period. The indicator of spread and shrinking seen earlier captures this specific form of electoral wave.

Considering the two major historical swings in European electoral history – the socialist positive swing and the liberal negative swing between the last decades of the 19th century and the immediate aftermath of World War I – the question that arises is how much of these swings is determined by spread in new countries, or by the shrinking of party families, as opposed to gains and losses of already existing parties. Looking back at Figures 4.3 and 4.6 where percentages of countries with uniform swings are calculated for the total number of countries with democratic elections, one sees that *positive swings may in fact be due to the appearance of parties in new countries*, namely when positive swings (the solid lines) correspond to the decline of dotted lines indicating in how many countries a family does not exist. Similarly, a negative swing may be due in part or mostly to the disappearance of party families in a number of countries at the same time. Again this would appear in the inverted relationship between the dotted lines indicating in how many countries the family is not existent and, in this case, the dashed line of negative uniform swing. Only when the dotted line remains flat are we in the presence of swings between existing parties. This is different compared to what Schattschneider described for the United States.[35]

While looking at the graphs in Figures 4.3 and 4.6 may reveal such a relationship between spread and uniformity of swings visually, a firmer ground can be gained from correlation analysis. Starting with the two long uniform swings of socialist rise and liberal decline, Figure 4.7 reveals two different patterns. In the case of the uniform positive swing of socialists in the five-year periods identified through the operational definition in Table 4.1, the correlation between the percentage of countries in which this, at the time, new family is present and the percentage of countries in which it increases its votes is high and significant ($r = 0.802**$).[36] This indicates that the uniform positive swing is not so much caused by increase of votes for these parties in the various countries where they already existed, but by the *appearance of these parties where they did not exist* in the previous periods.

A closer look, however, reveals a more complex pattern. When does this spread with uniform swing take place? The striking trajectory in the left-hand graph of Figure 4.7 is the one between 1885 and 1895. Here one sees two moments of strong spread (increased percentages of coverage) and strong swing: (1) *between 1885 and 1894* (both percentages increase dramatically) and (2) *between 1890 and 1899*. After this a slight increase occurs again between 1895 and 1904 (and also before between 1875 and 1884 there is

---

[35] The disappearance of party families is obviously less likely as parties may decline, even abruptly, but tend to survive. In fact, as a large amount of research has claimed both in classical analyses (Rokkan, 1999: 254–8) and more recent research (Boix, 1999), the introduction of PR almost simultaneously throughout Europe around World War I was the attempt by old elites to secure their survival. This scenario applies, for example, to the liberals in Italy. The decline without disappearance of liberals, however, can also be seen where plurality was kept, as the United Kingdom.

[36] Significance level at 0.01. The correlation is computed with five-year periods as cases and limited to the period 1870–1924.

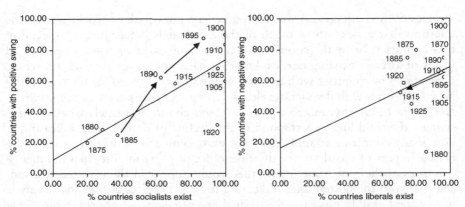

FIGURE 4.7. Relationship between spread and uniform socialist and liberal swings.
Note: Dates in the graphs indicate five-year periods (for example, 1920 = 1920–4).

a slight increase). It is between 1885 and 1900 that socialists spread. These 15 years are the ones that determine, through spread, the long positive swing for socialists, *after which swings stop being related to spread*. The left-hand graph in Figure 4.7 shows one main outlier (the period 1920–4) in which the absence of uniform swing is explained by the loss many socialist parties suffered in terms of votes as a consequence of the communist split during those years.

The other major historical uniform swing is the negative swing against liberals during the same period, that is from the last decades of the 19th century and the period after the end of World War I. As is visible in the right-hand graph in Figure 4.7, the levels of uniformity of the negative swing are not dependent on the territorial coverage across Europe (the correlation coefficient is $r = 0.303$). Swings, therefore, seem unrelated to either spread or shrinking. The levels of swing are clustered towards the 100 per cent level of territorial coverage, which indicates that negative swings are not related to swings towards 0.0, that is, disappearance of these parties in some countries. The exception that appears in the graph and marked with the arrow is between the period 1910–14 and 1915–19 during which the liberals seem to "disappear" from a number of countries. In fact, this is an artificial effect of the increasing overall number of countries included among which – Austria, Estonia, Iceland, Luxembourg, and Poland (and later also Czechoslovakia, Latvia, and Lithuania) – no liberal party exists. The decreasing percentage of coverage (spread) is a result of the larger denominator (the number of democratic countries).

The link between spread and uniform positive swing is also visible – albeit at a reduced scale – for the more recent green and populist waves. For these two party families the correlation coefficients between territorial coverage and percentage of countries swinging in the same direction are $r = 0.845^{**}$ and

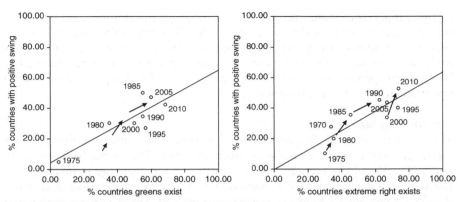

FIGURE 4.8. Relationship between spread and uniform green and extreme-right swings.
Note: Dates in the graphs indicate five-year periods (for example, 1990 = 1990–4).

$r = 0.862**$, respectively.[37] This indicates that a large part of uniformity in the positive swings towards greens and extreme-right parties is due to territorial spread, that is from the passage from 0 per cent to some level of support in the countries in which these parties appear as new players.[38] As the arrows in the two graphs in Figure 4.8 show the period of time when the spread combined with uniform positive swing occurs is similar for the two party families, namely between 1975 and 1985 (1990 for extreme-right parties) and then again more recently (that is since 2000). As for socialists a century earlier, *Europeanization as a uniform swing takes place through territorial spread* for greens and neo-populists too.

The strongest positive uniform swing that occurred in the 150 years of European electoral history covered by this study – the socialist rise through class and mass politics – takes largely the form of territorial spread and derives from swings from nothing to something, from 0.0 per cent of support to some electoral strength. Once again, the results of this study support the thesis that *Europeanization is in the first place a matter of class politics* imposing itself. The socialists' spread translates into the major case of positive uniform swing since democratic elections take place. The 15 years from 1885–1900 can be seen as "the" moment of their Europeanization and thus of the Europeanization of a large chunk of electoral politics more generally. Rather than swings strictly speaking – and as Schattschneider understood them in the 1960s United States – we are in the presence of an episode of spread of parties

[37] Significance level at 0.01. The correlation is computed with five-year periods as cases and limited to the period 1970–2012.

[38] It should not be forgotten that, as Table 4.2 shows, the strength of these recent swings are not comparable to those of a century earlier and involve small amounts of votes for party families that remain, overall, marginal in the European landscape.

of this family appearing and diffusing through new territories. While this is the case also (but the scales of events are hardly comparable) for greens and right-wing populists since 1975, the major case of negative swing – the liberals in the first decades of the 20th century – is not caused by "disappearance", but by a genuine general and simultaneous loss of votes for this party family in the transition from elite to mass politics.

Amount and Size
The passages of combined spread and uniform swing just described are not the largest occurrences in terms of shifts of votes. The swing between 1885 and 1890 shifted on average across countries 7.1 percentage points of votes towards socialist parties. The subsequent swing between 1890 and 1895 shifted 4.1 percentage points of votes towards them. These were encompassing swings in terms of how many new countries were involved in socialist advances in Europe, but were not strong ones in terms of votes. It was primarily spread across European countries. The strongest swing towards socialist parties is the one that takes place after World War I in the period 1915–19 (mostly elections taking place in 1918 and 1919). Here the shift of votes towards socialists is on average across all countries 11.0 percentage points (see Table 4.1).[39] This is also the period when the swing against liberals is strongest with an average loss of −13.9 percentage points across countries.

How uniform has the swing been in terms of size? The last two columns in Table 4.1 give the minimum and maximum swings from which the range can be derived. Let us start with the two major socialist swings combined with territorial spread. In 1890–5 the swing ranges between a minimum of +2.3 (Switzerland) and a maximum of +13.2 (Belgium). In 1895–1900 the swing ranges between +1.2 (United Kingdom) and +10.1 (France). If now we take the largest uniform swing towards socialists (1915–19), the swing ranges between −1.7 percentage points (actually a loss of votes) for Finland and +27.3 percentage points for Belgium. Also for the other two socialist swings of 1900–4 and 1910–14 the range is similar. This hardly points to uniformity in size. While such swings are uniform in direction (percentage of countries swinging in the same direction) and are strong (above 3.0 percentage points of votes shifted), they are not uniform in size: in some countries the increase of vote is minimal and in others it is very high. Such a pattern reveals country-specific factors beneath the general swing towards socialists.

The same very much applies to negative swings. At the largest negative swing – the one against liberals during World War I – in Bulgaria liberal parties lost −41.9 percentage points of votes with respect to the previous period while in Finland they lost −0.4 percentage points (in Italy the loss was −22.5; in Belgium and Finland they gained votes). As far as the other large negative

[39] The socialist uniform swings of 1900–4, 1910–14, and 1915–19 (see Table 4.1 and Figure 4.7) occur without spread.

swing is concerned – conservatives' loss in 1880–4 – the minimum swing was –1.8 (United Kingdom) and the maximum –32.3 (Italy). In that period German liberals lost-2.3 percentage points and Danish liberals –3.2 while the French liberals lost –19.7. The differences between countries, even if the direction (i.e. loss) is uniform, are considerable. The next largest negative swing is that against extreme-right parties after World War II in 10 countries out of 19 (1945–9). The maximum loss is that suffered from the German Nazi party with –43.9 percentage points with respect to the 1933 election (in fact, an instance of disappearance of this family) and of the Romanian PTT (–15.8 percentage points compared to the 1937 election) while in all other countries the losses were less than –5.0 percentage points.

It can be concluded that even if there are instances of uniform swings in terms of direction (a general and simultaneous change in the same direction), and even if such uniform swings are sometimes very consistent in terms of votes towards or against specific families, *the differences between single countries in the size of swings remain large*. In some countries the gains or losses (depending on whether we are dealing with positive or negative swings) can be of very different size – large in some countries, small in others. Such differences *do not indicate a uniformity of size* even when we are in the presence of uniformity of direction. Such differences also point to the persistence of country-specific factors during Europe-wide tides of change affecting most or even all countries.

Conclusion

The classic literature on parties and party systems has captured the momentous change from elite to mass politics with the rise of class politics in the wake of enfranchisement and mobilization through socialist parties. The analysis in this chapter shows the power of this change quantitatively and in sheer vote strength. To "see" graphically the size and strength of this transition in the long socialist swing at the end of the 19th century, and the contraction of liberal politics shortly afterwards, is indeed impressive. Such a momentous transformation is reinforced in its meaning by the fact that nothing comparable has happened since, in spite of claims of radical change in the recent decades.

As for Chapter 3, evidence presented in that chapter points to Europeanized processes that were much stronger in the 19th century up to World War I compared to the period after World War II to the present. *Europeanization is an "early" phenomenon* typical of the radical socio-economic and political transformation of the late 19th and early 20th centuries. Uniform swings are large for periods of party systems' formation when electoral shifts towards and away from specific party families are large. Today, on the contrary, swings are simply too weak to appear as major Europe-wide "waves" in a context of comparatively consolidated party systems. The three major uniform swings from World War II to the present take place exactly in the first elections after the end of the war and were all of negligible strength as seen earlier.[40] What is more, the recent period of time does not include any swing between left and right, although much of the attention among observers stresses the commonality of alternation between the two ideological camps. The party families on which much of the recent academic literature has focussed – new regionalist mobilization, far-right populism, and green politics – fade away in comparison with swings of the past.[41]

Looking at the major swings throughout European electoral history focuses our attention once again to parties of the *left–right dimension,* mainly the socialists with liberals and conservatives. Europeanization in terms of general, similar, and simultaneous change occurs first and foremost with the *transition from elite to mass politics* at the end of the 19th century and the first two decades of the 20th. First, this entails the "long socialist swing" between the 1880s and 1919 but really concentrated in the 15 years between 1885 and 1900 with the territorial spread of this, at the time, new party family. Second, this entails the "long (negative) liberal swing" roughly in the same period during which liberals decline. The cleavage model seen in Chapter 2 appears here with the supremacy of the left–right class cleavage imposing itself, as does the division of the left with the communist split after the Soviet Revolution which mirrors the negative swing for socialists in the first half of the 1920s.

Importantly, the analysis in this chapter shows that these major uniform swings have a strong territorial component as they are related to the *appearance and spread* of a new party family in the case of socialists (especially in the 15 years between 1885 and 1900). The most important swing is, therefore, related to and correlates with territorial spread.

Territoriality is not involved in a further proof of the early Europeanization of electorates and party systems in the late 19th century and the early 20th century according to this indicator. Yet very similarly to what Schattschneider observed for the United States during a similar period of time, conservatives and liberals in the period of restricted suffrage display alternating but parallel swings over the period 1885–1919, one "gaining ground" generally in Europe when the other "lost ground" and the other way around in the following phase. These, too, are patterns of an early Europeanized electorate and nothing comparable takes place since, reinforcing the conclusion of a historical process of Europeanization.

---

[40] In favour of communist parties and against agrarians and far-right parties.
[41] Only two swings are noted in the past decades: the negative swing against left parties in the second half of the 1980s and the negative swing against religious parties after 2010. The latest election results for 2013 and 2014 – not included in the analysis – indicate that a stronger swing towards populist parties for the period 2010–14 may be under way.

5

Correspondence

Overlapping versus Distinctive Electorates in National and European Elections, 1974–2012

Introduction

Correspondence refers to the overlap or, conversely, the distinctiveness between the two levels of elections in Europe, national and supra-national. This chapter investigates the extent to which there is a distinct electorate and party system at the EU level, independent from national issues, party platforms, and alignments. The vertical correspondence of electoral behaviour between national and European elections is analyzed through a comparison of national elections and elections to the EP.[1] Is there, and, if so, to what degree, a differentiated European party system or, on the contrary, is electoral behaviour in European elections a reflection of national political contests?[2] And is there a trend in the progressive "emancipation" of the European party system from national politics over 30 years of European elections? This chapter investigates the origins of distinctiveness based on swings towards and against party families based on the previous chapter.

Since the first direct elections to the EP in 1979, European elections have been described as "second-order elections" (Reif and Schmitt, 1980). This label implies not only that European elections are (perceived as) less important than national elections in the member-states of the EU, but also that European elections are dominated by national factors. European electorates vote for the EP according to national criteria, campaigns are run on national issues, voters are guided in their voting choices by national party affiliations and electoral alignments, and leaders seek support on national policies and platforms. In sum, European elections are national contests "by other means".[3]

---

[1] Grateful thanks to Trond Kvamme of NSD in Bergen for his help in completing the collection of the European Parliament election results.

[2] Bartolini (2005: 392) speaks of alignments at the European level that are "isomorphic" with most national cleavage systems.

[3] See Van der Eijk and Franklin et al. (1996) for a comprehensive analysis. See Hix (2002) for an overview of the literature and Hix and Marsh (2011) for one of the most recent analyses.

Over the past 30 years the EP has acquired new competences and strengthened those it already had. Decision making is systematically affected by European party federations, and groups consolidated in the EP.[4] More generally, the process of integration has moved at an accelerated pace and public debates have gained strength in the wake of referenda on accession, common currency, and treaties and with the process of the EU's "constitutionalization". As seen in Chapter 1, integration is the crucial moment that the literature has identified as affecting lines of contestation by introducing a pro/anti-integration cleavage. Transfer of shares of sovereignty may have created new dimensions at the European level – a cleavage on basic integration choices – that translates into both a *distinct offer* in European elections (different parties, alliances, and programmes) and a *differentiated electoral response* translating into a shift of votes between national and European elections.[5] If this is indeed the case, one expects to find a *progressive divergence* of electoral behaviour between European and national elections. This chapter asks whether a pro/anti-Europe dimension is indeed challenging other dimensions in EP elections or if, on the contrary, "second-order" effects (such as protests and votes for small parties) are the explanation for distinctiveness.

To test the degree of correspondence empirically, European elections are placed into a time perspective beginning in the early 1970s and ending with the most recent national elections in 2012 and the election to the EP in 2009. The analysis covers mostly 27 EU member-states.[6] Voting behaviour is analyzed through an approach comparing national and European elections based on indices of electoral volatility. This indicator allows focussing on voters and their voting behaviour rather than on elites.[7] First, descriptively, this chapter charts cross-nationally and longitudinally the degree to which national and European electoral behaviour overlaps. Second, explanatorily, this chapter tests hypotheses about the origin of volatility between national and European "orders" based on electoral swings towards/against specific party families building on the previous chapter. Triangulation between different methods (multiple and logistic regression, and qualitative comparative analysis) is used.

---

[4] This was observed already back in the 1990s. See Hix and Lord (1997: 18). Kreppel speaks of a "transformation of the EP from a chamber of debate to a legislative body" (2002: 151). Hix, Kreppel, and Noury (2003) come to the conclusion that the European party system is "ready for power".

[5] The classical nationalization literature speaks of "stimuli–response" mechanisms (see Chapters 1 and 4).

[6] Iceland, Norway, and Switzerland do not vote in European elections as they are not part of the EU. They are excluded from the analysis, although national volatility figures are provided in the graphs and tables.

[7] The level of mass electorates is often neglected in integration studies, which focus instead on MEPs, party groups, and elite-level negotiations. Hix et al. (2003) distinguish an organizational and a competitive dimension in the EP, leaving aside the dimension of the electoral process.

Framework for Analysis

Main Indicator and Hypotheses

Most analyses of the EU party system conducted through the comparison of European and national elections consider two dimensions of electoral behaviour: electoral participation (turnout) and the support for political parties. More generally, these dimensions appear in work comparing *different orders of elections* trying to explain why voters turn out and vote differently in different types of elections or when they are held at different times. In this vein authors have analyzed US elections and advanced explanations for the weaker performance of incumbents in midterm elections compared to elections taking place in presidential election years. One of these theories – the theory of "surge and decline" – has stimulated authors to describe the European party system by comparing it with the US one.[8]

Research on different orders of elections has proved useful in analyzing elections to the EP. This work has pointed to the lack of salience of European elections in the eyes of many voters as they do not lead to the selection of an executive and as the EP has had only limited power (Reif, 1985a, 1985b). This is expected to lead to (1) lower turnout rates in elections to the EP[9]; (2) a loss of votes for major parties in European elections; and (3) poorer performances of national incumbent parties. Because in European elections there is "less at stake" the propensity to vote sincerely is expected to increase, that is disregarding tactical or strategic considerations which would on the contrary encourage citizens to vote for large and/or incumbent parties that have a realistic chance of winning office.[10]

The concept of "differential" voting behaviour between the two orders of elections represents a useful heuristic tool. This is the main indicator used here to investigate *if – and to what extent – there is a trend towards a EP party system, increasingly distinct from national party systems*, based on a different party offer, with different platforms and stressing different issues and dimensions.

---

[8] The literature on this comparison is quoted in the Conclusion to this volume. For a systematic juxtaposition see Raunio (2002: 273). On "surge and decline" see Campbell (1960 and 1966), Campbell (1987), and Niemi and Weisberg (1993: 207–21).

[9] Explanatory factors accounting for the few cases in which turnout in European elections approaches national levels include compulsory voting (Blumer and Fox, 1982), positive views on Europe (Van der Eijk and Oppenhuis, 1990), and time until the next national election (Marsh and Franklin, 1996). Because of the focus on party alignments turnout is not considered in this chapter.

[10] Schmitt (1990) has described the tendency of "wasting votes" and "voting with the heart". Others interpret such cycles in terms of a "punishment effect" against incumbents in national governments (Erikson, 1988; Reif, 1985a). On the "theory of second-order elections" see also Marsh (1998) and Reif (1997). Two more elements are presented in this literature. First, the loss of votes for incumbent parties is caused by the lower turnout in midterm or European elections. Second, second-order elections are interpreted as referenda on the performance of the government.

What is the degree of differentiation or, conversely, correspondence between the two levels, what is the trend over time, and is there cross-country variation? It is clear that a *low differential* between the two orders of elections shows the absence of differentiating elements, such as different alignments active at one level but not the other, issues, alliances, and so forth that would account for a deviating electoral behaviour in EP elections with respect to national elections. It would mean overlap and similarity in electoral behaviour between the two levels. A *high – and increasing – differential* can, on the contrary, have different origins. Three main hypotheses are considered.

- A high differential may be caused by *sincere voting* factors leading to shift votes towards green, new left, pirate, and generally small "libertarian" parties.
- Alternatively, it may capture *Euro-specific dimensions* and the tendency of voters to consider EP elections as a distinct arena in which parties compete on European rather than national issues, that is a distinct alignment activated mainly at the EU level by voting for extreme-right and anti- or pro-EU parties or personal candidacies.
- Finally, it may be due to *punishment effects* against the large, mainstream, social democratic, centre-right (conservatives and people's parties), and liberals.

The operationalization of these hypotheses about the origin of differentiation consists of the swings towards or against specific party families between national and EP elections.

Method, Data, and Cases

To provide empirical insights into the degree of differentiated alignments underlying national and European party systems and electorates, this chapter uses aggregate data and, in particular, electoral support for parties over the period starting (depending on the country) with the national election before the first EP election in 1979 until 2012. The measure used to establish the degree of differential between national and EP elections is that of *electoral volatility* – a measure of the change of votes between elections.

The well-known "Pedersen index" of volatility is applied (see Appendix 3 for the formula). The index is constructed by summing the absolute differences (disregarding plus and minus signs) between the percentage of votes for each party in election t and the percentage in $t-1$. The sum is then divided by two to avoid double counting (gains for one party meaning losses for another or several other parties), and to make the index vary between 0 and 100. Based on this formula, the combination of national and European elections leads to three types of volatility:

- *National volatility* (NV) between national elections only (in the graphs this type of volatility is represented through solid lines). Computations include

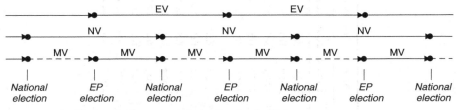

FIGURE 5.1. National, European, and mixed volatility.

all national elections in a country since the election before the first EP election. NV has always been computed on the previous election. For example, the level of volatility in the British 2010 general election has been computed with respect to the 2005 general election.

- *European volatility* (EV) between elections to the EP only (dotted lines). Similarly to NV, EV has always been computed on the previous election (for example, the 2009 EP election with respect to the 2004 EP election). For the first EP election in a given country there is no level of EV because no previous EP election exists.

- *Mixed volatility* (MV) between national and European elections and the other way around (dashed lines). The levels of MV in national elections have been computed with respect to the previous European election and, conversely, the levels of MV in European elections have been computed with respect to the previous national election. When two or more national elections took place between two EP elections, only one has been considered.[11]

These various combinations are depicted in Figure 5.1. Unlike NV and EV, for MV two different directions are possible: (1) mixed volatility from national *towards EP elections* (MV value for EP election year, dashed arrows) and (2) mixed volatility from EP *towards national elections* (MV value for national election year, solid arrows). This allows establishing in which direction the propensity to change vote is higher or lower.

Table 5.1 gives the details about which elections have been analyzed. The number of member-states included in the analysis varies over time according to accession. For the first 1979 election to the EP there were ten countries. Greece joined the EU in 1981 and voted to elect its representatives to the EP after accession. Similarly, Portugal and Spain voted in 1987 after accession and this vote has been considered with the 1984 European election in the other countries. The same applies to the subsequent round of accessions in 1995 when Austria, Finland, and Sweden joined the EU, bringing the total number of member-states to 15. In Sweden the vote was held in 1995, whereas in the

---

[11] So far this has measure been applied to different "orders" of elections only in Caramani (2006). Values of volatility are computed for each election.

TABLE 5.1. *European and National Elections for EU Member-States*

Country	Nat.	EP	Nat.	EP	Nat.	EP	Nat.	EP	Nat.	EP	Nat.	EP	Nat.	EP	Nat.
	1976.5	1979	1981.5	1984	1986.5	1989	1991.5	1994	1996.5	1999	2001.5	2004	2006.5	2009	2011.5
Austria							1990	(1996)	1995	Yes	2002	Yes	2006	Yes	–
Belgium	1978	Yes	1981	Yes	1987	Yes	1991	Yes	1995	Yes	2003	Yes	2007	Yes	2010
Bulgaria											2001	(2007)	2005	Yes	2009[a]
Cyprus											2001	Yes	2006	Yes	2011
Czech Republic											2002	Yes	2006	Yes	2010
Denmark	1977	Yes	1981	Yes	1987	Yes	1990	Yes	1998	Yes	2001	Yes	2005	Yes	2011
Estonia											2003	Yes	2007	Yes	2011
Finland							1991	(1996)	1995	Yes	2003	Yes	2007	Yes	2011
France	1978	Yes	1981	Yes	1986	Yes	1993	Yes	1997	Yes	2002	Yes	2007	Yes	2012
Germany	1976	Yes	1980	Yes	1987	Yes	1990	Yes	1998	Yes	2002	Yes	2005	Yes	2009[a]
Greece	1977	(1981)	1981	Yes	1985	Yes	1993	Yes	1996	Yes	2000	Yes	2007	Yes	2012[b]
Hungary											2002	Yes	2006	Yes	2012
Ireland	1977	Yes	1981	Yes	1987	Yes	1992	Yes	1997	Yes	2002	Yes	2007	Yes	2011
Italy	1976	Yes	1983	Yes	1987	Yes	1992	Yes	1996	Yes	2001	Yes	2006	Yes	–

Latvia										2002	Yes	2006	Yes	2010
Lithuania										2000	Yes	2008	Yes	–
Luxembourg	1974	Yes	1979[a]	Yes	1984[a]	Yes	1989[a]	Yes	1994[a]	Yes	1999[a]	Yes	2004[a]	Yes	2009[a]
Malta										2003	Yes	2008	Yes	–
Netherlands	1977	Yes	1981	Yes	1986	Yes	1994[a]	Yes	1998	Yes	2002	Yes	2006	Yes	2010
Poland										2001	Yes	2007	Yes	2011
Portugal			1983	(1987)	1987	Yes	1991	Yes	1995	Yes	2002	Yes	2005	Yes	2009[a]
Romania										2000	Yes	2008	(2007)	–
Slovakia										2002	Yes	2006	Yes	2010
Slovenia										2000	Yes	2008	Yes	2011
Spain			1982	(1987)	1986	Yes	1993	Yes	1996	Yes	2000	Yes	2008	Yes	2011
Sweden							1991	(1995)	1998	Yes	2002	Yes	2006	Yes	2010
United Kingdom	1974[c]	Yes	1983	Yes	1987	Yes	1992	Yes	1997	Yes	2001	Yes	2005	Yes	2010

Notes: Years for EP elections in parentheses means that election has been considered together with other countries in the preceding EP election year. In Luxembourg European and national elections are held on the same day.

[a] National election in same year as EP election.

[b] May election.

[c] October general election.

– No national election after 2009 (at the time of analysis, that is January 2013).

other two countries it was held in 1996. Ten new countries joined before the 2004 European election, bringing the number of member-states to 25. To these, the 2004 election adds the elections in Bulgaria and Romania both held in 2007 for a total of 27 cases in 2004. Finally at the 2009 EP elections all 27 member-states voted simultaneously.

Seven elections to the EP since 1979, the first direct election, and until 2009 have been considered.[12] The 10 countries already members of the CEE/EU at the time have voted in all seven European elections. For countries that joined later the time series is obviously shorter. The shortest is for countries that voted only in the 2004 and 2009 European elections (Central-Eastern Europe, Cyprus, and Malta). All national elections have been considered since the early 1970s.[13]

Table 5.1 also provides information about which national elections have been included to calculate MV. MV is the level of change between a national election and a European election. To calculate MV one election before the first EP election for each country is needed and one after the last EP election of 2009 has been taken, as well as one national election between each of the various European elections.[14] Between two European elections (five years apart) more than one national election may take place, but only one has been considered. In choosing which national elections to take, as far as possible elections roughly in the middle of two European elections have been taken. This was not always possible as documented in Table 5.1.[15]

To increase cross-country comparability and for ease of presentation in tables and figures, these national elections have been re-coded to give them a similar year (because national elections never take place in the same year in all countries). These "fictitious years" appear on top of Table 5.1, whereas in the cells real election years are given. In the data file this is a surrogate of "simultaneity" in national elections. Because the number of years between two European elections is even (say, between 2004 and 2009) a 0.5 has been added to make the fictitious year appear right in between the two European elections. The closest national election has then been chosen as documented in Table 5.1 to calculate MV. EV, finally, includes only volatility from one EP election to the next. For countries in which only two European elections took place, therefore, there is only one value of EV.

---

[12] The analysis was carried out before the 2014 EP election.

[13] For the countries that joined later than 2009 two national elections have been considered before the first EP election in order to have NV values for roughly the same period of time as for EV and MV.

[14] For four countries no national election took place between 2008 and 2012 (at the moment of completion of the data collection), and therefore there is no national election after the last European election in 2009.

[15] In some cases national and European elections take place in the same year. If a previous national election was available, this has been preferred. In Luxembourg this is particularly problematic as the two types of election take place on the same day.

As in the rest of this book, national results include the election of lower houses according to the criteria specified in Chapter 2. Concerning the selection of parties for the computations, the criterion has been to include parties receiving at least 1 per cent nationwide in EP elections. This allows the analysis to include regionalist parties and more generally small parties which – in European elections – usually score better than in national contests.

The basic cases are elections by country. For each country, at each election, there is a volatility value (calculated from the previous election). In total, there are 260 values of NV (209 for Western Europe and 51 for Eastern Europe). For EV the number is obviously much lower as there have been fewer elections to the EP (the total figure is 91; 81 and 10 for Western and Central-Eastern Europe, respectively). Finally, there are 230 MV cases (193 and 37 for Western and Central-Eastern Europe, respectively).

Descriptive Analysis

Overall Figures: A Fundamental Correspondence

Table 5.2 provides the basic descriptive figures of the levels of volatility in and across Europe for NV, EV, and MV. The first aspect to notice is the large difference in volatility levels between Western and Central-Eastern Europe (as seen in Chapter 3). While in the former the average volatility is around 16.10, in the latter it is 35.27, about double. Second, while in Central-Eastern Europe all countries are affected by high levels of electoral volatility, in Western Europe there are large differences between the countries, with cases of very low volatility (such as Malta) and cases of high volatility (such as France and Italy). As far as NV is concerned Malta, Germany, Switzerland, the United Kingdom, and Cyprus have particularly low levels of cross-election change. On the contrary, France, Belgium, Italy, and the Netherlands have the highest scores. The United Kingdom, however, displays a high level of EV, as do Cyprus and Germany. Third, between Western Europe on one hand and Central-Eastern Europe on the other there is a difference regarding MV. This measure of change between national and EP elections is generally higher than NV in Western Europe. This means that there is a higher propensity for voters to change votes between the two orders of elections than in national elections only. On the contrary, in Central and Eastern Europe NV is higher as it appears in the last column of Table 5.2.[16]

Indeed, one of the most important pieces of information is not so much how high MV is (the volatility between national and EP elections), but rather *the extent to which MV is higher than NV*. Finding high MV may not mean

[16] It is maybe useful to remind readers that the geo-political category of Central-Eastern Europe includes the 10 countries part of the democratic transition after the breakdown of communist regimes. It does not refer to the latest round of EU enlargement, which includes Cyprus and Malta. These two countries have been counted as "Western Europe".

TABLE 5.2. *Levels of Electoral Volatility by Country (1970–2012)*

Country	National Volatility (NV)	(N)	European Volatility (EV)	(N)	Mixed Volatility (MV)	(N)	Mean Volatility (All Types)	Overall N	Differential (MV–NV)
Overall (30 countries)	17.54	(260)	19.63	(91)	20.26	(230)	19.14	(581)	2.72
Standard deviation	14.25		10.96		11.01		12.07		
Western Europe									
Overall (20 countries)	12.61	(209)	17.46	(81)	18.22	(193)	16.10	(483)	5.61
Standard deviation	8.63		8.65		9.41				
Denmark	12.99	(15)	18.54	(6)	32.06	(14)	21.20	(35)	19.07
United Kingdom	8.24	(10)	18.10	(6)	21.51	(14)	15.95	(30)	13.27
France	20.14	(9)	32.32	(6)	32.58	(14)	28.35	(29)	12.44
Sweden	10.41	(11)	18.29	(3)	21.31	(8)	16.67	(22)	10.90
Germany	7.70	(10)	13.20	(6)	15.90	(14)	12.27	(30)	8.20
Malta	2.29	(8)	7.08	(1)	10.28	(3)	6.55	(12)	7.99
Austria	9.01	(12)	14.74	(3)	15.24	(7)	13.00	(22)	6.23
Ireland	10.79	(11)	14.54	(6)	15.75	(14)	13.69	(31)	4.96
Cyprus	8.64	(6)	16.03	(1)	11.37	(4)	12.01	(11)	2.73
Finland	9.42	(11)	11.48	(3)	11.73	(8)	10.88	(22)	2.31
Greece	14.51	(14)	14.84	(6)	16.63	(14)	15.33	(34)	2.12
Spain	12.48	(10)	16.81	(5)	14.13	(12)	14.47	(27)	1.65
Netherlands	18.82	(12)	18.54	(6)	20.06	(14)	19.14	(32)	1.24
Italy	18.46	(10)	27.85	(6)	18.58	(13)	21.63	(29)	0.12
Portugal	14.99	(12)	12.16	(5)	14.61	(12)	13.92	(29)	-0.38
Luxembourg	11.96	(7)	11.98	(6)	10.59	(14)	11.51	(27)	-1.37
Belgium	18.23	(12)	15.57	(6)	12.38	(14)	15.39	(32)	-5.85
Iceland	16.08	(11)	–		–		–		–
Norway	13.60	(9)	–		–		–		–

	(1)	(2)	(3)	(4)	NV
Switzerland	7.51 (9)	—	—	—	—
Central-Eastern Europe					
Overall (10 countries)	37.76 (51)	37.20 (10)	30.85 (37)	35.27 (98)	-6.91
Standard deviation	14.99	12.29	12.71	13.33	-2.28
Romania	35.56 (5)	45.41 (1)	39.30 (3)	40.09 (9)	3.74
Slovenia	33.07 (4)	30.23 (1)	35.58 (4)	32.96 (9)	2.51
Czech Republic	26.47 (6)	24.56 (1)	27.05 (4)	26.03 (11)	0.58
Estonia	35.36 (5)	46.20 (1)	35.43 (4)	39.00 (10)	0.07
Latvia	48.69 (5)	60.24 (1)	41.89 (4)	50.27 (10)	-6.80
Bulgaria	42.08 (5)	23.42 (1)	33.89 (3)	33.13 (9)	-8.19
Hungary	25.28 (5)	26.71 (1)	15.99 (4)	22.66 (10)	-9.29
Poland	38.50 (6)	43.39 (1)	27.21 (4)	36.37 (11)	-11.29
Lithuania	56.37 (4)	43.95 (1)	37.95 (3)	46.09 (8)	-18.42
Slovakia	40.51 (6)	27.86 (1)	18.84 (4)	29.07 (11)	-21.67

Notes: The overall mean and standard deviation includes 30 countries for national volatility but 27 for European and mixed volatility (Iceland, Norway, and Switzerland are excluded). The same applies to the mean and standard deviation for 20 (or 17) West European countries. Countries are ordered by difference between MV and NV (last column). The N indicates the number of pairs of elections (t and $t-1$) on which volatility indices have been computed. The overall N includes volatility between pairs of national elections, pairs of European elections, and pairs of national and European elections.

Sources: For the sources of national elections see Appendix 6 and previous chapters. As far as European elections are concerned the main source has been the data set prepared by Trond Kvamme of NSD in Bergen. These data have been double-checked and complemented with data from National Statistical Yearbooks (several years), National Ministries of Interior (electoral services), National Statistical Offices, European Parliament (poor data), Grunberg, Perrineau, and Ysmal (2000), Lodge (1986, 1990, 2001), Mackie (1990), Mackie and Craig (1985), and Perrineau and Ysmal (1995).

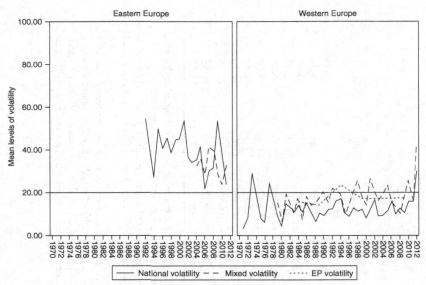

FIGURE 5.2. Levels of volatility in Europe (1970–2012).

much in a country which is "congenitally" very volatile – as reflected in high NV. More revealing is the additional MV compared to the "normal" NV in a given country. As mentioned, Central-Eastern European countries are highly volatile at the national level, and much less so when it comes to switching votes between national and EP elections. Instability takes place mainly between national elections or even between EP elections, but less so between national and EP elections. In Western Europe one finds the opposite. On average, MV is 5.61 higher than NV. Only in three countries (Portugal, Luxembourg, and Belgium) is MV lower than NV and in one country it is basically the same (Italy, in which both NV and MV are around 18.00). For a number of countries, on the contrary, there is a much higher propensity for voters to shift votes between the two orders of elections than from one national election to the next. Denmark clearly stands out with 19.07 of additional volatility between the two orders compared with its "normal" NV. This country is followed by the United Kingdom and France, and then by Sweden (see last column in Table 5.2). Finally, Germany, Malta, and Austria are above the average of 5.16 of "additional" volatility. These are the six countries in which the propensity to switch votes when different arenas (national or EP) are involved is higher and on which the comparative analysis will focus.

Figure 5.2 shows the evolution of the three types of volatility. The fundamental difference between Western Europe and Central-Eastern Europe appears clearly. Also remarkable is the steep increase of volatility in Western Europe in 2010–12 which is especially influenced by elections in Ireland, Greece, and

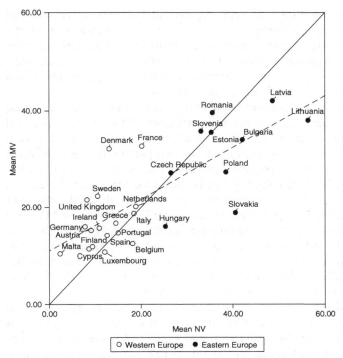

FIGURE 5.3. Country distribution for national and mixed volatility.
Note: Solid line: bisector; dashed line: regression line.

the Netherlands. For Western Europe the levels of volatility tend to stay below the 20.00 level since the beginning of the 1970s. One can also observe that the levels of EV – that is volatility between two subsequent European elections – is systematically higher than NV because of the unstructured nature of alliances and coalitions that take place in elections to the EP. As one can also see, the levels of MV are higher than the congenital volatility levels in national elections in Western Europe, basically since the mid-1980s. Overall, however, the differences between the three types of volatility are not dramatic. Since 2000 MV departs from NV in Western Europe and becomes higher, but only slightly. The relationship between MV and NV is depicted in Figure 5.3, where the cluster of Central and Eastern European countries for which both types of volatility are high also appears. One sees that most Central-Eastern European countries are located below the bisector (meaning MV is lower than NV), whereas the opposite is the case for Western European countries.

How can these overall results be interpreted? If the thesis of the progressive differentiation of a European electorate from national politics was true, one would expect to find a divergence between party vote in national and European elections over 30 years. This happens to a limited extent since the mid-1980s. If we do not find an increasing level of volatility when national elections are combined with European elections, we have an indication that – in EP elections – voters refer to the same issues, platforms and leaders (a similar political offer) as in national elections. Operationally, if over the seven elections to the EP since 1979 a distinct European competition sphere has indeed developed, we must find that MV increases over time.

From these Europe-wide figures over the past 30 years, one sees that electoral behaviour in EP elections has not been dramatically different from electoral behaviour in national elections. This basic result of the analysis appears from the first rows in Table 5.2. What appears in the comparison between different types of volatility is that there is only a slight difference in the levels of NV, EV, and MV. The lowest level of volatility can be observed for national elections in Western Europe. But the more important information about the thesis of the differentiation of the European sphere of competition is given by MV. This type of volatility shows that there are only small differences between electoral behaviour in national and European elections. Instead, these figures give a first indication that electoral behaviour in elections to the EP and national parliaments is fundamentally similar and overlapping, speaking against the thesis of a distinct European arena and in favour of isomorphism.

This initial result is confirmed by trends over time as appearing in Figure 5.2. As far as national elections are concerned (solid curve), there is an increase of volatility in the mid-1970s and early 1980s due to instability in the Netherlands (1977), Greece, and Spain (1982). Later, during the 1990s until the present, volatility levels slightly increase.[17] But the most important information in Figure 5.2 is conveyed by the evolution of MV (dashed curve). The trend of electoral volatility between national and European elections follows very closely the other two types of volatility – between national elections only and between European elections only. *At no moment, during the 30 years of European elections, has electoral behaviour in elections to the EP drastically differed from electoral behaviour in elections to national parliaments.* The curves follow the same trajectory. Furthermore, *trends do not suggest any divergence* which would indicate that European electoral behaviour progressively "departs" or "detaches" itself from national patterns.

According to these findings, therefore, it is possible to argue that, over the seven elections to the EP from 1979 to 2009, *a distinct European electoral and partisan arena* – a competitive sphere autonomous from national parties, issues, and alignments – *has not as yet emerged*. Data suggest on the contrary that, overall, in Europe the same electoral lists run for both national and

---

[17] NV data reproduce trends that previous research identified. Some differences are due to the choice of countries. Gallagher, Laver, and Mair (2001: 260–5), as well as Bartolini and Mair (1990), do not include Greece, Portugal, and Spain, which are considered here since the 1970s and were highly volatile until the early 1980s. Finally, data are not directly comparable with Dalton and Wattenberg (2000: 38–42) because of their inclusion of non-European countries.

European elections and that these lists receive very similar levels of support in national and European elections. This indicates that voters do not modify their behaviour on the basis of a distinct offer in elections to the EP and that they do not react to the European platforms of parties as presented in campaigns before European elections. As a first conclusion, therefore, it is possible to say that there is a fundamental similarity or overlap between national and European elections.

Trends of the three types of volatility levels by country display a familiar pattern. One sees high moments of NV at the beginning of the 1970s for countries like Belgium and the Netherlands which underwent processes of restructuring of the party system, as well as towards the end of the 1970s in countries like Portugal and Spain soon after the transition to democracy.[18] In Italy the peak of volatility corresponds to the transition towards the so-called second republic in the mid-1990s with the disappearance of the Christian democrats and the rise of the Northern League and Forza Italia. In Greece the recent turmoil with a shift of votes towards extreme parties of the left and right reflects in the scores for the two 2012 elections. Furthermore, patterns in Central and Eastern Europe are overall very volatile in spite of reductions observable in countries like Estonia, Lithuania, Poland, Romania, and Slovenia.[19]

Overall the three types of volatility correlate closely. The graph in Figure 5.3 shows the relationship between NV and MV. The correlation coefficient is high and significant ($r = 0.769^{***}$), as are the correlations between NV and EV and between EV and MV ($r = 0.849^{***}$ and $r = 0.836^{***}$, respectively, with $N = 27$). However, for some countries MV is systematically higher than NV or EV and these are the interesting cases where European elections seem to constitute a distinct competitive arena. Such a case is Denmark, which, as seen earlier, displays the highest level of MV and is the only country in which this feature of electoral behaviour is persistent since the 1970s. For other countries in which MV is high compared to NV this is a more recent feature as in France and the United Kingdom as well as, but to a lesser extent, in Germany and Sweden.[20] This leads us to discuss MV in a comparative perspective.

Comparative Perspective

As mentioned earlier, the most important piece of information concerns not so much MV as such – as it may just mirror the congenital volatility inherent

---

[18] In Belgium the main change has been the division of the main Catholic, liberal, and socialist parties along the linguistic cleavage, whereas in the Netherlands it is the merging of the major religious parties into the large inter-confessional CDA.

[19] Countries such as Cyprus, Finland, Luxembourg, Malta, Norway, and Switzerland are mostly characterized by stable voting patterns.

[20] For some countries in Western Europe the time points of MV are only three or four depending on whether there has been a national election after the 2009 EP election. The same applies to the 10 Central and Eastern European countries.

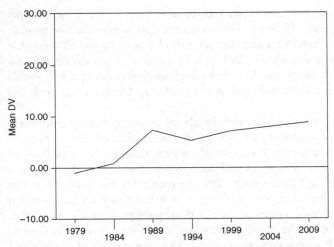

FIGURE 5.4. Differential volatility over time for Western Europe.

to a country – but *how much higher* MV is compared to NV. This measure
is called "differential volatility" (DV). The variable measures the difference
between MV in a specific European election and NV in the previous national
election in each country. By looking at how much more MV is with respect to
NV, DV is stripped of the inherent level of volatility in a specific country that
could be considered "normal", that is usual in national elections. Figure 5.4
shows that with the exception of 1979 and 1984 MV has been higher than
NV by roughly 8.0 percentage points in all the remaining EP elections up to
2009. Interestingly there is no significant increase of DV after 1989, meaning
that the propensity to shift votes between national and European electoral
arenas has not increased in the past 20 years. The level of DV, rather than indicating the formation of a distinct arena at the European level, is influenced by
strong country differences with some countries showing low DV and others
very high ones.[21]

The countries in which MV is high are, as seen earlier, primarily Denmark
and France. Looking at the two countries from the perspective of DV, however, reveals that the additional volatility when shifting between the two orders
of elections is much higher in Denmark (19.82), as it appears in Table 5.3,
whereas in France the additional volatility is 11.52, indicating that a higher

[21] This chapter focuses on Western Europe from this point onwards because time series are longer
with more national elections and up to a maximum of seven European elections. Also, as seen,
levels of MV are lower than NV in Central-Eastern Europe while this chapter attempts to
account for higher propensity to shift votes between national and EP electoral arenas. For
obvious reasons Iceland, Norway, and Switzerland are excluded from here onwards leaving an
N = 17 in terms of countries analyzed. The correlation between MV and DV is $r = 0.665^{***}$
(N = 98 couples of elections).

TABLE 5.3. *DV and MV Towards European and towards National Elections (Western Europe)*

Country	Mixed Volatility (MV)	(N)	Differential Volatility (DV)	Mixed Volatility towards EP Elections (MVe)	(N)	Difference (MV–MVe)
Overall	18.22	(192)	5.72	18.75	(98)	−0.53
Denmark	32.06	(14)	19.82	32.31	(7)	−0.25
United Kingdom	21.51	(14)	15.79	23.26	(7)	−1.75
France	32.58	(14)	11.52	30.22	(7)	2.36
Malta	10.28	(3)	8.53	10.44	(2)	−0.16
Germany	15.90	(14)	8.31	15.64	(7)	0.26
Cyprus	11.37	(4)	7.29	14.90	(2)	−3.53
Sweden	22.24	(7)	7.12	22.53	(4)	−0.29
Ireland	15.75	(14)	6.58	16.31	(7)	−0.56
Italy	18.58	(13)	5.46	21.76	(7)	−3.18
Finland	11.73	(8)	2.65	12.01	(4)	−0.28
Austria	15.24	(7)	2.33	16.09	(4)	−0.85
Greece	16.63	(14)	1.98	15.68	(7)	0.95
Luxembourg	10.59	(14)	1.70	12.85	(7)	−2.26
Spain	14.13	(12)	1.53	15.18	(6)	−1.05
Portugal	14.61	(12)	0.10	16.77	(6)	−2.16
Netherlands	20.06	(14)	−0.79	19.33	(7)	0.73
Belgium	12.38	(14)	−2.98	12.13	(7)	0.25

proportion of MV in France is part of the congenital volatility than it is in Denmark. DV is about 61 per cent of the MV in Denmark, whereas it is only about 31 per cent in France. The analysis reveals three further countries with high MV, namely Sweden, the United Kingdom, and the Netherlands. Of these, however, only in the United Kingdom is the differential high (15.79, almost at Danish levels), indicating that high MV does not simply mirror congenital levels of volatility but, on the contrary, is due to shifts specific to the change of arenas (about 65 per cent).

Italy has high levels of MV (18.58), but the differential with NV is small (5.46), meaning that most MV is not due to the change of arenas in MV but rather to its inherent instability. On the contrary, most of Malta's level of MV (10.28) seems to be due to differences between the two arenas as the differential with NV is 8.53 (about 80 per cent). Summing up, the two countries standing out for high additional volatility between the two orders (MV) with respect to the "normal" national volatility (NV) are Denmark and the United Kingdom, then France, followed by Germany and Malta, as well as Sweden, Cyprus, and Ireland (all above the DV average of 5.72 for 17 countries). In this order, these are the countries in which European elections are a competitive arena distinct from the national one, in which other parties and coalitions, issues, and alignments are at work. It will be the task of the multivariate analysis to account for the sources of higher DV in these countries.

Which shifts of votes cause this high differential in these countries? In Denmark since 1979 the main factor of volatility is the creation of a specific anti-EU movement which contests as an electoral alliance European elections since 1979 (*Folkebevægelsen mod EF*). This alliance does not run in national elections. Because most of the groups participating in this alliance are left-wing, the second factor accounting for a high DV in Denmark is the weakness of social democrats in European elections.[22] In the United Kingdom the high differential between the two electoral arenas is a combination of variation of support for large parties and the increase of votes for small parties in European elections. The European election of 1989 was characterized by the decline of the Conservative Party (from 42.3 per cent to 33.0 per cent), as well as of the Liberal Party (almost half the votes). In contrast, the Labour Party increased its support. Furthermore, the Greens received 14.5 per cent. Since 2000 the main factor of volatility is Labour scoring poorly in European elections, but also the extreme-right vote for the BNP and the anti-EU vote for UKIP. In France too, the strong fluctuations between the two orders is the result of ad hoc alliances and new lists on European themes. This concerns particularly the 1994 and 1999 European elections in which the Gaullist Rassemblement pour la République built an alliance with the liberal Union pour la Démocratie Française. Other lists include Energie Radicale and Autre Europe, a right-wing splinter of the Gaullist party, as well as the Rassemblement pour la France et l'Indépendance de l'Europe. In 1984, in addition, the Front National increased its votes from close to nothing to more than 10 per cent, pointing to a significant dimension in the party system between pro- and anti-Europeans. The examples taken for these three countries point to which factors are at the origin of DV.

Until now MV has been considered in both directions, that is in terms of change from national to European elections and from European to national elections. A further distinction concerns the *direction of MV*, whether MV is higher when changing from national to European elections (MVe) or from European to national elections (MVn). Table 5.3 also includes the column giving the information about MVe. If these figures are higher than MV, it would indicate that change towards European elections is more important. If these figures are similar to MV, it would indicate that change towards European and national elections is the same and that MV is not predominantly produced in

---

[22] The anti-EU movement regroups candidates from different parties (most of them are left of centre such as Socialistisk Folkeparti, Socialdemokrater, Venstresocialisterne). It includes also the liberal Retsforbundet (Justice Party). The Radikale Venstre scored less in European elections during the 1980s.

one direction. As it appears from the last column in Table 5.3 the differences are small, indicating that MV is not predominantly produced in one direction only, but rather a back-and-forth change between the two orders of elections – national and European.

The Origins of Mixed and Differential Volatility

How can one account for higher and lower levels of volatility between the two orders of elections across countries? What type of electoral behaviour is at the origin of higher MV and DV in given countries – or at given elections – and from which vote shifts does this type of volatility come? This chapter now turns to the explanatory perspective and aims to test the hypotheses formulated earlier in regard to the origin of MV and DV.

Independent Variables and Indicators

Volatility is caused by shifts of votes between parties across two (subsequent) elections. Following the definition in the previous chapter, these shifts are referred to as "swings". Volatility is the aggregation of such swings. In terms of explanatory perspective this section searches for the origin of higher levels of volatility between national and European elections in the nature of swings – whether, for example, MV is caused by swings away from established parties when voting for the EP or, on the contrary, it is caused by swings between major established parties. A strong association between swings towards/against, for example, anti-EU parties would reveal a different origin of MV than a strong association between swings towards/away from green parties. Swings in electoral behaviour are the independent variables used in this part of the chapter.

Ultimately, therefore, the explanatory perspective relies on the analysis of the "composition" of MV. Which swings (towards/against which parties) compose volatility? Swings are changes in the amount of votes for a party between two elections in a specific country. For example, a strong swing (20 per cent more votes compared to the last national election) towards a Eurosceptic party in a given EP election causes a high level of MV. Because, however, in given countries/elections there may be two or more anti-EU parties, figures for single parties have been aggregated into party families and calculations of swings have been done based on families rather than single parties.[23] In such a case it is the aggregate swing towards (or against) two or more Eurosceptic parties that would explain a high level of MV. Furthermore, for the sake of hypothesis-testing and to gain a more general picture, broader categories have in some cases been used. For such broader categories the swings towards/against single parties have been added together.[24]

---

[23] For the classification of parties and their aggregation see Appendix 1 and Chapter 2.

[24] The broader categories are the following: (1) AEU includes anti-EU parties and extreme right-wing populist parties, as well as personal parties; (2) MCR includes main centre-right

Calculations of swings have been done between European elections and the "fictitious" elections years (and the other way around), that is, one national election before the first EP election in each country, one between each European election, and one after the 2009 European election. Depending on the countries there is a maximum number of seven European elections. In total, the number of cases (that is swings and MV figures between EP-national elections, and swings and MV figures between national-EP elections, for all the countries) is 228.

Two types of swing have been calculated for each family:

- *Absolute swings*: For each party family the *absolute amount of vote change* is used (disregarding whether it is losses or gains of votes between a national and EP election, and conversely). Because a family may gain votes in EP elections and then lose them again in the next national election, in order to produce correlations with MV these figures need to be considered in absolute terms. This allows taking MV in national and European elections together.

- *Positive/negative swings*: For each party family *both the amount and the direction of vote change* (whether it is losses or gains of votes between a national and EP election, and conversely) are used. In these figures a negative sign (–) means that MV is caused by the loss of votes and a positive sign (+) means that MV is caused by the gain of votes of a particular party family. Positive/negative swing figures are used when analyzing MV or DV towards European elections only (MVe or DVe) or towards national elections only (MVn or DVn). Correlations between swings towards/against party families and MVe reveal where votes change when voting for EP elections.

Both types of swings are presented. When all 228 elections couples are taken together (MV between national and European elections and the other way around), then absolute swings are used. When elections couples are taken distinctly (MVe from national to European elections, and MVn from European to national elections), positive/negative swings are used.[25]

Country Analysis
As pointed out earlier MV may just mirror the congenital levels of electoral instability present anyway in a country and not caused by a specific propensity

---

parties such as conservatives, inter-confessional, and people's parties; (3) EREG includes both ethnic and regionalist parties; (4) LBT includes libertarian parties such as greens, new left, and social liberals. All other party families have been kept unchanged, in particular socialists and liberals, for whom the main party in each country has been taken for the calculations.

[25] For example, one could expect a strong positive (+) swing towards anti-EU parties in a European election compared to the previous national one (MVe) and then a strong negative (–) swing against these parties in the next national election (MVn). If one were, however, to consider all elections together (national and European), then absolute swings would be needed to calculate a correlation between swings and MV or between swings and DV.

to change vote when shifting arenas. It is, therefore, more appropriate to consider the additional volatility between arenas, that is, MV as compared to NV. This measure is DV.

The multivariate analysis addressing the origins of DV is approached first by zooming into the countries which display the highest levels of DV in correlation matrices. Table 5.4 gives the correlation coefficients between DV and swings for/against parties for the six countries which the previous analysis has revealed have the highest levels of DV: Denmark, the United Kingdom, France, and, to a lesser extent, Germany, Sweden, and Ireland. These are the countries for which DV is above the average of all 17 countries considered in this part of this chapter.[26] The table indicates each of the countries in which DV is high, where the additional volatility when voting for the EP comes from.

Because MV is considered in one single direction (when shifting votes from national to EP elections), it is possible to use positive/negative swings as independent variables. The first aspect to note about Table 5.4 is that correlations between DVe and swings for/against parties are very different in the six countries. This testifies to different party constellations and electoral behaviour across them, which do not lead to one single conclusive result. The sources of MV seem to be manifold and different for the various countries.

Starting with Denmark, correlations are high and positive for the extreme right. This means that the volatility occurring when changing from national to European elections correlates with an increase of votes for extreme-right parties in Denmark. DVe is particularly high, meaning that the increase of votes for the extreme right correlates in particular with the additional volatility of MV as compared to the "normal" NV in this specific country. Further high correlations appear for the conservatives, this time with a negative sign, meaning that MV is caused by a loss of votes in European elections for these parties compared to national elections. In the United Kingdom MV correlates highly with an increase of votes in the European elections of anti-European (UKIP) and extreme-right parties (BNP), as well as the Greens, and with a loss of votes for Labour and the Liberal Democrats (social liberal family).[27] In France volatility from national to European elections correlates with gains of votes for the conservatives (Gaullist party, later the UMP) and with loss of votes for socialists (as well as for the liberals, UDF mainly).

In Germany the high MV is partly an artificial effect of the changing position of the CSU between national and European elections whereby it runs as

---

[26] Cyprus and Malta have been excluded from this table because only two European elections have taken place in these countries producing correlation coefficients of 1.0. For the other countries N = 7 with the exception of Sweden (N = 4), that is one for each election of the EP since 1979. Because of the low number of cases coefficients are, therefore, not significant.

[27] The high correlation with an increase of Protestant votes in the United Kingdom refers to the very small Christian Party "Proclaiming Christ's Lordship".

TABLE 5.4. *Sources of Mixed Volatility by Country: Correlations between Swings and DVe And MVe in Six Countries*

Swing towards/against party families in EP elections	Denmark DVe	Denmark MVe	United Kingdom DVe	United Kingdom MVe	France DVe	France MVe	Germany DVe	Germany MVe	Sweden DVe	Sweden MVe	Ireland DVe	Ireland MVe
Catholics							−0.78*	−0.81*			0.11	0.29
Anti–EU parties	−0.21	−0.05	0.77*	0.87*	0.16	0.05	−0.15	0.05	0.73	0.64	0.66	0.86*
Pro–EU parties		−0.61	−0.18	0.07	0.23	0.36						
Protestants	0.00		0.62	0.69					0.81	0.88		
Regionalists		−0.28	−0.40	−0.11								
Social liberals	−0.10		−0.50	−0.81*	0.27	0.34			0.60	0.70		
Agrarians									−0.78	−0.85		
Socialists	0.11	0.02	−0.75*	−0.78*	−0.34	−0.61	−0.82*	−0.79*	−0.57	−0.46	0.76*	0.87**
Communists	0.66	0.18			0.24	−0.04	0.49	0.52			−0.36	−0.20
Conservatives	−0.57	−0.05	−0.07	−0.21	0.66	0.72	0.41	0.43	−0.04	−0.17	−0.55	−0.79*
Extreme right	0.87	0.46	0.79*	0.85*	−0.15	0.23	−0.17	−0.22	−0.36	−0.24		
Greens	−0.28	0.41	0.65	0.62	0.31	−0.01	−0.09	0.06	−0.38	−0.26	−0.96**	−0.69
People's parties							0.82*	0.78*			0.23	0.21
Liberals	−0.02	−0.34	−0.35	−0.01	−0.67	−0.57	0.27	0.13	−0.73	−0.64	−0.29	−0.36
New left	−0.75*	−0.52	0.39	0.35			−0.05	−0.13	−0.50	−0.60	−0.08	0.15
Number of EP elections	(7)		(7)		(7)		(7)		(4)		(7)	

Notes: Coefficients are Pearson's r. Negative signs mean DVe and MVe are due to loss of votes in EP elections compared to the previous national election for a specific party family. Positive signs mean DVe and MVe correlate with a gain of votes between a national and an EP election. The distinction does not apply to MV, whose coefficients indicate correlations with absolute swings.
Statistical significance **(p < 0.01), * (p < 0.05) in two–tailed test.

an independent party in the former arena and in alliance with the CDU in the latter. This affects the value of both CSU (under Catholic parties) and CDU (under people's parties). Apart from this artificial effect, the strongest correlation with MV in Germany is that of the loss of votes for the SPD (socialist parties) in European elections and that of the gain of votes for Die Linke (communist parties).

In Sweden, for which only four European elections took place, as compared to seven for the other countries in the table, MVe correlates mostly with negative performances in European elections of all parties with the exception of the anti-European June List that runs exclusively in elections to the EP and performed particularly well in 2004. In Ireland, finally, the change of vote from national to European election correlates with strong wins for the Irish Labour Party, as well as for smaller anti-European lists, and with strong losses of votes for the mainstream conservative party (Fianna Fáil) that dominated Irish politics over the past couple of decades together with the liberal Progressive Democrats.

Summing up, while in some of the countries for which the volatility from national to European elections (MVe) is high and correlations indicate an effect of an increase of anti-European parties and extreme-right parties capturing the same anti-integration rhetoric, in other countries there seems to be an anti-incumbents effect with shifts away from either socialists or mainstream centre-right parties such as conservative or people's parties.

In a further step the country comparison involves 15 Western European countries and analyzes the association between family swings and MV more broadly.[28] From the graphs in Figure 5.5, the hints derived from the case studies included earlier are confirmed on a more general level. There is a strong association among the 15 countries between the swing from socialist parties between national and European elections on one hand, and the additional volatility between these two arenas with respect to NV on the other.[29] The coefficient of correlation is $r = 0.840**$. Absolute swings do not tell us the direction, but give an idea of the amount of losses and gains in the "back-and-forth" switch of votes between the national and EP arenas. The higher the swing for socialists, the higher the differential of MV with respect to the congenital volatility in a country. The same applies to the swing for extreme-right parties, anti-European parties, and personal lists running on Eurosceptic platforms ($r = 0.784**$), whereas it is weaker for swings of the main centre-right

---

[28] In this part of the analysis aggregates values at the country level are used (for the entire period covered) rather than values for single elections. For reasons of space, only absolute swings have been reported (values measuring the amount of votes changed "back and forth" between the national and EP arenas, rather than positive/negative swings). Party family aggregations are used with anti-EU and extreme-right parties together and with the category main right-wing parties (conservatives, people's, and inter-confessional parties).

[29] Note that the DV is negative for Belgium and the Netherlands insofar as MV is lower than NV in these two countries.

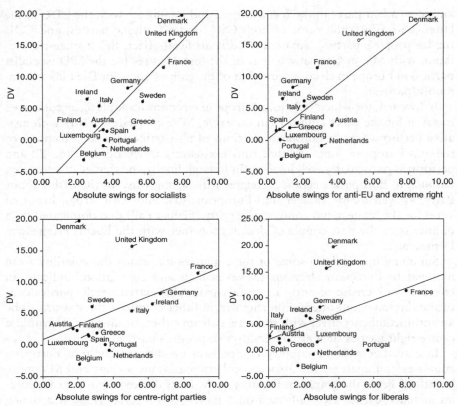

FIGURE 5.5. Association between swings and DV in 15 Countries.

parties such as people's parties, conservatives, and inter- confessional parties ($r = 0.371$). For the remaining party families the association between their swings back and forth between the two arenas and DV is even weaker. The two groups of party families which associate most with DV (the additional volatility between the national and EP arenas with respect to NV) are the socialists and extreme-right/anti-EU.

If one shifts for a moment the perspective from variable-oriented to case-oriented analysis, the position of a number of countries in the scatterplots is revealing of patterns of multiple causation of high DV. The high DV in Denmark is associated with high swings for both socialists and extreme-right/ Eurosceptic parties. The United Kingdom is a similar case, although the swing towards/against the BNP and UKIP plays a lesser role than the swing for similar parties in Denmark. Socialist swing also plays a role in France and Sweden, but the swing towards/against extreme-right and anti-EU parties much less. In France, on the contrary, DV associates with swings of liberals and the main centre-right parties, as is the case in Germany, Italy, and Ireland.[30] On the contrary, this type of swing does not play any role in explaining high DV in Denmark. Again, these results point to the lack of one single factor accounting for high levels of DV across all the countries, but rather to multiple factors at the origin of DV in various countries.[31] It remains, furthermore, that only for a few countries is MV more than 5.0 percentage points higher than NV pointing to a fundamental overlap between electoral behaviour in the national and European arenas.

Multivariate Analysis

The analysis turns now to single elections as basic cases. Before addressing the multivariate model this section looks at the bivariate association between swings towards/against various families on one hand, and DV and MV on the other.

Looking overall at Western Europe (with the exclusion of Cyprus and Malta), the volatility from national to European elections (MVe), and the additional component of volatility specific to this shift in comparison to the "natural" NV existing in the various party systems, from Table 5.5 it appears clearly that *the highest correlations are with swings towards extreme-right parties and anti-European parties*. It is the increase of votes of these party families in European elections that correlates more strongly with MVe and DVe (and for which coefficients shown in the table are most significant). Other party families for which swings show an increase in European elections as compared to national elections are agrarians, pro-European parties, and the main centre-right parties such as conservatives and people's parties.

All these party families do better in European elections than in national elections (as the positive signs show). However, none of these shifts is associated with mixed volatility as much as the increase of votes for extreme-right and Eurosceptic parties. Volatility between the two orders of elections is caused also by the loss of votes in European elections for a number of party families. The strongest associations with MVe and DVe are those coming from the *loss of votes for socialist and liberal parties*, while the coefficients for Catholics, communists, and ethno-regionalists are negligible. While the loss of votes between the two arenas for these families is not large enough to cause higher levels of mixed volatility, the loss of votes for socialists and liberals is significantly associated with MVe and DVe.

The six graphs in Figure 5.6 depict the relationship between mixed volatility and swings for the two party families mostly associated with it, that is

---

[30] The role of liberals applies also to Denmark and the United Kingdom, as well as to Portugal, whose MV is, however, quite low.

[31] For this reason a qualitative comparative analysis (QCA) is performed after the multivariate section.

TABLE 5.5. *Correlations between Swings for 11 Families and MVe/DVe in 15 Countries*

Party Families	MVe	DVe
Agrarians	0.141	0.073
Catholics	−0.033	−0.137
Communists	−0.028	−0.048
Pro–European parties	0.246*	0.116
Liberals	−0.277**	−0.216*
Protestants	−0.088	−0.106
Socialists	−0.277**	−0.234*
Extreme-right and anti-EU parties	0.411***	0.395***
Main centre-right parties (conservatives, people's parties)	0.183*	0.099
Ethno-regionalist parties	−0.074	−0.046
Libertarian parties (greens, new left, social liberals)	0.007	−0.030
Number of elections	(94)	(94)

Note: Coefficients are Pearson's *r*.
Statistical significance *** (p <0.001), ** (p < 0.01), * (p < 0.05) in two-tailed test.

socialists and extreme right-wing parties with anti-European parties.[32] Because the graphs include data on swings in both directions (from national to EP elections and the other way around), absolute swings are used. Insofar as MV is also an absolute measure according to the volatility formula given earlier, both axes of the graphs are positive. On the contrary, DV can be negative as MV can in principle be lower than NV.[33] It should be noted straightaway that very large swings towards/against party families are rare and that most swings are in the region of ±5.0 percentage points compared to the previous (either national or European) election. This is the case especially for extreme-right and anti-EU parties, for which most swings are very small and the relationship with both MV and DV is influenced by a rather limited number of elections with large swings.

The picture for socialist parties is different, with a much higher number of elections displaying larger swings. The association of swings with MV appears

[32] For each family two graphs have been produced, one with MV as a dependent variable (the cross-arena volatility from national to European elections) and one with DV as a dependent variable. The graphs with DV as a dependent variable include European elections only (because DV measures the additional volatility of MV at a specific European election as compared to the previous national election in each country).

[33] As seen earlier this is rarely the case but it occurs in Belgium, Greece, the Netherlands, and Spain for a limited number of elections.

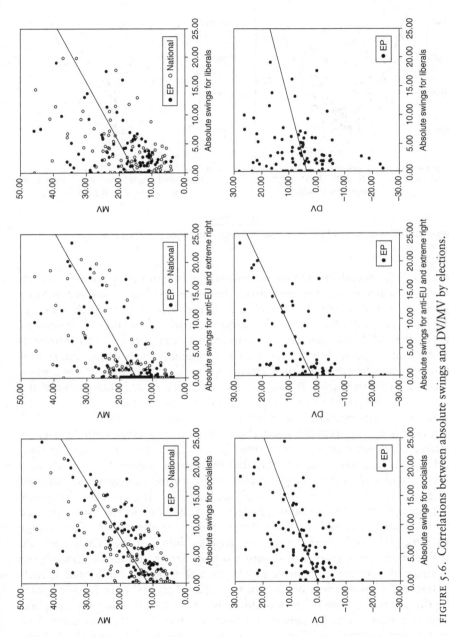

FIGURE 5.6. Correlations between absolute swings and DV/MV by elections.

Note: The graphs with DV as a dependent variable include European elections only because DV measures the additional volatility of MV at a specific European election as compared to the previous national election in each country.

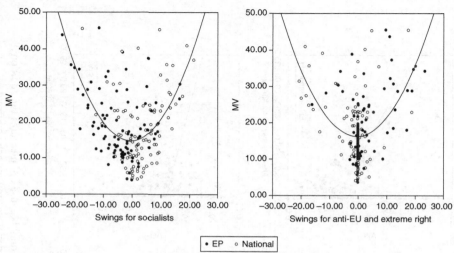

FIGURE 5.7. Correlations between positive/negative swings and MV by elections.

more clearly for socialists than for extreme-right and anti-EU parties for which the dots are scattered further away from the regression line. There seems to be no clear pattern distinguishing black and white dots, indicating that swings in the two directions have a similar impact on MV. One should remember, however, that MV is a measure of volatility between national and European elections that, in part, simply captures the congenital levels of instability present in countries between national elections only and, therefore, DV is a more telling indicator measuring the additional volatility in switches between the two orders as compared to the congenital levels of instability.

In the three lower graphs the pattern is quite similar to the one described earlier, that is a more regular association for socialist swings than for swings towards/against extreme-right and anti-EU parties. In quite a number of elections DV is, in fact, *negative*, meaning that *the change of votes between the two orders is smaller than the change of votes between the two previous national elections*. This is the case in highly volatile countries. Importantly, this result points again to the overlap between electoral behaviour in the two orders of elections. Finally, with DV as a dependent variable, the effect of absolute swings for extreme-right and anti-EU parties is stronger than that for socialist parties.

In the three upper graphs of Figure 5.6 both losses and gains between the two orders of elections contribute to MV, as well as to the additional volatility between the two orders of elections compared to NV only (as it appears in the three lower graphs). One should, however, remember that the direction for the two party families considered here is opposite: while socialists lose votes between national and European elections, extreme-right and anti-EU win votes; it is the opposite between European and national elections.

This appears clearly when considering positive/negative swings instead of absolute ones in Figure 5.7. The swing axes of the graphs now include both positive swings (gains of votes) and negative swings (losses of votes). In both graphs for socialists on one hand, and for extreme right and anti-EU parties on the other, there is a clear separation of black and white dots. Clearly, socialist swings are negative between the previous national and the subsequent European election; and clearly positive for extreme-right and anti-EU parties (black dots). Conversely, socialist swings are positive between the previous European and the subsequent national election; and clearly negative for extreme-right and anti-EU parties (white dots).[34] The comparison of the two graphs shows again that the amount of swing in percentage points is higher for socialists than for extreme-right and anti-EU parties with dots scattered much more widely away from the zero point.[35]

The last step in the multivariate analysis is two regressions (multiple and logistic) with three different dependent variables: MV (volatility back and forth between the two arenas), MVe (volatility from national to European elections), and DV (additional volatility in switches between the two arenas as compared to NV). The results of the multiple regression are reported in Table 5.6.

The multiple regression is performed with elections as cases for 15 Western European countries over the entire period from the national election before the first EP election in 1979 to the last national election after the 2009 EP election. The total number of cases is 186 for MV and 94 (one-directional volatility) for MVe and DV – roughly half. Standardized regression coefficients are reported, allowing for comparison of the effect on dependent variables. In the first model with MV as dependent variable, all major party families (or groups of families) have been entered. Results are significant and the adjusted R^2 is 0.78. Regression coefficients confirm the insights from the bivariate analysis, with the absolute swings for extreme-right and anti-EU parties displaying the strongest effect (0.445***), double that of swings for liberals and socialists (0.269*** and 0.262***, respectively). Unlike what we have previously seen, swings for main centre-right parties display now a stronger effect than that of liberals and socialists (0.316). If we turn to MVe as a dependent variable (one-directional volatility from national towards EP elections), the number of cases decreases and therefore a number of effects are not significant any longer. The two significant results concern both anti-EU parties (together with extreme right) as before and pro-EU parties (with coefficients of 0.477*** and 0.277***, respectively). The positive sign indicates that MVe is affected by the increase

---

[34] There are obviously exceptions, such as the increase of votes for socialists in Ireland (Irish Labour Party) or the loss of votes for extreme-right parties in European elections in Germany (NPD, Republikaner, and DVU). See also coefficients in Table 5.4.

[35] The pattern for liberals is similar to that for socialists but appears more squashed towards the zero point. No clear pattern appears for the main centre-right parties. Graphs with DV as a dependent variable have not been produced as they would include only EP elections.

TABLE 5.6. *Multiple Regression: Family Swings and Mixed Volatility*

Swing for Party Families	MV	MVe			DV		
	(1)	(1)	(2)	(3)	(1)	(2)	(3)
Communists	0.167*** (0.150)	0.057 (0.360)			-0.028 (0.470)		
Pro-Europeans	0.132*** (0.210)	0.277** (0.542)	0.268** (0.523)	0.258** (0.518)	0.128 (0.707)	0.134 (0.682)	0.133 (0.672)
Liberals	0.269*** (0.084)	-0.167 (0.242)	-0.206* (0.195)	-0.253** (0.163)	-0.242 (0.316)	-0.210 (0.254)	-0.217 (0.211)
Socialists	0.262*** (0.074)	-0.036 (0.224)	-0.083 (0.163)	-0.156 (0.120)	-0.146 (0.293)	-0.088 (0.212)	-0.099 (0.156)
Extreme-right and anti-EU parties	0.445*** (0.070)	0.477*** (0.227)	0.437*** (0.170)	0.392*** (0.147)	0.341* (0.297)	0.386** (0.221)	0.397*** (0.191)
Main centre-right parties	0.316*** (0.068)	0.133 (0.187)	0.092 (0.143)		-0.028 (0.244)	0.014 (0.187)	
Ethno-regionalists	0.158*** (0.215)	-0.043 (0.489)			-0.028 (0.638)		
Libertarian parties	0.184*** (0.097)	0.043 (0.254)			-0.043 (0.332)		
Constant	3.266	16.259	16.314	15.985	2.818	2.700	2.640
Adj. R²	0.78	0.29	0.31	0.31	0.17	0.19	0.20
N	(186)	(94)	(94)	(94)	(94)	(94)	(94)

Notes: Standardized regression coefficients (betas) shown with standard errors in parentheses. Collinearity above VIF = 5.0 in italics. The dependent variable is volatility for single elections in 15 countries (MV, MVe) and the differential between MV and NV (DV). For MV independent variables are absolute swings. For MV independent variables are absolute swings. For MVe and DV independent variables are positive/negative swings. Estimation: OLS. Statistical significance *** (p < 0.001), ** (p < 0.01), * (p < 0.05) in two-tailed test.

of votes for these party families in EP elections, as compared to national ones. Once a number of non-significant independent variables are removed, the only other family for which results are significant is that of the liberals, with a coefficient of $-0.253**$, indicating that MVe is affected by the decrease of votes for these parties in EP elections.[36] The most surprising result, however, is that of the lack of effect of socialist swings with low and non-significant coefficients (even though the direction of the sign is the expected one based on what was seen earlier, and even though for the last model it is almost significant).[37]

While both MV and MVe are measures of volatility which may just reproduce levels of instability present anyway in the countries, the third dependent variable (DV) is really the additional volatility in cross-arena electoral behaviour with respect to NV. Consistently with the results it is, once again, the extreme-right and anti-EU family displaying strong and significant results (already in the baseline model). No other party family, with the exception of the liberals (whose loss of votes in EP elections contributes significantly to DV), displays significant coefficients. The additional volatility to normal national levels of instability coming from the shift of arenas is mainly due to the increase of support for Eurosceptic parties, be it in the form of ad hoc anti-EU coalitions, specific anti-EU issue parties running in EP elections only, or extreme-right parties whose platform is one of anti-European rhetoric.

For the logistic regression the dependent variable (DV) has been recoded into a dichotomous indicator for high and low DV. The dichotomization has been done for each value of DV (i.e. for each EP election compared to the previous national one) on the basis of the mean additional MV with respect to NV.[38] Table 5.7 includes two models. For both models the number of elections predicted correctly (i.e. either with high or low DV) is around 72–73 per cent (from a benchmark of 52.1 per cent classified correctly "by chance") and the omnibus tests are 0.000, meaning an improvement over the null hypothesis. Out of 45 elections with high DV (1), the models predict 29 correctly and 16 incorrectly. Once again the role of swings for extreme-right and anti-EU parties appears clearly. Contrary to the multiple regression, the role of swings for socialists and main centre-right parties is striking. In the second model only four variables are kept and the results remain to a large extent unchanged.

---

[36] Results, not shown in the table, for the opposite direction (i.e. volatility when shifting from EP to national elections) include again two main significant results: the decrease of votes for both pro- and anti-EU (as well as extreme right) parties. These families gain votes in EP elections and lose votes in national elections. To be noted is also the consistently high standard error for pro-European parties.

[37] The adjusted R^2 for these models is around 0.30. Note the high constant, which indicates a much higher one-directional volatility towards EP elections than for the two-directional MV. The significance level for socialists in model (3) is 0.149, i.e. almost one star.

[38] The mean DV over 94 cases (EP elections in various countries) is approximately 5.50. DV has been recoded with the codes 1 for DV > 5.6 and 0 for DV < 5.6. The logistic regression has not been performed with countries as cases because of the small N.

TABLE 5.7. *Logistic Regression: Family Swings and High Levels of Mixed Volatility*

Swing for Party Families	Model 1	Model 2
Communists	0.023	
Pro-Europeans	0.000	
Liberals	2.370	2.434
Socialists	3.116*	3.968*
Extreme-right and anti-EU parties	4.175*	4.704*
Main centre-right parties	4.349*	3.142*
Ethno-regionalists	1.321	
Libertarian parties	2.328	
% correct	73.4	72.3
R^2 (Cox and Snell / Nagelkerke)	0.295 / 0.393	0.248 / 0.330
Hosmer and Lemeshow test	0.603	0.896
N	(94)	(94)

Note: Coefficients in the table are Wald.
Statistical significance * ($p < 0.05$) in two-tailed test.

Summing up, one must read the results from the perspective of the basic overlap between electoral behaviour in national elections and electoral behaviour in European elections as already pointed to in the descriptive analysis. The only exception to this is the propensity to vote more for European-issue parties in elections to the EP, and mainly in an anti-EU vote for extreme-right and Eurosceptic parties. This involves some "punishment effect" mainly for liberal parties but, surprisingly, much less so for socialists and the main centre-right parties (conservative and people's parties). The lack of effect on DV of these two families remains somewhat a puzzle that should again be interpreted in terms of overlap of electoral behaviour between the two orders of elections: the effect on MV shows in fact that socialists and main centre-right parties contribute to the overall volatility in the systems, meaning that they are losing support in both arenas and not only in the shift to the European arena. Also the non-existent effect of a more sincere vote towards greens, new left, and social liberals points to the overlap between the two orders. With the exception of swings across the two arenas along the pro/anti-Europe dimension, these results point to isomorphism. However, what the analysis also shows is that such patterns vary greatly by countries, which leads us now to address variation in volatility at this level of analysis.

Qualitative Comparative Analysis

Looking back at the graphs of Figure 5.5 it becomes evident that a high level of DV – the additional volatility across orders compared to the normal NV volatility – can have *multiple origins* depending on the countries. The logic of multiple causation typically captured by Qualitative Comparative Analysis

(QCA) shows that DV is associated with high swings for socialists and extreme/anti-EU parties in Denmark but that the configuration for Germany and Ireland is different, with swings for main centre-right and (to a lesser extent for liberals, socialists, and libertarian parties) playing a role. In France and the United Kingdom, on the other hand, there are many more family swings at the origin of DV and, finally, for Sweden, it is mainly socialist and liberal swings that are responsible for cross-order volatility. Such different patterns of causation across countries lead to addressing the issue of DV from a case-oriented perspective.[39]

The QCA is based on dichotomization of seven variables in which the cut-off point is the mean of the values for the 15 countries. This value is reported in Table 5.8 as well as the 1/0 values for each country whereby 1 means above the mean. The table reports for each variable (i.e. source of swing) figures of coverage and contingency. According to the usual definitions of necessity and sufficiency, one can start by eliminating three variables: swing for pro-European parties, communists, and ethno-regionalists.[40] All three have very limited coverage (indicator for necessity) insofar as among the six countries with high DV five do have this condition and therefore it is hardly necessary (coverage of 0.17). Further, among the two countries with high pro-European swing, in only one does this produce high DV (consistency, or sufficiency, of 0.50). The degree of sufficiency is even lower in the case of communists and ethno-regionalist parties. These families are thus not included in the analysis.

QCA is performed on the remaining five variables. Socialist swing has the highest scores for coverage and consistency. Of the six countries in which DV is high, five (Ireland being the exception) have high socialist swings (coverage of 0.83). Conversely, DV appears in five (Greece being the exception) out of the six countries with high socialist swing (consistency of 0.83). A similar pattern (but with lower scores) is that of main centre-right parties. For liberals and libertarians (including greens), coverage is 0.50 (too low to indicate any necessity) but consistency is 0.75 (i.e. a certain degree of sufficiency). Finally, sufficiency is 1.00 for extreme-right and anti-EU parties. Where there is a swing for these parties, this appears as a sufficient condition to produce high DV. However, there are only two countries with this type of swing (Denmark and the United Kingdom).

[39] This different approach to causal explanation stressing multiple causation and configurational analysis owes most to the pioneering insights of Ragin (1987). For recent developments in QCA and related techniques see Rihoux and Ragin (2009) and Schneider and Wagemann (2012). For an overview of the comparative method and Boolean algebra see Caramani (2009).

[40] A necessary condition is a factor in whose absence the dependent variable never takes place. A sufficient condition is a factor always leading to the outcome. Necessity and sufficiency relax the terms *never* and *always* by considering degrees. Necessity (coverage) is the ratio between the number of cases in which the independent variable is 1 (when DV is 1) and the total number of cases in which the dependent variable is 1. Sufficiency (contingency) is the ratio between the number of cases in which the independent variable is 1 (when DV is 1) and the total number of cases in which the independent variable is 1.

TABLE 5.8. *Truth Table (QCA)*

Country	Swing Socialists	Swing Extreme Right Liberals and Anti-Eu	Swing Liberals	Swing Main Centre-Right	Swing Libertarians and Greens	Swing Pro-Europeans	Swing Communists	Swing Ethno-Regionalists	DV High
Denmark	1	1	1	0	0	0		0	1
France	1	0	1	1	1	1	0	0	1
Germany	1	0	0	1	0	0	1	0	1
Ireland	0	0	0	1	0	1	0	0	1
Sweden	1	0	0	0	1	0	0	1	1
United Kingdom	1	1	0	1	1	0	0	0	1
Austria	0	0	0	0	0	0	0	0	0
Belgium	0	0	0	0	0	0	0	1	0
Finland	0	0	0	0	0	0	0	0	0
Greece	1	0	0	0	0	0	1	0	0
Italy	0	0	0	1	0	0	0	1	0
Luxembourg	0	0	1	0	1	0	1	0	0
Netherlands	0	0	0	0	0	0	0	0	0
Portugal	0	0	0	0	0	0	1	1	0
Spain	0	0	0	0	0	0	0	1	0
Mean	4.4	2.4	2.5	3.8	2.2	1.7	1.2	0.5	
Coverage	0.83	0.33	0.50	0.67	0.50	0.17	0.17	0.17	
Consistency	0.83	1.00	0.75	0.80	0.75	0.50	0.20	0.20	

The advantage of QCA, however, is not only that of identifying causality in terms of necessity and sufficiency in a setting with small N, but also that of identifying configurations of causality. Its combinatorial logic relies on configurations of values of the explanatory factors leading to the outcome, here a high DV.[41] QCA in this respect is particularly useful to identify various combinations of factors which explain why DV is high in some cases. These combinations do not always need to be the same in the logic of multiple causation (a high DV may have different origins depending on the country). Performing QCA analysis with the QCA module in R (Thiem and Duşa, 2013 and 2014) leads to the following result after both minimization and factorization have been performed:[42]

F1: SOC *(LBT + MCR + AEU*LIB)

Factorization clearly shows that the socialist (negative) swing is a necessary condition for DV to be high (all five cases have it). It also shows that there are three equivalent combinations that lead sufficiently to high DV. First, socialists and either main centre-right swing (Germany, but also France and the United Kingdom) or libertarian swing (Sweden, but also France and the United Kingdom) or the couple (liberal * anti-EU) swing (Denmark). These are three possible alternative causal combinations leading to high DV. *Without a high negative socialist swing, however, none of them would occur.* No other condition is necessary apart from high negative socialist swing. As it appears high DV in France and the United Kingdom are explained by both the combination between socialist and libertarian swing and the combination between socialist and main right-wing swing.

Conclusion

The analysis carried out in this chapter finds a fundamental correspondence between electoral behaviour at the two main levels of elections – the national and EU – in the multi-level European party system. There is a basic overlap of the party systems at the national and European levels with only a few countries clearly showing distinct patterns between the two "orders". The main conclusion, based on the indicator of "mixed volatility" and how much "differential" there is with respect to the congenital national volatility, is one of vertical isomorphism which applies both to Western and Central-Eastern Europe.

[41] Among the remaining combinations only in the case of Ireland is one factor only (main centre-right swing) responsible for high DV. In the other five countries it is combinations of factors. For Ireland this factor is MCR, which covers both Fianna Fáil and Fine Gael (conservatives and people's, respectively) while the Irish Labour Party plays an irrelevant role. Therefore Ireland has not been included in the analysis.

[42] For full details on the code see Appendix 4. The same results have been obtained with Ragin's software (fs/QCA). Minimization refers to the exclusion of factors that appear in one combination but not in another, and factorization to identifying (1) necessary conditions and (2) causally equivalent sufficient combinations.

The evidence confirms that there is no distinctive European party system based on other alignments than those also existing in national cleavage constellations. The same dimensions structure the electoral process at both levels, and there is a persistent overlap of party offers between national and EU arenas. What does this tell us about Europeanization? Does this mean that there is not a Europeanized party system according to this indicator? The fact that there is no *distinct* European electorate does not mean that there is no European electorate whatsoever, and the "correspondence" between national and European elections does not indicate the absence of a European electorate. Data seem rather to point to a party system that looks like the *two- or multi-level* electorate and party system some authors have proposed – in which the same dimensions dominate at all levels.[43] Such an interpretation of the data is strengthened by the general trends of volatility presented in this chapter pointing to *commonality between levels*.

Rather than concluding that there is no European party system because there is no distinct party system, data presented in this chapter support the thesis that it is precisely the overlap between national and EU electorates – both synchronically (same cleavages and party families in most countries) and diachronically (similar trends and change over time) – that indicates the existence of a Europe-wide electorate, which is sensitive to the same issues and structured along the same dimensions transpiring at all electoral levels. In particular, the same dimension that dominates nationally at the level of member-states – namely, the left–right alignment – imposes itself also at the EU level. The left–right dimension that imposed itself everywhere in Europe, and that, as seen in Chapters 3 and 4, makes Europe homogeneous, today *permeates the EU party system* too. Evidence of correspondence supports the conclusion that the main national alignment also structures the EU party system. Not only horizontal homogeneity and uniformity, but vertical correspondence as well.

The similarity of the political offer and response in the two orders of elections confirms that the left–right dimension predominates in the EU cleavage constellation and that there is no significant national/territorial dimension in the form of a pro/anti-integration that cuts across and weakens it. A homogeneous left–right dimension which imposed itself everywhere over pre-industrial territorial and cultural cleavages displays its strength at the EU level today. It is the similarity between member-states seen in the previous chapters which homogenized Europe soon after democratization in the 19th century that creates the preconditions for a EU level structured along the same dimension. As seen in this chapter, the levels of correspondence do not increase over time. They are not a product of EU integration. On the contrary, today's correspondence results from earlier homogenization of electoral behaviour and party systems in Europe.

---

[43] See, in particular, Hooghe and Marks (2001) and the various publications in the wake of this book discussed in Chapter 1.

The comparative analysis of which factors account for the cases of "distinctiveness" between the two orders (Denmark, France, Ireland, Sweden, and the United Kingdom mainly) complements this conclusion. On one hand, multivariate analysis and QCA point to a mix of factors such as an anti-establishment and anti-incumbent vote in some cases and to protest more generally, while pointing to a more sincere vote in others (greens and libertarians). On the other hand, the anti-EU and extreme-right vote stands out as a factor of differentiation between the two orders of elections.

All in all data do not allow identifying a different dimensionality able to disrupt the vertical bottom-up pervasiveness of the left–right dimension at the upper level of the multi-level European party system. Whereas the nationalization of politics took place, first, during a period of great social and geographical mobilization (Industrial Revolution) and, second, in conditions of unprecedented and unrepeated levels of political mobilization (National Revolution), such conditions are absent today in Europe, with lower turnout, ideological dilution, and the weakening of organizational party structures. This makes it difficult even for a historical change as momentous as giving up national sovereignty and identity to disrupt allegiances that proved resilient over a century. It is not surprising that the new forming electoral space at the EU level structures around the same dimension as before. At the European level today a sizable "challenge" to the left–right dimension has not manifested itself yet. In spite of the differences in the conditions under which the integration of electorates occurred nationally and today at the European level, the presence of left–right everywhere in Europe does suggest that this dimension – once again – will play a strong role as a factor of integration of a Europe-wide democratic citizenship as it did a century earlier at the national level.

6

Cohesion

Ideological Convergence within European Party Families, 1945–2009

Introduction

Following three chapters on the Europeanization of party systems from the perspective of their "format", the analysis in this and the next chapter turns to the perspective of their "contents". One of the critiques made against studies of the national integration of parties and party systems is precisely that – in spite of similar levels of support and change over time – the content of the ideology and policy programmes of local "branches" are too different to consider them the "same" party. The names and symbols may be the same, but the local context imposes its constraints so that, say, the French Communist Party in Bretagne is a very different thing from the French Communist Party in the eastern *banlieue* of Paris.

The critique has been formulated against nationalization approaches, especially for some countries.[1] In most cases, the strong centralization of party organizations at the national level and the fact that competition is national rather than local (or, more precisely, becomes national in the process of nationalization), makes cross-regional ideological variation rather unproblematic.[2] At the European level the problem of "sameness" of parties of different countries bundled together in European party families, however, needs to be addressed

---

[1] This is especially the case for highly decentralized (federal) countries such as Switzerland and the United States where the ideological content and competitive strategy of branches of the same party in different cantons or states vary to a great extent. Yet these are also the cases that the analysis of formats indicates as the least nationalized – proving that nationalization measures are reliable proxies for ideology. Similar critiques can be formulated for countries with strong local patronage.

[2] Manifestos, for example, are national and there are no significant instances of national parties with different regional manifestos.

in a systematic manner. The classification of national parties into families is the first step (seen in Chapter 2). The analysis of the *ideological cohesiveness* of parties belonging (or classified as belonging) to the same party family is the second step. This is the goal of the present chapter.

With Europeanization one observes homogenization of electoral support over time, similar cleavage structures and party systems across countries and across levels of governance, and simultaneity of change. Given that party families are the units of analysis and that these families are composed of parties from countries with different historical trajectories, a variety of socio-economic and cultural contexts, and specific institutional determinants of competition (elected or nominated presidents, different electoral laws, size and composition of parliaments, etc.), Europeanization presupposes a certain amount of sameness of these parties beyond name and symbol and broad ideological orientation. This calls for an analysis of their programmes. The role of the analysis in this chapter is thus, first, to give meaning to the Europeanization of formats seen previously and, second, to analyze a further dimension of Europeanization in its own right, namely the cross-country convergence of ideology between parties of the same family. As seen in Chapter 1, such a dimension is a crucial indicator of Europeanization.

This chapter analyzes the ideological convergence of national parties within Europe-wide families from 1945 to the most recent point in time for which reliable comparable data are available at the moment of the analysis. To what extent do parties belonging to the same family but located in different countries converge towards similar positions? Is it possible at all to speak – empirically – of European "families" of parties, or are national parties ideologically and programmatically too diverse to allow one to use this term? And is it possible to identify ideological similarities only at the *"elite" level* – in party programmes – or also at the *"mass" level* – among the voters of these parties? Ideological cohesion should not only apply to the elite level of party organizations, but also to the preferences and positions of the voters of the parties.

Ultimately, the goal of this chapter is to provide, in a broad comparison and in a longitudinal perspective, a picture of ideological convergence or divergence between parties across national borders. It makes no attempt to explain converging or diverging patterns (which is dealt with in Chapter 7). This chapter starts with a discussion of the relevance of within-family ideological convergence for the emergence of a Europe-wide electorate and party system. Then, it addresses methodological issues concerning the measurement of party positions, data sources, and the creation of times series. The largest sections are devoted to the presentation of empirical results. First, this chapter draws the broad picture of converging patterns comparatively for all party families (at both the elite and electorate levels). Second, it looks at converging versus diverging patterns by distinguishing cultural from economic dimensions of left–right.

Ideological Convergence

Much has been written on whether an ideologically integrated Europe-wide electorate is needed for the emergence of a democratic supra-national polity which holds legitimacy. Although it was suggested that output legitimacy and long-term commitments can be achieved via the shift from political intervention to agency-type regulation disregarding ideological preferences (Majone, 1996), by the end of the 1990s, with the furthering of European integration, a growing part of research has pointed to the importance of input legitimacy and of making "citizens' voice" heard (Habermas, 2001; Hooghe and Marks, 2008). In this perspective, the democratic deficit, which is the lack of democratic delegation, contest, deliberation, and accountability, undermines the support for European integration (Bartolini, 2005; Beetham and Lord, 1998; Scharpf, 1999; Schmitter, 2000).

In view of the importance of ideology, research has begun to focus on the impact of European integration on democratic processes at the EU and national levels. A number of studies have addressed the impact of Europeanization on the ideology of political parties (Enyedi and Lewis, 2006; Holmes and Lightfoot, 2011; Ladrech, 2002; Von dem Berge and Poguntke, 2013). Other studies have investigated policy contestation in the EP (Diez, 2001; Hix, Noury, and Roland, 2007) and the ideological orientation of individual parties on European policies and integration (Gaffney, 1996). Recently, research has compared ideological transformations in national party systems in major Western European countries. As seen in Chapter 1, most of this literature has conceptualized Europeanization as a top-down process looking at the impact of European integration on national party systems and policy making.

Converging and eventually cohesive ideologies within party families cutting across national and territorial identities represent an important step in the integration of Europe from an *electoral perspective*. The persistence of territorially fragmented and diverse ideologies – as well as the lack of Europe-wide functional alignments – has often been interpreted as an obstacle to accountability and effective representation in the EU. The extent to which ideologies and programmes are "comparable" across borders, at both the elite and mass levels, is a crucial premise for the structuring of a supra-national political space along *non-territorial Europe-wide functional alignments*. So far they have been at the centre of important comparative studies mostly focussing on MEPs and party federations (Hix et al., 2007), political cleavages in national politics (Kriesi et al., 2008 and 2012; Marks and Wilson, 2000), or the translation of national into Europe-wide cleavages (Marks and Steenbergen, 2002). Yet the important research contribution of the mapping of policy preferences and spatial analyses devoted little attention to cross-national convergence over time. Also, in spite of "triangulations" between sources of data, a systematic analysis at both the elite and mass levels has been missing.[3]

Furthermore, most spatial analyses and efforts to map party ideologies focus on convergence *between families*. Yet the Europeanization of electorates and party systems is not so much revealed by the fact that party families become more similar among one another. Rather, Europeanization becomes apparent in the fact that parties in different countries, but belonging to the same family, converge towards similar ideological and policy positions. Such an analysis should rely primarily on assessing convergence of different equivalent parties and ideologies *within families*. Similar ideological positions of different families do not necessarily allow one to detect Europeanized alignments because national differences may still be very strong, pointing to persistent national factors. It is, on the contrary, *the cohesion among parties within the same family* that defines Europe-wide alignments.[4] While the distance between families defines the *depth of cleavages*, the distance between parties within families defines the *territoriality* of cleavages. In the definition of Europeanization in Chapter 1, *the weaker the territoriality of a cleavage, the more Europeanized the electorate can be considered* as a weak territoriality is an indicator of alignments overcoming national borders.

To carry out the analysis empirically two sources of data are explored. First, at the *elite or party level* this chapter assesses the degree of convergence of programmes through electoral manifestos (from 1945 to 2009). Second, at the *mass or electorate level* it measures the convergence of ideological preferences of voters of equivalent parties in different countries through survey data (from 1970 to 2008).[5]

The dual analysis of party and electorate levels allows one also to evaluate the degree of correspondence or, conversely, discrepancy between the two levels with regard to ideological positions. In the first part of this chapter the analysis focuses on the ideological dimension in European party systems that the analyses in the previous chapters have identified as the most important and dominant cleavage, namely the *left–right dimension*. The analysis concentrates

[3] A major symposium on the comparison of measures of party positioning and policy preferences was published in a special issue of *Electoral Studies* in 2007 (volume 26, issue 1, pp. 1–234). This represents the most important attempt to "triangulate" between expert surveys, party manifestos, and survey data with a first part of the volume devoted to the issue of European integration and a second party of the volume devoted to the left–right dimension.

[4] The convergence between families is what several spatial analyses on centripetal competition since Downs (1957) have described. After the classic Budge, Hearl, and Robertson (1987), more recent research includes Stonecash, Brewer, and Mariani (2003), Adams, Merrill, and Grofman (2004), Grofman (2004), and Hale (2008), in addition to work quoted earlier.

[5] As specified later the analysis of the elite level of ideological cohesiveness relies on a data set of party manifestos (Comparative Manifesto Project), for which data for periods prior to World War II are not available. Also for survey data, longer time series are unfortunately not possible for reasons of comparative data availability.

on families that exist in at least half of the 30 European countries analyzed, in both Western and Eastern Europe. The families considered in the analysis are again those identified as more important in the previous chapters (especially in the period for which data are available: above all socialists, liberals, conservatives, and religious parties, but also greens, far-left parties, and far-right parties). In the second part, the analysis distinguishes *cultural and economic dimensions of left–right*, and assesses the degree to which party families become more cohesive on either or both of these dimensions.

Why focus on the left–right ideological dimension? Left–right has been the traditional "layman's 'index' of politics" since the 1970s (Sartori 1976: 79; see also Sigelman and Yough, 1978 and Putnam, 1971). As seen earlier, most national political systems are structured along this dimension with the main parties of these systems defining themselves as either left or right. Cumulatively, these parties receive almost all votes. Furthermore, it is a dimension that has dominated party systems since the emergence of the working-class movement, therefore allowing for long-term longitudinal analysis.[6] EP party federations have coalesced along similar lines. Furthermore, the process of Europeanization leads party families to become more similar as a result of the increased cooperation and opportunities in the EP (Bardi, 2002). In this vein, Marks and Wilson (2000) study party families' stances on European integration between 1984 and 1996 and find support for the hypothesis that party positions on European integration are assimilated "into pre-existing ideologies of party leaders, activists and constituencies that reflect long-standing commitments on fundamental domestic issues" (Marks and Wilson, 2000: 433; Hooghe, Marks, and Wilson, 2002).[7] Left–right is numerically the most important, and ideologically the most encompassing, dimension in European electorates, justifying a focus on this ideological dimension in the following analysis.

---

[6] For this reason the CMP includes this dimension since 1945. On the contrary, the dimension of opposition or support for European integration is included since 1990 only (see Gabel and Hix, 2002, and Pennings, 2006, for positions on Europe related to family). Furthermore, as Budge et al. (2001) have argued, the left–right dimension captures the basic cleavages of industrialized societies. Castles, Mair, and Pedersen (1997) offer a comparison of left–right scales (see also Mair, 2007b), whereas Knutsen (1995) presents a comparative study. Most of the literature points to the lack of convergence among party families. Volkens and Klingemann (2002) have found that families vary significantly in their left–right placement. Thomas (2006), using a ten-point left–right scale, finds support for a narrowing of parties' scope, but data does not highlight convergence among party families. On the left–right dimension and party positions see also Albright (2010), Dinas and Gemenis (2010), and Hug and Schulz (2007).

[7] Harmel, Zeynep, and Smith (2005) analyze Euromanifestos (of European party federations) since 1979 and conclude that instances of divergence are outnumbered by those of convergence. On Europarties see also Johnsson and Zervakis (2002).

Data and Method

Data Availability

The comparison of the left–right position of parties and electorates, and of the degree of ideological family cohesion and convergence over time, relies on data at two levels:

- *Elite level*: The left–right position of a party is operationalized using scores on the left–right scale based on *party manifestos*; the source of data is the Comparative Manifestos Project (CMP);
- *Electorate level*: The left–right placement of a party's electorate is operationalized using *survey data*: the average self-placement values on the left–right scale of the voters of a specific party; the sources of data are Eurobarometers (EB, Mannheim Trend File) and European Social Surveys (ESS).

Data availability over time since 1945 and across 30 countries for the two levels is presented in Table 6.1.[8] In regard to surveys, data availability concerns the concomitant presence of data for two variables: (1) *party preference* (either closeness to, or vote intention for, a party) and (2) self-placement on the *left–right scale*. Both sets of information are needed to establish the left–right position of the electorate of specific parties. The EBs stop asking the question about vote intention after EB54.1 (year 2000). However, it is possible to extend the time series beyond this date by using the ESS, which provide comparable data since 2002 in four survey rounds (at the moment of the analysis). This problem does not concern party manifestos for which left–right positions are defined for each party in the CMP data set.

Beside the time-series discrepancy between party manifestos (1945–2009) and surveys (1970–2008), Table 6.1 also displays the difficulties in achieving equivalent time series across countries.[9] The major comparative problem arises between Western Europe and Central-Eastern Europe as a consequence of the timing of democratization. In addition, EB files have different starting dates as a consequence of the timing of accession to the EU. For most countries data on the left–right self-placement by vote intention or closeness are available since 1973, but for countries that joined the EU subsequently the time series are shorter. Furthermore, not all countries participate regularly in ESS. Finally,

---

[8] Text data have been preferred to expert surveys because they allow broader comparison and longer time series. Among major expert survey projects see Benoit, Hunt, and Laver (Benoit and Laver, 2006; Laver and Hunt, 1992; Mikhaylov, Laver, and Benoit, 2008) and the Chapel Hill projects (Ray, 1999; Marks et al., 2006; Steenbergen and Marks, 2007). On expert surveys see also Castles and Mair (1984), Huber and Inglehart (1995) and Knutsen (1998). For a comparison between expert surveys and content-based data see Benoit and Laver (2007).

[9] The analysis does not intend to compare the two levels (parties and their electorates), but rather to portray convergence at both levels. A comparison would indeed require that the same scale is used, as well as the same time series.

TABLE 6.1. *Data Availability by Country and Year (Surveys and Manifestos)*

Country	Electorate Level		Party Level		
	EB	ESS[a]	CMP I	CMP II	CMP update[a]
Austria	1995–2002	2002–6	1949–95	1999–2002	n.a.
Belgium	1973–2002	2002–8	1946–95	1999–2003	n.a.
Britain	1973–2002	2002–8	1945–97	2001–5	n.a.
Bulgaria	n.a.	2006–8	n.a.	1990–2001	2005
Cyprus	n.a.	2006–8	n.a.	1996–2001	n.a.
Czech Republic	n.a.	2002–4	n.a.	1990–2002	n.a.
Denmark	1973–2002	2002–8	1945–98	2001	2005
Estonia	n.a.	2004–8	n.a.	1992–2003	n.a.
Finland	1993–2002	2002–8	1945–95	1999–2003	n.a.
France	1973–2000	2002–8	1946–97	2002	2007
Germany	1973–2002	2002–8	1949–98	2002	2005–9
Greece	1980–2002	2002–4	1974–96	2000	n.a.
Hungary	n.a.	2002–6	n.a.	1990–2002	n.a.
Iceland	n.a.	2004	1946–95	1999–2003	n.a.
Ireland	1973–2002	2002–6	1948–97	2002	n.a.
Italy	1973–2000	2002	1946–96	2001	n.a.
Latvia	n.a.	n.a.	n.a.	1993–2002	n.a.
Lithuania	n.a.	n.a.	n.a.	1992–2000	n.a.
Luxembourg	1973–2002	2002–4	1945–94	1999	n.a.
Malta	n.a.	n.a.	n.a.	1996–8	n.a.
Netherlands	1973–2000	2002–6	1946–98	2002–3	n.a.
Norway	1990–5	2002–8	1945–97	2001	n.a.
Poland	n.a.	2002–8	n.a.	1991–2001	2005
Portugal	1985–2002	2002–8	1975–95	1999–2002	2005
Romania	n.a.	n.a.	n.a.	1990–2000	n.a.
Slovakia	n.a.	2004–6	n.a.	1990–2002	n.a.
Slovenia	n.a.	2002–8	n.a.	1990–2000	n.a.
Spain	1985–2002	2002–8	1977–96	2000	2004–8
Sweden	1995–2002	2002–8	1948–98	2002	n.a.
Switzerland	n.a.	2002–8	1947–95	1999–2003	n.a.

Notes: For Eurobarometers (EB) and European Social Surveys (ESS) data availability refers to the combined availability of both "intention to vote" (specific parties) and "left–right placement" (on a 1–10 scale). For EB data are not always available for each year. In the EB, Germany covers West Germany only and Britain excludes Northern Ireland. This limitation does not apply to ESS. Concerning Comparative Party Manifestos, for CMP II the table includes only the years not already included in CMP I to avoid overlaps.

[a] At the moment of the analysis. Available online only.

Table 6.1 indicates which time periods are covered by the two rounds of the CMP project, plus the online update for some countries for the period 2005–9.

Measurement

A first important issue for the measurement of left–right positions at the mass level is the operationalization of a party's electorate. Which respondents to surveys should be considered as the electorate of specific political parties? EB data offer two main possibilities (excluding a third one based on membership of individual voters): (1) *vote intention* for a specific party and (2) *feeling of closeness* to a specific party. For the analysis in this chapter the latter choice was made because it allows avoiding short-term and election-specific considerations that can influence vote intention (for example, protest or tactical voting). Furthermore, the variable of the feeling of closeness is also available in the ESS (whereas for voting intention there is only retrospective voting intention).[10] In the ESS the variable of retrospective voting intention has been considered to check for significant deviations from the party closeness variable.[11]

A second issue in the measurement of left–right positions is the comparability of scales used by different data sources (on this point see Castles et al., 1997; Mair, 2007b). As far as the measurement of the electorate's placement on the left–right scale is concerned, the EBs use a scale from 1 to 10, whereas the ESS use a scale from 0 to 10. To standardize the two scales, the ESS scale has been re-coded by grouping individuals placed on the value "0" (extreme left) with those placed on the value "1". This affects a negligible number of respondents.[12] As far as CMP data are concerned, the aggregate left–right indicator as defined by Budge et al. (2001: 228) and Klingemann et al. (2006: 163) has been used. This is the well-known "left_right" or "rile" variable which varies from –100 (left) to +100 (right). To match the 1–10 scale and to make it comparable the scale has been re-coded.[13]

---

[10] EB include three variables: closeness to a party (feelclo), prospective vote intention (voteint), and inclination to vote (inclvote). The ESS includes two variables: retrospective vote intention (questions B14 then B12 since 2004, variable prtvt) and closeness to a party (questions B25b then B20b since 2004, variable prtcl). Both sources provide information on party membership, which this chapter does not consider. Using vote intention does not reveal differences with respect to closeness to a party.

[11] A related issue concerns response rates. Parties with response rates on vote intention and feeling of closeness below 50 respondents have been excluded. In most cases the N of respondents for parties is above 100. This reduces risks of biased estimates of the position of electorates.

[12] Concerning the position of parties on the left–right axis, in case of alliance ESS give closeness and vote intention for all parties in the alliance. However, for this analysis the ESS position of the largest party in the alliance has been used. The EB and ESS wording in the questionnaire about self-placement (variable "lrs") is similar (questions B28 then B23 since 2004, variable "lrscale").

[13] A cultural and economic dimension of left–right is distinguished later. For details see Appendix 2 on scales as well as later in this chapter. The analysis does not rely on the alternative scale Lowe et al. (2011) suggested based on the logarithm of odds-ratios.

The main purpose of the analysis that follows in this chapter is to measure the convergence or divergence over time of party positions on the left–right scale. This requires the measurement of *spread of party positions within a family over different points in time* (time and family are discussed in the next two sub-sections). As a general measure of spread (or "ideological inequality") the standard deviation is used. The measure varies from a minimum of 0.0 (when all the parties of a family are on the exact same ideological position on the left–right scale from 1 to 10) to a maximum of approximately 6.36, which has been rounded down to 6.0 in the graphs for ease of interpretation. This is the maximum possible value of the standard deviation calculated with the minimum number of possible cases (two parties) where one is placed on the left extreme of the scale (1) and the other on the right extreme (10). The lower the value of the standard deviation, the larger ideological homogeneity within the family across parties of different European countries.

Time Points

Two issues are related to the temporal dimension of the analysis beside the already mentioned problems of time series length. First, different sources of data are based on different time points for the reporting of left–right positioning. Basic time points of the database as described in Chapter 2 are election years in each country. These are also the time points of the CMP data for which party positions are reported at each national election (although for only the main parties). Data for EB and ESS, however, do not always fit these time points. The time point for each data source closest to the election year has been chosen (for example, ESS data of 2004 has been used for an election taking place in 2005). Second, in comparative perspective time points differ across countries because elections take place in different years according to countries and CMP data are collected for election years. As in the rest of this book, therefore, *five-year aggregations* have been used.[14]

Families

First, case selection concerns *parties*. Each party has been allocated to a party family. As in the previous chapters all parties receiving at least 1 per cent of the votes in a specific national election, or at least one seat, have been classified. Appendix 1 on party family classification indicates the various families into which parties have been grouped. However, data concerning the ideological position (at the level either of party programme or of the electorate of the party) are not available for all parties. This is an important point on which the basic pool of cases differs from previous chapters. Pragmatically, all parties

---

[14] As far as ESS data are concerned, these surveys are available every two years. This means that sometimes not all the available information has been used, as elections do not take place that often.

TABLE 6.2. *Parties' Left–Right Position by Family and Country (Analysis of Variance)*

Independent Variables	Univariate Analysis (means)			
	Parties (CMP data)		Electorates (survey data)	
	(Eta)	(Eta squared)	(Eta)	(Eta squared)
Party family	0.613***	0.375***	0.869***	0.754***
Country	0.248***	0.061***	0.204***	0.042***
	Multivariate Analysis (general linear model)			
	Parties (CMP data)		Electorates (survey data)	
	(Partial eta squared)		(Partial eta squared)	
Party family	0.404***		0.803***	
Country	0.205***		0.227***	
Country* party family	0.316***		0.431***	
N	(1,908)		(1,118)	

Dependent variable: 1–10 left–right scale; N = parties at single elections.
Statistical significance *** ($p < 0.001$), ** ($p < 0.01$).

for which data are available have been considered in the analysis here, meaning the joint availability of data for CMP and EB/ESS. This means that the analysis covers all parties with a given relevance in terms of size and continuity over time.

If one uses this classification into party families to explain the position of single parties on the left–right axis, it becomes clear that such a classification has a strong and significant effect. Even if just on a preliminary basis, this is already an important result in the perspective of the question of cohesiveness within party families in Europe. The classification based on party families is systematically higher than the classification based on the national belonging of a party. As shown in the analysis of variance in Table 6.2, "genealogy" (the family) is more powerful than "nationality" (the country) in explaining the ideological position of a party on the 1–10 scale, in both univariate and multivariate terms, with coefficients for party family triple or more those for country, both for electorates (survey data) and elites (party manifestos). This tells us that the classification of national parties into Europe-wide party families makes sense in terms of the left–right dimension.

A second issue of case selection concerns *families*. To make the analysis of a Europe-wide, within-family convergence meaningful, it must focus on *families that exist in at least half of the 30 European countries* considered in the analysis. The coverage analysis in Chapter 3 is applied here to establish whether a party family exists in at least 50 per cent of the countries.[15] According to this criterion, the analysis concentrates on the following families:

- *Far left*: Communists and new left parties have been aggregated (see Table 2.3).
- *Socialists*: As defined in Chapter 2 and Appendix 1.
- *Greens*: Compared to other families the time series are shorter starting early 1980s.
- *Religious parties*: Includes Christian democrats, people's parties, and denominational parties; Orthodox parties have been excluded.
- *Liberals*: Social liberals have not been aggregated to this family.
- *Conservatives*: Sometimes with religious as "right-wing parties" (see Table 2.3).
- *Far right*: Neo-populist parties, nationalists, and extreme-right parties.[16]

Evidence of Ideological Convergence

Party Families on the Left–Right Dimension

Before presenting evidence of within-family convergence, this section shows the left–right position of each family over time. This allows depicting the overall spatial map of electorates and parties in Europe, as well as to addressing discrepancies of positioning between the two levels. Figure 6.1 portrays the position of party families for electorates (since 1970, upper graph) and parties (since 1945, lower graph). The left–right position of electorates of each family has been measured by taking the mean self-placement on the 1–10 scale of respondents to EB and ESS surveys according to their closeness to a party. The position of parties of each family has been measured with the CMP left–right aggregate scale from −100 to +100 (re-coded to match the 1–10 scale).[17]

The position of families on the left–right axis meets expectations, with minor discrepancies in the ranking, such as the more pronounced right position of conservatives with respect to far-right parties. Also there are few changes over time, the major one being the radicalization of far-right parties at the level of party programmes. A more important point appearing from the analysis

---

[15] To establish which party families exist in at least half the 30 European countries the decade 2000–10 has been considered rather than the average of presence for the entire period since 1945.

[16] Mainly because regionalist and ethnic parties exist in few countries, a "minority parties" family has mostly been excluded from the analysis. Similarly, because of sporadic presence in elections – both spatially and temporally – agrarians and social liberals have not been considered in detail.

[17] The graphs include both Western and Central-Eastern European countries. Omitting Central-Eastern European parties does not alter the general trend of Figure 6.1. The figure, in addition to the seven party families analyzed in this chapter, shows trends for agrarians, minority parties, and social liberals.

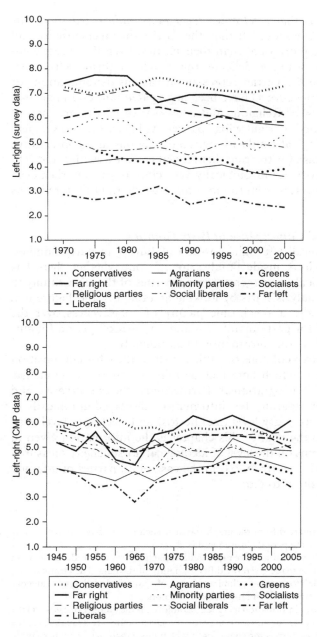

FIGURE 6.1. Left–right position by family: electorates (survey data: 1970–2008) and parties (manifesto data: 1945–2009).

of electorates and elites is that *electorates seem more radicalized than parties*: left-wing electorates are more left than the parties they feel close to, and right-wing electorates are more right than their parties. Even if a direct comparison between the two scales is delicate, this would confirm well-known party strategies. In Figure 6.1 parties representing various denominations or levels of religiosity (see Appendix 1) have been aggregated into one single category of "religious parties".[18] Religious and conservative parties are merged into a more general category of "right wing" parties. As Figure 6.2 shows, there is a high degree of ideological similarity between religious and conservative families, supporting the case for treating them together. Conservative and religious electorates and parties are ideologically very close to one another, even though conservative electorates seem to move more to the right than religious ones in recent decades.[19]

Overall Homogeneity and Convergence of Party Families

After having seen the overall left–right position of European party families, this section proceeds to look inside families to find out whether there has been a process of ideological convergence among parties of the same family in Europe. To this end the analysis starts by looking at Table 6.3 and Figure 6.3. Whereas Table 6.3 provides a synchronic picture of cohesiveness over the entire 1945–2004 period for party manifestos and 1970–2008 period for survey data, Figure 6.3 displays the information longitudinally.

For reference, the first two columns of Table 6.3 show the left–right position of the main party families, which here include minority parties (regionalists and ethnic parties), as well as agrarians.[20] Furthermore, the conservative and religious families are kept separate. The information, displayed graphically in Figure 6.1, is given for both party level (manifestos) and electorate level (surveys). More important to the goal of this chapter is the information given in the third and fourth columns on the level of ideological homogeneity measured through the standard deviation (from 0.0 in the case of all parties of a family on the same left–right position to 6.0).

---

[18] Orthodox parties have been omitted from the graph (because such parties have contested only two elections in Greece during the period covered in this chapter).

[19] In this graph one sees again that electorates are more radical than parties in their ideologies even if a direct comparison cannot be made given the different nature of the data. The erratic movement inter-confessionals display for 1955–9 is limited to the only party included in this category in that period, which is the German Christian-Democratic Union.

[20] An important additional piece of information included in Table 6.3 is the number of cases: (1) the number of countries in which data for at least one party of a given family are available; (2) the number of observations, that is, parties for countries in which more than one party per family exists. The number of countries also varies during the period considered because of new data and accession to the EU (and the consequent inclusion in the EB). Values in Table 6.3 represent overall averages for the period 1945–2004. As before, the latest period from 2005 to 2009 has been excluded from the computation because data are only available for eight countries.

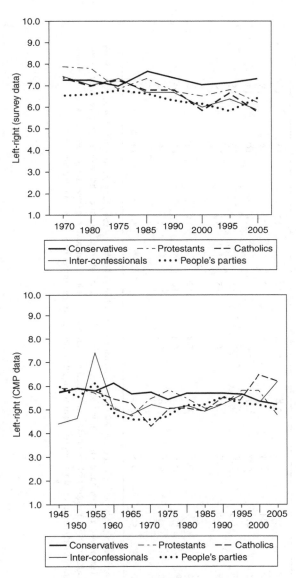

FIGURE 6.2. Left–right position of religious and conservative families: electorates (survey data, 1970–2008) and parties (manifesto data, 1945–2009).

TABLE 6.3. *Left–Right Position and Ideological Homogeneity within Families: Overall Period for Electorates (Survey Data) and Parties (CMP data)*

Family	Left–Right Position (Mean)		Ideological Homogeneity (Standard Deviation)		Discrepancy	Electorate Data: Average Number of		Manifesto Data: Average Number of	
	Electorates	Parties	Electorates	Parties		Countries	Observations	Countries	Observations
Far left	2.7	3.7	0.8	0.8	-0.1	10	17	11	17
Far right	7.0	5.4	1.3	0.9	1.6	7	9	6	9
Greens	4.1	4.2	0.7	0.7	-0.1	9	12	10	13
Liberals	6.1	5.3	0.8	0.9	0.8	11	19	15	25
Right wing overall	6.9	5.6	0.8	0.9	1.3	15	33	19	40
Conservatives	7.2	5.8	0.6	1.0	1.4	10	14	13	20
Religious	6.8	5.4	0.8	0.8	1.4	10	19	12	20
Socialists	4.0	4.1	0.7	0.8	-0.1	15	25	19	32
Overall	6.0	5.2	0.8	0.9	0.8	9	16	11	20

Notes: Families have been ordered alphabetically. Values represent averages for the overall period of 1945–2004 for party manifestos and 1970–2008 for surveys of electorates. The period 2005–9 has been excluded because of limited CMP data at the moment of the analysis. "Discrepancy" is the difference between the mean left–right position of electorates and parties. Number of countries indicates in how many countries a family exists. Number of observation indicates the number of parties of a family for all elections. Both averages have been rounded up.

The main message conveyed by these two columns is that in terms of *both electorates and parties, European families display a high degree of cohesiveness* with all figures below a standard deviation of 1.0 with the exception of far-right parties (1.3). This confirms the partial results of the previous sections, indicating that *parties belonging to the same family have similar ideological positions on the left–right scale, as well as the electorates who feel close to these parties*. The fifth column in Table 6.3 indicates the "discrepancy" of the position on the 1–10 left–right scale between the party (based on its manifesto) and its electorate (based on surveys). In Figure 6.1 it was observed that electorates tend to be more radical than parties. This is confirmed by figures in Table 6.3. Generally, right wing electorates are more right than the parties they vote for or to which they declare feeling close. This is the case for agrarians, far-right parties, liberals, and right-wing parties (both conservatives and religious parties). Symmetrically, left-wing electorates are more left than "their" parties. One sees this for far-left parties, greens, and socialists.[21] The pattern clearly attests to the fact that electorates are more "extreme" than parties, although this conclusion is based on different types of data and should not be exaggerated. The size of the discrepancy is higher for right-wing parties (between 1.4 and 1.6 for right-wing parties and far-right parties), whereas it is smaller for left-wing parties (–0.1 for far-left parties, socialists, and greens).

Both graphs in Figure 6.3 – parties and electorates – confirm the within-family cohesiveness over the entire period covered with the partial exception of far-right electorates (parties which are not ideologically very similar as the upper graph shows).[22] Cohesiveness, however, does not mean convergence, which is a temporal process of reduction of ideological differences between parties of the same family. As seen in the previous section, there are feeble signs of within-family convergence among socialists, right-wing parties, and liberals. Figure 6.3 provides a more general picture. In this figure, declining curves indicate smaller standard deviations and a reduction of ideological differences on the left–right axis among parties of a same family. From a longitudinal perspective from the upper graph on parties' position it appears that *there is a feeble but continuous process of ideological convergence between parties of the same family from 1945 to the present*, which seems more accentuated in the recent decades. On the contrary, at *the level of electorates the pattern seems to be rather one of slight divergence*, especially for liberals, conservatives, and religious parties.

A closer look at specific families, limited here to the three main ones, confirms this finding – starting with the socialists. The socialist family is the only one for which at least one party exists in all 30 European countries as seen in Chapter 3. Socialists are one of the largest party families and usually considered

---

[21] A negative value of discrepancy means that electorates are more left than what appears through manifestos. A positive value means that electorates are more right than the party.

[22] In the upper graph on parties far-right parties in the 1950s have a value close to zero because the graph includes two parties only, namely the Italian Social Movement and the Austrian FPÖ until the 1980s.

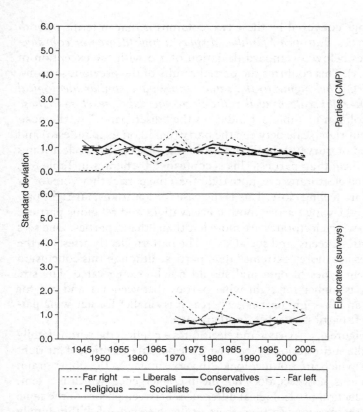

FIGURE 6.3. Ideological homogeneity on the left–right scale within the main families.
Note: Families present in few countries omitted from the graph: agrarians and minority parties.

a party family with high ideological homogeneity. Figure 6.4 shows the position on the left–right axis of socialist electorates in the different European countries. Survey data are available since the early 1970s for members of the EU. The number of countries included in the graph increases over time. The graph in Figure 6.4 displays *cohesiveness but a feeble ideological convergence* at the electorate level. The result is made more important by the fact that the level of cohesiveness not only does not decrease, but actually increases in spite of additional countries added to the sample. The graph in Figure 6.5 at the party level *shows cohesiveness and slight convergence.*[23] Figure 6.6, which

---

[23] For both graphs the time period differs between countries as documented in Table 6.1 because of democratization processes, but also data availability. In Figure 6.4 Bulgaria, Cyprus, and Iceland have been excluded because there is only one time point in the ESS and none in the EB. In Figure 6.5 Cyprus and Malta have been excluded because of short time series.

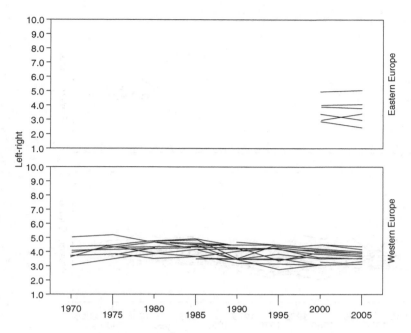

FIGURE 6.4. Left–right position of socialist electorates (survey data, 1970–2008).

displays the level of ideological spread across socialist parties in Europe, indicates that *party programmes converge since 1945*, with ideological differences (measured through the standard deviation) constantly decreasing in spite of an increasing number of countries included.[24]

In spite of little convergence, there are *strong similarities*: all European socialists are close to one another on the left–right scale, which leaves little room for further convergence. There are no major outliers, with the very marginal exception of Poland, whose socialists are slightly more left (as is the case of France and Switzerland in Western Europe) and Estonia slightly more right (as is the case of the Labour Party in Britain in the past 10 years). Finally, there are no major differences between Western and Eastern Europe even if the socialist parties that are more at the centre of the spectrum are those of Central-Eastern Europe. In Figure 6.5 outliers or national parties with major

[24] Figure 6.6 includes selected years only and the period 2005–9 has been excluded because there are only eight countries in the CMP online update for this period at the moment of analysis. In comparing the cohesiveness between party families, the size of parties does not play any role so that, differently than in Chapter 3, it is not necessary to employ indices that control for different size of party families.

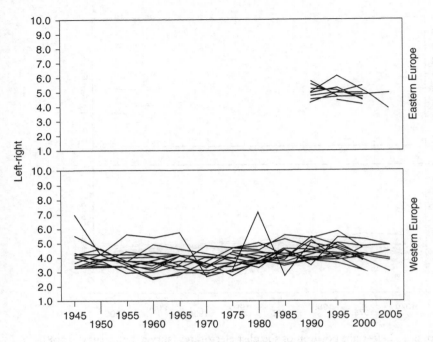

FIGURE 6.5. Left–right position of socialist parties (manifesto data, 1945–2009).

changes over time include Finland and Sweden in Western Europe and Bulgaria in Central-Eastern Europe. To sum up on the socialist family, one can say that there is little evidence of ideological convergence over time, mainly because of an already high degree of ideological similarity among parties of this family, in both Western and Central-Eastern Europe.

For the right-wing family, data lead to similar results. Because of space constraints this section does not include the same number of figures. As for the socialists one sees that there is a higher ideological homogeneity between electorates than between parties, and that electorates are more radical (in this case right-wing) than the parties they vote for.[25] The comparison between electorates and parties reveals that electorates are more homogenous ideologically than parties, and more right-wing. There are few specific national deviations from the pattern that deserve lengthy comments. The Italian right-wing electorate (voters of the Christian Democrats since 1945 and Forza Italia since 1994) and the Belgian Christian Democrats (Flemish

[25] At the electorate level Bulgaria, Cyprus, and Iceland have been excluded because of a short time period. At the party level Cyprus and Malta have been omitted for the same reason. In Figure 6.7 the period 2005–9 has been skipped because of too few countries.

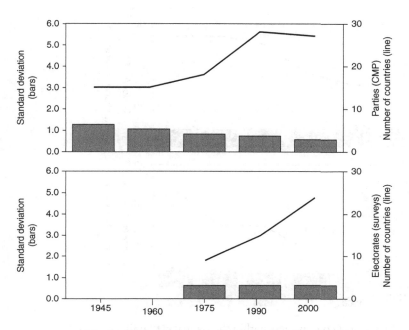

FIGURE 6.6. Ideological cohesiveness within the socialist family.

Notes: The scale for the standard deviation varies between a minimum of 0.0 (all parties of a family on the exact same ideological position on the left–right scale from 1 to 10) and a maximum of approximately 6.36 (half of the parties at one extreme 1 and the other half at the other extreme 10) calculated with the minimum number of cases possible, that is two parties. For presentation matters, in the graph it has been rounded down the maximum value to 6.0.

and Walloon) appear to be placed more towards the centre with respect to other European parties of this family. This is also the case of Estonia in Eastern Europe.

Similarly to the socialists we see a *feeble ideological convergence at the party level*, whereas there is *no such convergence at the electorate level*. Again, such patterns are due to an *already high ideological cohesiveness* that leaves little room for further homogenization.

This appears more clearly in Figure 6.7. In spite of a growing number of countries included in the computations (because of democratization, first in Southern and then in Central-Eastern Europe), *the standard deviation of the position of right-wing parties decreases slightly* since the 1960s, attesting to ideological convergence. This is not the case for electorates (lower graph in Figure 6.7) which, on the contrary, show signs of a divergence, albeit a very small one, with a standard deviation remaining below 1.0 throughout. Finally,

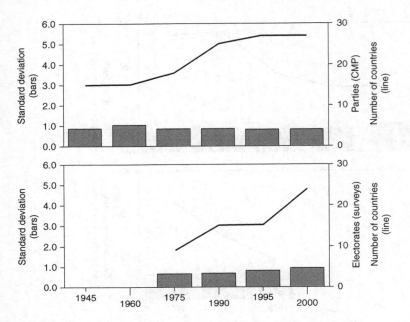

FIGURE 6.7. Ideological cohesiveness within the right-wing family.
Note: See note to Figure 6.6.

unlike socialists and right-wing parties, liberals exist in fewer countries. As for socialists and right-wing parties, the pattern of the liberals is one of *slight or no ideological convergence, but clear overall similarity* with a spread between parties' positions on the left–right scale almost always below 1.0 standard deviation. This is the main message from Figure 6.8.[26]

As far as electorates are concerned, most liberal voters are located between 5.0 and 7.0 on the left–right scale (in both Western and Eastern Europe) with little movement over time. Noteworthy is the French liberal electorate, which converged towards the centre after most of the members of the Union for French Democracy joined the former Gaullists to form the new Union for the People's Movement (UMP). A similar pattern is that of the Danish liberal party, whereas the Swedish liberals present a harsh move towards the left in the period 1965–9. The level of the standard deviation remains constant as far as

[26] Because of too few observations Bulgaria, Cyprus, Iceland, Poland, and Slovakia have been excluded at the electorate level. For the Austrian Liberales Forum (LIF) classified as liberal, data are available for 1995–9 only and therefore they do not appear here (the FPÖ has been classified as far right). Again, because of insufficient observations on party manifestos, Austria, Cyprus, Greece, Iceland, Ireland, and Latvia have been left out.

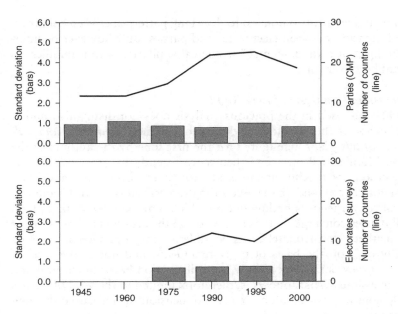

FIGURE 6.8. Ideological cohesiveness within the liberal family.
Note: See notes to Figure 6.6.

the ideological position of parties (manifesto data) is concerned. In Figure 6.8 one sees that this measure is continuously below 1.0 and does not show signs of convergence because of the already existing fundamental similarity. Also electorates display policy positions that are very homogenous in spite of an increase of the standard deviation above 1.0 for the period 2000–5 (as for the previous graphs the latest five-year period has been omitted for lack of sufficient cases).

The overall message from this exploration is thus one of a certain degree of bifurcation: *divergence between "electorates"* on one hand, *convergence among "parties"* on the other. While the ideological position of *electorates* (that is the voters) of different national parties of a same family becomes slightly more diverse, the position of the *parties* themselves, measured though their programmatic positions, appears to become slightly more similar, attesting to a process of Europeanization. On the basis of this result one can conclude that there is an ideological *Europeanization of party systems, but less so of electorates*, even though at both levels the degree of cohesiveness is very high with standard deviations rarely above 1.0. This result supports what has been reported in Chapter 3, where systemic factors such as turnout – and to some extent also fragmentation and volatility – pointed to diverging patterns between countries. The slight bifurcation between electorates and parties must however be interpreted in the light of a fundamental ideological similarity within families, as well as of stability over time.[27]

A Two-Dimensional Analysis of Left–Right

The left–right scale used in the previous analysis does not distinguish underlying components of this ideological dimension, namely *economic and cultural elements of left–right* highlighted for the first time by the authors of the Comparative Manifesto Project and then more recently by other scholars as well (Budge et al., 2001; Klingemann et al., 2006; see also Castles and Mair, 1984; Kriesi et al., 2008 and 2012). Accordingly, a crucial issue in the analysis of ideological convergence is finding out on which dimension(s) it takes place. Do national parties converge on the cultural or on the economic dimension, or on both or neither? Unfortunately, it is possible to carry out such an analysis longitudinally only on the basis of party manifestos and not at the level of electorates as survey data do not allow for a distinction between cultural and economic dimensions. What follows is, therefore, limited to the level of parties and their ideological position along the two dimensions as measured through their programmes.

The two left–right dimensions are the following (for details see Appendix 2):

- *Economic dimension*: Role of the state in the economy (planning and state ownerships), industrial relations and decision-making processes (corporatism), incentives for free enterprise versus Keynesian management, extension of welfare.
- *Cultural dimension*: National pride and identity, law and order, state authority, attitudes towards multi-culturalism and national traditions, tolerance of diversity, social justice, solidarity with the developing world, and internationalism.[28]

To operationalize the two dimensions the analysis in this chapter departs from the two aggregated indicators provided by the CMP data set even though the economic dimension in this chapter includes the two variables making up CMP's "markeco" indicator (per401 and per414) and the cultural dimension includes one of the two variables of CMP's "welfare" indicator (per503). The reason for this choice is that the two CMP aggregate indicators do not provide enough variation across cases. In 90 per cent of the cases (the cases being

---

[27] The correspondence between the party and electoral level is supported by the correlation between the 1–10 left–right position of parties' electorates and the position of parties based on their manifestos, which is generally high with a Pearson's $r = 0.603$, whether electorates are considered based on feeling of closeness or voting intention.

[28] Unlike other research (including CMP) in the present analysis it has been decided to include "welfare" in the economic dimension rather than the cultural one (see the variable "per504" in the CMP data set, which is used in that study as a cultural variable).

parties at a specific election) the number of quasi-sentences is below 10 per cent of positive mentions of per401 and per414, and in 80 per cent of the cases values are below 10 per cent of positive mentions of welfare. This means that there is no real variation across cases, making it problematic to re-code the variable and render it comparable to the 1–10 left–right scale used elsewhere in this chapter.[29]

Instead, for the purpose of the present analysis two new aggregated indicators have been created with a total of 26 variables (see Table A.2.1 in Appendix 2).[30] These indicators have been calculated through the number of quasi-sentences in favour of right-wing categories as a percentage of the total number of quasi-sentences in favour of both left- and right-wing categories. The higher the numerator, the more right-wing the party's position. Then the result has been divided by 10 to make it vary between 0 and 10 and, finally, re-coded 0 into 1 to make the left–right scale vary between 1 and 10 as before. The procedure has been applied to both cultural and economic dimensions.[31]

It is now possible to place party families in a two-dimensional space with a cultural and an economic left–right dimension (Figure 6.9), as well as to follow the placement of party families on these two dimensions over time since 1945 (Figure 6.10). The graph in Figure 6.9 is divided into four quadrants based on the mean value for each of the two dimensions.[32] The mean position of party families on the economic dimension is 4.2 and on the cultural dimension 4.9 on the 1–10 left–right scale. Clearly two groups of parties appear with three border cases: the social liberals (at the centre of the economic axis) and the agrarians and liberals (at the centre of the cultural axis).

If one observes the dynamics of families' placement on the two axes since 1945 (except for the greens, which appear later), we see that right-wing parties such as far-right parties, conservatives, and religious parties are characterized by a *divergence between cultural and economic dimensions*. For these three families Figure 6.10 shows that *while on the economic dimension these parties tend to move towards the left, on the cultural dimension they move towards the right*, in both cases in correspondence with more protectionist attitudes

---

[29] The CMP data places parties on the left–right scale by counting the number of either positive or negative mentions ("quasi-sentences") for 56 items from which various scales, including the left–right one, are then derived.

[30] See, for a similar procedure, Benoit and Laver (2006: 100), who use slightly different categories.

[31] As mentioned earlier, the analysis in this part of the chapter does not follow Lowe et al. (2011). The original items based on the number of quasi-sentences include *positive* mentions so are not subject to criticism that what is actually measured is the *salience* of an issue (whether or not it is important) rather than the left-right *position* of the party on this issue (whether it is positive or negative).

[32] In the graph positions represent averages for the entire period since 1945. For specific periods party families would be positioned slightly differently as in the case of far-right parties that in the more recent decade are placed at the left of the reference line for the economic axis (upper-left quadrant). The graph also includes agrarians and social liberals even if in most of this chapter they are not included in the analysis as they are present in less than half the countries in Europe.

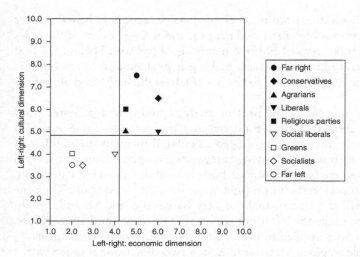

FIGURE 6.9. The positioning of families on the economic and cultural left–right dimensions: overall period (CMP data).

Note: Reference lines represent overall means.

observed by recent research. This trend can be observed also for the socialists, whereas such a discrepancy seems to have always existed for the far-left parties. On the contrary, in the case of the greens there is a clear move towards the left also on the cultural dimension.

Leaving aside the question of the position on the two left–right dimensions, let us investigate the *issue of the convergence on these two axes*. Do parties of the same family converge on either or both or none of the economic and cultural dimensions – and for which families? Figure 6.11 provides the longitudinal depiction of the levels of ideological cohesiveness of parties on the two axes measured through the standard deviation which are given in more detail in Table 6.4. This figure shows the level of diversity among parties of the same family.[33] Three aspects can be noted:

- First, there are *no significant trends towards either convergence or divergence on either dimension*. This applies to all party families. As mentioned earlier, one can witness a feeble trend towards convergence, but none of the patterns displays dramatic reductions of diversity.

---

[33] Because of the different composition of items used to build the two dimensions with respect to the aggregate left–right scale seen earlier in this chapter – and used in the CMP studies – the overall levels of cohesiveness are not comparable between the families in Figure 6.11 and those in the aggregate figures above.

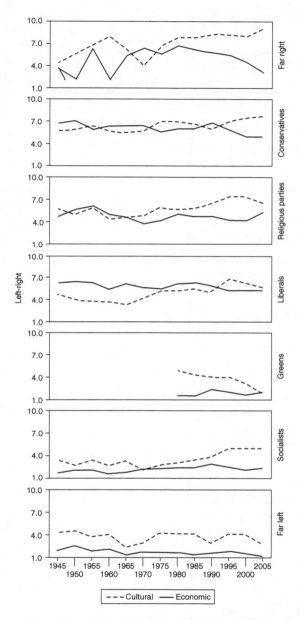

FIGURE 6.10. The positioning of party families on the economic and cultural left–right dimensions: 1945–2009 (CMP data).

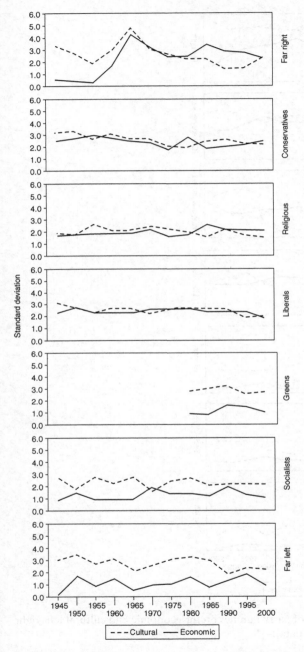

FIGURE 6.11. Ideological cohesiveness within families on the economic and cultural left–right dimensions: 1945–2004 (CMP data).

- Second, *left-wing families seem more homogenous than right-wing families in regard to the economic dimension*. The solid lines are lower, indicating a lower standard deviation and a higher level of cohesiveness in the economic programme.
- Third, *left-wing parties have a much lower cohesiveness on the cultural dimension* than on the economic one. The dashed curves (cultural dimension) are consistently higher than the solid ones (economic dimension), indicating more diversity on cultural matters than on economic ones.

Summing up, the analysis shows that the overall level of *ideological cohesiveness is high among parties of the same family*. The various families analyzed in this chapter have remained cohesive throughout the periods considered: since 1945 for party manifestos and 1970 for survey data.

There has been little further convergence during these periods, most likely because of the already high levels of ideological homogeneity among parties of the same family. This chapter has nonetheless shown that ideological convergence has taken place in parties' ideology, albeit not among their electorates. It has also shown that electorates are placed on more radical positions than the parties they feel close to, or they intend to vote for. Finally, the analysis of the two economic and cultural dimensions of left–right attests to a greater homogeneity on economic issues in left parties than on cultural ones.

Conclusion

The main message from the previous discussion is that electorates and party families are "Europeanized", in the sense that *parties belonging to the same ideological family and voters supporting and sympathizing with the same political side are located on similar positions along the left–right axis* across political systems. The variance of single parties around the European average position is small. National parties are similar across borders when they belong to the same family. Does this attest to a *process* of "Europeanization"? This is certainly not the case during the period of time that data availability allows us to consider, since 1945 for parties' position on left–right and since 1970 for voters' placement on the scale. During this period one does not see a pronounced trend towards Europeanization. The curves in the various graphs look rather flat, and the levels of ideological diversity within families do not decrease dramatically during the period covered.

How should this finding be interpreted? It is possible to put forward two lines of interpretation. First, the data presented earlier show that high levels of ideological cohesiveness for the most important party families making up for most of the party systems have been constant since the very beginning of the periods considered. In other words, ideological homogeneity has always been so high as to limit the room for further convergence. *Once Europeanized, there can be only little further Europeanization of electorates and party systems.*

TABLE 6.4. *Level of Ideological Homogeneity on the Economic and Cultural Dimensions of Left–Right (CMP Data) within Party Families (Standard Deviation)*

Five-Year period	Far left		Socialists		Greens		Liberals		Religious		Conservatives		Far right	
	Economic	Cultural	Economic	Cultural	Economic	Cultural	Economic	Cultural	Economic	Cultural	Economic	Cultural	Economic	Cultural
1945–49	0.1 (1.9)	3.0 (4.3)	0.8 (1.7)	2.7 (3.7)			2.2 (6.2)	3.1 (4.7)	1.7 (4.7)	1.8 (5.7)	2.5 (6.7)	3.2 (5.8)	0.5 (3.7)	2.6 (4.3)
1950–54	1.7 (2.5)	3.4 (4.5)	1.5 (2.0)	1.8 (2.8)			2.7 (6.3)	3.1 (3.8)	1.7 (5.7)	1.7 (5.0)	2.7 (7.2)	3.3 (5.9)	.4 (2.2)	3.3 (5.5)
1955–59	0.9 (1.9)	2.7 (3.8)	0.9 (2.1)	2.8 (3.4)			2.3 (6.2)	2.2 (3.7)	1.9 (6.1)	2.6 (5.9)	2.9 (6.5)	2.7 (6.4)	0.3 (6.3)	2.7 (6.8)
1960–64	1.5 (2.0)	3.1 (4.1)	1.0 (1.6)	2.2 (2.7)			2.3 (5.4)	2.7 (3.6)	1.8 (5.0)	2.0 (4.4)	2.7 (6.6)	3.0 (5.6)	1.7 (2.2)	1.9 (7.9)
1965–69	0.5 (1.3)	2.1 (2.3)	0.9 (1.8)	2.8 (3.2)			2.2 (6.0)	2.6 (3.3)	1.9 (4.6)	2.1 (4.5)	2.4 (6.5)	2.7 (5.4)	4.2 (5.3)	2.9 (6.2)
1970–74	0.9 (1.6)	2.5 (2.9)	1.9 (2.3)	1.5 (2.1)			2.5 (5.6)	2.3 (4.2)	2.2 (3.8)	2.5 (4.8)	2.4 (6.3)	2.6 (6.0)	3.2 (6.4)	4.9 (4.1)
1975–79	1.0 (1.7)	3.0 (4.2)	1.4 (2.3)	2.4 (2.9)			2.5 (5.5)	2.6 (5.0)	1.6 (4.2)	2.2 (5.9)	1.7 (5.5)	2.1 (7.1)	2.4 (5.6)	3.1 (7.0)
1980–84	1.6 (1.7)	3.3 (4.1)	1.4 (2.5)	2.7 (3.1)	0.9 (1.5)	2.8 (4.9)	2.6 (6.2)	2.8 (5.1)	1.7 (5.0)	1.9 (5.6)	2.8 (6.1)	2.0 (6.8)	2.4 (6.7)	2.6 (7.8)

1985–89	0.8 (1.4)	3.0 (4.1)	1.2 (2.5)	2.0 (3.5)	0.8 (1.6)	3.0 (4.2)	2.4 (6.3)	2.7 (5.5)	2.6 (4.7)	1.6 (5.8)	1.9 (5.8)	2.5 (6.6)	3.4 (6.2)	2.2 (7.9)
1990–94	1.3 (1.7)	1.8 (2.9)	1.9 (2.9)	2.2 (4.0)	1.6 (2.4)	3.2 (4.1)	2.3 (5.9)	2.5 (5.0)	2.1 (4.7)	2.1 (6.5)	2.1 (6.7)	2.6 (5.9)	2.9 (5.8)	2.2 (8.3)
1995–99	1.8 (1.8)	2.4 (4.2)	1.3 (2.6)	2.2 (5.1)	1.5 (2.0)	2.6 (3.9)	2.3 (5.2)	1.9 (6.7)	2.2 (4.2)	1.6 (7.3)	2.2 (5.7)	2.2 (7.0)	2.8 (5.5)	1.4 (8.1)
2000–04	0.9 (1.6)	2.2 (4.0)	1.1 (2.1)	2.1 (5.2)	1.0 (1.7)	2.7 (3.2)	1.8 (5.2)	2.0 (6.2)	2.1 (4.2)	1.5 (7.4)	2.5 (4.8)	2.2 (7.5)	2.3 (4.5)	1.5 (8.0)
Overall	1.0 (1.7)	2.6 (4.0)	1.3 (2.2)	2.3 (3.6)	1.1 (1.9)	2.6 (3.7)	2.3 (5.8)	2.5 (4.8)	2.0 (4.8)	2.9 (5.8)	2.3 (6.1)	2.5 (6.4)	2.2 (4.9)	2.5 (7.0)

Note: Mean position on the left–right cultural and economic dimensions (1–10) in parentheses. The period 2005–9 has been omitted because of the limited number of cases.

Only in the case of some families, first and foremost the socialists, do levels of ideological diversity further contract during the period since 1945.

Second, electorates and party systems may have converged before the period considered, and families have always been cohesive perhaps even since the beginning of parliamentary life. Data do not allow us to answer the question of whether ideological convergence has taken place during earlier periods, even though processes of integration at the national level seem to suggest that such a hypothesis is plausible (Caramani, 2004; Marks and Steenbergen, 2002). Furthermore, the findings of Chapters 3 and 4 support the interpretation that crucial pushes of Europeanization take place when party systems form at the end of the 19th century. For certain, the level of homogeneity of party families across Europe seems independent of the factors usually called upon to account for integration, whether it is technological change in communication, growing labour mobility across national markets, or supra-national political integration and economic/financial coordination. Ideological integration seems to have occurred *prior to and independently of* such factors, pointing rather to similar national factors such as transformations triggered by the National and Industrial Revolutions.

In the light of what has been seen in the previous chapters on homogeneity, uniformity, and correspondence, the ideological similarity and family cohesiveness should not come as a surprise. Findings on the format of party systems attest to Europeanization. Furthermore, cleavage models explaining the genesis of party systems in Europe stress the similarity and simultaneous appearance of ideologies in most countries, as well as their persistence up to the present as stressed in Chapter 2. Also research on party families and the history of ideology shows that Europe-wide oppositions and alignments have developed in common and at the same time (Von Beyme, 1985).

Looking from a broad historical perspective ideological commonalities across Europe are at the basis of the transformation of the institutional as well as the social order in all countries. The opposition between liberals and conservatives during periods of restricted suffrage, but more important, on the basic issues of *liberalism* – that is the liberalization of civil and political rights, representative democracy, secularization, and abolition of privilege, as well as free enterprise and fiscal relations between individuals and the state. It should further be recalled that such dominating ideology in the 19th century was closely coupled with nationalism, aspirations of national unification, and/or national independence. As historical studies show, contacts across countries between liberal–nationalist elites were frequent, with the leading role of some supra-national figures supporting nationalism at home and abroad. Nationalism, in this sense, was a "trans-national" ideology, as was Marxism and social democracy that developed later in the 19th century, and as was the degeneration of nationalism after World War I in the form of fascism. The main difference between liberalism–nationalism and socialism was the degree to which the latter was supported by international organisations and coordinated political and electoral strategies, as well as debated ideological issues (Bartolini, 2000; Przeworski and Sprague, 1986).

Even in the absence of manifesto data before World War II, the evidence on ideological cohesiveness within party families together with evidence of horizontal Europeanization (homogeneity and uniformity) points convincingly to trends that started during earlier phases of electoral development.

Finally, ideological similarity within party families across borders suggests that ideological differences (between party families) are more important than territorial differences (between countries), as the analysis of variance presented in Table 6.2 also confirms. The *ideological identity* of parties and voters is much stronger than the *geographical identity*. Genealogy trumps nationality. As also noted in the conclusions of the previous chapters, such conditions should be considered as setting the premise for electoral integration at the supra-national European level, and to move from territorial to functional alignments whereby ideological differences wipe out national ones.

7

Closure

The Europeanization of Cabinet and Coalition Politics, 1945–2009

Introduction

The chapters so far have analyzed processes of cross-country convergence that the literature seen in Chapter 1 mostly traces back to within- and trans-country processes. This chapter introduces aspects that may be ranged under "top-down" effects, namely factors located at the supra-national level that affect countries in a similar way and thus create convergence. At the same time this chapter extends Chapter 6. While including an analysis of long-term trends since 1945, it focuses on Europeanization in the more usual definition of the impact of European integration on member-states. The hypothesis about the impact on cross-country convergence is addressed in an explanatory perspective. Beyond this impact, however, this chapter addresses further supra-national factors such as the breakdown of communist regimes in 1989 and the impact of such a momentous juncture on cross-country convergence.

Furthermore, while this book has so far focussed on the Europeanization of electorates and party systems, this chapter turns to the arena of cabinet and coalition politics. The move to the *executive arena* is needed first and foremost because the top-down effect from supra-national factors such as European integration is felt primarily in cabinets' format and policy. It is at the level of cabinets and governmental coalitions that one observes programmatic changes that affect policy making. While small, extreme protest opposition parties are not called to translate their platforms into actual policies, programmes of parties with cabinet responsibility provide the basis for executive action.

Indeed, it is the programmatic action of cabinets that has been most affected by Europe-wide changes such as the end of the Cold War and European integration. On one hand, the breakdown of communist regimes in Central and Eastern Europe had the effect of de-radicalizing leftist politics and reducing the alternatives in foreign and economic policy. This has led to claims about the policy convergence through liberalizations and privatizations, as well as calls for a reduction of the welfare state and of general state intervention in the economy. On the other hand, the acceleration of the process of European integration since the Single European Act of 1986 and the Maastricht Treaty of 1992 has constrained the margin for action on the part of national governments. The Maastricht criteria on inflation, interest rates and deficit, together with the EMU, have deprived national governments of most options in economic policies, reducing variety across Europe. As seen in Chapter 1, the literature on Europeanization has thus pointed to patterns of convergence. In addition, the literature on cleavage structures has pointed to the similar impact of European integration on national party systems, through the "sovereignty dimension".

Against this broad background, this chapter aims at finding out empirically the extent to which, and at which point in time since World War II, cabinets' policy positions across Europe have become more similar. It does so through indicators looking at the degree of homogenization in the executive landscape in Europe. Further, it establishes whether cross-national convergence of national cabinets is, first, due to the simultaneous presence of similar parties in government ("same composition") or, second, may be independent of which party is in power if there is a fundamental and increasing ideological similarity between party families ("family similarity"). Average positions are calculated from the combination of information on parties in government with manifesto data on their ideological positions. Policy convergence is measured on the left–right dimension as in Chapter 6. It is a further goal of this chapter to find out whether policy convergence takes place on the economic dimension or on the cultural dimension.[1]

This chapter starts by discussing the concept of closure. After addressing methodological issues, the main bulk of the chapter is devoted to the presentation of results. First, evidence of cross-country ideological homogeneity and convergence of cabinets' composition and programmes over time is presented. Second, explanations for converging patterns between national cabinets are tested through regression analysis.[2]

Analyzing the Europeanization of Executive Politics

Governmental Closure and Cabinets

The concept of closure (Mair, 1996) is used in this chapter as it specifically refers to the executive arena, to the governmental formula, and to alliances and

---

[1] First, it looks at homogeneity and convergence in the *composition* of cabinets (left, centre-left, centre, centre-right, right, or consociational coalition) and *type* of cabinet (single-party majority or minority, minimum winning coalition, minority, or oversized coalition). Second, it looks at homogeneity and convergence in the cabinets' placement on the left–right dimension.

[2] The term *cabinet* is used interchangeably with the terms *government* and *executive* to refer, in European parliamentary or semi-presidential systems, to the executive branch (prime minister and ministers). This chapter avoids the use of the term *administration*, applied mostly to the United States and other presidential systems.

coalitions as the most central element of the general concept of party system collaboration (as a complement to competition). The underlying meaning of closure is the stability, structuring, and institutionalization of the features of party systems and – more specifically – of alliances and coalitions at the executive level (especially in parliamentary systems requiring an absolute majority in parliament to support and vote the confidence of cabinets). In addition to what has been seen in the previous chapters, which mainly focussed on the *competitive aspects* of party systems in national elections, the concept of closure allows a move to the *cooperative aspects* of party systems in national cabinets.[3] It is these cooperative aspects in alliances and coalitions that this chapter is concerned with.

The concept of closure is analyzed in its Europe-wide dimension – namely the extent to which governing formulae and the stability of their policy positions are similar across national cabinets. Is it possible to identify a Europe-wide institutionalization and predictability of cabinet alliances and coalitions? So far neither the literature on closure nor the rich literature on cabinets has investigated long-term converging trends among national cabinets in Europe.[4] The following analysis of closure focuses on whether there are *periods during which specific governing formulas have predominated* across Europe. Two different aspects of closure are investigated:

- *Cabinet composition*: the governing formula in terms of which alliances between party families prevail in Europe (for example, left-wing, centre, right-wing, etc.).[5]
- *Cabinet type*: the governing formula in terms of the size and type of alliance between party families that prevail in Europe (for example, single-party majority or minority cabinet, oversized coalition, etc.).

After the descriptive analysis, it is the task of the explanatory analysis to inform about systematic exclusions of some party families from governing formulas (access to government) or if some party families are favoured under the impact of supra-national factors such as European integration and the end of the Cold War. During different periods of time one or the other type or composition may become institutionalized and consolidated across Europe as a

---

[3] The concept of closure entails three dimensions (Mair, 1996), the first one being alternation (wholesale, partial, or absent), which is related to the analysis of uniform swings in Chapter 4. The other two dimensions are the governing formula (composition in the analysis presented later) and access to government (whether it is open to all parties or from which some are systematically excluded). To these dimensions Mair (2007a) adds the frequency of composition change.

[4] On cabinet politics see Blondel and Cotta (2000), Cheibub (2007), Laver and Schepsle (1990, 1994, 1996), Laver and Schofield (1990), Müller and Strøm (2000), Strøm (1990), and Strøm, Müller, and Bergman (2007).

[5] The classification of cabinets relies on the classification of party families discussed in Chapter 2. It has been modified here with more aggregate combinations of families better adapted to include broad coalitions in the executive.

consequence of varying supra-national factors. Furthermore, this analysis will allow establishing a balance between rather familiar compositions and types versus more innovative formulas. The analysis then goes a step further and includes *contents* aspects, that is the ideological placement of cabinets. The analysis of convergence focuses on the left–right dimension – for the reasons specified in Chapter 6 – and on whether national cabinets have been converging towards similar positions, and under which circumstances such converging patterns have taken place.

Europeanization as Cross-National Policy Convergence

As seen in Chapter 1, Europeanization as convergence of policy programmes results from two types of processes. First, the *top-down, vertical perspective* follows the typical definition of Europeanization in terms of changing national policies and administrative structures under the impact of European integration, namely the formation of a supra-national level of governance, the centralization and integration of policies, and the transfer of legislative competences to the EU.[6] The top-down mechanism of Europeanization refers primarily to an indirect impact *reducing policy alternatives for national parties* – and in particular for executive coalitions – resulting in cross-country convergence. The example of the EMU in particular shows how the EU has an impact on national structures and how this leads to convergence as a result of the narrowing of the policy alternatives for national actors caused, on one hand, by economic and monetary integration (the loss of exchange-rate and interest-rate instruments) and, on the other hand, by the "internalization" of economic imperatives.[7]

The *horizontal transfer perspective* is a second type of process that the literature has identified as a source of cross-national coordination and convergence of policy programmes. Concepts of policy transfer, diffusion, and learning all point to mechanisms by which policies, administrative arrangements, and ideas from other settings are used for policy making. Recently, more specific research has looked at *trans-national transfer among political parties*, especially parties belonging to the same ideological family. Similarly to top-down Europeanization, *diffusion narrows down the spectrum of policy programmes variation*, as work on market ideology and economic liberalism demonstrates. Cross-national convergence is here a consequence of policy transfer, learning, and lesson drawing. This is directly relevant for the process of Europeanization in terms of cross-country convergence and spatial homogenization.[8]

---

[6] Among the longer list of references quoted in Chapter 1, for work on member-states see Knill (2001), while for work on countries outside the EU see Schimmelfennig (2007).

[7] On the EMU in this perspective see Dyson (2002). On convergence see Bennett (1991) and Börzel (1999) and, for a more recent special issue, see Knill (2005). See also Featherstone and Radaelli (2003) and Green Cowles, Caporaso, and Risse (2001).

[8] Specifically on political parties and their policies see Paterson and Sloam (2005) on social democracy in Eastern Europe, and see Sloam (2005a) and Zaborowski (2005). In this regard,

What Chapter 1 has also discussed is research on *trans-national transfers among political parties*, especially parties belonging to the same ideological family. The cross-national coordination and "linkage" between national parties of the same family is a consequence of the top-down effect of the integration of national parties into trans-national federations and parliamentary groups in the EP.[9] Groups and party federations have become more integrated and organized. The forming multi-level party system in Europe thus implies a strong element of coordination, which in turn has a direct impact on the degree of cross-national convergence among parties of the same ideological family.

The more specific hypothesis to be derived from this literature is that supra-national factors, especially European integration, limit policy alternatives, which reduces and directs the governing formulae in Europe with the result of homogenizing them. This hypothesis points to the economic policy impact on the construction of European integration and thus to convergence mainly on the economic policy dimension.

A broader take on converging ideological positions across national systems is the one describing the emergence in most countries of a new cleavage responsible for increasing cross-national similarity. The main contribution from this approach is to consider the impact on national patterns of contestation of the formation of a supra-national level of governance, with a new cleavage imposing itself on the national party systems – namely, a pro- versus anti-European integration cleavage.[10] While leftist parties have long opposed further economic integration because of the fear it would undermine welfare and economic policies, as well as the possibility to conduct monetary policy, they later came to favour political integration as a solution to the loss of policy instruments at the national level.

The general impact of European integration on national party systems is thus one of *transformation of the ideological space* in which a predominant left–right dimension is challenged by a sovereignty dimension between "nationalism" and "supra-nationalism". While, initially, empirical results pointed to a high degree of overlap between the two dimensions (the left side of the axis being more anti-European and the liberal right being more pro-European), with the ideological change of social democrats, the two dimensions became "orthogonal" with the extremes of the left–right axis (the so-called losers of integration and modernization) opposed to integration for either economic or cultural reasons, and to *mainstream parties with executive ambitions being in favour of integration*. In terms of closure this would point to large-scale

recall that Europeanization is not synonymous with convergence, but that convergence can be seen as a *consequence* of Europeanization (Radaelli, 2000: 6).

[9] On Europarties see in particular see Bardi (1992, 1994, 1996, 2002), Hix (1996), and Pedersen (1996).

[10] See the seminal article by Marks and Wilson (2000) and other contributions in its wake (Hooghe and Marks, 2001, in particular chapters 8 and 10; Marks, Wilson, and Ray, 2002; Marks and Steenbergen, 2002; Ray, 1999).

governmental coalitions. Mainstream parties with cabinet aspiration and potential bundle towards similar economic policy positions. This has led some authors to conclude that the left–right dimension is defined mainly in terms of *libertarian versus authoritarian positions*, as well as other *"cultural"* features rather than in terms of economic policy.[11]

It would be limiting, however, to consider EU integration as the only possible source of closure at the coalition level. Factors other than EU integration can have similar cross-country converging effects. A second major juncture taking place simultaneously, and which also had a strong impact on the re-alignment of European cleavage landscapes, consists of the end of communist regimes in Central and Eastern Europe. The re-alignment of the left along pro-European positions occurred following the disappearance of the main alternative to the liberal capitalist democracy promoted by the EU and has freed up space, most notably for the mobilization of the working class by extreme-right populist parties that fed into the opposition to European integration. In this view, the convergence of de-radicalizing left-wing parties towards pro-European integration economic policies is a consequence of the end of the Cold War. This process, too, fed into the *increasing similarity of policy positions of party families with governmental aspirations*, especially on economic-policy issues, independently of who is in power. The literature on dimensions of contestation thus reinforces the hypothesis derived from the literature on Europeanization that convergence among parties with cabinet responsibility results from similar ideological shifts on economic policy.

Data and Method

Data Availability
The analysis of the executive arena relies on two data sources:

- Cabinet *composition*: These data are used to analyze the homogeneity of *cabinet composition* across Europe. Cabinet composition is determined from the parliamentary parties that provide ministers. It excludes cases in which parties provide "external support" – vote bills proposed by the government – but do not participate in it. These data are also used to analyze the homogeneity of the *cabinet type* (whether single party or a type of coalition, as well as whether the party or coalition is a minority or a majority or is "oversized"). The source of data is the ParlGov database (Döring and Manow, 2010).
- Cabinet *placement*: The left–right position of a cabinet is operationalized by using scores on a left–right scale based on party manifestos. This allows the

---

[11] See the literature quoted in Chapter 1 but particularly Kitschelt (1994) and the related research programme on the transformation of national party systems under the impact of globalization (Kriesi et al., 2008 and 2012).

analysis of ideological homogeneity and convergence of executives across Europe. The data sources are the two rounds of the Comparative Manifestos Project (Budge et al., 2001; Klingemann et al., 2006), as well as online updates as in Chapter 6.[12]

Availability for *cabinet composition* data is displayed in Table 7.1 and includes information on which party or coalition is in government. This information is necessary for depicting the cabinet landscape at any particular time. As far as information about the party composition of cabinets is concerned, time series depend on patterns of democratization. For most Western European countries time series start in 1945–6. Cyprus and Malta are included since 1977 and 1962, respectively. Democracy resumed in the mid-1970s for Greece, Portugal, and Spain. Finally, Eastern European countries are included since the breakdown of communism. For all countries information is included until 2010.[13]

Time series are shorter in regard to the information on the *ideological placement of cabinet parties*. This information is necessary to measure the position of cabinets on the left–right dimension and to describe patterns of ideological convergence between national governments. Availability of CMP data is the same as in Chapter 6 (Table 6.1). As it appears, data on placement do not match perfectly the data on composition. Again, many countries are included since democratization or later. For Cyprus and Malta times series are particularly short (and are excluded from some of the analyses). In addition, CMP data are missing for a number of cabinet parties, even if this never concerns major coalition partners. There is only one case of CMP data for a victorious electoral coalition – the PD-PNL coalition in Romania in 2004 – which broke up before forming a cabinet. CMP data do not correspond to the parties in the cabinet in this case. The most important issue is that manifesto data are not available for the Bavarian Christlich-Soziale Union. The placement for this party has been estimated on the basis of the Germany-wide sister party Christlich-Demokratische Union.[14]

---

[12] As for Chapter 6, text data have been preferred to expert surveys because they allow longer time series. For major expert survey projects see references in Chapter 6.

[13] As a general rule, the cabinet existing at the beginning of the calendar year 2010 has been taken, rather than cabinets sworn in after a general election in the first half of 2010. Before separation Czechoslovakia is considered under the label Czech Republic. Because of issues of data quality Latvia in 1991, Lithuania in 1990, Poland in 1989, and Slovenia until 1992 have been excluded.

[14] Additional missing data concern the following parties. Belgium: Communist Party in the 1940s–50s, and Socialist Party and Parti Réformateur Libéral in 2003. Czech Republic: Unie svobody / Demokratická unie in 2002. France: Parti Républicain in 1960s–70s, Mouvement Républicain de Gauche in 1970s–80s, Nouveau Centre in 2007. Germany: Deutsche Partei and Bayernpartei in 1940s–50s. Ireland: Clan na Plobachta, Clann na Talmhan, National League in 1940s–50s. Italy: Centro dei Cristiani Democratici in 1994, Nuovo Partito Socialista in 2001. Latvia: Green Party, Farmers' Union in 1995. Portugal: Partido Popular-Monárquico.

TABLE 7.1. *Cabinet Data Availability by Country*

Country	Cabinet Composition
Austria	1945–2010
Belgium	1946–2010
Bulgaria	1991–2010
Cyprus	1977–2010
Czech Republic	1990–2010
Denmark	1945–2010
Estonia	1992–2010
Finland	1945–2010
France	1945–2010
Germany	1949–2010
Greece	1974–2010
Hungary	1990–2010
Iceland	1946–2010
Ireland	1945–2010
Italy	1946–2010
Latvia	1993–2010
Lithuania	1992–2010
Luxembourg	1945–2010
Malta	1962–2010
Netherlands	1946–2010
Norway	1945–2010
Poland	1991–2010
Portugal	1976–2010
Romania	1990–2010
Slovakia	1990–2010
Slovenia	1997–2010
Spain	1977–2010
Sweden	1945–2010
Switzerland	1947–2010
United Kingdom	1945–2010

Notes: Dates are calendar years. For the availability of CMP data see Table 6.1.

Time Points

The basic time unit of the analysis is the calendar year. The data file has been constructed in a way as to have all necessary information for each year since 1945. As far as party composition is concerned, this means that for the years in which there was no change in government, the information of the previous year applies. CMP data, on the other hand, are available for election years only, that is at the beginning of a legislature period. For all cabinets within the same legislature, the CMP of the election has been taken and copied for all cabinets within that legislature period even if there has been a cabinet change without a general election. Therefore, CMP data may apply to multiple cabinets within the same legislature period. For cases of more than one cabinet during the same year, Appendix 5 explains how they were dealt with.

Operationalization

The analysis is based on two main indicators. The first indicator is the *overall left–right placement of cabinets*. The position on the left–right scale of a cabinet is determined by the position of the parties that compose the cabinet. For example, the placement of a specific cabinet in a given year is derived from the left–right position of the various parties that compose the cabinet.[15] To establish the left–right position of parties CMP data have been used, in particular the aggregate left–right indicator as defined by Budge et al. (2001: 228) and Klingemann et al. (2006: 163), that is the "left_right" or "rile" variable, which varies from −100 (left) to +100 (right) that has also been employed for the analysis in Chapter 6. Also the recodification of the scale into a 1–10 scale follows the same procedure as in the preceding chapter (see Appendix 2 for details).

Based on the cabinet parties' values on this dimension two measures have been defined.

- First, the *average* of the values of the different parties in the coalition (in the case of coalition). In the case of single-party government the placement of the party corresponds to that of the cabinet.
- Second, the *weighted average* based on the size of parties in government. The larger a party, the more weight it should have in the average placement of the cabinet. The share of a specific party has been calculated in terms of *numbers of parliamentary seats of a party, as a percentage of the total number of seats for all cabinet parties*. In this way, the value of cabinet parties with a larger share in cabinet weights more in the overall cabinet left–right position than the value of parties with smaller shares.[16]

For each year, therefore, it is possible to calculate the *degree of spread* (through the standard deviation) of cabinets' left–right position across European countries, and assess the degree to which there have been patterns of convergence over the decades. For reference, Table 7.2 shows the average position of national cabinets for each country over the entire period considered. The number of years varies and for several countries data availability is limited (Slovenia and Malta are such cases, with only seven years covered, but Cyprus and Central-Eastern European countries are also generally below 20 years). There is considerable variation across national governments in terms of cabinets' left–right placement (between the left-most country, Norway, with an average of 3.9 over the entire period from 1945 to the present, and the most right one, Iceland,

---

[15] Cabinets' placement on the left–right scale is, therefore, a *programmatic* one, based on their platforms as expressed in the manifestos, rather than a *policy* one.

[16] In cases of single-party government the two indicators are the same.

TABLE 7.2. *Cabinets' Left–Right Placement on 1–10 Scale by Country (World War II–Present)*

Country	Average	Weighted average	Average number of parties in cabinet	Number of years
Norway	3.8	3.9	1.8	60
Malta	4.0	4.0	1.0	7
Sweden	4.0	4.0	1.6	61
Luxembourg	4.3	4.3	2.1	59
Romania	4.6	4.4	2.2	14
Spain	4.5	4.5	1.0	34
Greece	4.6	4.6	1.1	30
Finland	4.8	4.6	3.8	62
Belgium	4.9	4.8	3.5	57
Netherlands	5.0	4.8	3.2	61
Cyprus	4.8	4.9	1.9	10
France	5.1	4.9	2.8	66
United Kingdom	4.9	4.9	1.0	65
Italy	5.1	5.0	3.4	60
Portugal	5.1	5.0	1.3	33
Slovenia	4.8	5.0	3.6	7
Latvia	5.3	5.1	4.0	13
Austria	5.1	5.1	1.8	54
Bulgaria	5.3	5.1	1.6	18
Denmark	5.1	5.1	2.0	62
Germany	5.2	5.1	2.8	62
Poland	5.2	5.2	2.3	16
Estonia	5.2	5.2	2.6	15
Hungary	5.5	5.2	2.3	16
Ireland	5.2	5.2	1.9	62
Slovakia	5.2	5.3	3.3	16
Czech Republic	5.4	5.3	2.5	16
Switzerland	5.3	5.3	3.9	60
Lithuania	5.6	5.6	2.4	12
Iceland	5.6	5.9	2.3	61

Note: Countries are listed according to the weighted average. Period covered varies according to country from earliest to most recent year for which CMP data are available (see Table 7.1).

with 5.9) and the average number of parties that usually compose a government in the different countries (from 1.0 for Malta to 4.0 for Latvia).

The second indicator is the degree of *homogeneity of cabinets' composition* in terms of parties. The larger the number of national cabinets with the same composition (say, centre-left), the higher the homogeneity. This indicator can be expressed in percentages where 100 per cent for a specific composition

TABLE 7.3. *The Classification of Cabinets*

Cabinet Composition	Cabinet Parties and Alliances	Left–Right Placement		
		Average	Weighted Average	Number of Years / countries
Left	Alliances between socialists and communists or new left	N.a.	N.a.	5
Centre-left	Alliances between socialists, social liberals, greens	4.2	4.2	284
Centre	Alliances between centre-left and centre-right parties	4.7	4.6	159
Centre-right	Alliances between Christian democrats, liberals, conservatives, agrarians	5.4	5.3	455
Right	Alliances between Christian democrats, liberals, conservatives and extreme right-wing parties, radical religious parties, nationalists, neo-populists	5.3	5.2	39
Other	Consociational coalitions, *grosse Koalitionen*, over-sized cabinets of national emergency or with constitutional purposes, as well as technocratic cabinets	4.9	4.9	232

Note: The number of years is equal to the sum of years for all countries.
Legend: N.a. = CMP information not available.

indicates perfect homogeneity (all countries have the same cabinet). Larger percentages indicate greater homogeneity for years.

A related issue is the *classification of cabinets*. Cabinets need to be classified according to their ideological compositions. Cabinets have been classified into six categories as it appears in the first column of Table 7.3. For example, a coalition between socialists and communists is classified as left cabinet, or a coalition between liberals and conservatives as centre-right. To do this, the classification of parties into families discussed in Chapter 2 has been used. Table 7.3 also includes the average and weighted average left–right position. As one can see, there are very few cases of "left" or "right" cabinets.[17] The table also shows that the classification of cabinets is consistent with the left–right

[17] See also Figure 7.5. The five years of "left" in Table 7.3 refer to Cyprus when communists were in government alone. CMP data for these cases are not available.

placement of the parties that compose them as measured through manifesto data, even if "centre-right" coalitions have slightly higher averages on the scale than "right" ones. The coefficients of associations are 0.52 and 0.50 (eta) for the average and the weighted average, respectively.

Cabinets have further been classified into single-party majority cabinets (SPMA), single-party minority cabinets (SPMI), minimum winning coalition cabinets (MWC), minority coalition cabinets (MC), and over-sized coalition cabinets (OC) (see Table 7.6). The classification is based on the number of parties in the cabinets and on the size of their majorities in terms of shares of seats in the legislature, and follows the one used in the *Political Data Yearbook*. This classification allows the analysis of homogeneity across Europe of *types* of governments in power, alongside that of homogenous composition and converging placement.

Converging Coalition and Executive Politics in Europe

This section includes the analysis of the Europeanization of cabinet politics along the two indicators of *placement* and *composition/type* just described. The analysis of the placement of national cabinets over time is presented first, before moving to the question of convergence of policy programmes and the homogeneity of cabinet composition and type across Europe. In a further step this section turns towards the *explanatory analysis* of larger cabinet homogeneity across Europe.

Placement: Policy Programme Positions
Before moving to the central question of this chapter about the convergence of policy programmes and governmental formulae among national cabinets since World War II, Figure 7.1 displays the *overall placement of cabinets* in Europe on the left–right scale operationalized as both the simple average of the position of cabinet parties (solid line) and as the weighted average based on the relative size of coalition partners (dashed line). While the left graph shows a basic stability of Western European cabinets (around 5 on the 1–10 scale), the right graph for Central and Eastern European cabinets since 1990 shows a progressive change from slightly above position 5 towards slightly below position 4.5. When looking more closely at the past 20 years in Western Europe it appears that such a trend towards the left is also taking place in this set of countries.

In Figures 7.2 and 7.3 on Western Europe and Central-Eastern Europe, respectively the information about the position of cabinets is disaggregated for 28 countries. At the same time, this set of graphs begins answering the question about the cross-national convergence of cabinet programmes over time. The upper graph in Figure 7.2 includes countries in which there is a basic stability of cabinet placement since 1945, as well as France and Portugal displaying a trend towards more left-wing positions. The lower graph includes countries in which the trend has been from left towards centre positions. Two

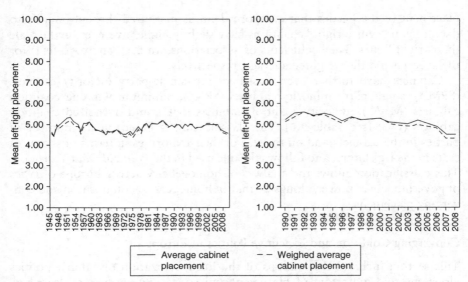

FIGURE 7.1. Left–right placement of European cabinets since 1945 (Western Europe) and 1990 (Central-Eastern Europe).
Note: Annual data points even if not all years appear in the category axis. The last time point considered because of data missing for recent years is 2008.

aspects can be noted regarding the trends for single countries. First, there are neither strong fluctuations over time nor frequent "jumps" between left and right positions (which one would assume when governments change hands). Trends of the countries are progressive. Second, and more important for the purpose of this chapter, the graphs display convergence among countries over the past 60 years. This is especially the case for the countries included in the lower graph in which the convergence seems to be due to a *change from left to centre placement*.

Figure 7.3 on Central and Eastern European countries in particular points to three main aspects. First, in spite of the shorter period of time covered for this group of countries, the curves on the left–right placement of national cabinets are more erratic than for Western Europe. For several countries the range of shifts in placement is considerable. Second, among these countries there appears to be no pattern of convergence over the 15 years considered since the transition to democracy in the wake of 1989. Third, the overall placement of the countries is similar to that of Western European countries.

Let us now turn more directly to the basic question of this chapter, namely whether ideological differences between national cabinets decrease since World War II. As seen previously, the ideological position of cabinets is calculated based on the left–right position of the parties composing the governing coalition. How similar are national cabinets in Europe measured on their left–right

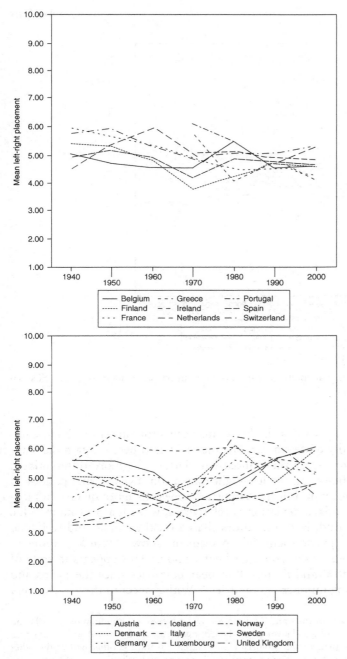

FIGURE 7.2. Left–right placement of cabinets by country since 1945 (Western Europe): Figures by decade.

Note: Cyprus and Malta not included in graphs because of short period of time covered by available data at the moment of the analysis.

Analysis

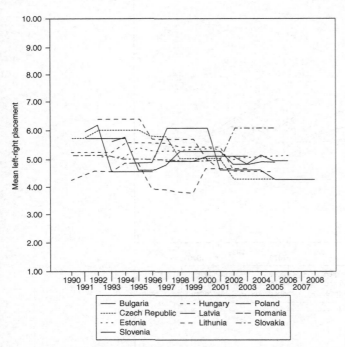

FIGURE 7.3. Left–right placement of cabinets by country since 1990 (Central-Eastern Europe): Annual figures.

placement? Table 7.4 provides the basic answer to this question. First, cabinets seem ideologically quite similar. The measure used here is again the standard deviation.[18] The larger the standard deviation, the more differentiated the placement of cabinets on the left–right dimension. Even during periods in which national cabinets in different countries appear as more diverse in ideological terms, the standard deviation is relatively low with a maximum value of 1.07 or 1.08. Second, both indicators (based on the simple and weighted averages of coalition parties' left–right placement) show a *sizable homogenization among cabinets in the 1990s and early 2000s*. This appears in spite of the inclusion of Central and Eastern European countries since the 1990s and in spite of the growing number of countries.[19] With respect to the 1970s, there

[18] As in Chapter 6, the scale for the standard deviation varies between a minimum of 0.0 (all cabinets on the exact same ideological position on the left–right scale from 1 to 10) and a maximum of approximately 6.36 (half of the cabinets at one extreme 1 and the other half at the other extreme 10) calculated with the minimum number of cases possible, that is two cabinets.

[19] Figures for "Western Europe" and "all countries" are obviously the same for the decades 1940s–80s. The number of countries increases from 20 to 30 with the inclusion of Eastern Europe, as well as Cyprus and Malta in 1996. Greece, Portugal, and Spain are included since the mid-1970s.

TABLE 7.4. *Level of Cabinets' Cross-Country Programmatic Homogeneity on the Left–Right Dimension (CMP Data) by Decade (Standard Deviation)*

Decade	Cross-Country Variation in Left–Right Position (Based on Mean of Coalition Parties)			Cross-Country Variation in Left–Right Position (Based on Weighted Mean of Coalition Parties)			Number of Years for All Countries	Average Number of Countries during Decade
	Western Europe	Central-Eastern Europe	All countries	Western Europe	Central-Eastern Europe	All countries		
1940s	1.04	–	1.04	1.03	–	1.03	61	12.2
1950s	1.01	–	1.01	1.05	–	1.05	150	15.0
1960s	0.95	–	0.95	0.97	–	0.97	150	16.3
1970s	1.08	–	1.08	1.07	–	1.07	163	18.0
1980s	0.91	–	0.91	0.99	–	0.99	180	27.0
1990s	0.80	0.56	0.76	0.82	0.61	0.78	270	27.0
2000s	0.65	0.42	0.59	0.65	0.49	0.60	195	27.7

Notes: Number of countries for each decade for which CMP data are available. The 1940s decade includes the years from 1945 to 1949 (5 years). The 2000s decade includes the years from 2000 to 2010 (11 years) for the years in which data are available. The weighted mean is based on the share of seats (within the coalition) of each coalition party.

FIGURE 7.4. Cross-country differences in cabinets' left–right placement: 1945–present. *Note*: Annual data points even if not all years appear in the category axis. The last time point considered because of data missing for recent years is 2005.

is a 30 per cent (or 28 per cent on the weighted indicator) reduction of the standard deviation in the 1990s and a 45 per cent (or 44 per cent) reduction in the 2000s. That is to say that *diversity in cabinet ideology across Europe has almost halved* between the 1970s and the 2000s. This trend with data by year is depicted in Figure 7.4 showing the steady reduction of cross-country differences in the placement of national cabinets on the left–right scale between the end of the 1980s and the mid-2000s.[20]

The fundamental similarity of programmes of Central and Eastern European cabinet parties with those of Western Europe after 1990 is a particularly interesting result supporting qualitative analyses on the transfer via political parties and their programmes of economic policies (see, for example, the various contributions published in a special issue of the *Journal of Communist Studies and Transition Politics* in 2005) coupled with the strong will on the part of the newly elected elites to anchor the democracies in Central and Eastern Europe to the EU as reflected in the adoption of compatible constitutions, human right

---

[20] After this point the quality of the CMP data available at the moment of the analysis deteriorates with the number of countries diminishing. The resurgence of differences in 2005 should be taken with caution.

standards, and most of the *aquis communautaire* as pointed out by the conditionality literature reviewed in Chapter 1 and mentioned at the beginning of this chapter.

At the Origin of Convergence: Cabinet Composition and Family Similarity

To explain the convergence between parties with government responsibility in national cabinets over time, what follows relies on two main hypotheses. The first one is that programmatic convergence in certain years is due to the fact that countries have similar cabinet compositions. For example, according to the dimensions of closure, one would expect little ideological diversity in Europe if most countries had centre-right governments at the same time. One can call this the *same-composition hypothesis*: the less fragmentation across Europe in cabinet composition, the more ideological homogeneity across national cabinets. A second (alternative) hypothesis is that programmatic convergence is due to the fact that parties from different families have ideologies and programmes that are increasingly similar. Composition does not play any role here as parties from different families (left, centre-left, etc.) are ideologically similar. One can call this the *family-similarity hypothesis*: the less ideological diversity across party families with governmental responsibility, the more ideological homogeneity across national cabinets.

Let us first analyze composition and type of cabinet, as well as the ideological distance between families. Concerning the degree of homogeneity of composition and type of cabinets, evidence is based on the share (percentages) of countries with similar cabinets (incumbent parties) according to the classification outlined earlier. From Table 7.5 on *cabinet composition* it appears clearly that two types of *cabinet composition* are predominant in Europe: centre-left and centre-right cabinets. In almost half (about 45 per cent) of the cumulative years, European countries had either centre-left or centre-right cabinets. It also appears that purely left or right cabinets are rare (with the exception of Cyprus, where left cabinets have existed for some years, and Latvia and Slovakia, where right cabinets have been quite frequent). As for great coalitions, oversized coalitions, technocratic cabinets with large majorities in parliament, and so on, the typical consociational cases stand out, in particular Switzerland, where 93.8 per cent of the time such large coalitions have taken place since 1945, but also Austria, Luxembourg, Belgium, and the Netherlands (the "other" category in Table 7.5).

The pattern about a number of countries with large consociational coalitions is confirmed by looking at Table 7.6 on the *type of cabinets*: oversized coalitions (OC) occur especially in the five countries listed earlier. What also appears from this table is that the large majority of cabinets in Europe since 1945 have been the minimum winning coalition (MWC) type 41.8 per cent of the time across the whole of Europe. Single-party majority (SPMA) is rather the exception, and the United Kingdom (with Malta and Greece) really stands out as the only country in which this type of cabinet is predominant. In some

TABLE 7.5. *Cabinet Composition by Country 1945–2010 (Percentages)*

Country	Left	Centre-left	Centre	Centre-right	Right	Other	Total
Austria	0.0 (0)	19.7 (13)	6.1 (4)	6.1 (4)	10.6 (7)	57.6 (38)	100.0 (66)
Belgium	0.0 (0)	1.5 (1)	18.5 (12)	30.8 (20)	0.0 (0)	49.2 (32)	100.0 (65)
Bulgaria	0.0 (0)	10.0 (2)	20.0 (4)	70.0 (14)	0.0 (0)	0.0 (0)	100.0 (20)
Cyprus	14.7 (5)	23.5 (8)	14.7 (5)	47.1 (16)	0.0 (0)	0.0 (0)	100.0 (34)
Czech Republic	0.0 (0)	19.0 (4)	0.0 (0)	61.9 (13)	0.0 (0)	19.0 (4)	100.0 (21)
Denmark	0.0 (0)	39.4 (26)	13.6 (9)	47.0 (31)	0.0 (0)	0.0 (0)	100.0 (66)
Estonia	0.0 (0)	15.8 (3)	21.1 (4)	63.2 (12)	0.0 (0)	0.0 (0)	100.0 (19)
Finland	0.0 (0)	6.1 (4)	42.4 (28)	22.7 (15)	0.0 (0)	28.8 (19)	100.0 (66)
France	0.0 (0)	19.7 (13)	9.1 (6)	63.6 (42)	0.0 (0)	7.6 (5)	100.0 (66)
Germany	0.0 (0)	11.3 (7)	21.0 (13)	56.5 (35)	0.0 (0)	11.3 (7)	100.0 (62)
Greece	0.0 (0)	56.8 (21)	0.0 (0)	40.5 (15)	0.0 (0)	2.7 (1)	100.0 (37)
Hungary	0.0 (0)	9.5 (2)	47.6 (10)	38.1 (8)	4.8 (1)	0.0 (0)	100.0 (21)
Iceland	0.0 (0)	20.0 (13)	0.0 (0)	41.5 (27)	0.0 (0)	38.5 (25)	100.0 (65)
Ireland	0.0 (0)	0.0 (0)	28.8 (19)	69.7 (46)	0.0 (0)	1.5 (1)	100.0 (66)
Italy	0.0 (0)	10.8 (7)	35.4 (23)	36.9 (24)	15.4 (10)	1.5 (1)	100.0 (65)
Latvia	0.0 (0)	0.0 (0)	0.0 (0)	27.8 (5)	72.2 (13)	0.0 (0)	100.0 (18)
Lithuania	0.0 (0)	31.6 (6)	47.4 (9)	21.1 (4)	0.0 (0)	0.0 (0)	100.0 (19)
Luxembourg	0.0 (0)	0.0 (0)	7.6 (5)	36.4 (24)	0.0 (0)	56.1 (37)	100.0 (66)
Malta	0.0 (0)	36.7 (18)	0.0 (0)	63.3 (31)	0.0 (0)	0.0 (0)	100.0 (49)
Netherlands	0.0 (0)	0.0 (0)	12.3 (8)	26.2 (17)	21.5 (14)	40.0 (26)	100.0 (65)
Norway	0.0 (0)	69.7 (46)	0.0 (0)	30.3 (20)	0.0 (0)	0.0 (0)	100.0 (66)
Poland	0.0 (0)	20.0 (4)	20.0 (4)	55.0 (11)	5.0 (1)	0.0 (0)	100.0 (20)
Portugal	0.0 (0)	45.7 (16)	0.0 (0)	48.6 (17)	0.0 (0)	5.7 (2)	100.0 (35)
Romania	0.0 (0)	30.0 (6)	35.0 (7)	25.0 (5)	0.0 (0)	10.0 (2)	100.0 (20)
Slovakia	0.0 (0)	19.0 (4)	0.0 (0)	33.3 (7)	47.6 (10)	0.0 (0)	100.0 (21)
Slovenia	0.0 (0)	21.4 (3)	28.6 (4)	50.0 (7)	0.0 (0)	0.0 (0)	100.0 (14)
Spain	0.0 (0)	61.8 (21)	0.0 (0)	38.2 (13)	0.0 (0)	0.0 (0)	100.0 (34)
Sweden	0.0 (0)	69.7 (46)	9.1 (6)	21.2 (14)	0.0 (0)	0.0 (0)	100.0 (66)
Switzerland	0.0 (0)	0.0 (0)	0.0 (0)	6.3 (4)	0.0 (0)	93.8 (60)	100.0 (64)
United Kingdom	0.0 (0)	45.5 (30)	0.0 (0)	54.5 (36)	0.0 (0)	0.0 (0)	100.0 (66)
Overall	0.4 (5)	23.8 (324)	13.2 (180)	39.4 (537)	4.1 (56)	19.1 (260)	100.0 (1,362)

Note: In parenthesis the number of years/countries. The four years during which a different type of cabinet existed in Switzerland are the years from 1955 until the 1959 election, during which the socialists were not part of the coalition.

countries, finally, the dominant type of cabinet is the minority one, either single party (SPMI) or coalition (MC), in particular in Denmark and Sweden, but also in Spain (for a shorter period of time).

Figure 7.5 displays the composition of cabinets in terms of which family is in power across Europe from 1945 to 2010. Looking at the evolution tells us first

TABLE 7.6. *Type of Cabinet by Country 1945–2010 (Percentages)*

Country	SPMA: Single-Party Majority	SPMI: Single-Party Minority	MWC: Minimum Winning Coalition	MC: Minority Coalition	OC: Oversized Coalition	Total
Austria	24.2 (16)	1.5 (1)	16.7 (11)	0.0 (0)	57.6 (38)	100.0 (66)
Belgium	6.2 (4)	0.0 (0)	44.6 (29)	0.0 (0)	49.2 (32)	100.0 (65)
Bulgaria	30.0 (6)	30.0 (6)	40.0 (8)	0.0 (0)	0.0 (0)	100.0 (20)
Cyprus	17.6 (6)	29.4 (10)	52.9 (18)	0.0 (0)	0.0 (0)	100.0 (34)
Czech Republic	0.0 (0)	23.8 (5)	76.2 (16)	0.0 (0)	0.0 (0)	100.0 (21)
Denmark	0.0 (0)	34.8 (23)	9.1 (6)	56.1 (37)	0.0 (0)	100.0 (66)
Estonia	0.0 (0)	15.8 (3)	84.2 (16)	0.0 (0)	0.0 (0)	100.0 (19)
Finland	0.0 (0)	4.5 (3)	57.6 (38)	7.6 (5)	30.3 (20)	100.0 (66)
France	0.0 (0)	4.5 (3)	68.2 (45)	3.0 (2)	24.2 (16)	100.0 (66)
Germany	0.0 (0)	0.0 (0)	83.9 (52)	4.8 (3)	11.3 (7)	100.0 (62)
Greece	97.3 (36)	0.0 (0)	0.0 (0)	0.0 (0)	2.7 (1)	100.0 (37)
Hungary	9.5 (2)	0.0 (0)	90.5 (19)	0.0 (0)	0.0 (0)	100.0 (21)
Iceland	0.0 (0)	4.6 (3)	87.7 (57)	0.0 (0)	7.7 (5)	100.0 (65)
Ireland	28.8 (19)	13.6 (9)	51.5 (34)	6.1 (4)	0.0 (0)	100.0 (66)
Italy	0.0 (0)	13.8 (9)	72.3 (47)	12.3 (8)	1.5 (1)	100.0 (65)
Latvia	0.0 (0)	5.6 (1)	72.2 (13)	22.2 (4)	0.0 (0)	100.0 (18)
Lithuania	21.1 (4)	0.0 (0)	26.3 (5)	31.6 (6)	21.1 (4)	100.0 (19)
Luxembourg	0.0 (0)	0.0 (0)	43.9 (29)	0.0 (0)	56.1 (37)	100.0 (66)
Malta	100.0 (49)	0.0 (0)	0.0 (0)	0.0 (0)	0.0 (0)	100.0 (49)
Netherlands	0.0 (0)	0.0 (0)	56.9 (37)	3.1 (2)	40.0 (26)	100.0 (65)
Norway	24.2 (16)	39.4 (26)	24.2 (16)	12.1 (8)	0.0 (0)	100.0 (66)
Poland	0.0 (0)	10.0 (2)	75.0 (15)	15.0 (3)	0.0 (0)	100.0 (20)
Portugal	42.9 (15)	34.3 (12)	17.1 (6)	0.0 (0)	5.7 (2)	100.0 (35)
Romania	4.8 (1)	28.6 (6)	14.3 (3)	47.6 (10)	4.8 (1)	100.0 (21)
Slovakia	0.0 (0)	0.0 (0)	100.0 (21)	0.0 (0)	0.0 (0)	100.0 (21)
Slovenia	0.0 (0)	0.0 (0)	100.0 (14)	0.0 (0)	0.0 (0)	100.0 (14)
Spain	44.1 (15)	55.9 (19)	0.0 (0)	0.0 (0)	0.0 (0)	100.0 (34)
Sweden	7.6 (5)	63.6 (42)	15.2 (10)	13.6 (9)	0.0 (0)	100.0 (66)
Switzerland	0.0 (0)	0.0 (0)	6.3 (4)	0.0 (0)	93.8 (60)	100.0 (64)
United Kingdom	92.4 (61)	6.1 (4)	1.5 (1)	0.0 (0)	0.0 (0)	100.0 (66)
Overall	18.7 (255)	13.7 (187)	41.8 (470)	7.4 (101)	18.3 (250)	100.0 (1,363)

Note: In parenthesis the number of years.

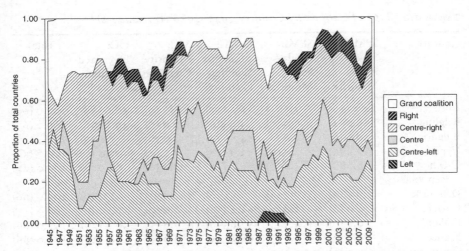

FIGURE 7.5. Proportion of countries by ideological composition of cabinets (1945–2010).
Note: Annual data points even if not all years appear in the category axis.

of all if there are periods during which a certain composition of cabinets has dominated in Europe. For example, observers have often claimed that the 1980s were a time of neo-liberal and conservative governments in Europe as well as elsewhere. Second, the pattern over time tells us if the fragmentation in composition across Europe decreases over time, which would be a sign of increasing homogeneity in who is in power. Over time it is hard to detect clear trends towards a less fragmented picture, nor does it seem possible to identify periods of clear predominance of one composition over the others. One notes that the share of great coalitions and consociational governments slightly decreases over time and that there is a surge of right-wing cabinets associated with the inclusion of Central and Eastern European countries. However, based on this figure it is impossible to conclude that there have been phases in which one ideology predominated in Europe. There is no Europeanization in this sense over time.[21]

The first hypothesis formulated earlier is that convergence may be due to the fact that countries have the same parties in power (*same-composition*). Figure 7.5 indicates that this is not the case, but one needs to test the hypothesis quantitatively. To this end, an indicator of the degree of homogeneity of composition has been created for every year in the data set based on Rae's fractionalization index (see Appendix 3).[22] The lower the index, the more uniform

---

[21] The same conclusion applies to the type of cabinets. The equivalent figure on the European pattern of the type of cabinet has not been reproduced in this chapter. For reasons of space also the tables with the data over decades have not been included.

[22] For each year the share of left, centre-left, centre, centre-right, right, and other compositions has been calculated (as in Figure 7.5). These shares have been squared and then added together. This

the composition landscape in Europe. A strong correlation between low fragmentation of composition and programmatic convergence between national cabinets would be an indication that convergence is due to the fact that the same parties are in power in a large number of countries.[23]

The correlation coefficient between these two variables (Table 7.7) is negative (Pearson's $r = -0.429^{**}$), meaning that the lower the fragmentation of composition, the higher the standard deviation measuring programmatic convergence (conversely, the lower the programmatic convergence). This runs opposite the hypothesis, and means that programmatic convergence, in fact, increases as the composition of cabinets in Europe is more diverse. The relationship is depicted in the upper graph in Figure 7.6, where it becomes clear that programmatic homogeneity is higher when different parties are in power in the various European countries. The more fragmented the composition of party families (i.e. great diversity of who is in power in the different European countries), the lower the standard deviation (i.e. the more programmatic convergence there is across cabinets). This points to the result that convergence cannot be due to the fact that the same parties are in power everywhere at the same time. Based on these results one can reject the "same-composition hypothesis".

As seen earlier, the alternative hypothesis is that, independently of who is in government, ideological similarity between party families is at the origin of the large convergence between cabinets in the past two decades (*family-similarity*). To operationalize the degree of similarity between party families the range between the most left-wing family and the most right-wing family has been calculated on the 1–10 scale for each year.[24] If this hypothesis were true, one would expect that the lower the range between families, the lower the standard deviation measuring the degree of programmatic homogeneity between national cabinets across European countries.

The strength of the positive correlation between ideological distance between families and programmatic diversity between national cabinets appears in the second row of Table 7.7 (Pearson's $r = 0.608^{**}$) as well as in the second graph in Figure 7.6. The strong correlation means that the lower the

---

figure has then been subtracted from 1 to obtain an index varying between 0 (no fragmentation whatsoever; all countries have the same government) to a maximum of 1.

[23] As before, programmatic convergence is measured each year through the standard deviation of the placement of national cabinets on the left–right scale from 1 to 10. The weighted measure has been used taking the average of cabinet parties weighted by their share of seats within the coalition.

[24] Note that only families with cabinet responsibility have been considered here. It should also be stressed that, to measure most left-wing or most right-wing positions, the *empirical* measurement has been used. It is not always the case that right-wing cabinets are actually those placed most right when measured through CMP data. Often "centre" cabinets are placed more to the right than centre-right cabinets. Finally, to compute the range the placement of party families has *not* been weighted by the share of seats within the cabinet. In this case the size of party families does not matter.

TABLE 7.7. *Correlation Coefficients Between Indicators and Level of Programmatic Homogeneity across National Cabinets (Standard Deviation)*

Indicators	Pearson's *r*	Mean placement (entire period)	Difference with overall mean of 4.88
Cross-country fragmentation in the composition (party families) of cabinets (Rae fragmentation index)	−0.429**	N.a.	N.a.
Range between ideological placement of most left and most right cabinet composition (1–10 scale)	0.608**	N.a.	N.a.
Left-right placement of centre-left cabinet coalitions (1–10 scale)	−0.623**	4.03	0.85
Left-right placement of centre-right cabinet coalitions (1–10 scale)	0.474**	5.28	0.40
Left-right placement of centre cabinet coalitions (1–10 scale)	0.080	4.66	0.22
Left-right placement of great coalitions and consociational cabinets (1–10 scale)	−0.223	4.95	0.07

Notes: The number of cases (years) is 66.
Statistical significance ** ($p < 0.01$).

range between the placement of the most left-wing and most right-wing party families, the lower the standard deviation measuring the programmatic convergence between national cabinets across Europe. This points to the fact that territorial convergence is due to the increasing ideological similarity between families (especially, as it appears, when they have government responsibility). These results support the "family-similarity hypothesis".

To investigate further the relationship between family similarity and cross-country convergence, Figure 7.7 displays the temporal trend of the left–right placement of the five compositions of government distinguished earlier. What appears clearly is first of all the *strong convergence on the 1–10 scale in the 1990s*. Different compositions of government based on different party families are extremely close together during this decade. What appears in the second place is the clear trend towards *de-radicalization or moderation of the centre-left cabinets and of the large social-democratic parties* that make up most of this composition. From the early 1970s the position of centre-left cabinets converges towards the centre of the left–right axis with a placement that basically overlaps with those of centre and centre-right governments in

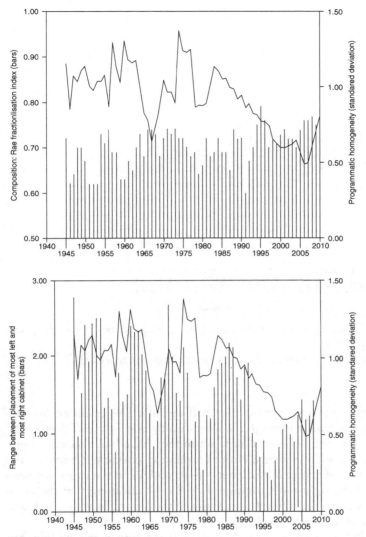

FIGURE 7.6. Relationship between programmatic convergence across Europe over time and (1) fractionalization and (2) range.

Note: Annual data points even if not all years appear in the category axis.

the 1990s. No other cabinet composition displays such a clear trend over the six decades covered. Are the social democrats responsible for the overall convergence among cabinets in Europe?

A provisional answer is yes: indeed, social democrats seem to be the cause of the reduction of the ideological spread (measured on the left–right axis) among

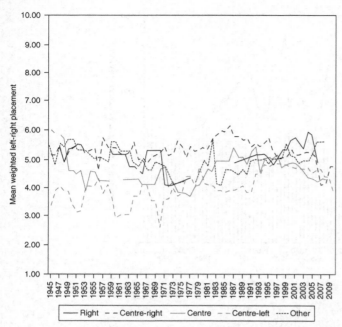

FIGURE 7.7. Ideological convergence between cabinet compositions: left–right placement (weighted indicator).

Note: Annual data points even if not all years appear in the category axis.

national cabinets in Europe over the past half-century. This result points to a *process of Europeanization through the de-radicalization of social democratic parties*, especially during periods of time when they have had executive functions. In support of such evidence is the correlation coefficient between the left–right placement of centre-left cabinets (1–10 scale) and the range between the left-most and the right-most cabinet of –0.861**, meaning that the more centre-left parties converge towards the centre of the left–right scale, the lower the ideological spread across families.

Table 7.7 includes a number of indicators that strengthen this finding, but also complement it with additional information. First, we see the strong effect of the left–right placement of centre-left cabinets on the overall ideological homogeneity across national cabinets (–0.623**), meaning that the more social democrats go towards the centre (higher scores on the 1–10 scale), the lower the ideological diversity across national cabinets (measured with the weighted standard deviation). Second, however, it also appears that a significant effect on the reduction of ideological diversity in Europe's executives is displayed by the placement of centre-right cabinets (0.474**). This means that there is a *correlation between lower scores on the left–right scale for centre-right*

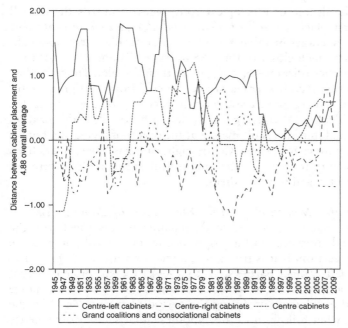

FIGURE 7.8. Distance between left–right placement of party families and overall mean on the 1–10 scale for the entire period (1945–2010).
Note: Annual data points even if not all years appear in the category axis.

cabinets (therefore towards the centre of the axis) *and smaller ideological diversity among cabinets in Europe*. This finding shows that the homogenization of executive politics in Europe is not only a story of de-radicalizing social democrats, but also one of centripetal shift of centre-right parties. The effect is weaker compared to that of the placement of the centre-left cabinets. Finally, the last two figures for centre cabinets, and for great coalitions or consociational governments, report that the placement of these two groups of party families does not have an effect on the Europeanization of executive politics in terms of converging policy programmes (correlation coefficients of 0.080 and −0.223, respectively).

Such results indicate the effect of converging ideological placements between party families (those who compose centre-left and centre-right cabinets in particular) on the level of programme homogeneity across European executives. *This homogenization is the result of converging ideologies rather than similarity of who is in power at the same moment*. Figure 7.8 depicts the distance between the overall mean of placement of all cabinets for the entire period (equal to the position 4.88 on the 1–10 scale) and the annual placement of each cabinet composition (left, centre-left, centre, etc.). Visually, it appears quite clearly that the degree of ideological convergence towards the overall average is in the first place a *result of ideological change among centre-left party families*.[25] The averages in Table 7.7 show that, overall, centre-right cabinet parties have been much closer to the 4.88 average (distance of 0.40) than centre-left cabinet parties (distance of 0.85, more than double). The two compositions closest to the overall average are centre coalitions and great coalitions (with average distances of 0.22 and 0.07, respectively, on the 1–10 scale). This confirms that ideological convergence is driven by the de-radicalization of left-wing parties and that this is ultimately at the origin of increasing homogeneity in executive politics in Europe. Centre-right cabinets have always been more towards the centre (except for the mid-1980s) and it is the centre-left cabinets that have converged towards them.

Ideological Change after Maastricht and the Breakdown of Communism

The last part of the analysis presented in this chapter is concerned with the empirical test of the hypothesis on the origin of the ideological convergence seen in the previous section. If it is true that cabinet convergence is primarily the effect of centre-left cabinet parties and, to a lesser extent, of centre-right ones, it remains to be seen under which circumstances this ideological change has taken place and at what point during the period of time covered by the analysis. To do this, what follows uses the hypothesis that such a convergence has taken place through the Europeanization of economic and monetary policy in concomitance with two Europe-wide junctures.

First, the *Maastricht criteria* on inflation, interest rates, and deficit together with the transfer of competences in economic policy through the *European Monetary Union* for many countries have deprived national governments of most options in economic policies, thus reducing variety across Europe. The Maastricht Treaty has significantly constrained the margin for action on the part of national governments which transferred most competences previously in the hands of national governments in matters of economic and monetary policies to the European Union (inflation, interest rates, exchange rates, etc.), requiring much stronger-cross country coordination. Second, the ideological change follows the *end of communism in Central and Eastern Europe* as a viable alternative of economic policy (state ownership of infrastructures and industries, planned economies, etc.), with strong effects on the platform of socialist and social-democratic parties in the western part of Europe. The breakdown of communist regimes in Central and Eastern Europe has reduced

[25] Figure 7.8 and the coefficients in Table 7.7 are based on the deviation of the left–right placement of each family and the overall mean for the entire period (position 4.88 on the 1–10 scale). Results do not change if instead of the overall mean the mean for each year is taken. In Figure 7.8 centre-left cabinets appear on the upper half of the graph as their left–right position (usually below the mean of all cabinets) has been subtracted from the mean of 4.88 resulting in a positive figure.

the ideological spectrum on the left–right dimension in particular on its left side, and reduced alternatives in economic policy with claims about the policy convergence on liberalization and privatization, as well as calls for the reduction of state intervention in the economy.

While such a hypothesis is frequently mentioned, empirical evidence has never supported it. It is this gap that this section aims at closing. The "watershed" represented by Maastricht and the end of communism is operationalized through the date of 1992. At the same time, the analysis summarized in the regression in Table 7.8 allows us to strengthen results from the previous section by testing the impact of ideological convergence of centre-left and centre-right cabinet parties controlling for such a change over time. The baseline model in Table 7.8 includes the variables analyzed earlier.[26] The regression model confirms the lack of impact of the degree of similarity of national cabinets during the same year (operationalized with Rae's index of fractionalization). Also the position of centre cabinets and of great-coalition and consociational cabinets does not produce significant results, confirming the correlation coefficients seen earlier. The model displays a strong collinearity between the position of centre-left parties and the ideological range, meaning that the scope of the range in a national political system is affected by the position of left-wing parties.[27]

In the second model, the variable "range" has been removed. As a result, the effect of the position of centre-left parties becomes clear and highly significant (the beta, not reported in the table, is −0.514). This effect is higher than the one for centre-right parties which appears as slightly less significant and less strong. Also, any sign of collinearity between the independent variables disappears from the model. Finally, one sees again that the position of centre cabinets or great coalitions has no impact on the degree of programmatic homogeneity of cabinets across Europe. For this reason the third model excludes these two variables.

At the same time the variable about the junctures of Maastricht and breakdown of communism is introduced in the form of a dummy variable (time before 1992 and time after 1992). The effect of this variable is very strong and, as can be seen in Table 7.8, also significant (the beta coefficient is −0.501). Interestingly, we see that while introducing this variable alters only marginally the effect of the position of centre-right parties (0.165** as opposed to 0.187** in the second model), it affects strongly the effect of the position of centre-left parties (−0.111* as opposed to −0.217*** in the second model with

---

[26] Although from the graphs it is clear that the stationarity assumption is violated (mean and variance are not constant across different sub-sets of cases), a time series estimation has not been used insofar as there is no auto-regressive component in the dependent variable (its value at time t is not a function of its value at $t-1$, $t-2$, etc., even if the test for the partial autocorrelation function indicates that a first-order effect exists). Furthermore, there are no lagged effects of other variables on the dependent variable in the model.

[27] The correlation coefficient between the two variables is very high, as seen earlier (−0.861**).

TABLE 7.8. Regression Analysis: Programmatic Convergence and Left-Right Placement of Cabinet Compositions

Variables	Entire period				Before 1992	After 1992	Entire period
	(1) Baseline	(2)	(3)	(4)	(5)	(6)	(7)
Cross-country fragmentation in the composition of cabinets (Rae index)	-0.942 (0.501)	-0.899 (0.493)					
Range between most left and right cabinet composition (1–10 scale)	0.041 (0.069)						
Left-right placement of centre-left cabinet coalitions (1–10 scale)	-0.176* (0.079)	-0.217*** (0.039)	-0.111* (0.044)	-0.239*** (0.036)	-0.100 (0.051)	-0.223 (0.107)	
Left-right placement of centre-right cabinet coalitions (1–10 scale)	0.174** (0.065)	0.187** (0.061)	0.165** (0.047)	0.229*** (0.050)	0.169* (0.067)	0.183** (0.058)	
Left-right placement of centre cabinet coalitions (1–10 scale)	-0.020 (0.040)	-0.015 (0.038)					
Left-right placement of great coalitions and consociational cabinets (1–10 scale)	-0.055 (0.050)	-0.050 (0.049)					
Dummy variable for period before 1992 and after 1992			-0.218*** (0.051)				

	(1)	(2)	(3)	(4)	(5)	(6)	(7)
Left-right placement of centre-left cabinet coalitions on *cultural* dimension (1–10 scale)							−0.090*** (0.015)
Left-right placement of centre-left cabinet coalitions on *economic* dimension (1–10 scale)							−0.076 (0.032)
Left-right placement of centre-right cabinet coalitions on *cultural* dimension (1–10 scale)							0.050** (0.017)
Left-right placement of centre-right cabinet coalitions on *economic* dimension (1–10 scale)							0.038* (0.015)
Constant	1.681	1.758	0.566	0.683	0.499	0.770	0.908
Adj. R^2	0.529	0.534	0.644	0.526	0.146	0.327	0.641
N	66	66	66	66	47	19	62

Notes: Unstandardized regression coefficients shown with standard errors in parentheses. Collinearity above VIF = 5.0 indicated in italics. The dependent variable is the standard deviation of the weighted mean left–right placement of cabinet parties across national executives for every year from 1945 to 2010 (1–10 scale). The coding for the dummy variable before/after 1992 is before = 0 and after = 1. Estimation: OLS. Statistical significance *** ($p < 0.001$), ** ($p < 0.01$), * ($p < 0.05$) in two-tailed test.

a loss of significance). This suggests indeed that *the ideological change across the juncture has predominantly taken place on the left* and that the effect of the juncture on the *overall degree of programmatic homogeneity among European cabinets has been mediated by the converging pattern of centre-left parties in the first place.*[28]

It seems at this moment that centre-left parties have converged towards more liberal economic platforms.[29] The fact that the effect of centre-left parties re-emerges significantly and stronger than for centre-right parties (and with smaller standard error) as soon as the dummy variable before/after 1992 is removed (fourth model) confirms that the effect of the shift towards more "centre" positions of centre-left parties on economic matters on one hand and the time point 1992 are related. This is confirmed in the models produced for each of the two periods of time. The fifth and sixth models have been run with just two variables for the periods 1945–91 and 1992–2010, respectively. It appears clearly that *within* these two periods of time the effect of the two variables is highly reduced (with adjusted R^2 of only 0.146 for the first period and 0.327 for the second). This strengthens the previous result that programmatic convergence is due to ideological changes that take place *across* these two periods of time.

Yet to gain a more precise picture it is necessary to run an analysis of the nature of the shift by social democrats. While Europeanization in terms of cross-country policy coordination and reduction of alternatives in economic policy refers to an *economic* type of convergence on the left–right dimension (socialist vs. liberal policies), evidence of left–right disaggregated for the economic and cultural dimensions shows a different picture.[30] Figure 7.9 is very explicit in showing that *while on the economic dimension the shift across the "watershed" is sudden but not permanent* (centre-left cabinets revert to more left-wing positions in the mid-1990s), *on the cultural dimension it is more permanent* – in line with what is depicted for the socialist family in Figure 6.10 in the previous chapter. The long-term centripetal move of social democrats seems *more a cultural type of ideological shift* than an economic type, supporting theories of *changing patterns of domestic politics competition* rather than Europeanization theories in terms of adaptation to constraints by European integration. The additional variables included in model 7 in the regression table above confirm the stronger impact of cultural elements in the convergence of centre-left parties (the betas, not shown in the table, are –0.631 for the cultural

[28] The negative sign before the coefficients indicates that the effect of the period post-juncture (coded 1) has a negative effect on the programmatic spread (measured with the standard deviation among national values of the weighted cabinet average on the 1–10 scale).

[29] Note that there is a slight appearance of collinearity for the dummy variable and the position of centre-left parties (VIF of 2.094 and 1.908, respectively) due to its correlation with the programmatic change of centre-right cabinet parties.

[30] The construction of the cultural and economic dimension is described in Appendix 2 (see also Chapter 6).

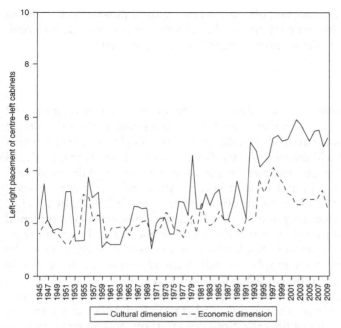

FIGURE 7.9. Left–right placement of centre-left cabinet parties on the cultural and economic dimensions.

dimension against –0.251 for the economic dimension) compared to economic elements of policy adaptation.[31]

This additional result complements the finding about cross-country policy homogeneity due to Europeanization, the constraints on domestic economic policies, and the limitation of policy alternatives through economic integration. It shows that convergence is also and, in the long term, foremost taking place on the cultural dimension of the left–right axis. First, from both Figure 7.9 and the regression table one sees that *the shift towards the right on the part of centre-left parties is primarily taking place on the cultural dimension.* Second, one also sees that on *the economic dimension after a converging pattern around 1992 centre-left parties revert to more left-wing positions.* Both patterns seem to point to a concern of social democrats to respond to the challenge right-wing populist parties posed in the mobilization of a specific electoral constituency on issues of national protection, law and order, multi-culturalism, and authoritarianism. While the literature on Europeanization stresses the convergence of cabinet policy positions on economic matters (and in particular *liberal* economic policies), these results point to a more important element of convergence

---

[31] The dummy for before/after 1992 has been excluded here because of collinearity with the variable measuring the left–right position of centre-left parties on the cultural dimension.

based on national retrenchment, not only on the cultural dimension but also in terms of protecting domestic labour markets, as the return towards economically more left-wing positions appearing in Figure 7.9 suggests.

Conclusion

Evidence broadly points to the relationship between social democracy and European integration, in particular during the crucial phase of the reshaping of the national–EU balance around the adoption of the Single European Act first and, subsequently, the Maastricht Treaty. Results also indicate that ideological and programmatic change took place less so following the breakdown of communist regimes in Central and Eastern Europe when the open liberal market economy project of the EU came to dominate and was left without a major alternative. Social democracy – a historical party family with governmental vocation – initially converges towards the centre of the left–right axis in these years, thus producing a fundamental homogeneity in cabinet politics across the continent. The curves in the graphs, as well as the regression analysis, clearly identify 1989–92 as the moment when this shift takes place.

From this perspective, the relationship between the left and European integration, in fact, is not simply the relationship between social democracy and the market economy, policies of liberalization, privatization, and de-regulation, as well as the dismissal of the main instruments of economic and monetary policies such as inflation, currency, and interest rates, on which the entire European project rests. It is also, as demonstrated by the impact of the cultural dimension of the change, the relationship between social democracy and free people's movement, immigration, open borders, and integrated labour competition.[32]

Centre and right-wing parties have played a lesser role in the homogenization of governmental programmes in Europe. Europe was mainly their project and did not require the same degree of policy adaptation in the crucial years of integration. Furthermore, these party families were not affected by the end of communism. The end of international ideological confrontation during the Cold War and the end of strong foreign policy divergence between European countries affected the left, not the right.[33]

The long-term analysis presented in this chapter rather points to policy position convergence among national cabinets in which the centripetal move from left to centre-of-left coalitions plays a crucial role, a finding that supports the

---

[32] This evolution of social democratic parties was first analyzed by Marks and Wilson (2000). As Dimitrakopoulos notes in reference to social democrats, "European integration was, to a large extent, the product of their domestic political rivals" (2011: 2). On de-regulation and privatization policies in Britain and the United States see Pierson (1994).

[33] The main contribution of the volume edited by Dimitrakopoulos (2011) focuses on the explanation of cross-country differences in the relationship between national social democratic parties and European integration.

"family-similarity hypothesis" and rejects the "same-composition hypothesis". On the other hand, such an interpretation lacks, first, other elements of convergence of centre-left parties, namely on the cultural dimension, and second, what happens *after* the "watershed". In interpreting this result the top-down view of Europeanization contributions stressing the impact on positions of the narrowing down of policy alternatives due to supra-national integration and the end of communism is probably not sufficient.

The distinction between cultural and economic left–right dimensions of the centre-left centripetal convergence shows that competitive *concerns of electoral mobilization* raised by what the literature has identified as the populist challenge also seem to play a strong role. Centre-left convergence since the 1990s is, in the long term, primarily cultural. Convergence among cabinet parties takes place through the re-positioning of social-democrats towards more right-wing positions on issues of national protection (of the labour market in particular), law and order, and multi-culturalism, and thus points to the re-alignment of left–right along the cultural rather than the economic dimension. If anything, economically, social democrats reverted to more leftist positions, which runs against the interpretation in terms of policy constraints and limited economic alternatives.

The centripetal convergence as the cause of homogenization of cabinet politics in Europe thus has origins rooted in the re-alignment of social democratic parties less on an economic dimension between "socialist" and "capitalist" policies and more on a cultural dimension between "integration" and "demarcation". Economically, after the convergence towards the centre, social democrats revert to more left positions (to be interpreted in terms of domestic labour market protection) in their competition for a specific electoral constituency with right-wing political actors. This points to a sudden and short-term process of convergence on the part of leftist cabinets across the crucial years of European integration between the end of the 1980s and the early 1990s. This seems to be the case for economic adaptation, but only temporarily, whereas the response on the cultural dimension – a clear shift towards the right – appears as long term and permanent. An interpretation in terms of class structure and dimensionality points to the renewal of matters of leftist politics as a response to the populist mobilization of "globalization and integration losers" often, as documented in a number of case studies, accompanied by a renewed emphasis on matters of national identity and priority in the labour market.[34]

---

[34] See the various case studies in Dimitrakopoulos (2011). Furthermore, on France see Bell (2003); on Britain see Kriesi et al. (2008: 183–207); on Germany see Wimmel and Edwards (2011) as well as Sloam (2005b); and on Italy see Bordandini, Di Virgilio, and Raniolo (2008).

PART III

ASSESSMENT

8

Sources of Europeanization

Supra-, Within-, and Trans-national Explanations

Introduction

Empirical evidence presented in the five chapters of Part II provides ample support for the thesis of the Europeanization of politics. The crucial phases in the late 19th and early 20th centuries of the formation of party systems witness steady homogenization processes and simultaneous waves of change across the continent – in both Western and Central-Eastern Europe. Similar alignments are put in place which – in the past 30 years – have also permeated the EP. The ideological cohesiveness within Europe-wide party families has been high since World War II and it is likely that this indicator, too, has its roots in early periods of party systems' formation. Executive politics has undergone cross-national convergence under the impact of the recent events of European integration and the end of the Cold War.

The main line of interpretation that transpires through the evidence points to the role of the left, that is the role of socialists and social democrats: "class politics" and the left–right cleavage. This is the dimension that, by structuring national party systems, is the fundamental feature of their similarity. Its emergence in the late 19th century represents the main swing which, up to the present time, has remained unparalleled. In its wake territorially differentiating factors of a cultural nature and pre-industrial age are replaced by a functional alignment cutting across territories. Social democrats appear as the most integrated party family and it is their ideological shift in the early 1990s that causes the convergence of cabinet politics. Europeanization is to a large extent the story of the left and its relationship to the market economy.

The goal of this chapter is to investigate more systematically the sources of Europeanization along the explanatory scheme sketched in Chapter 1.

Europe-wide similarity and convergence result from three mechanisms (see Figures 1.1 and 1.2):

- *Supra-national* events, processes, and factors affecting similarly all countries as a top-down mechanism of Europeanization;
- Parallel but independent *within-country* factors leading to similar party systems as a national-level mechanism of Europeanization;
- *Diffusion* from country to country in processes of imitation, influence, imposition, and learning as a trans-national mechanism of Europeanization.

Which of these mechanisms has been operating relative to the five dimensions of Europeanization seen in Part II of this book? This chapter starts with a summary of results (Table 8.1) and then discusses the methodological issues of the causal analysis of broad common cross-space structures and cross-temporal change. It then reviews macro-historical work before addressing evidence in support of the three mechanisms.

Summary of Results

Indicator 1: Homogeneity (1848–2012)
1. *Measures of party support.* – Between 1850 and 1885 Europeanization manifests itself as the decline of cross-country diversity in the electoral support for party families, that is soon after the democratic revolutions of the 19th century. Subsequently, there is a progressive convergence in the format of national party systems in spite of an increasing number of countries included in the analysis. The aggregate distinctiveness of single-party systems from the European average declines continuously over the entire period covered and strong country deviations are absent even when Central and Eastern European countries are included.

The quantitative re-interpretation of the cleavage model shows that the similarity between countries is a product of the dominance of class politics with left–right expressing in, initially, a liberal–conservative constellation and, later, in the homogenizing presence of socialism. Socialist parties exist in all countries with similar levels of support and are an element of commonality. National Revolution and Industrial Revolution families from the state–church and class cleavages have a homogenizing impact and the resulting families are the truly "European" ones.[1] De-homogenizing party families – as features of cross-country deviation – are quantitatively too weak to cause party systems' deviations (pre-industrial families such as religious, ethno-linguistic/regionalist parties, and agrarians) from the centre–periphery and rural–urban cleavages. Their small size has little impact on cross-national deviation.

2. *Systemic measures.* – Systemic measures of homogeneity such as turnout, volatility, and fragmentation show the degree of similarity of electorates, rather

[1] To these families the communists from 1919 until 1989 should be added (in terms both of homogeneity and of the simultaneity of their appearance and decline).

than party systems: varying levels and styles of participation, institutional differences, structuration, and temporal consolidation of party organizations. Evidence points to more divergent patterns compared to measures of party support, in particular between Western Europe on one hand and Central-Eastern Europe on the other:

1. *Turnout*: Since the 1960s data on electoral participation point to a divergent process with increasing differences between (1) countries in which turnout is high and remains stable (mostly Western Europe) and (2) countries in which turnout is declining (mostly Central-Eastern European nations but also a number of Western European ones).[2] On this dimension "two Europes" have grown apart since 1989.
2. *Volatility*: Large differences exist between Western and Central-Eastern Europe in the propensity to change vote between elections and in the continuity of party organizations. However, volatility is increasing in Western Europe and decreasing in Central-Eastern Europe, leading to more similar levels today than in the past. Overall, volatility levels increase with the addition of new countries (after waves of democratization) and soon decrease afterwards, pointing to repeated processes of structuration of party systems in new democracies.[3]
3. *Fragmentation*: Similarly to volatility the measures of ENP point to differences between the two halves of Europe that, however, lessen with the increase of ENP in the West and the decrease in Central-Eastern Europe. Like for volatility, structuration seems to follow a cyclical pattern of increase of diversity with the inclusion of new countries which are, however, soon "absorbed" afterwards. If ENP is computed on families rather than parties homogeneity is higher. This indicates that cross-country differences reside primarily in party organizations rather than in basic alignments.[4]

Indicator 2: Uniformity (1848–2012)

The analysis of temporal change – trends, spread, and above all swings – confirms that the main phases of Europeanization coincide with the structuration of party systems towards the end of the 19th century, whereas phases after World War II are characterized by stability. Uniform swings, that is electoral change that is similar, simultaneous, and general in Europe, occur in parallel to the radical transformation from elite to mass politics between the last decade of the 19th century and the 1920s. This is a period when European

---

[2] These are Finland, France, Ireland, Portugal, and the United Kingdom (as well as Switzerland, which has had historically low levels of turnout compared to other countries).
[3] Similar results are obtained with single party and family figures.
[4] This alternative measurement is equivalent to one of "effective number of families". The analysis has not revealed significant differences between ENPP and ENEP.

TABLE 8.1. *Summary of Results: Europeanization of Electorates and Party Systems in Historical Perspective*

Period	1848–World War I	Inter-War period	World War II–1989	1989–present
Context	State formation and nation-building, democratization, industrialization	Massification of politics (universal suffrage, mass parties, PR), war de-mobilization	International security (Cold War), economic growth, welfare state development, value change	European integration, end of Cold War and communist rule, globalization
Electorates	Restricted	Mass	Full Democratization	
INDICATOR 1 *Homogenization*	Homogenization of cleavage structures (left–right): conservative and liberal party families (NR), later socialists (IR)		Decrease of country "distinctiveness"	Increase of territorial heterogeneity of electoral participation (turnout)
INDICATOR 2 *Uniformity*	Long socialist swing from 1885 to 1919 and long (negative) liberal swing from 1885 to 1924 (from elite to mass politics) – Communist swing (1919–25) – Fascist swing (not electoral)		Anti-fascist swing in 1945–50	Weak green and populist swing

INDICATOR 3 *Correspondence*		Vertical correspondence of alignments and party systems between national and EP arenas; distinctive pro/anti-EU dimension in EP elections
INDICATOR 4 *Cohesion*	High within-family ideological cohesion between parties in various countries with little room for further convergence (applies to main party families of the left–right dimension)	
INDICATOR 5 *Closure*	Cross-country cabinet similarity: – *Coalitions (cabinet composition)*: no convergence – *Policy*: convergence independent of composition	Effect of end of Cold War and Maastricht Treaty

Notes: Dashed arrow indicates probable earlier origin of process (but no evidence because of lack of data). NR = National Revolution, IR = Industrial Revolution.

party systems undergo similar structural change that manifests, in particular, in two swings:

- A long positive socialist swing (1885–1919); and
- A long negative liberal swing (1885–1924).

These represent the largest uniform swings in Europe over the entire 1848–2012 period and are unmatched by any subsequent change. After World War II no shift of votes is strong enough to be captured by the operational definition of uniform swing used in Chapter 4.[5] While there are examples of swings towards communists (after World War I), against extreme-right parties (after World War II), and, more recently but to a lesser extent, towards greens and populists, they do not cover the whole of Europe and are weak in terms of votes shifted. The analysis of spread reveals that the main swing towards mass and class politics between 1885 and 1919 is mainly made up by the progressive diffusion of socialist parties in countries in which they previously did not exist: it is a specific type of swing with gains of votes from nothing (0.0 per cent where such parties did not exist) to some level of electoral support with their appearance.[6] Rather than *swings* strictly speaking, one witnesses the *spread* of a new party family.[7]

Like for homogeneity, uniformity shows that the main dimension along which European party systems are integrated is the left–right one with its party families – socialists, conservatives, and liberals. Uniform swings take place along this dimension while change on other dimensions, in particular religion, ethno-regionalism, and environmental politics, is not uniform in Europe and thus does not contribute to the definition of a Europeanized electorate.

Indicator 3: Correspondence (1974–2012)

1. *Overall pattern.* – The third indicator of Europeanization measures the degree of overlap in the vertical dimension (rather than horizontally, across countries) between the two main arenas of party competition in Europe – national party systems and the EP. The overall analysis of distinct electoral behaviour between the two levels reveals a fundamental overlap, attesting that in EP elections voting behaviour is not distinct from voting behaviour in national elections. The same parties and alliances dominate at both levels, with similar issues and dimensions structuring competition.

---

[5] The swing must take place in at least half the countries in which democratic elections exist and in at least 75 per cent of the countries in which the family exists. Furthermore, the amount of votes shifted must be at least 3 per cent. The analysis considers only periods with at least four democratic countries.

[6] Classical analyses of swings in the United States contemplated uniquely swings back and forth between existing parties. The analysis here shows that the main swings are those of appearing and spreading parties.

[7] Such is not only the case of the major socialist swing, but also of greens and populists in the recent decades.

2. *Comparative analysis.* – Besides the distinctive electoral behaviour caused by change along left–right, the comparative analysis shows that one other party family is responsible for distinctiveness, namely the extreme-right, Eurosceptic, and anti-EU family that fares particularly well in EP elections. Such a distinctive support in EP elections compared to national elections points to the presence of a pro/anti-European dimension at the EP level, which makes it distinct from the national arenas.

Indicators of "differentiation" of electoral behaviour between the two arenas (mixed and differential volatility, MV and DV) show that, while left–right party alignments dominate at the national level, this is also the case at the EP level with few deviations from this basic configuration around socialists, liberals, and conservatives/Christian democrats. Only marginally are non-mainstream families (greens, populists, regionalists) favoured in the "second-order" elections to the EP. Furthermore, when a distinct behaviour is observed it originates rather from "punishment effects" for the main left–right parties: especially centre-right parties and socialists.[8]

The vertical correspondence between arenas in the European multi-level party system is based on the left–right alignment that proved a source of Europeanization also when measured cross-nationally (homogeneity and uniformity). The origin of this correspondence is to be sought in the preconditions set by the imposition of left–right at the national level in periods prior to EP elections since 1979. Such a constellation was already in place everywhere nationally and today permeates the EP system.

Indicator 4: Cohesion (1945–2009)

While the previous indicators focus on the format of party systems – either horizontally or vertically – the fourth indicator analyzes the ideological contents of voters' positioning and party manifestos. Having identified left–right as the main party system dimension in Europe, the indicator of cohesion focuses on the main socialist, liberal, and conservative/Christian democratic parties to find out the degree of cohesiveness of their ideology at two levels:

- *Mass level*: Voters' left–right positioning based on survey data (EB and ESS);
- *Elite level*: Parties' left–right positioning based on selected text items from party manifesto data (CMP).

The content analysis reinforces the conclusion of Europeanized party systems as similar levels of support for parties of the same family across countries

---

[8] Levels of differential volatility (DV) – the additional propensity to change vote from national to EP elections and back compared to national volatility – is higher for some countries, Denmark and United Kingdom in particular, but also for France, Germany, Sweden, and Ireland. The QCA ran to complement econometric analyses shows that the socialist volatility is a necessary condition for national and EP behaviour to diverge, coupled with other sources of differentiation.

(homogeneity) and simultaneous shifts towards/against parties of the same family (uniformity) are meaningful indicators only if these families are ideologically cohesive. In the balance between ideological and territorial variations of party ideology the analysis shows that the "family it belongs to" explains much more the ideological position of a party than the "country it comes from": genealogy is more important than nationality. This proves that party alignments are functional divides rather than territorial ones in Europe, attesting to a high level of integration. Differences between ideologies are larger than differences between geographical areas.

The longitudinal analysis shows little convergence over time between parties of the same family as levels of ideological cohesiveness were always high, pointing to the likely origin of cohesiveness in periods prior to those considered in Chapter 6. Since 1945 there seems to be little space left for further convergence, at both the mass and elite levels.[9] Europeanization – as a process – is feeble for electorates and party systems already Europeanized. In the light of the two historical chapters (Chapters 3 and 4) it is legitimate to assume that at content level, too, Europeanization is an older process, most probably set in motion by the National Revolution and the Industrial Revolution in the 19th century.[10]

The distinction between economic and cultural dimensions of left–right shows that, for socialists, cohesion and convergence is higher on the former than on the latter.

Indicator 5: Closure (1945–2009)
The last indicator considers the Europeanization of coalition politics at the executive level from both format and content (policy position) perspectives. Results show high levels of policy proximity between executives and – over time – there are no signs of geographical differences emerging with the addition of Central-Eastern European countries after 1989. The origin of such similarity among cabinets has been investigated through two major hypotheses:

- *Same-composition hypothesis*: Closure implies that policies are cohesive insofar as the same parties (that is parties from the same family) are in power at the same time across Europe. This hypothesis has been rejected.
- *Family-similarity hypothesis*: Disregarding which parties are in power, policy converges insofar as programmes of different families are increasingly similar. This hypothesis has been confirmed.

The between-family programmatic convergence (second hypothesis) is caused mainly by the move towards the centre of the left–right axis on the part of socialist parties. This centripetal move of de-radicalization takes place across

---

[9] To be exact, there is some convergence at the level of party manifestos.
[10] This excludes, as causes of ideological convergence, factors such as technological change, increased communication, labour mobility, supra-national integration, and economic and financial coordination after World War II.

the "1992" juncture which combines Maastricht (European integration) and the aftermath of the fall of the Berlin Wall (end of the Cold War and its global ideological confrontation).[11] The result is cross-country convergence in spite of diverse cabinet compositions in various nation-states. Such a converging pattern – at the cabinet level – does not occur before 1992 or after, but across this date.[12] On the cultural dimension of left–right such a convergence is also visible after this juncture.[13] On the economic dimension the centripetal shift of centre-left cabinets (which is at the origin of cross-country similarity of cabinet politics) takes place across the crucial narrowing of policy alternatives established by the Maastricht Treaty but also by the end of communism.

The analysis of closure shows once more the role of the left as a motor of Europeanization – alongside the indicator of homogeneity (socialists are the only family existing continuously in all 30 countries), uniformity (the main swing is, historically, the socialist one), and cohesion (the socialist party family is ideologically the more cohesive one). As the transfer literature shows, Central-Eastern European socialist parties have heavily borrowed from their Western European counterparts in setting up their policy programmes. Finally, and differently than the other indicators, the analysis of closure points clearly to the top-down effect of supra-national factors on national systems.

Converging Dimensions versus Diverging Regimes

The electoral history of Europe emerging from what has been briefly summarized is one of common dimensionality. The basic argument of this book – Europeanization of electoral politics – relies on evidence of one main dimension that is similar in the various European countries. While evidence is convincing, it cannot be forgotten that it is also limited: in particular, it is limited to *periods of liberal-democratic regimes when free competitive elections* take place with *political parties* as the main actors. Undeniably, this is not the full picture of European political history.

In particular, the previous chapters are limited to one specific type of regime (liberal democracy) and exclude periods prior to this type of regime (*ancien régime*) and periods of interruption when other, namely totalitarian, forms of mass political mobilization led to fascist and communist regimes.[14] As mentioned in the research design, elections in non-free and non-competitive regimes (one-party states) are not included in the analysis. Before the discussion of the

---

[11] Besides the centripetal convergence of left cabinets, there is also a similar move of centre-right ones, albeit not as sizable.

[12] See the dummy variable in Table 7.8 used to operationalize this juncture.

[13] The centripetal move on the part of socialists can be seen as a response to the populist challenge on issues of opening up of labour markets, cultural threat, and, concretely, immigration.

[14] Measures of Europeanization in Chapters 3 and 4 are compiled based on party votes, disregarding the extension of the electoral franchise. The term *democratic* refers to free competitive elections even when most of the adult population was still excluded from the electoral franchise.

mechanisms of commonality can take place, the implications of such an exclusion need to be addressed. How, in a broad view, do illiberal regimes fit into the picture of European similarity brought forward by Part II of this book?

In many ways the evidence of Europeanization runs against the picture that emerges from the tragic confrontation during and between the two world wars, namely a picture *associating whole countries with specific regimes* – be it Anglo-Saxon liberal democracies, the communist East, or the fascist South. Inevitably, such an association points to diversity and divergence rather than commonality, and to strong territoriality between nations rather than ideological and functional divisions cutting across them. Indeed, a view of divergence is what emerges from macro-sociological work done in historical perspective, and comparatively, on the conditions for success of specific regimes – liberal democracy, communism, and fascism (to summarize schematically). This work, which includes pioneering studies such as Moore (1966), Skocpol (1979), Rogowski (1989), Luebbert (1991), and Acemoglu and Robinson (2006), among others, has pointed to dramatically diverging patterns among European countries with different regimes imposing themselves in different countries.[15] Whether on the basis of agrarian structures, levels of state capacity, outcomes of wars, state finances, and debt, or on the basis of varying alliances and coalitions between labour, land, and capital, countries were directed on different trajectories. How can such a view of divergence be reconciled with evidence of Europeanization? Two broad points can be made.

First, it can be argued that in the mentioned literature, divergence in the resulting institutional regimes is limited to the inter-war period. The countries supposedly on a divergent historical trajectory have in fact been so for limited periods of time in Europe, namely after World War I. In most cases such divergence in regime outcome is discontinued after World War II when countries revert back to the long-term track of democratization.[16] Furthermore, a reading of these works purely in terms of divergence of outcome in the inter-war period should not be decoupled from the long-term trajectory since the beginning of the 19th century of commonality in terms of constitutionalization, parliamentarization, extension of civil and political rights, accountability of executive

---

[15] Sometimes referred to as macro-historical comparative sociology, this perspective often goes under the labels of "historical institutionalism" (Hall and Taylor, 1996; Skocpol, 1995, Steinmo, Thelen, and Longstreth, 1992, Thelen, 1999) or "political economy" (Acemoglu and Robinson, 2006). This is just to mention the main book contributions, as the literature is extremely extensive. The theoretical breadth and historical detail of these analyses cannot be addressed exhaustively here. Rokkan is not included in this list as his model of Europe does not address different regimes (with the exception of brief considerations on the rise of fascism) and does not include Central and Eastern Europe. His model is mainly concerned with cleavages in liberal democracies.

[16] This is the case for many countries in Central and Eastern Europe before Soviet intervention, as it was after World War I and in the aftermath of the breakdown of the Tzarist, Habsburg, and Ottoman Empires. The two main exceptions in Western Europe are Portugal and Spain, which did not return to democracy until the deaths of Salazar and Franco.

power, and so forth. Countries that turned fascist after World War I had often pioneered liberal and democratic reforms as in the Spanish Constitution of Cádiz (1812), the German Frankfurt Parliament (1848), or the secular Statuto Albertino extended to Italy with unification in 1861. The same applies to many constituent "nations" in the Habsburg parliament, including Bohemia, Poland, and Hungary itself.[17] On the other hand, countries that remained liberal during the inter-war period had experienced protracted phases of undemocratic rule as, for example, in Bonaparte's France until 1870. The divergence between the two wars should thus not divert the attention from the broader picture of common democratic progress in Europe – before and after the two world wars.

Second, limiting the argument of divergence to the outcome in terms of regime – liberal democracy, fascism, or communism – without paying proper attention to the ideological confrontation and political struggle unduly magnifies differences between countries and ranges them almost monolithically in different camps.[18] The emphasis on divergent outcomes shadows the commonality of the confrontations *inside* each country and blurs the similarity of the battle within the countries. The outcome in terms of regime may have been different in different countries, but the opposed groups were quite similar in most of them. In fact, in spite of different outcomes, most countries went through the same confrontations with the outcome often resting on contingent factors of varying alliances and coalitions between the main social actors – as the macro-historical comparative literature clearly shows.[19]

Reconciling historical evidence of the Europeanization of the vote with divergent institutional patterns does not mean that outcomes in terms of regime are irrelevant or marginal in the analysis of commonality and divergence in Europe, but rather that (1) countries should not be considered monolithic blocs because of their outcome in the inter-war period and (2) the dimensionality, struggle, and opposition is very similar in all countries in spite of different (often contingent) outcomes. A *long-term perspective* including periods before and after the two world wars and a *focus on confrontation* rather than outcome brings to the fore a much more homogenous picture of Europe for periods in which

[17] As far as Central and Eastern Europe is concerned after World War II, the deviation caused by the outside "influence" of the Soviet Union should not be underestimated in countries like Czechoslovakia, Hungary, and Poland, among others.

[18] The international war between liberal democracies and fascist regimes in 1939–45 has obviously exacerbated its territorial dimension. After World War II political science literature in the United States has also accentuated the cross- and whole-country dimension with arguments of political culture (for example Almond and Verba, 1963).

[19] These confrontations over basic regime choices between socio-economic/cultural groups (workers, peasants, the Catholic Church, peripheries, bourgeoisie, landlords, etc.) is what emerges in all these classical accounts. Even in the United States, the Civil War has been portrayed by Moore as a "civilization" struggle (see the chapter on the United States in Moore, 1966). What also emerges from these detailed accounts is that the outcome could often have been different. While the structures of the confrontation are common, the outcome is not. On the contingent element of critical junctures see Capoccia and Kelemen (2011).

electoral data cannot be used to compute indicators. This is a picture in which *functional divisions within and across countries* predominate over territorial divisions between them.

This book does not cover periods of undemocratic regimes and yet the classical studies on regimes mentioned earlier point to the need to address *the dimensionality of politics* in non-democratic settings to get a full picture of commonality in Europe. Such common dimensionality (left–right) appears in Part II of this book through the analysis of party families and electoral behaviour. *It does not mean that a similar dimensionality is absent in regimes without elections and free competition between parties.* The indicators of the present book cannot extend to fascist and communist regimes in Europe. It is a work on electoral politics in the liberal-democratic setting.

Sources of Europeanization

Supra-national Mechanisms

The first mechanism leading to Europe-wide convergence and increased commonality is the mechanism through which *one or several supra-national factors affect similarly all units (national party systems)*. This is the typical definition of "Europeanization" as reviewed in Chapter 1 in terms of impact of European integration on national structures (institutions, administrations, or, as in the case here, party systems). Differently from the literature on this narrow definition of Europeanization, other supra-national factors must be contemplated, beyond and before that of European integration or even "globalization".

Table 8.2 summarizes the empirical evidence, pointing to *top-down factors* as a first source of Europeanization – that is territorial similarity and convergence in electoral behaviour and party systems – by enumerating chronologically its main manifestations. The analyses in Chapters 4, 6, and 7 have identified five major instances of cross-country convergence through the top-down effect of supra-national factors. Three of these instances affect the "uniformity" dimension of Europeanization, that is a common supra-national factor creates a general, similar, and simultaneous electoral change (the operational definition given to uniform swings in Chapter 4) in Europe.[20] This affects the format of party systems. In addition, two instances affect the content of party systems: ideological and programmatic convergence among parties of the same family and cabinets.

The three sources of uniform swings are taken first. The first instance of uniform swing caused by a common supra-national source is the general and simultaneous negative swing against extreme-right (mostly fascist) parties in the first elections after the end of World War II. As seen in Chapter 4 this is not

---

[20] The effect on homogeneity is indirect. Similar change in most European countries (uniform swing) results in a higher degree of homogeneity (in parentheses). As seen, however, populists and greens are not factors of homogeneity in Europe because of their small size.

TABLE 8.2. *Supra-national Mechanisms: Top-Down Effects*

Event	Dimensions	Effect	Period
Outcome of World War II	Uniformity (homogeneity)	Swing against fascist parties in the immediate aftermath of the conflict	1945–50
"Post-industrial revolution"	Uniformity (homogeneity)	Weak swing towards green parties from value and attitude change following period of international peace/security and economic growth	1970s–80s
Outcome of Cold War	Cohesion	Ideological convergence of socialists with the narrowing of left–right spectrum following the breakdown of communism in Central-Eastern Europe	1989–present
Maastricht Treaty	Closure	Ideological convergence of socialists with (or aspiring to) cabinet responsibility on the left–right spectrum	1992–present
Globalization	Uniformity (homogeneity)	Defensive response (economic and cultural protectionism) from extreme-right populists with consequent weak swing towards them	1985–9

Notes: For a depiction of supra-national mechanisms see Figure 1.2.

one of the strongest swings as most fascist partisan mobilization did not take place in competitive settings and therefore is not included in this analysis. Yet there is a clear move away from these parties in the second half of the 1940s when these elections are compared with the last democratic elections in the 1920s and 1930s.[21] The common supra-national factor causing this backlash for extreme-right parties is the outcome of World War II with the defeat of the regimes based on fascist-Nazi one-party rule like in Germany, and with the defeat of these parties in civil war–ridden countries like Czechoslovakia, Italy, France, Greece, and Romania, among others.[22] While in some countries extreme-right parties disappeared or were banned, in others they suffered major losses as a consequence of the war and the inter-war experience of fascist regimes.

The second instance of uniform swing caused by a supra-national factor is the general increase of votes for green parties (as the major case of an emancipatory party family) in the 1980s as documented in Chapter 4. As a supra-national factor the emphasis is here on the conditions of international peace and security (coupled with global economic growth) during the Cold War which led to the transformation of value priorities from materialist to post-materialist. It should be noted that, in terms of its effects, this supra-national factor needs to be treated as a necessary or background condition for the emergence of environmental movements and parties across Europe. As a supra-national factor, international peace and security is present in all countries covered by the analysis of the 1970s–80s (that is, Western Europe only): there is no case of a green party without this condition.[23]

The third instance of uniform swing caused by a supra-national factor is the increase of votes across Europe for far-right, populist parties as a response to "globalization" intended as the opening up of labour markets, the blurring of national boundaries, the dislocation of production towards emerging economies, and the threat to job security and hostile cultural identities coming from immigration. In Europe, such a process is associated with European integration, the free movement of persons and capital, and the pooling of decision-making processes above the level of nation-states. While such a positive swing towards populist parties is usually associated with the most recent period since 2010, data in Chapter 4 indicate that such a swing takes place earlier, in the second half of the 1980s, while in the period from 2010 to 2012 there is a strong

---

[21] Elections in the five-year period of 1945–9 also include Central-Eastern European countries such as Czechoslovakia and Romania.

[22] Elections during 1945–9 are not included for Portugal and Spain, where fascist regimes continued until well into the 1970s. As mentioned in the previous section the analysis in this book does not capture deviations stemming from non-democratic sections. Yet it is possible to assume that the ideological confrontation in these two countries were similar to that of other countries with a fascist experience during the two wars.

[23] It is not a sufficient condition as the presence of this condition does not always lead to the emergence of green parties.

populist swing but covers less than half the European countries and therefore cannot be considered "general".[24]

These three instances of uniform swings following supra-national factors are weak. As seen in Chapter 4 (Tables 4.1 and 4.2) these swings are not strong in terms of votes and do not cover most countries. This is not a strong indication of Europeanization as caused by common supra-national factors. Yet from Table 8.2 one sees that supra-national factors can be identified as causing Europeanization on the content dimension of party systems, too, besides the format dimension. Chapters 6 and 7, in particular, have identified two patterns of parties' cross-national ideological convergence – both relating mainly to the socialist family.

The first instance of within-family ideological convergence caused by a common supra-national factor takes place with the end of the Cold War and democratization in Central and Eastern Europe. On one hand, the programmes of socialist and social democratic parties in the newly democratic countries appear as moulded on their Western European counterparts, causing a high degree of Europe-wide cohesiveness when measured at both the electorate (surveys) and party (CMP) levels. On the other hand, the end of the international ideological confrontation and the end of communism in Central and Eastern Europe has forced several, more radicalized socialist parties to operate a centripetal move, bringing them in line with most other mainstream socialist parties – thus leading to more cohesiveness within this party family. The outcome of the Cold War can clearly be treated as supra-national factor common to all countries.

The increased ideological cohesiveness among socialist parties in different national party systems is affected by a second supra-national factor, which is European integration proper, more specifically the shift of the major economic policy instruments from the national to the EU level. Such a process of typical "Europeanization" has a top-down effect on socialist parties in forcing a centripetal move on the left–right axis parallel to their acceptance of European integration. The Maastricht criteria have reduced the space of manoeuvre for socialists on the left side of the ideological spectrum, forcing the more radical ones to reform their programmes towards liberal economic policies. As the analysis of closure in Chapter 7 shows, such a process of ideological convergence among socialist parties occurs across the crucial years of the Maastricht Treaty especially for parties with cabinet responsibility, or aspiring to it, as is the case of the major socialist parties. In this case Europeanization operates via a top-down effect on the content dimension of party systems.

---

[24] For the greens, the swings cover about half the democratic countries. For extreme-right populists, the swing is strong with, on average, a 9.62 per cent increase in the period since 2010 compared to the previous five-year period. However, data since 2010 include only 19 countries (because the others did not vote between 2010 and 2012 when the data set has been completed). Furthermore, of the 19 countries with elections, in only 14 does this family exist and the positive swing took place in 10 countries (71.43 per cent of the countries where populists exist, that is below the 75 per cent threshold used in the analysis in Chapter 4).

Summing up, the analysis of supra-national factors seems to point to recent periods as the ones during which such factors act as sources of Europeanization. It is the two recent supra-national factors of (1) the end of the Cold War (and the simultaneous end of communist regimes in Central-Eastern Europe) and (2) European integration in its crucial manifestation through the Maastricht Treaty of 1992 that have a top-down effect on cross-country convergence. This convergence takes place primarily at the ideological level, and primarily on the main party family of the left.[25] However, it should also be noted that over-all ideological cohesiveness is quite high among parties of a same family, so that supra-national factors such as international peace and security could not further compress already high levels of cohesiveness, and therefore cannot be detected by the analysis. Top-down mechanisms do not have a strong impact on the format of party systems as proved by the weak impact of supra-national factors on the Europe-wide uniformity of electoral change between subsequent five-year periods. While Europe-wide ideological cohesiveness can be traced back to supra-national sources, for other dimensions of Europeanization one needs to look for different sources.

Within-National Mechanisms

As seen in Chapter 1 (Figure 1.2), the second mechanism through which cross-country convergence occurs is the within-country mechanism, whereby *similar party systems* (composed by similar party families with similar over-time transformations and a high degree of ideological cohesiveness within the families) *are brought about by similar factors* – say, similar class structure or ethnic/religious composition or a similar electoral system change. Similarity, however, in this case does not mean commonality of a single supra-national event that all countries experience. It is developments within the countries which happen to be similar.[26] Fundamentally, this is the design on which the cleavage model presented in Chapter 2 is based and which Chapter 3 has assessed quantitatively.

What are the instances of party system Europeanization that can be traced back to national-level factors that are similar in most countries? As reported in Table 8.3, such instances relate primarily, although not exclusively, to the emergence of left–right as the dominant dimension of contestation in most national party systems in the course of the 19th century and the early 20th century. It is not supra-national factors that are at the origin of the major party families of the left and right that emerge in almost all European countries – liberals and conservatives first, under restricted suffrage, and social democrats later, under conditions of mass enfranchisement. This crucial dimension of

---

[25] As the analysis in Chapter 7 shows, a similar but less significant process takes place for centre-right parties. It should also be reminded that the content analysis cannot take place before 1945 because of the lack of data. A conclusion pointing to the recent nature of top-down mechanisms should take this caveat into account.

[26] Conversely, in this type of mechanism "deviations" of given party systems can be traced to differences in the structural socio-economic, cultural, and institutional development of the countries.

TABLE 8.3. *Within-national Mechanisms: Country-Level Effects*

Factor	Dimensions	Effect	Period
"National Revolution"	Homogeneity	Organization of liberal-nationalist bourgeois parties and conservative parties under conditions of restricted electorates (party families of "internal origin")	19th century
"Industrial Revolution"	Uniformity (homogeneity)	Simultaneous rise of socialist, social democratic parties for the mass mobilization of the working class (party family of "external origin")	Late 19th century
	Cohesion	Within-family ideological cohesion between parties in various countries with little room for further convergence (main party families of the left-right dimension)	1945–present
"Post-Industrial Revolution"	Uniformity	Rise of green parties from the value and attitude change following a period of international peace/security and economic growth (see *supra-national mechanisms*, Table 8.2)	1970s–80s

Notes: For a depiction of within-country mechanisms see Figure 1.2.

271

Europeanization – homogeneity of party systems' structures – can be traced back to conditions that are internal to each national political system and that are the conditions mainly identified by the cleavage model:

- The rise of the entrepreneurial bourgeoisie in agriculture and manufacture set in motion by technological change and its demands for participation in political decision making and distribution of power (parliamentarism and suffrage), coupled with the cultural change set in motion by the Enlightenment (secular individualism, individual representation, and national citizenship) – and the corresponding religious/conservative resistance to such changes.
- Industrialization, urbanization, and the process of commodification of manufacturing labour at the mass level, leading to the rise of the working class and demands for social and economic security and equal opportunity within the capitalist economy (social rights) and liberal institutions (universal suffrage and PR).

Together these factors compose the concepts of National and Industrial Revolutions as they appear in Table 8.3.[27] While under conditions of restricted suffrage the liberal family "Europeanizes" European countries, under conditions of mass suffrage the socialist family takes up this role. These two families have been the main feature of Europeanization at the electoral level with no other families playing a similar role in the homogenization of European party systems in subsequent times.[28] The rise of liberals first (which is concomitant to, and in fact establishes, competitive electoral parliamentarism) and of socialists later transpires in the dimension of uniformity (Europe-wide simultaneous swing towards these party families) as shown in the analysis in Part II.[29] These factors are similar in all countries and transformations that all countries witness.

These transformations affect the uniformity and homogeneity of the format of party systems. Through the electoral waves that bring liberal dominance and, later, the consolidated presence of social democrats, homogenous party systems establish themselves across Europe. This shows the link between the two dimensions of Europeanization with a focus on the format of party systems: it is through uniformity (similar and simultaneous changes in most

---

[27] The concept of National Revolution includes other aspects of state formation and nation-building, namely the centralization and standardization of administrative structures and the cultural integration and socialization (not least through schooling and military conscription) of the newly constructed citizenship. This dimension of the National Revolution is, however, more a policy of liberalism than one of its causes.

[28] As seen, this is in part a consequence of treating the conservative and Christian democrat families as separate entities to stress the dis-homogenizing role of religion as an element of differentiation of national party systems alongside language and agrarian politics.

[29] To be precise, the analysis does not show evidence of uniform swings towards the liberals since the first elections considered in the time series already include the liberals as the dominant party family and therefore cannot be compared to a "previous" election in which liberals did not exist or were weak in terms of votes. The liberal wave is simultaneous with the establishment of liberal democracy itself.

countries) that homogeneity across national party systems is reached. There is a link between uniformity and homogeneity, whereby uniformity (a dynamic factor) puts in place party systems (a static factor) everywhere. This link appears in particular from the fact that, as seen in Chapter 4, the strongest and more general uniform swings are associated with *appearance patterns*. Rather than increase/decrease of votes between elections due to swings from left to right and vice versa, shifts of votes go to "new entrants" in the party systems. From a format point of view the analysis shows the impact of within-country factors and how these factors affect the homogeneity of the format of European party systems.[30]

Table 8.3, however, also includes the content dimension of cohesion, that is the similarity in the ideological content of party programmes of parties belonging to the same family in different countries. The cleavage model has always remained at the level of party systems format and has been criticized for not taking into account the country-specific contents behind similar labels. To what extent is it possible to speak of homogeneity among national party systems based exclusively on party names and symbols? This problem concerns in particular the large party families of the left–right dimension that make up most of the homogeneity existing among European party systems. As seen in Chapter 6, the degree of within-family cohesion in regard to party programmes and, to a large extent, also party voters is high since 1945, and slightly increasing over time. The main issue facing the analysis at this stage is that such a content-based analysis cannot be pushed back before 1945 and especially not to the formative decades of Europeanized party systems, namely between the 1880s and the aftermath of World War I. The high degree of cohesion within the social democrat, right-wing (conservatives and Christian democrats), and liberal families right after 1945 suggests that the origin of this cohesion can be traced back to earlier periods, and indeed to the periods during which these party families formed and spread across Europe in the second half of the 19th century and the early 20th century.

The classical cleavage model is based on the idea that similar structural factors based at the national level have a generative effect on party systems. The empirical analysis in Part II shows that commonalities in party systems are significantly stronger than deviations. Where the classical cleavage model is deficient is, first, in not considering supra-national factors and, second, in not considering trans-national effects. Only recently, most notably with the research on the impact of globalization (Kriesi et al., 2008 and 2012), have

---

[30] The table also includes the value change that takes place after World War II under conditions of international security and economic growth. As seen under supra-national mechanisms, this instance of Europeanization is not very significant as it does not give rise to a strong and general swing and because it does not contribute much to the degree of homogeneity of party systems. Furthermore, while the value change takes place in all countries, it can be questioned if its origin is national (generational change) or supra-national (post-war growth and security).

these elements been taken into account. While homogeneity does not require the simultaneous effect of structural factors to, eventually, put in place similar party systems, *the analysis of the degree of simultaneity of electoral change across Europe* (especially the crucial changes of mass and class politics) and the link between the dimensions of uniformity and homogeneity (i.e. homogeneity as resulting precisely from simultaneous change), makes it necessary to include mechanisms other than the purely within-national one.

From the perspective of format, *structural factors* (National and Industrial Revolutions to summarize) as independent variables explaining the origin of similar party systems across Europe *cannot be reconciled with the simultaneity with which the same party families have emerged.* If, on one hand, broad processes of state formation and nation-building, democratization, industrialization, and urbanization take place in all countries, on the other the timing of such transformations and their extent vary dramatically cross-sectionally.[31] Yet evidence of the emergence of party families in Part II shows remarkably simultaneous and general electoral patterns. Simply remaining within the scheme provided by the cleavage model based on national structural factors, *the temporal discrepancy between staggered structural transformations and party systems' simultaneous formation cannot be explained.*[32] On the contrary, it points to other mechanisms and to a perspective in which agency plays a role that structure-based models cannot capture. From the perspective of content, the radically different socio-economic, cultural/historical, and institutional contexts in different countries can hardly be reconciled with the high level of commonality in the ideological content of party programmes across countries.

Mechanisms other than within-national ones are, therefore, at work which, on one hand, leads one back to the effects on Europeanization of *supra-national factors*, but, on the other, points to more agency-oriented factors at work in *trans-national mechanisms* based on the diffusion of ideas and practices through international communication, contacts, and exchanges.[33] This is a

---

[31] Evidence of cross-sectional variation in the structural factors generating specific party families is not provided here. Data on socio-economic and institutional change can be accessed through a number of data- and documentation-rich works such as Bartolini (2000), Caramani (2000), Flora (1983), Flora, Krauz, and Pfenning (1987), Mitchell (2007), Nohlen and Stöver (2010), and Stasavage (2003), among others.

[32] Such factors include the timing, pace (tempo), and reversals (Bartolini, 1993) of the formation of the state, as well as reforms towards centralization, nation-building with the introduction of compulsory schooling and a conscript army, the timing of democratization (for example extension of the franchise and universal suffrage), and the shift to proportional electoral systems, the transformation from a predominantly agrarian to predominantly industrial and urban economy, and so on.

[33] Part of all this is the diffusion of ideas and the influence of writings, imitation of political strategy, and organization, but also learning processes stemming from collaboration in supra-national organizations. Such effects are visible in the political actions of nationalists, socialists, and communists but also, more recently, of the greens.

major complement to the cleavage model provided by the empirical analysis carried out in Part II. Furthermore, not only should one focus on diffusion effects at the level of party families, but also at the level of the very structural factors that generate these party families. Processes of state formation and nation-building, democratization, technological innovation, and industrialization are also subject to diffusion. These complements to the cleavage model based on within-national structural factors are addressed next.

Trans-national Mechanisms

The fact that supra-national and within-national factors have an effect on the degree of similarity of party systems in Europe does not exclude that trans-national effects, too, act in explaining homogeneity, uniformity, and cohesion as the major dimensions of Europeanization identified by the analysis in Part II of this book. An instance of convergence can originate from more than one mechanism. In fact, a number of instances of Europeanization listed in the two previous tables appear again in Table 8.4.

The factors that according to the cleavage model have led to similar party families in most European countries – namely the factors that can be summarized by the terms of "Revolutions" (National, Industrial) – are similar structural factors acting within many countries that lead to the emergence of similar party families. In a macro-sociological perspective these factors are the structural preconditions for specific agents (parties) to develop. Yet this does not exclude that at the same time diffusion effects exist and that the factors listed as "within-country" do not act in isolation in the various political systems. Also in regard to a further "Revolution", namely the international one, diffusion effects cannot be excluded in addition to the supra-national effects (for example, those produced by the Soviet Revolution on homogeneity and uniform swing towards communist parties with their emergence).[34] It is quite obvious, therefore, that trans-national effects must be incorporated into explanations alongside supra- and within-national factors.

Diffusion effects seem to be ubiquitous and are difficult to single out because of their presence at two levels:

- First, trans-national diffusion effects are present at the *level of "independent variables"*, that is the structural factors that act as preconditions for the development of specific party families in different countries.
- Second, trans-national diffusion effects are present at the *level of "dependent variables"*, that is the specific party agencies themselves that develop in different countries.

---

[34] The lack of attention Rokkan devoted to the interactions between national systems constitutes the core of Charles Tilly's critique of the cleavage model, especially the omission of the international system from the model and more particularly the role of wars as a form of contact between national systems (Tilly, 1990; see also Kuhnle, 1975).

TABLE 8.4. *Trans-national Mechanisms: Diffusion Effects*

Origin	Dimensions	Effect	Period
"National Revolution": United States, France, Britain	Homogeneity	*Europe-wide*: Liberal-nationalist movements and party organizations, ideology of constitutionalism, popular sovereignty, and parliamentary representation	1848–90
"Industrial Revolution": Britain, Germany	Uniformity, homogeneity	*Europe-wide*: Rise of workers' movement and creation of socialist and social democratic parties with creation of trans-national organizations (Second International, 1889–1916)	1890–1919
"International Revolution": Russia	Uniformity	*Europe-wide*: Division of workers' movement and spread of communist parties through separation from socialists in all European countries (division of the left)	1919–25
Fascist reaction: Italy	Uniformity	*Europe-wide*: Rise of reactionary response to international socialism and crisis of parliamentarism, totalitarian role of state, and corporatist organization of economy	1922–39
Third wave of democratization: Western Europe	Cohesion	*Central-Eastern Europe*: Adoption of ideological positions and party programmes in countries after third wave of democratization for most party families	1989–present

Notes: For a depiction of trans-country mechanisms see Figure 1.2.

In the first case it is the structural change that spreads across countries, thus homogenizing the conditions for the emergence of a specific party family. For example, technological change and subsequent industrialization in the 19th century have spread across countries through trade, mercantilism, communication, and so forth, thus prompting, in most countries, the type of socio-economic change that led to the rise of labour movements and social democratic parties. In the second case, it is the model of political mobilization itself to spread across national borders with forms of organization of labour being introduced in given countries and then emulated in others. While in the first case trans-national factors concern the *structural conditions that lead to party families*, in the second case trans-national factors concern *party creation, organization, and ideology*. Whereas in most cases the literature on diffusion of party families, and their organization and ideology, focuses on this second level, the first one on the diffusion of the socio-economic and cultural conditions favouring their appearance in large parts of Europe should not be forgotten, and the analysis of diffusion effects should not be limited to one level only.[35] Even if it is arduous to empirically separate the levels, only by considering both can convergence in Europe be conceptualized properly.

The first row of Table 8.4 mentions results for the Europe-wide spread of liberalism as an indicator of early Europeanization. Empirical data in Part II of this book show that the high levels of homogeneity (first indicator) are due to the opposition between liberals and conservatives (or Catholics depending on the countries) during phases of restricted suffrage. This opposition is present in all countries with competitive elections. According to the cleavage model such a similarity is explained – as seen in Chapter 2 and under within-country mechanisms discussed earlier – by the conflict over the degree of liberalization and equalization of political participation (parliamentarism and franchise), but also over fundamental *Weltanschauungen* concerning the individual, science, and religion.

Empirical data, however, do not show an impact of the National Revolution on the dimension of uniformity (a similar, general, and simultaneous electoral shift) which would support the mechanism of trans-national diffusion. While the lack of this type of evidence can be explained by the fact that homogeneity was in place at the very moment of the first elections (and therefore cannot be captured by an indicator based on a change with the previous election), it

---

[35] The distinction made here is one between *structure* (first level) and *agency* (second level). Unrelated to the issue of diffusion, Mahoney and Snyder provide a useful distinction of the effects of structure as "constraining" or "generative" (Mahoney and Snyder, 1999). More generally, on the agent–structure problem see discussions in Berejikian (1992), Flanagan (1993), Taylor (1989), and Wendt (1987). In the literature based on the cleavage model, Bartolini and Mair (1990) provide a similar distinction in their definition of cleavage whereby the *social base* of a cleavage (class, religion, ethnicity, etc.) is distinguished from its *organizational expression* (typically, unions and parties).

is very likely that the homogeneity of liberalism, and of the liberal–conservative opposition more generally, includes a significant element of cross-border
diffusion.[36] The homogeneity of party systems during phases of restricted suffrage is not caused uniquely by processes of state formation, nation-building,
and democratization that take place in all countries independently, but also by
interactions between elites. In fact, what this homogeneity reveals is that processes of state formation, nation-building, and democratization took place in
various countries to a large degree because they took place in neighbouring –
often rival – countries.[37] The homogenization of liberalism as an indicator of
Europeanized electorates is a product both of within-country changes brought
about by the diffusion of "independent variables" (i.e. state formation and
nation-building) and of diffusion factors at the level of the "dependent variable" (i.e. liberal party formation, organization, and ideology).

Where the effect of trans-national diffusion appears more clearly in the data
in Part II is the instance of uniform swings of socialists at the beginning of
the 20th century (with the concomitant negative swing for liberals) – the tide
of mass and class politics leading to the entry of socialist, social democratic,
and labour parties in the party systems in all European countries (second row
in Table 8.4). As seen in Chapter 4 the rise of electoral socialism is the single
major instance of uniform swing during the whole European electoral history
and shows the appearance of new socialist parties in an increasing number
of countries.[38] Unlike the liberal family, therefore, data here clearly show a
trans-national diffusion effect. Similarly to the liberal family, on the other
hand, diffusion effects must be considered at both the "independent variables"
level and the "dependent variable" level.

Concerning the former, most of the structural conditions under which socialism arose in various countries are related to technological change in agricultural
production and manufacture. While the improvement of production can be conceived as occurring independently in different countries, this would certainly be a
limited view. Production technology spread across borders and affected progress
in most countries, albeit at different times and varying paces. A within-national
mechanism in this sense must necessarily be complemented by a trans-national

---

[36] It is thus not surprising to find (also in periods previous to democratization) episodes of simultaneous push towards liberalization following the 1789, 1830, and 1848 revolutions. The
most obvious form of diffusion of liberalism is the spread of ideas, in particular among highly
inter-connected and multi-lingual elites (cultural and political) throughout Europe. However,
other vehicles of diffusion include the Napoleonic wars (the "time bomb" of people's sovereignty in Rokkan's terms) and the general affirmation of the idea of "nation" which incorporated those of "liberalism" and "progress". The diffusion of liberalism takes place also in
periods prior to the national unifications of Germany and Italy at the *Kleinstaat* level.

[37] This image is conveyed perhaps most famously in Tilly's phrase that "war made the state and the
state made war" (Tilly, 1990).

[38] As discussed in Chapter 4, the rise of socialism is an instance of territorial "spread" across countries rather than "swing" properly speaking, namely a change of vote from an already existing
family to another already existing family.

mechanism regarding the structural conditions for the emergence of socialism as the most significant "wave" in European electoral history.[39]

Yet diffusion of structural factors would lead to an almost simultaneous timing of industrialization, which is not the case. Electoral waves seem to be of the second type (formation, organization, ideology), that is at the agency level. The birth of trade unions and subsequently socialist parties, too, did not happen in isolation from developments in neighbouring countries and the labour movement defined itself precisely as an international movement with trans-national contacts. Most of the national parties conceived themselves as national "sections" of an international organization. There is a strong element of agency – the creation of unions and parties, their internal organization and ideology – in the uniformity of the electoral swing detected by the indicators in Chapter 2.

Two more instances of uniformity appear in Table 8.4 during almost the same period, that is after World War I. The first is the appearance of the communist party family splitting away from the socialists in all European countries in the aftermath of the Soviet Revolution of 1917. The second is the rise of extreme-right fascist parties.[40] Concerning the former instance, data show that this is not a very large swing but that its territorial coverage is Europe-wide. Whatever the causes or the origins of the Soviet Revolution in Russia, this event can be assimilated to a supra-national event that had a similar effect in many European countries. The fact that this event takes place in one specific country and is followed by the birth of communist parties in most European countries in the next five-year period speaks in favour of a diffusion effect. The fact, furthermore, that the birth of communist parties in various countries takes place in spite of a huge diversity of socio-economic, cultural, and political conditions[41] suggests that the origin of the spread of communist parties cannot be attributed to parallel transformation at the national level (within-national mechanism). Also the brief time during which the division of the left occurs does not support the idea that diffusion effects acted through "independent variables" as in the case of the spread of socialists with technological change and industrialization. The diffusion mechanism operating in the case of communist parties is at the level of agency.

The last instance of diffusion that the analysis has detected concerns the ideological convergence within party families measured through text data

---

[39] Such a diffusion of technology, if nothing else, is driven by economic competition (the market) between firms and – in mercantilist perspective – by national economies as a whole.

[40] As mentioned, the quantitative indicators do not capture the magnitude of this swing as many of these parties rise in contexts of non-democratic polities and therefore are not included in the data set on which the analysis is based.

[41] By political conditions what is meant is the variety of patterns of state formation and nation-building (patterns of secession and independence, territorial unification, and break-up of multi-national empires), as well as of democratization with various levels of franchise in different countries and parliamentarism.

(party manifestos) in Chapters 6 and 7. As seen earlier, at the Europe-wide level there is a supra-national top-down impact through European integration and the outcome of the Cold War with the fall of the Berlin Wall on the cohesion of socialist programmes in particular (but also concerning other party families). With democratization in Central and Eastern Europe after 1989, there is also a horizontal diffusion process with party programmes in Central and Eastern Europe being very similar to those of their Western European counterparts when measured on the general left–right scale and on the more specific economic and cultural dimensions of this scale. Differently than other instances of diffusion, in this case one observes a flow from one half to the other half of Europe. The effect is a Europe-wide ideological convergence among parties of a same family.

Summing up, what emerges from this discussion is that trans-national diffusion mechanisms across political systems complement in two main ways the analysis of the origins of convergence in Europe's electorates and party systems.

First, the analysis of diffusion complements that of within-national mechanisms by separating the *structural level* of the preconditions that are favourable to the emergence of given party families from the *agency level* of their actual emergence. The uniform spread of given party families in the absence of Europe-wide similar conditions cannot be traced back to these conditions and must be explained by diffusion mechanisms.[42] Further, the uniform spread of given party families cannot be traced back to structural favouring conditions that appear in different national contexts at different points in time such as technological change, industrialization, and the transformation of class structure, but also democratization and enfranchisement. These are all favourable conditions for the emergence of given party families that, at some point or another, have brought about similar party families all over Europe. Yet it is the temporal simultaneity of appearance of these parties that cannot be explained by favourable factors displaced in time and across countries.

The observation of trans-national mechanisms thus points to agency much more than to structure. The diffusion of liberal movements, of the organization of labour and of communist splinters from it after World War I must be traced back to political action entailing the formation of such parties, their organization, and the definition of ideology. More than structures, it is the force of ideas that spread across Europe in brief periods of time in spite of the differential timing of favourable structural conditions. As seen, the role of left–right is crucial in homogenizing Europe first with nationalist-liberal parties (vs. conservative reaction) during periods of elitist politics and the idea of equal political participation through parliamentary representation, and then with social democracy and the idea of social equality and the role of the state in compensating for economic inequality caused by privilege and capitalism. Structural factors

---

[42] Especially if the diffusion of party families throughout Europe takes place also in the absence of a common supra-national factor and when it takes place over a short period of time.

are different across Europe, but such ideas spread nonetheless, bringing about similar alignments in most national party systems. In addition, nationalism and liberalism first, and social democracy later with the massification of politics, are both factors that functionally aim at integrating national territories and discard internally cultural fault lines such as language, ethnicity, and religion.[43] This further diminishes the degree of dissimilarity between national territories which become similar in the way the "new" national citizenship (based on civil, political, and social rights) is integrated. It is in this sense that processes of nationalization are a precondition for the Europeanization that takes place at the same time and along similar functional alignments.

Second, trans-national diffusion effects bring additional understanding about why the left–right dimension (the party families that develop from it, in particular the social democrats) plays such an important role in processes of Europeanization. "Structure" elements of technological change and industrialization, but also democratization and secularization, are *diffusion-prone* and therefore create converging conditions for the emergence of party families of the left–right dimension. Structure elements such as ethnic or religious composition of given countries and the geo-morphology of territory (which is connected to the origin of ethno-regionalist, agrarian, and denominational parties) are *diffusion-resistant* and thus do not lead to convergence through this mechanism.[44] Because it is the structural factors at the origin of left–right party families that are diffusion-prone, it is these party families (rather than those emerging from diffusion-resistant structural factors) that are present in a large number of European countries.[45]

Finally, from the three tables summarizing the effects of the three mechanisms one should note the absence of the dimension of "correspondence", the vertical homogeneity between levels in the multi-layered European party system. The degree of similarity between electoral behaviour and alignments at the national level and the EP results from a lack of major dimensions of contestation present at one level but not the other (Chapter 5). The major dimension of contestation present in most national systems permeates from the "lower"

---

[43] The integrative function of the nation especially during the phases of industrialization is analyzed by the classical literature on nationalism, first and foremost in Gellner (1983), but also in Anderson (1991), who points to the "spread" of the nation as a modern phenomenon.

[44] The ethno-linguistic composition of a country cannot spread to other countries, nor is it something that can be copied. It is difficult to emulate an ethno-linguistic party if there is no culturally distinct minority or if favourable conditions (for example, geographical isolation) are not given.

[45] As seen in Chapter 3 it is the industrial families (left–right) that are the most homogeneous throughout Europe while pre-industrial families (mainly based on cultural groups) are responsible for diversity in Europe. From the perspective of cultural factors, the one idea that did diffuse across Europe is the one of culturally homogenous nation-states with a correspondence between cultural traits (language, religion, ethnicity), territory, and political sovereignty, eventually leading to repeated attempts of border shifting, population migrations ("cleansing" in the more tragic cases), and cultural assimilation.

level to the "upper" EP one. Such isomorphic correspondence cannot be traced back to parallel national factors, a common supra-national factor, or diffusion, but rather to a sort of "bottom-up" effect from national structures to the EP one.

Conclusion: One Europe versus Several Nation-States

At different moments in the history of European elections and party systems' formation all three mechanisms – parallel change due to common factors and structural transformation, trans-national diffusion effects, and supra-national factors with similar effects in all national units – have played a role in homogenizing national systems, bringing them closer to one another and making them more similar. Empirically, observing these mechanisms highlights a consistent degree of commonality in European societies even if it is difficult to keep the three mechanisms separate from each other with more than one playing a role in convergence processes simultaneously.

Yet, while all three mechanisms have been confirmed in at least some of the dimensions of Europeanization, they all start from the premise that national electorates and party systems in Europe are different units. The basic units of the whole analysis are *separate and discrete* national systems. There is a high and increasing level of commonality between them, but the fundamental assumption is that one is dealing with several units. From the perspective of political organization this is obviously a reasonable point of view as there are different sovereign states that form, centralize, and integrate over the past 150 years. Nonetheless, as this book approaches its conclusion a different image starts forming – especially when contemplating European politics from a *mass electoral perspective* rather than from an institutional or regime one. This image is not one of many different and separate units, but rather of *Europe as one single unit*.

The methodological question that arises from the empirical analysis carried out in this book is about the criteria justifying an analysis of 30 different national units, as a different starting point – namely taking Europe as one single unit – would lead to a different interpretation of the data. How much sense does it make to speak of "parallel transformation" if rather than 30 units, Europe is considered as "one"? There is nothing parallel or similar if there is only one unit. How much sense does it make to speak of "diffusion among units" if there is one unit only? Diffusion requires at least two units. How much sense does it make to speak of "common, supra-national, top-down effects" on different systems if, instead of having different systems, there is only one? If Europe is considered as one unit there is nothing "common", nothing "supra-national", and nothing "top-down". The very basic concepts of convergence and commonality – as well as the operational indicators of homogeneity, uniformity, coherence, and closure – would make little sense if at least two different units are not considered. Even linguistically, the idea of commonality (and, conversely, deviation) requires the existence of a plurality of units of comparison. If empirical evidence points to a high degree of similarity between units, on what grounds, looking back at the beginning of the study, can one justify the separation of Europe into discrete territorial units?

The answer to this question has obviously to do with the fact that politics in Europe is organized in territorial and sovereign states which are still the most important locus of power and competition. It is the methodological choice made at the outset of this research. It is the standard answer in comparative politics. Can this choice be reconciled with the vision – supported empirically – of one European electorate and party system rather than many?

Yes if the existence of adjacent territorial states, with aspirations of unification and independence, characterized by similar parliamentary institutions and parallel phases of democratic transformation (civic, political, and social) – if this specific system itself, *a system of governance based on territorial states, is considered as one system.*[46] Europe is one system of governance and the fact that in all parts of Europe the nation-state imposes itself appears as an element of similarity: similarity of political structures which are typical of Europe. *Europeanization* – as defined in this book – *thus really becomes nationalization as a process of internal structuration* and the nation-states assume a similar status to US states and Swiss cantons before the formation of the federal states. Aspirations of fitting "state" and "nation" through unification or secession are processes of territorial structuration that involve the whole of Europe as one political unit of governance.

The analysis of Europeanization, thus, makes sense methodologically if considered as the process of integration at mass electoral perspective *among distinct units indeed but, at the same time, units belonging to one single system.* The weakening of territoriality with one main functional alignment – the left–right one – through different mechanisms thus becomes something that happened "in Europe", primarily from the second half of the 19th century until the 1920s.

---

[46] This process of institutional convergence and of formation of a specific form of Europe-wide governance based on adjacent nation-states shows through the dissolution of "multi-national" empires. As Kumar noted, "European civilization marked itself off from all past civilizations precisely by its principle of diversity, which, paradoxically, also gave it its unity" (Kumar, 2003: 37).

Conclusion

Towards Europe-wide Representation

In 1774 Edmund Burke, addressing the electors of Bristol, said:

> Parliament is a deliberative assembly of one nation, with one interest, that of the whole – where not local prejudices ought to guide, but the general good, resulting from the general reason of the whole. You choose a member, indeed; but when you have chosen him he is not a member of Bristol, but he is a member of Parliament.[1]

Since its first use in the English parliament, representation was based on a territorial, geographical, indeed local principle. Burgesses and knights summoned by the king were representatives of towns and counties (the Commons). For long representation was imposed from above and with democratization the local geographical definition of representation did not change immediately (Morgan, 1988: 43–6).[2] With Burke, however, representation acquires a new meaning: not the representation of particular interests from various territorial constituencies but, as famously stated in the same quote, the vision that "Parliament is not a congress of ambassadors" but rather the site where the same interests *across* territorial units – say, trade interests in places such as Bristol or Birmingham – are represented. Further, as Pitkin discussed in her seminal treatise on political representation, even towns or regions not enfranchised or represented territorially through a member of parliament may nonetheless be "virtually" represented in a communion of interests and feelings (Pitkin, 1967: 173). More recently, Manin too has written about the importance of representation being "national" rather than local in its historical development (Manin, 1997: 163). In the terminology used in this book, the

---

[1] The quote is from the *Speech to the Electors of Bristol (at the Conclusion of the Polls)* (1774). While this famous quote entails many important points – not least the one concerning "general reason of the whole" – the following discussion is limited to the aspects of interest in this book.

[2] The composition of the House of Commons was defined by the king in assigning representation to new boroughs and counties.

functional dimension of representation, as opposed to the territorial one, predominates (see Chapter 1).[3]

Historically, in national political systems the actors through which nation-wide cross-local interests are represented since the earliest phases of democratization are political parties. Political parties have the role of aggregating the different interests in coherent programmes and ideologies but also of linking the different territorial bits of a country together – in other words, making national representation possible.[4] This is done through the cross-district "linkage" or "coordination" of parties (Cox, 1999) or, what in a different terminology is referred to as their "nationalization,[5] that is the progressive replacement of territorial divisions in the representation process through functional dimensions of contestation. Parties, in modern democracies, not territorial constituencies, are the "link between local wishes and national interests" (Pitkin, 1967: 148) through the presentation of national programmes and a national vote.[6] Cross-territorial convergence becomes, therefore, a crucial *indicator of the electoral/democratic integration* of a political system. While constituency-based representation enhances the representation of the territorial parts, party-based representation enhances the aggregate representation of the whole.

This applies also to the European level. From a normative point of view, the existence of functional electoral alignments, the replacement of a vision of fragmented, territorially segmented electorates with a cross-territorial one, the integration of party organizations, and ideological convergence across territorial units play a crucial role at the European level – as similar processes did at the national level during earlier periods of time – in *enhancing the quality and efficiency of representation*.[7] The transition from a vision of territorially

---

[3] "Although the city of Birmingham elects no members to Parliament, it can still be virtually represented there because Bristol sends members; and these are really representative of the trading interest, of which Birmingham, too, is a part" (Pitkin, 1967: 174, more generally 171–80). In Pitkin's terminology "virtual" representation, that is cross-local, is juxtaposed to "actual" representation, that is through territorial constituencies. See also the concept of "surrogate" representation (Mansbridge, 2003: 523).

[4] The function of aggregation of political parties is stressed in functional-systemic theory (Almond, 1956).

[5] As nationalization literature has stressed the process is strengthened by PR. Duverger points to the role of PR in bringing about nationwide rather than regionally limited representation (Duverger, 1951: 331–2). See also Rokkan (1970: 350), Rose and Urwin (1975: 19), Sartori (1986), and Urwin (1982: 192), as well as Caramani (2004: 228–30) and Chapter 1.

[6] Similarly, Pierce stresses that "[t]he main alternative to the party model is the constituency-centred model ... In the party model, the national electorate conveys instructions to national parties" (Pierce, 1999: 10).

[7] As mentioned in Chapter 1, the study presented in this book does not take into account the organizational dimension of parties and the control of local/national stances, programmes, or personalities which would also guarantee a better visibility (or "identifiability") with respect to territorially fragmented party systems. For the concept of responsibility in the sense of "who is in charge" see Powell (2000).

fragmented representation to one stressing cross-territorial dimensions of contestation modifies our perception of both the accountability and responsiveness of representing elites. The perception of commonality from electorates of the Europe-wide issues that are more pressing stimulates integrated policy responses from representatives. The impact of common expressions of voice is increased compared to separate claims directed to several national systems and conveyed through different legislative chambers. Accountability, rather than working through 30 separate electorates, operates through integrated fronts across national boundaries.

At the EU level representative institutions with comparable power and legitimacy as national institutions still have to develop – if they ever will. It is not for this study to evaluate the possibility of a political union in Europe in the near or far future. What this study can show, however, is that the electoral and partisan/ideological structures would allow for a Europe-wide representation along partisan dimensions of confrontation rather than national ones and that the absence of territorially segmented electorates can enhance the democratic process. As Bartolini suggests in the conclusion of his seminal study on European integration, political structuring at the European level can be analyzed along territorial and functional dimensions, and "cross-border coordination among national social, political, and corporate actors with similar interests/values … is the core of the 'Europeanization' hypothesis" (Bartolini, 2005, 389–92).[8] The present investigation has addressed precisely this question and reached the conclusion that the functional dimension predominates over the territorial one in the European electorate.

In Europe today the construction of a political and democratic citizenship is at the centre of the debates on the "democratic deficit" of the EU. The integration of system-wide electorates and party systems represents a crucial step towards the structuring of political parties necessary for a "truly European" accountable party system to emerge (Andeweg, 1995: 67), that is (according to Marquand's phrase quoted in the Introduction) from a *Europe des patries* (in which European politics is structured around national identities and interests) to a *Europe des partis* (in which European politics is structured along non-territorial, functional, and Europe-wide alignments). The main conclusion this book reaches is that Europe is "Europeanized" from an electoral point of view, and that it has been so for a long time.

Europeanization reaches back to periods of time prior to European integration proper. It is a long-term process that has its origins in factors that go beyond the top-down impact of European integration in the more recent decades

---

[8] Bartolini goes on to note that "[n]ext to the above-mentioned alignments *among territories*, others are increasingly *across territories*" (Bartolini, 2005: 392). This results for the most part from the alignments that are, at the European level, "isomorphic with the predominant national cleavage system" (p. 403), what the analysis of correspondence in Chapter 5 confirms empirically.

TABLE C.1. *A Comparison of Europeanization and Nationalization*

Period	Europeanization			Nationalization		
	Coverage (%)	Standard Deviation	IPR	Coverage (%)	Standard Deviation	IPR
	All Countries with Elections			**All Constituencies**		
1850–1914	54.4	11.64	0.74	52.2	18.49	0.72
1915–44	55.2	10.82	0.74	75.0	9.59	0.61
1945–present	49.7	8.91	0.76	77.7	6.58	0.54
Entire period	53.0	9.91	0.74	70.7	10.10	0.60
	Only Countries where Families Present			**Only Contested Constituencies**		
1850–1914	–	10.04	0.49	–	17.43	0.49
1915–44	–	10.61	0.54	–	9.86	0.50
1945–present	–	8.65	0.52	–	6.54	0.43
Entire period	–	9.37	0.52	–	9.87	0.46

Notes: Nationalization figures indicate average for 17 Western European countries. Europeanization figures include Central and Eastern Europe. The more recent period is slightly different between Europeanization and nationalization, that is 1945–2012 for the former and 1950–2000 for the latter. For Europeanization figures, party families are aggregated as documented in Chapter 3.
Source: Chapter 3 and Caramani (2004: 79).

of European history as theorized in Chapter 1 and summarized in Chapter 8. Although the conclusions reached in the various chapters are much more nuanced than this, overall empirical evidence points to patterns of commonality and convergence. But just how robust is such a conclusion in comparison? Over time one observes a process of homogenization and increased cohesiveness in Europe, and there is evidence of "waves" of change that wipe across Europe simultaneously. Yet cross-sectionally Europe stands out as a unique case: without comparison it is difficult to assess its degree of integration.[9] At the end of this study, it is useful to address the scope of Europeanization alongside other instances of formation of electoral space more broadly.

The indicator of homogenization (the first of the five considered in the empirical analysis in Part II) is the closest one to research on nationalization and can be used for a comparison with electoral integration processes between European and national levels.[10] Table C.1 includes a comparison of figures

---

[9] The N = 1 problem is familiar to scholars of European integration. For a debate of this issue see Caporaso et al. (1997). All major studies have debated the challenge of testing hypotheses on integration (Haas, 1958; Milward, 1992; Moravcsik, 1998; Pollack, 2003).

[10] A comparison would in principle also be possible between Europe-wide swings (uniformity in Chapter 4) and swings that take place at the national level as done by Stokes for the United

with averages for Western European countries. As seen in Chapter 2, and as it appears again in Table C.1, the average coverage in Europe (the presence of parties in the various democratic countries) is 53.0 per cent on average for the whole period analyzed. This is comparable to the average coverage at the country level for the period up to World War I (52.2 per cent). At the national level the average increases to roughly 75.0 per cent after World War II, attesting to a higher degree of nationalization than Europeanization. The indicator of coverage, however, does not weight parties by their size, and therefore the standard deviation is a more appropriate indicator when putting together parties and party families to obtain a system-wide figure. For both nationalization and Europeanization the overall figure is around 10.0, and both national and European data attest to a process of integration over the three periods distinguished in the table. European nation-states, on average, do not appear more integrated than "Europe" when considered as one unit. On the contrary, for the period covering the 19th century until World War I, single nation-states were internally more diverse than Europe as a whole. This conclusion is made more significant by the fact that nationalization figures include only 17 Western European cases, whereas Europeanization figures include also Central and Eastern European cases – albeit not for all periods.[11]

Table C.2 provides a more precise comparison of European levels of homogeneity with single countries rather than overall country averages as in Table C.1. The case "Europe" is placed in the list of countries ranked according to the standard deviation (computed on all territorial units, be it countries for Europeanization or constituencies for nationalization). As it appears, *a number of countries are less integrated* nationally than Europe overall.[12] "Europe" appears as quite average in this list. The coverage measure points to countries in which parties are present in a small number of constituencies, like Spain and its many regionalist parties. However, when taking into account the fact that these regionalist parties are quite small in terms of votes, the standard deviation for the whole system points to a nationalized party system for the main large parties. In countries like Switzerland, Belgium, and the United Kingdom

Kingdom and the United States (Stokes, 1965 and 1967), as well as a comparison of correspondence (Chapter 5) between regional and national levels. A comparison on the other dimensions analyzed in this book would require survey, cabinet, and manifesto data at the regional level for single countries (Schakel, 2013).

[11] For reference Table C.1 includes the IPR, another indicator controlling for the size of parties (small and large parties weight the same in the systemic average). Figures computed only on territorial units (constituencies or countries) in which parties are present do not lead to very different results except for the obvious fact that they point to higher homogeneity.

[12] Low levels of territorial integration concern in particular "territorialized" party systems like Switzerland and the United Kingdom (in which the main parties are unevenly distributed across constituencies), "segmented" party systems like Finland, Germany, and Italy in the past 20 years (in which there is one main, solid region with its distinctive party), and "regionalized" party systems like Belgium (in which the main parties are unevenly distributed plus there are regionalist parties). For this typology see Caramani (2004: 151–3).

TABLE C.2. *Comparison of Homogenization between Europe and Nation-States* *(1945–Present)*

Countries	Coverage (%)	All Units (Constituencies or Countries)		Only Units in which Party Families are Present	
		Standard Deviation	IPR	Standard Deviation	IPR
Switzerland	42.1	9.46	0.79	10.57	0.44
Belgium	59.4	9.39	0.66	6.05	0.39
UK-Britain	55.1	9.25	0.67	10.57	0.44
Finland	85.5	9.04	0.52	9.66	0.46
"Europe"	49.7	8.91	0.76	8.65	0.52
Germany	77.9	8.26	0.55	5.38	0.40
France	96.1	6.66	0.57	6.86	0.49
Iceland	91.8	6.63	0.45	6.67	0.39
Ireland	71.1	6.50	0.55	6.48	0.41
Greece	90.2	6.13	0.44	6.17	0.40
Austria	96.8	6.04	0.40	6.27	0.38
Netherlands	99.9	5.26	0.44	5.26	0.44
Norway	95.6	4.97	0.43	4.83	0.41
Spain	37.8	4.56	0.79	5.58	0.45
Italy	76.5	4.52	0.59	7.20	0.51
Sweden	98.6	4.34	0.37	4.39	0.36
Denmark	94.9	3.79	0.42	3.99	0.39

Notes: Countries ordered by standard deviation (all units). Europeanization figures include Central and Eastern Europe. Periods are different between Europe and single countries: 1945–2012 for the former and 1950–2000 for the latter. Spain since the mid-1970s. Germany since re-unification (and CDU/CSU as separate parties). United Kingdom does not include Northern Ireland.
Source: Caramani (2004: 86 and data set).

it is the large parties themselves that are unevenly distributed across regions. Table C.2, furthermore, does not take into account the fact that for the past 20 years countries like Belgium, Italy and the United Kingdom have become more regionalized compared to the average for 1950–2000 reported in the table.[13]

The nationalization literature from which this study on Europeanization is inspired can be traced back to Schattschneider's classic book *The Semi-Sovereign People* (1960) in which one chapter is devoted to the existence and subsequent dissolution of "solid sections" in the United States, the emergence of

---

[13] Similar conclusions that Europe is not less homogenous than many nation-states can be reached also with a comparison with Latin America. Such data are provided in particular by Harbers (2010). The average Gini coefficient for Latin American countries is 0.29 even if the version that controls for the size of parties is 0.71. For Europe the equivalent figures are 0.35 and 0.41.

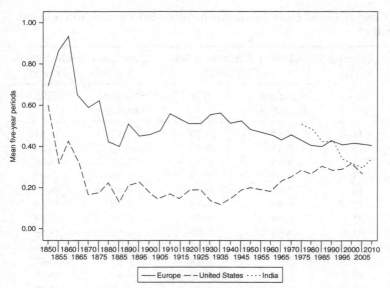

FIGURE C.1. Europeanization and Americanization of party systems: 1850s–present (Gini2W).
Source: For India and the United States data are taken from the Constituency-Level Elections Archive (CLEA). Territorial units are districts (Lok Sabha and House of Representatives). For India longer time series are not available.

nationwide issues and policies, and simultaneous shifts of votes between elections. As a major case for comparative analysis it is thus tempting to compare Europeanization with Americanization.[14]

The overall pattern of this comparison since the mid-19th century for both territorial units (Europe and the United States) appears in Figure C.1. Since 1977 also data for India are added as a further unit of comparison with another large and stable democracy. As it appears, the United States is more homogeneous than Europe, and India has comparable levels (with a pattern of homogenization since 1977). The longitudinal pattern of Europe and the United States is quite similar with a shift towards similar party system structures across territory in the second half of the 19th century when the US two-party system established itself at the end of the Civil War in 1865 and when in Europe more countries are included in the wake of democratization processes. More important, however, this is the moment when class politics imposes itself with its economic and political mobilization. While never reaching the levels of

[14] A number of studies on the territorial structures of Europe and the United States have been recently conducted. See, in particular, Ansell and Di Palma (2004) and Fabbrini (2004, 2005, 2007), who speaks of "compound democracies". On the use of the term *Americanization* see in particular Brady, D'Onofrio, and Fiorina (2000) and Claggett, Flanigan, and Zingale (1984).

structuration and simplicity of the two-party system in the United States, the basic dominant left–right dimension – as seen throughout this book – shapes in a similar way most European national party systems.

Overall, in this comparison with other nation-states, "Europe" taken as a unit does not stand out as particularly heterogeneous. Its levels of internal diversity are even lower than those of certain European countries which nationalization research has identified as territorially diverse. In normative terms, thinking of future possible pushes towards political union at the EU level and democratization of its institutions, this level of diversity is comparable to other well-established national democracies – Germany, Switzerland and the United Kingdom for example. Party system structures and party family ideologies are *similar to a degree that, in a number of national contexts, has not hindered the emergence of stable democratic institutions and competition.* The preconditions for a type of functional cross-territory representation which Burke identified as truly "national" representation thus seem to apply to Europe and seem to have been in place for a long period of time. Importantly, this study has not identified "solid sections" or regions of Europe that stand out for their diversity with respect to the European party systems – significantly, this does not apply to Central and Eastern Europe.

The comparison between Europeanization and processes that took place at the level of nation-states, however, should not be taken too far. Europeanization as defined in this study misses one of the central elements of electoral integration at the national level, namely a sovereign centre carrying out policies aimed at state formation, administrative-economic integration, and nation-building based on the legitimate use of force. Furthermore, nationalization processes were embedded in unprecedented social and political mobilization: the radical change of the Industrial Revolution, with urbanization and the commodification of labour, coupled with ideological projects and visions of society, as well as the powerful political organization represented by the mass party. Today, both types of mobilization are weak with decreasing participation rates and individual rather than collective forms of participation. While the national-liberal endeavours were the project of elites that only later incorporated the masses (vote and welfare), the European project cannot be carried out without the support of citizens.

Ultimately, in this comparison between national and European integration there is an irony. Nation-states integrated under conditions of democratically illiterate masses that were excluded from the political process or, at best, were only just learning how to be participant citizens. Regional diversity, with religious, ethno-linguistic, and urban–rural differences, was high. National integration was imposed by largely undemocratic elites and constraining means of socialization like compulsory schooling and conscript military service. The preconditions were not favourable, but centralization could be imposed. Europe today, on the other hand, presents favourable conditions with a democratically literate citizenry and a high degree of cross-national homogeneity originating from the predominance of the left–right dichotomy across national borders. However, it lacks a centre with the strength and legitimacy to impose centralization even to a level approaching that of decentralized countries like Switzerland. The preconditions are favourable, but political centralization cannot be imposed – precisely because of the expectation of democratic participation created by nation-states.

What is more, the electoral conditions for integration identified earlier are such that integration would not necessarily have to occur in a consociational way. The cultural and socio-economic diversity of Europe has often invited comparisons with polities based on consensual agreement and consociational politics.[15] The electoral picture that emerges in this book, however, points to a rather different possibility, namely that a homogeneous and dominant left–right dimension that pervades European party systems horizontally, but also vertically, in the multi-level governance structure is closer to the majoritarian, "Westminster" type of politics. Left–right as a homogenous dimension of contestation in Europe and one that spans levels of governance, not ethno-linguistic and religious dimensions, dominates this party system. European party federations in the EP already point to the possibility of such an aggregation (Hix, Noury, and Roland, 2005 and 2007).

Part of the irony is, then, that resistance to European integration comes from the very element that the elites who put forward the vision of a united Europe held as central – namely citizens' democratic participation in the project of bringing the European "peoples" closer and peacefully together. Democracy makes it impossible for an elite to "responsibly" impose political integration while "irresponsively" disregarding electorates. But part of the irony is also that this difficulty is set in an electoral and partisan context that the very democratization has rendered homogenous across national borders, in fact setting favourable conditions for political integration. Furthermore, it is through democratization (political and social) that the homogenous factors that cut across national territories as shown in the previous chapters become, in fact, increasingly bound to national centres as these are the centres from which political and social rights emanate. While similar in the different national units that make up Europe, these very common rights across the whole of Europe reinforce the legitimacy and identity of separate national polities.

As a result, Europe is divided into units that, from the perspective of electoral alignments, are structured similarly in a sort of division-of-similarity pattern, or "segmented similarity". This similarity unifies the different levels of the European "multi-level" party system vertically as it unifies the European

---

[15] On the features of consociational (or proportional) versus "Westminster" (or majoritarian) types of democracy see Horowitz (1985), Lijphart (1984), and Powell (2000). The most important features include PR, multi-party systems, and oversized cabinet coalitions to allow the representation of, mainly cultural, minority groups.

"multi-unit" party system horizontally.[16] Yet accountability and responsiveness as two crucial dimensions of representation processes – the degree to which citizens identify and sanction the action of representatives, and the degree to which representatives act according to citizens' preferences – are channelled through 30 separate political systems rather than a common one.[17]

Finally, there is the question of how Europe-wide convergence fits into the broader picture of globalization. Comparative political science oscillates between visions of global convergence and regional divergence. After the bloody confrontation between antagonistic models of mass mobilization represented by liberal democracy, communism, and fascism, writings in the aftermath of World War II optimistically pointed to convergence towards Western models of liberal–capitalist order only to be denied by the persistence of communist regimes in Eastern Europe and China, and authoritarian regimes in Latin America and Southern Europe, as well as by the rise of new patrimonialist regimes in decolonized Africa and the Middle East. The closer analysis of Europe also contributed to questioning the model of Anglo-Saxon democracies with the analysis of plural, but democratically stable and effective, and economically wealthy and egalitarian democracies.[18] With the "third wave of democratization" once again visions of convergence were put forward when alternative (mostly authoritarian) models collapsed in Eastern Europe, Latin America, and Southern Europe, or were radically reformed as in China.[19] More recent trends, however, point also to divergent directions with new forms of state capitalism in Asia, "competitive authoritarianism" in countries like Russia, or "Bolivarian" populism in Latin America. Also in relation to culture some have pointed to persistently distinct "civilizations", centre–periphery structures, and new North–South divisions.[20]

The question thus becomes whether Europeanization as shown in this book is simply part of a broader pattern of Westernization and globalization or is

---

[16] The concept of "multi-level" party systems is taken from Hooghe and Marks (2001). The concepts of "multi-unit" party systems and "segmented similarity" are made up.

[17] On accountability see Powell (2000, especially chapter 3), Przeworski, Stokes, and Manin (1999), and Strøm (2000). On responsiveness see Andeweg (2011), Powell (2009), and Schmitt and Thomassen (2000), besides the classical treatment by Pitkin (1967).

[18] See the contributions to Dahl's influential volume *Political Oppositions in Western Democracies* (1966) and work quoted in the Introduction, not only on Europe but also on Canada, South Africa, Lebanon, and India.

[19] Reference is made here to the thesis of the "end of history" and the definite establishment of liberal democracy but also to evidence of democracy promotion by Western states (the United States and the EU in particular) and international organizations.

[20] On distinct "civilizations" see Huntington (1996) and on new North–South divisions see Gartzke (2007). Other types of global territorial alignments include relics of the Cold War, anti-hegemonic bloc (Jackson and Sørensen, 2007) and world regionalization. Historical and cultural literature on "world systems" includes the distinction between core states, peripheries, semi-peripheries, and external areas (Wallerstein, 1974, especially chapters 5 and 6, 1980, 1989, and 2011).

a distinct pattern. Are the dimensions of politics that *unite* Europe also the dimensions that make it *distinct* from other areas? Or does convergence go beyond Europe to cover the West and maybe other regions and "modernities" too?[21] The latter possibility links to the core values on which European politics is based, namely the quest for equality and freedom mentioned in the Introduction, and for political and judicial institutions enshrining civil, political, and socio-economic rights. Yet what this book has shown is not so much the parallel development of these values and institutions.[22] It has shown the commonality of the *conflict*, the *cleavage*, over such values and over the balance between freedom and equality. Looking back to the goals of the analysis as defined in the Introduction, this book points to the similarity of the *political divisions and the cultural conflicts* over the degree of civil, political, and socio-economic equality and freedom: Which civil rights, what degree of inclusion for political rights, how deep the correction of socio-economic inequalities and privilege through state intervention? Not a commonality of values but commonality of the conflict over them.

Political divisions and cultural conflicts were and are strikingly similar across European countries. Is this unique to Europe, or is there something more universal in this basic choice which has crudely been summarized in terms of left and right?[23] Is it limited to Europe and excludes North America where social democracy never developed? Or does it include North America, where the debate on the welfare state is a major dimension in the political space, but excludes other regions? Or, on the contrary, is there something universal in the "dimensionality of politics" regarding the balance between state and market, between democratic input legitimacy and (not necessarily democratic) output legitimacy? Is this an underlying cleavage found in all regions cutting across the global geography, or is there a territoriality of this dimensionality?

These broad questions should not be answered in abstract terms but rather empirically. Yet even just their broad theoretical formulation seems to indicate that the territoriality of cleavages over basic social and policy choices is a major dimension of the globalization of politics and that the analysis of alignments worldwide and of "global cleavages" should be considered in future research.

---

[21] On multiple modernities see Eisenstadt (2002 and 2006).

[22] The global commonality of these values and the general trend towards human empowerment is the theme of Welzel's book (2013) on the rise of emancipative values (freedom and equality) in which within-societal differences (functional ones in the terminology used in this book) are "dwarfed" by national differences (i.e. territorial ones), as well as of the general literature on the geographical opposition between West (Europe mainly) and "rest" (Landes, 1998; McNeill, 1963; Morris 2010, and Pomeranz, 2000, among many others).

[23] On this thesis see Bobbio (1996) and Noël and Thérien (2008).

APPENDICES

HARPERTORCH

Appendix 1

Party Families

In many cases names of parties change over time. Because a detailed description is not a priority of this book, shortcuts and simplified names are used. Table A.1.1 indicates which parties are included in each family. For the general criteria for the attribution of codes, see Chapter 2.

For four small families no table has been produced:

1. Animalist parties: there is only one such party, namely the PvdD in the Netherlands between 2006 and 2010.
2. Pro-alcohol parties: there are only two instances: the SPP-Beer in 1992–6 in the Czech Republic and the PPPP in 1991–3 in Poland.
3. Feminist parties: three such parties existed in Iceland (WA in 1983–99), Latvia (SS in 1931), and Lithuania (LMP-Women's Party in 1996–2000), in addition to the Slovenian GZS and the Swedish Feminist Initiative (both in EP elections only).
4. Pro-European parties in national elections: the EK in Cyprus has been considered (1981–2001), as well as three Czech parties (SNK in 2002–10, DU in 1996–2002 and US 1998–2002). Most pro-European parties run in EP elections (see Table A.1.2).

In Table A.1.1 dates refer to election years with the indication of the first and last elections contested by each party and in which the party received at least 1 per cent of votes nationwide. Periods between the first and last elections during which a party did not exist or did not reach the 1 per cent threshold for inclusion in the analysis are not reported. Party families are listed alphabetically. Czech Republic as Czechoslovakia from World War I until separation. As far as European elections are concerned, parties that participate *exclusively* in elections to the EP (i.e. do not appear in figures for national elections) are listed in Table A.1.2.

TABLE A.1.1. *Party Families*

Several of the parties listed in the following tables may also be running in European elections (See Table A.1.2).

Agrarians

Country	Parties
Austria	Grossdeutschen u. Landesbund 1923–7, Landbund f. Oesterreich 1923–45, Bauernpartei 1919–20
Bulgaria	BNS 2005–9, NS 1991–7, BZNS 1899–1994
Czech Republic	SCSPZR 1992–6, AGR 1920–92
Denmark	A-BP 1898–1945
Estonia	ETE 1995, ML-Farmer assemblies-AWK 1932, Settlers 1923–32
Finland	Agrarian Union-Centre 1907–2011, Rural Party 1970–99, SPVP 1929–48, SPP 1962–70
Germany	BB 1898–1907, BdL 1898–1912, Landbund 1924–8, LvolkP 1928–32, DBP 1928–32, WV 1912–19
Greece	PADU 1926–61, AS 1926–46, Farmers and Labourers 1950–1
Hungary	FKGP 1990–2002, ASZ 1990–8
Iceland	PP 1916–2009, FP 1934–42, IF 1916–19
Ireland	FP 1922–33
Latvia	ZS 1920–2010, DCP-DPS 1993–2002, LZP-LKZS 1920–8, BAS 1920–2, BB 1920–2, JS 1922–31, J-S 1925–31, NZA 1925–8, LDZA 1928–31, LZPA 1931, JZA 1931
Lithuania	LVS-LVP-Peasant Party 1920–2008, ZS 1920–3, US 1920–6
Luxembourg	LLACMO 1937–45, PACM 1925–45
Netherlands	BP 1922–77, PLAT 1922–37, MSL 1929–33
Norway	Senter 1915–2009
Poland	PSL 1919–2011, SRP 1993–2011, PL-PSL-PZL 1919–97, ChhSR 1922–91
Romania	PNT-PNTCD 1927–2008, PDAR 1990–2, BNT 1926–7, PT 1928–37, BMT 1928–32, PNA 1932–7, PTD 1932–3, PUA 1933–46, PRT 1933–46, PTD 1946–90
Slovakia	SVP 1990–2
Sweden	Center 1917–2010, JR 1917–21
Switzerland	VLGV-JB-SVP 1914–67

Anti-Europeans

Country	Parties
Austria	Nein 1995–9
Czech Republic	Sovereignty 2010
Finland	True Finns 1999–2011
Greece	AE 2012
Poland	ROP 1997–2001
United Kingdom	Referendum Party 1997–2001, UKIP 2001–10

Catholics

Country	Parties
Belgium	DC 1919–49, Daens 1894–1919
Germany	CSU 1949–2009, Zentrum 1871–1953
Ireland	National Party 1997–2002
Malta	CWP 1962–71
Netherlands	KVP 1888–1977, RKVP 1925–37, KNP 1948–56
Poland	WAK-CNU-Fatherland 1991–7, Bloc for Poland 1997–2001, SKL 1919–22, ChZJN 1922–91
Romania	LANC 1926–37, PNC 1937–46
Switzerland	CVP 1848–2011

Communists

Country	Parties
Austria	KPÖ 1945–2008
Belgium	KPB-PCB 1925–87, PC 1971–4, KP 1971–4, UDRT 1981–7
Bulgaria	BKP 1920–2001
Cyprus	AKEL-EDEK-DIKO 1960–76, ADISOK-ADIK 1991–2006
Czech Republic	KSC-KSCM-Levy Blok 1925–2010, AB-Levy Blok 1935–98
Denmark	KP 1932–84
Estonia	Left Alternative 1992–5, Justice 1995–9, Communists 1920–92
Finland	Dem. League 1945–2011, Dem. Alternative 1987–91
France	PCF (Front de Gauche) 1924–2012, LO 1978–2007, Ligue Comm. Rév. 2002–7
Germany	PDS-Linke 1990–2009, KPD 1920–57
Greece	KKE-EDA 1926–2012, KKE-ES (Syriza) 1977–2012
Hungary	MSZMP 1990–2006, MDNP 1998–2002
Iceland	PA 1931–99
Ireland	SFWP-Workers' Party 1973–92, IWL 1927–32
Italy	PCI 1921–87, DP-PDUP 1976–92, RC 1992–2008, PDCI 2001–8
Latvia	LTF 1993–8
Latvia	KSZ 1928–31, PTA 1928–31, LDS 1928–31
Luxembourg	KPL 1934–2009
Malta	WP 1950–5
Netherlands	CPN 1922–86, SP 1994–2010
Norway	SV-SF 1961–2009, NKP 1924–73
Poland	Communists 1922, NPR 1922–91, SP 1991–3
Portugal	PCP-MDP/PEV (APU, CDU) 1975–2009, MDP 1975–6, UDP 1976–87, PSR 1979–95
Slovakia	KSS 1990–2010, ZRS 1994–2002
Spain	PCE/IU 1933–2011, MUC 1986–9
Sweden	Vaenster 1921–2010, SKP (Hoeglund) 1924–8
Switzerland	PdA 1922–99

Conservatives

Country	Parties
Belgium	PP 2010
Bulgaria	SDS (ODS) 1991–2009, DSB 2005–9, Blue Coalition 2009, PLP-ONPP 1899–31, NP 1899–1923
Cyprus	DEK-DISY 1970–2011
Czech Republic	ODS-KDS 1990–2010, NS 1935–46
Denmark	Right-KFP 1849–2011
Estonia	Pro Patria (Res Publica) 1992–2011, Res Publica 2003–7
Finland	Old Finns-NCP 1907–2011
France	RPR-UMP 1946–2012, Conservateurs-CNI 1876–93, Nouveau Centre (Maj. Pré.) 2007–12, MPF 2007–12, Chasse, Pêche, Nation, Trad. 2002–7
Germany	D Rechtspartei 1949–61, Vrep 1928–30, DRP 1871–1919, DkonP 1871–1919
Greece	ERE-GR-New Democracy 1956–2012, Pol. Spring 1993–2000, C 1926–8, CRP 1928–32, DS (G. Papandreou Party) 1936–52, New Party 1950–1, P 1951–61
Hungary	MDF 1990–2010, Fidesz (KDNP, MDF) 1990–2010
Iceland	IP 1923–2009, Citizen 1987–91, NPP 1953–63
Ireland	FF 1922–2011
Italy	Destra 1876–1913, Forza Italia-Popolo Libertà 1994–2008, IdV 2001–8
Latvia	LC 1993–2006, TP 1998–2010, JL 2002–10, JD 2006–10, PS 2010
Lithuania	TS-LK 1996–2008, NKS-Mod. Cons. Union 2000–4, Rising Nation 2008
Malta	CON 1921–55, DNP 1962–71
Netherlands	NMP 1971–2
Norway	Høire 1882–2009, KYST 2001–5
Poland	PiS 2001–11, UPR 1991–2007
Portugal	CDS-PP 1975–2009
Romania	PP 1926–37
Slovakia	HZD 2002–6
Slovenia	SDS 1996–2011
Spain	AP-PP 1977–2011
Sweden	MS 1911–2010
Switzerland	SVP 1971–2011, BDP 2011
United Kingdom	Conservatives 1832–2010

Appendices 301

Ethnic parties

Country	Parties
Austria	Tschechoslovaken 1919–20
Bulgaria	VMRO 1927–31, DPS 1991–2009
Czech Republic	Germans 1920–46, Slovaks 1920–35, Hungarians 1920–46
Estonia	Russians-UPP 1999–2007, Russians-VEE 1919–2003, Germans 1919–92
Finland	SFP 1907–2011
Germany	Poles, Alsacians, Welfs, etc. 1871–1919
Latvia	SLAT-TSP-Russians–Human Rights 1993–2010, Russians-ER-LSP 1993–8, Russians-LKPP 1993–8, Russians-SC 2006–10, Germans 1920–31, KPG 1920–5, EB 1920–5, CC 1920–2, APP 1922–31, AI 1922–31, PKLPS 1925–8, KPSD 1925–31, Mizrachi 1925–31, PKLPS 1928–31
Lithuania	LCRK-LLRA-Poles 1920–2008, LTMA-Nat-Minorities 1996–2000, RB-ZDS-LRS-Russians 1922–2000, LVK-KVP 1920–6, SG 1922–3, Polish Workers 1926
Poland	German Minority 1991–3, MN 1919–91, Ugrup Ukrainskie 1922–91
Romania	UDMR 1990–2008, BMG-Ethnic minorities 1927–2008, PE 1931–46
Slovakia	SMK 1990–2010, MOST-HID 2010
Slovenia	Italian Minority 1996–2000, Hungarian Minority 1996–2011

Extreme-right parties

Country	Parties
Austria	FPÖ 1949–2008, BZÖ 2006–8, Deutschnationale 1919–20, NSDAP 1930–45, Nat. Wirtschaftsblock 1930–45, Heimatsblock 1930–45
Belgium	FN 1991–2007, Rexists 1936–46
Bulgaria	Ataka 2005–9, PS 1994–7, RZS 2009
Czech Republic	VV 2010, NOF 1935–46
Denmark	Progress P. 1973–2001, Faelles Kurs 1987–94, DFP 1998–2011, DNSAP 1935–45
Estonia	Indep. Royalists 1992–5, Estonian Citizen 1992–9, MKOE 1995–9, Right-wingers 1995–9, ERSP 1992–5
Finland	Finnish Unity P. 1975–9
France	Boulange 1889–93, Poujade 1956–62, FN 1986–2012, Extrême droite 1956–62
Germany	NPD 1924–2009, REP 1990–2002, DVU 1998–2002, Antisemiten 1893–1912
Greece	Nat. Alignment 1977–81, FOP 1926–46, IR 1926–32, KA 2012

(*continued*)

Extreme-right parties (*continued*)

Country	Parties
Hungary	HVK 1990–4, MIEP 1994–2010, Jobbik 2010
Iceland	Nat. Party 1987–91
Ireland	Nat. League 1927–32
Italy	PNF 1921–46, MSI-AN 1948–2008, Fiamma Tricolore 2008–13, Monarchists-PMP 1946–62, UQ 1946–8
Latvia	TB-LNNK 1993–2010, JP 1998–2002, For Latvia 2006–10
Lithuania	Young Lithuania 1992–2008, Order and Justice 2004–8, Frontas 2008, LTS-LDP 1992–2000, LPKTS-LKPD 1992–2000, TPP 1922–6
Luxembourg	NB 1989–99
Netherlands	CD 1994–8, LN 2002–3, LPF 2002–6, PVV 2006–10, NSB 1937–46
Norway	SAMF-Progress P. 1933–2009, NS 1933–45
Poland	LPR 2001–11, Ruch Patriotyczny 2005–7, KPN 1991–7
Romania	PRM 1992–2008, PNG 2004–8, GCZC 1932–3, PTT 1937–46
Slovakia	HZDS 1992–2010, SNS 1990–2010, PSNS 2002–6
Slovenia	SNS 1996–2011, LIPA 2008–11
Spain	CEDA and alliance 1933–77
Sweden	NYD 1991–8, SD 2002–10
Switzerland	SD 1971–2003, Rep. 1971–9, FPS 1991–9, Front 1935–9, Gruet. 1919–25
United Kingdom	BNP 2010

Greens

Country	Parties
Austria	Grüne 1983–2008, VGÖ 1990–4
Belgium	Ecolo 1981–2010, Agalev-Groen 1981–2010
Cyprus	Greens-KEP 1996–2011
Czech Republic	SZ-LSU 1990–2010
Denmark	Gronn 1987–90
Estonia	EER 1992–2011
Finland	Vihrea Liitto 1987–2011
France	Verts (LV) 1981–2012, GE 1993–7
Germany	Grüne 1980–2009
Greece	Ecol. Greens 2007–12
Hungary	LMP-HP 2010
Iceland	LG 1999–2009
Ireland	Green P. 1992–2011
Italy	Lista Verde-Fed. dei Verdi-Arcobaleno 1987–2008
Latvia	ZAS 1993–5
Luxembourg	Die Greng 1984–2009, GLA 1999–2004, GLEI 1989–94
Malta	Dem. Alt. 1992–2008
Netherlands	GL 1989–2010

Country	Parties
Romania	PER 1990–2, MER 1990–2
Slovakia	SZ 1990–4, SZS 1992–4
Slovenia	SMS 2000–4
Sweden	MP 1982–2010
Switzerland	GPS 1983–2011, Green Lib. 2007–11
United Kingdom	Greens 2005–10

Inter-confessionals

Country	Parties
Estonia	CRE 1919–32, Christian Dem. 1999–2011
Germany	CDU 1949–2009
Latvia	LPP 2002–10, KNP 1920–8, KKZP 1925–8, KZK 1928–31, KA-S 1928–31, AVS 1928–31
Netherlands	CDA 1977–2010

Liberals

Country	Parties
Austria	LIF 1994–2008, Demokratische Partei 1919–20
Belgium	Liberals (PVV-PLP) 1848–1977, PRL-MR 1971–2010, VLD 1971–2010, Vivant 1999–2003
Bulgaria	NDSV 2001–9, BBB 1991–2001, SDS-Centre 1991–4, SDS-LIB. 1991–4, LP (NLP-MLP) 1899–1991, NLP 1899–1914, DP 1899–1931, MLP 1908–14
Cyprus	DIKO 1970–2011, ED 1996–2011
Czech Republic	TOP 2010, ODA 1992–8, OH 1992–6, KAN 1992–6, SB 1990–2, CND 1920–35, CZOS-DS 1920–90
Denmark	Venstre 1849–2011, Retsforbundet 1924–87, CD 1973–2007, New (Lib.) Alliance 2007–11, LRP 1895–1910, MV 1892–1910, Liberals of the capital 1947–50, LC 1966–71
Estonia	Centre 1992–2011, EEE-ERP 1992–2011, ETE Labour Party-RKE 1919–92, Economic group-Houseowners 1920–32
Finland	Young Finns-Progressive P.-Liberal P. 1907–91
France	Mvt. Réformateur-UDF-MD 1973–2012, Pole Rép. 2002–7, MNR 2002–7, Parti Rép.-UDR 1958–78, CDS 1981–6, RI 1906–78, ALP 1910–14, RD 1958–67
Germany	FDP 1949–2009, DDP 1919–33, WP 1924–32, NLP 1871–1919, LibRP 1871–7, LibV 1881–4, FrP 1884–1912, FoP 1871–84, FrVP 1893–1919
Greece	EK-Centre Union 1926–81, New Lib. Party 1977–81, Nat. Dem. Union 1974–7, INDR 1926–32, PU 1926–32, NPG 1928–51, NRF 1936–51, PIP 1950–1
Hungary	SZDSZ 1990–2010, VP 1990–4, OMC-Centre Party 2002–6

(continued)

Liberals (*continued*)

Country	Parties
Iceland	Liberal Party 1927–31, LP 1991–2009, Republican Party 1953–6
Ireland	PD 1987–2011, BPG 1922–3, NPD 1961–5, MR 1948–51
Italy	Sinistra 1876–1913, PLI 1913–94, PRI 1946–94, PdA 1946–8, CIND 1880–1913
Latvia	EkPA 1995–8, LVP 1995–8
Lithuania	Lib. Union-Centre Union (LLS) 2000–8, LCS-Centre Union-LCJ 1992–2004, Freedom Union 1996–2004, LRLS 2008, LUP 1996–2000, LLL 1992–6
Luxembourg	DP 1937–2009, EDF 1979–84, LJG-SL 1979–84, MIP 1964–8, PICM 1954–9, EST 1928–51, Parti Lib. 2 1945–51, Parti Radical Lib. 1934–45, Parti Lib. 1 1937–45, PPD 1931–7, Parti Indépendant 1919–37, Parti National Ind. 1919–31, Gauche Lib. 1925–31, Parti Ind. de la Droite 1925–31, Parti Pop. 1919–22, Cartel 1919–22
Netherlands	VVD 1888–2010, VDB 1888–1946, BVL 1909–22, EB 1918–22
Norway	Venstre 1882–2009, Nye Folkeparti 1973–7, MV 1888–91, FV 1927–30, FF 1930–45
Poland	AWS 1997–2005, DU (UW)-UD 1991–2005, KLD 1991–7, POC 1991–3, RP 2011
Portugal	PPD-PSD (CDS-AD) 1975–2009
Romania	PNL-CDR-PNTCD 1990–2008, CAP-LP 1996–2000, CDR-"2000" 2000–4, PNL-Campeanu 1926–2004, APR 2000–4
Slovakia	ANO 2002–10, DS 1990–8, DU-VPN-ODU 1990–8, LDS 1996–2011, DLGV 2011
Spain	UCD 1977–86, CDS 1982–96, Centre 1936–77
Sweden	FPL 1911–2010, SLP 1924–36
Switzerland	Radicals-FDP 1848–2011, LPS 1848–2011, Democrats 1848–1971, Dissident rad. 1860–3
United Kingdom	Liberal Party-Liberal Democrats 1832–2010

Nationalists

Country	Parties
Bulgaria	BNRP 1991–4
Denmark	DS 1943–50
Finland	IKL 1936–45
Germany	GDP 1949–65, GB BHE 1953–61, GVP 1953–7
Iceland	HRP 1916–23, IP 1916–23, IPAL 1916–19, IPAC 1916–19
Ireland	SF 1927–2011, CnaT 1943–65, CnaP 1948–65
Latvia	LNNK 1993–8
Lithuania	Sajudis 1992–6
Romania	PUNR 1990–2004

New left parties

Country	Parties
Austria	ALÖ 1983–6
Bulgaria	BEL 1997–2001
Denmark	VS 1968–88, EL 1990–2011
Estonia	TEE 1995–9
Germany	B90 1990–4
Ireland	DL 1992–2002
Luxembourg	Die Lenk 1999–2009
Netherlands	PSP 1959–86, PPR 1971–89
Norway	Roed 1993–2009
Portugal	BE 1999–2009
Slovenia	For Real 2008–11
Switzerland	Poch 1975–91

Orthodox

Country	Parties
Greece	Pop. Orth. Rally 2004–12
Latvia	LVCK 1922–5, PKO 1925–8, PVKO 1928–31, KVDTV 1931, PV 1931

Pensioners

Country	Parties
Czech Republic	DZJ 1992–2002
Estonia	EPL 1992–5
Finland	SEP 1987–91
Italy	Part. Naz. Pensionati 1983–7
Luxembourg	ADR 1989–2009
Netherlands	AOV 1994–8
Norway	PP 1993–7
Poland	KPEiR (RP) 1997–2001
Romania	PPR 1996–2000
Slovenia	DeSUS 1996–2011

People's parties

Country	Parties
Austria	ÖVP 1919–2008
Belgium	Catholics (CVP, PSC) 1848–1974, PSC 1971–2010, CVP 1971–2010
Bulgaria	GERB 2009
Czech Republic	KDU-CSL 1920–2010

(continued)

People's parties (*continued*)

Country	Parties
Estonia	People's Party 1919–32
Finland	Constitutional People's Party 1975–87, KP II 1951–66
France	CDP-DP-MRP 1932–78
Germany	DVP 1877–1953, DNVP, 1919–49
Hungary	KDNP 1990–2002
Ireland	FG 1922–2011, NCP 1933–7
Italy	Partito Cattolico-Dem. Cristiana-PPI (RI)-Margherita-Prodi 1909–2006, CCD-CDU-UDC 1996–2008
Latvia	LKDS 1993–2002, TKL 1995–5
Lithuania	KDS-Chr. Dem. Union 1996–2008
Lithuania	LKDP-Chr. Dem. Party 1920–2004, Chr. Cons. Social Union 2004–8
Luxembourg	CSV 1919–2009
Malta	Nationalist Party 1921–2008, UMP 1921–7
Poland	PO 2001–11, PC 1993–7, CD 1991–3, PCD 1991–3, ZNL 1919–22
Portugal	PDC 1979–80
Romania	UPM 1946–90
Slovakia	SDKU 2002–10, KDH 1990–2010, KSU 1994–8, SKDH 1992–4
Slovenia	SLS 1996–2011, NSI 2000–11, SKD 1996–2000, NS-KLS 2011

Personal parties

Country	Parties
Austria	DU 1999–2002, Martin 2006–8, Fritz 2008, DFP 1966–70, Uderverband 1927–30
Belgium	Dedecker 2007–10, ROSSEM 1991–5, CVB 1968–71
Bulgaria	KSII 2001–5, IMRO 2001–5, NUSII 2001–5, Alliance for the King 1997–2001, FTsB 1991–7, NV 2005–9, BSD 2005–9
Cyprus	PAME 1981–5, NDF 1981–5, Personal 2006–11
Czech Republic	NEI-Indep. Initiative 1992–6
Denmark	UAFH 1953–68
Estonia	Blue Party 1999–2003
Greece	DIANA 1989
Ireland	Anti H-Block 1981–2
Italy	Rete 1992–6, Patto Segni 1994–6, Rinnovamento It. 1996–2001, UDEUR-Dem. Europea 2001–8
Latvia	M-LNP 1995–8, LG 2002–6, TKL 1998–2002
Malta	Goz 1947–50, Jon 1947–50
Poland	BBWR 1993–7, Party X 1993–7
Slovakia	NS 1994–8, SPK 1994–8, HZPCS 1994–8, SAS 2010
Sweden	MS 1964–70

Protestants

Country	Parties
Denmark	KF 1971–2007
Finland	Chr. League 1970–2011, SKTL 1907–22
Germany	CSVD 1930–49
Netherlands	SGP 1925–2010, RPF 1981–2002, GPV 1971–2002, ARP 1888–1977, CHU 1894–1977, CU 2002–10, HGSP 1925–33, CDU 1933–46
Norway	KF 1936–2009
Sweden	KD 1964–2010
Switzerland	EK-EVP 1848–2011, EDU 1995–2011

Regionalists

Country	Parties
Austria	Kaerntner Einheitsliste 1923–7
Belgium	Volksunie-N-VA 1919–2010, VB 1978–2010, RW 1968–81, FDF (RW) 1965–95
Czech Republic	HSD-SMS 1990–6
Germany	BVP-BP 1920–57
Greece	Crete 1936–46
Iceland	South 1979–83
Italy	Lega Nord 1992–2008, Mov. Autonomia 2008
Lithuania	Klaipeda 1926
Spain	CiU 1977–2011, PNV 1933–2011, UC-DCC 1977–9, PSA-PA 1979–93, HB 1979–93, PTE 1979–82, BNG 2000–4, Unión Nacional 1979–82, CC 2000–4, ERC 1933–2011, Amaiur 2011, RC 1933–6, LR 1933–6
Switzerland	Lega Ticinese 1991–5
United Kingdom	SNP 1970–2010, Sinn Féin 1918–22, Irish Nationalists 1885–1922, Repealers-HR 1832–85

Social liberals

Country	Parties
Belgium	LS Cartel 1894–1961
Bulgaria	RDP 1908–31
Czech Republic	HSS 1992–6, SD-LSNS 1996–8
Denmark	RV 1906–2011
France	MRG-PRG 1973–2012, Rad. (RC-RR) 1893–2012
Germany	Pirate Party 2009, DFU 1961–9
Iceland	ULL 1971–9, AESJ 1987–91, Humanist Party 1987–95, Citizens' Mov. 2009

(*continued*)

Social liberals (*continued*)

Country	Parties
Italy	Rad.-PR-Rosa nel Pugno 1895–2008, AD 1994–6, PRI 1900–21
Lithuania	New Union 2000–8, People's Union "Fair" 2000–4, Civic Democracy 2008
Netherlands	Dem. '66 1967–2010
Poland	PD 2005–7
Romania	PD (FSN, USD)-PNL 1990–2008
Slovakia	SOP 1998–2002, SS 1990–2
Slovenia	LZJ-PS 2011
Spain	UPyD 2008–11
Switzerland	LdU 1935–99, LS 1935–47

Socialists

Country	Parties
Austria	SPÖ 1919–2008
Belgium	Socialists (BSP-PSB) 1894–1978, PS 1971–2010, SP 1971–2010, UDP 1974–7
Bulgaria	BRSDP-KzB-BSP 1899–2009, DAR 1994–7, SNI 1994–7, SF 1931–91, ORSDP 1931–91
Cyprus	EDEK-KISOS 1985–2011, Progressive Front 1960–76
Czech Republic	CSD(SD)-CSSD 1920–2010, SPR-RSC 1992–2002, CSS 1990–2, SPO-Z 2010, CSNS 1920–90
Denmark	SD 1872–2011, SF 1960–2011
Estonia	ESDTP-Moderates-SDE-STP 1919–2011, KMÜ-ECP-Safe Home 1992–2003, Socialists Revolutionaries 1919–26, National Union of Labour 1992
Finland	SDP 1907–2011, SDUWSF 1958–75, Progressive Party 1995–2003, Reform Group 1999–2003, SSTP 1922–33
France	PS 1893–2012, PRS 1914–45, RG-RS 1893–1978, PSU 1962–81
Germany	SPD 1871–2009, USPD 1919–24
Greece	Progressives-PASOK 1928–2012, DIKKI 1996–2007, Progressive Party 1981–5, DIMAR 2012
Hungary	MSZP 1990–2010, MSZDP 1990–8
Iceland	SPD-SDA 1916–2009, ASD 1983–7, Awakening 1995–9
Ireland	Labour 1922–2011, DSP 1989–92, SP 2011, People Before Profit 2011, National Labour 1944–51
Italy	PSI-PSIUP 1895–1996, PSDI 1948–94, PSIUP 1968–76, SR 1913–21, SI 1913–19, PDS-Ulivo-DS-PD 1992–2008
Latvia	DT 1995–8, LSDSP 1998–2010, SDS 2002–6, Dzimetene-SDLP 2002–10, LSDSP 1920–31, SDM&L 1922–31, LDP 1922–31, NS 1928–31
Lithuania	LSDP-SDP 1920–2008, Labour-LDDP-Youth 1992–2008, TPJ 1992–6, DF 1920–6, LSLDP 1920–3

Country	Parties
Luxembourg	LSAP 1919–2009, SDP 1974–84, PSI 1984–9, Parti Radical Socialiste 1925–31, Parti Radical 1928–37, Union des Gauches 1925–31, Gauche Indép. 1925–31
Malta	Labour 1921–2008, PCP 1953–76, DAP 1947–51
Netherlands	PvdA 1897–2010, DS70 1971–77, SDP 1918, RSP 1933–37
Norway	Labour 1900–2009, RF-AD 1906–30, NSA 1921–7
Poland	PPS-SLD-UP 1919–2011, SDPL 2005–7, UP 1993–2001, NSZZ-S 1991–7, SD 1991–3, USdRP 1993–7, NZR 1919–22
Portugal	PS (FRS) 1975–2009, FSP 1975–6, MES 1975–6, POUS-LST 1980–3, PRD 1985–91, PSN 1991–5
Romania	PSD (FDSN-PC-PU) 1931–2008, PSM 1992–2000, PS 1996–2000, PSMR 1996–2000
Slovakia	SDK (SDPS-HDH-SZ) 1990–2010, SDL 1992–2006, SDA 2002–6
Slovenia	SD 1996–2011
Spain	PSOE 1933–2011, PSP-US 1977–9, PR 1933–6, AR-UR-PRSI 1933–6
Sweden	SAP 1911–2010, VS 1917–24, SP 1932–40
Switzerland	SPS 1887–2011
United Kingdom	Labour 1895–2010, SDP 1983–92

TABLE A.1.2. *Additional Parties Exclusively in EP Elections*

Family	Parties
Agrarians	EPU (Estonia), Centre Party (Lithuania), PNTCD (Romania)
Anti-Europeans	Die Neutralen (Austria), FmEC, June Movement (Denmark), Alternative to EU (Finland), Mégret, RPF, Moins d'Impôts (France), BFB (Germany), Libertas Ireland (Ireland), TPP (Lithuania), GLS, Biergerlescht (Luxembourg), MEP (Portugal), Slovenia is Ours (Slovenia), June List (Sweden), No2 EU-Yes to Democracy (United Kingdom)
Communists	PDUP, DP, Alternativa Sociale, Sinistra e Libertà (Italy), PCTP-MPPP (Portugal)
Conservatives	Lider (Bulgaria), Familienpartei, Freie Wähler (Germany), Hunters (Greece), CL (Poland), PC (Romania)
Extreme-right	DF (Denmark), Centrumpartij (Netherlands), PIN (Romania), English Democrats (United Kingdom)
Europeans	SNK (Cyprus), EDS (Czech Republic), Majorité Autre Europe, Sarajévo (France), Europa Transparant (Netherlands), Pro-Euro Conservatives (United Kingdom)
Greens	Ecological Party (Finland), Mensch, Umwelt und Tierschutz (Germany), The Greens (Netherlands), Verdes Ecologistas (Spain)
Liberals	FS (Greece), PLD (Romania)
New left parties	Frieden (Germany), Respect (United Kingdom)
Pensioners	WOW (Belgium), Die Grauen (Germany)
People's parties	CSA (Austria), KKSS (Lithuania)
Personal parties	Tarand, Helme, Klenski (Estonia), Together We Are Strong, ZP (Lithuania), Laszlo, Elena, Pavel (Romania), Ruiz Mateo (Spain)
Protestants	Christian Party "Proclaiming Christ's Lordship" (United Kingdom)
Regionalists	Macedonian Front (Greece), Coalición Nacionalista (Spain), Democratic Unionists, Ulster Unionists, Plaid Cymru (United Kingdom)
Social liberals	SCP (Latvia), Pirate Party (Sweden)
Socialists	SP (Ireland), Libertas (Latvia), PSI (Luxembourg), LP Libertas (Poland), SDLP, SLP (United Kingdom)

Appendix 2

Scales

Recodification of the CMP variable

The left–right scale ranging from –100 to +100 has been recoded to match the other scales used in Chapters 6 and 7 from 1 to 10 where 1 represents far left. First, the value of the variable "left_right" (or "rile") has been increased by 100 to obtain a variable ranging from 0 to 200 and it was divided by 2 to obtain a variable ranging from 0 to 100. It has then been divided by 10 to obtain a variable ranging from 0 to 10.

$$LR = \frac{\dfrac{left\_right + 100}{2}}{10}$$

This new variable correlates perfectly ($r = 1.0$) with the original variable. Finally, all 0 values have been recoded into 1 (which in the original variable would correspond to values between –100 and –80). Also after the recodification the variable correlates perfectly with the original one as there are no values between –100 and –80.

Creation of Economic and Cultural Left–Right Dimensions

The distinction between economic and cultural dimensions is limited to CMP data. To create the left–right economic and cultural variables, the number of quasi-sentences in favour of right-wing categories as a percentage of the total number of quasi-sentences in favour of both left- and right-wing categories has been calculated. The higher the numerator, the more right-wing the party. Then, the result has been divided by 10 to make it vary between 0 and 10.

$$LR = \frac{\left(\dfrac{right\_items}{right\_items + left\_items} \right) * 100}{10}$$

Finally, o has been recoded into 1 to make the scale match the other scales used in the chapters. For a similar procedure see Marks (2007). Items for each of the economic and cultural dimensions for both left and right appear in the following table.

TABLE A.2.1. *Items for Economic and Cultural Left–Right Dimensions*

Dimensions	*Left-wing items*		*Right-wing items*	
Economic	per404	Economic planning	per401	Free enterprise
	per405	Corporatism	per402	Incentives
	per409	Keynesian management	per414	Economic orthodoxy
	per412	Controlled economy	per505	Welfare limitation
	per413	Nationalization	per702	Against labour groups
	per415	Marxist analysis	per704	Middle class and professional groups
	per504	Welfare expansion		
	per701	Labour groups		
Cultural	per103	Anti-imperialism	per109	Anti-internationalism
	per107	Internationalism	per305	Political authority
	per503	Social justice	per601	Nationalism
	per602	Anti-nationalism	per603	Traditions
	per604	Against traditions	per605	Law and order
	per607	Multi-culturalism	per608	Against multi-culturalism

Note: For details about the single items see Klingemann et al. (2006: 154–63).

Appendix 3

Computations

In the formulas included in Appendix 3 P denotes votes for a party family in percentages, S the seats in percentages, $\overline{X}$ the average across countries, N the number of countries. The terms t and $t-1$ refer to an election year (or five-year period) and the previous one.

1. Indices of Cross-Country Variability and Distinctiveness

Standard deviation: $S = \sqrt{\dfrac{\sum_{i=1}^{n}(P_i - \overline{X})^2}{N-1}}$

Coefficient of variability: $CV = \dfrac{S}{\overline{X}}$

Lee index: $LEE = \dfrac{\sum_{i=1}^{n}(P_i - \overline{X})}{2}$

Index adjusted for party size and number of regions: $IPR = \sqrt{\dfrac{N\sum_{i=1}^{n}(|P_i - \overline{X}|)}{2(N-1)\sum_{i=1}^{n}P}}$

Gini index (relative mean difference): $GINI = \dfrac{\sum_{i=1}^{n}\sum_{j=1}^{n}|P_i - P_j|}{\overline{X}/2}$

Gini adjusted for number of units: $GINI2 = \dfrac{\sum\limits_{i=1}^{n}\sum\limits_{j=1}^{n}|P_i - P_j|}{2\bar{X}N^2}$

Index of party system distinctiveness: calculated for individual countries where F is the total number of families in a country.

$$D = \dfrac{\sum\limits_{i=1}^{f}|P_i - \bar{X}|}{F}$$

Coverage: the degree of territorial coverage by party families is equal to the number of countries in which a given family receives at least 1 per cent of the vote nationwide as a percentage of the total number of countries in which democratic elections take place. The measure is also referred to as "presence" and "spread".

2. Party System Indices

Volatility (Pedersen, 1979): used to calculate national volatility (NV), mixed volatility (MV), and European volatility (EV). The measure of differential volatility (DV) is derived by taking the difference between NV and MV.

$$V = \dfrac{\sum\limits_{i}^{n}|P_t - P_{t-1}|}{2}$$

Effective number of parties (Laasko and Taagepera, 1979): used for votes and seats (ENEP and ENPP).

$$ENP = \dfrac{1}{\sum\limits_{i}^{n}P^2}$$

Fractionalization (Rae, 1971): $F = 1 - \sum\limits_{i}^{n}P^2$

Index of disproportionality (Gallagher, 1991): $LSQ = \sqrt{\dfrac{\sum\limits_{i}^{n}(P_i - S_i)^2}{2}}$

Swing: the definition of a "uniform swing" is one in which (for at least 50 per cent of the countries with elections) at least 75 per cent of the countries in which a given family exists the following difference is either positive or negative above 3.0 per cent of the votes.

$$SWING = P_t - P_{t-1}$$

Indices can be calculated (1) on countries in which a given family exists only; and (2) all countries with democratic elections. In the latter case, votes for a family that does not exist in a given country are set to 0.0 per cent. Indices (except LSQ) can be calculated on either votes or seat percentages. Country-specific indices can be calculated at the party and family levels.

Appendix 4

R Output for Chapter 5 (QCA)

```
> DiffVol <- read.csv("DiffVolData.csv", row.names = "Country")
> DiffVolNR <- superSubset(DiffVol, outcome = "DV", incl.cut = 0.9, cov.cut = 0.52)
> DiffVolNR
```

		incl	PRI	cov.r
1	SOC	1.000	1.000	0.833
2	LIB+MCR+LBT	1.000	1.000	0.625
3	AEU+MCR+LBT	1.000	1.000	0.714

```
> DiffVolTT <- truthTable(DiffVol, outcome = "DV", show.cases = TRUE, sort.by =
c("incl", "n"))
> DiffVolSC <- eqmcc(DiffVolTT, details = TRUE, show.cases = TRUE)
> DiffVolSC

n OUT = 1/0/C: 5/9/0
  Total    : 14

Number of multiple-covered cases: 0

S1: SOC*LIB*MCR*LBT + SOC*aeu*lib*mcr*LBT + SOC*aeu*lib* MCR*lbt +
    SOC*AEU*LIB*mcr*lbt
```

		incl	PRI	cov.r	cov.u	cases
1	SOC*LIB*MCR*LBT	1.000	1.000	0.400	0.400	France; UnitedKingdom
2	SOC*aeu*lib*mcr*LBT	1.000	1.000	0.200	0.200	Sweden
3	SOC*aeu*lib*MCR*lbt	1.000	1.000	0.200	0.200	Germany
4	SOC*AEU*LIB*mcr*lbt	1.000	1.000	0.200	0.200	Denmark
	S1	1.000	1.000	1.000		

```
> DiffVolTT  <- truthTable(DiffVol, outcome = "DV", show.cases = TRUE, complete =
TRUE, sort.by = c("incl", "n"))
> DiffVolSP <- eqmcc(DiffVolTT, include = "?", details = TRUE)
> DiffVolSP <- eqmcc(DiffVolTT, include = "?", details = TRUE, rowdom = FALSE)
> DiffVolSP$PIchart$p.sol
```

	18	19	24	29	32
AEU	–	–	–	x	x
LIB*LBT	–	–	x	–	x
LIB*MCR	–	–	x	–	x
MCR*LBT	–	–	x	–	x
SOC*LBT	x	–	x	–	x
SOC*LIB	–	–	x	x	x
SOC*MCR	–	x	x	–	x

```
> DiffVolSI <- eqmcc(DiffVolTT, include = "?", details = TRUE, direxp =
c(1,1,1,1,1))
> factorize(DiffVolSI)

C1P1S1: SOC*LBT + SOC*MCR + SOC*AEU*LIB

F1: SOC*(LBT + MCR + AEU*LIB)
```

Appendix 5

Cases with More than One Cabinet in the Same Year

The basic cases of the analysis in Chapter 7 are cabinets in a given year. When there is more than one cabinet during the same year, the cabinet formed after a general election has been retained. When no election took place, the last cabinet of the year has been retained if it is the one with the longest duration in the executive. In Table A.5.1 numbers in parenthesis indicate when more than two cabinets existed in the same calendar year. For 2010 the first cabinet in place has been retained.

TABLE A.5.1. *Calendar Years with more than One Cabinet*

Country	Years with Two (or Three) Cabinets
Belgium	1946 (3), 1950, 1958, 1974, 1977, 1980 (3), 1981, 2008
Bulgaria	1997
Czech Republic	1998
Denmark	1950, 1953, 1960
Estonia	1992
Finland	1951, 1953, 1954, 1957, 1972, 1982, 2003
France	1946 (3), 1947 (3), 1948 (3), 1949, 1950, 1951, 1952, 1953, 1957, 1958, 1962, 1968, 1974, 1981, 1988, 1995, 1997, 2007
Greece	1985, 1989, 1996
Iceland	1959, 1963, 2009
Ireland	1982, 2010
Italy	1947, 1953, 1954, 1960, 1963, 1968, 1970, 1972, 1974, 1976, 1979, 1980, 1982, 1987
Latvia	1997, 1998, 1999, 2004, 2006, 2010
Lithuania	1996, 1999, 2006
Netherlands	1977, 1982, 2010

Country	Years with Two (or Three) Cabinets
Norway	1963, 1981
Poland	1992, 1993, 2006
Portugal	1978, 1980, 1981, 2010
Romania	1996, 1998, 1999, 2004
Slovakia	1993 (3), 1994, 2006
Slovenia	2000, 2004
United Kingdom	1955, 1974

Appendix 6

Sources

The analysis presented in this book is based on four types of data:

- *Aggregate data* (electoral results): For national elections, the source is a new updated database compiled for the present study based on previous efforts in historical data collection (for the election of sources on Western Europe see Caramani, 2000: 1017–53; on Central and Eastern Europe the main source is Nohlen and Stöver, 2010). For elections to the European Parliament (EP) since 1979 the main source is the European Database at NSD in Bergen.
- *Individual data* (surveys): The sources of data are Eurobarometers (EB, Mannheim Trend File) and European Social Surveys (ESS).
- *Text data* (party manifestos): The source of data is the Comparative Manifesto Project (CMP). See Budge et al. (2001) and Klingemann et al. (2006), as well as online updates.
- *Membership data* (cabinet composition): The source of data is the ParlGov database (Döring and Manow, 2010).

References

Acemoglu, Daron, and James A. Robinson (2006). *Economic Origins of Dictatorship and Democracy*. Cambridge: Cambridge University Press.

Adams, James, Merrill, Samuel, and Bernard Grofman (2004). *A Unified Theory of Party Competition: A Cross-National Analysis Integrating Spatial and Behavioral Factors*. Cambridge: Cambridge University Press.

Albright, Jeremy J. (2010). The Multidimensional Nature of Party Competition. *Party Politics* 22: 1–21.

Alemán, Eduardo, and Marisa Kellam (2008). The Nationalization of Electoral Change in the Americas. *Electoral Studies* 27: 193–212.

Almond, Gabriel A. (1956). Comparative Political Systems. *Journal of Politics* 18: 391–409.

Almond, Gabriel A., and Sidney Verba (1963). *The Civic Culture: Political Attitudes and Democracy in Five Nations*. Princeton, NJ: Princeton University Press.

Anderson, Benedict R. (1991). *Imagined Communities: Reflections on the Origin and Spread of Nationalism*. London: Verso.

Andeweg, Rudy B. (1995). The Reshaping of National Party Systems. *West European Politics* 18: 58–78.

(2011). Approaching Perfect Policy Congruence: Measurement, Development, and Relevance for Political Representation. In Rosema, Martin, Denters, Bas, and Kees Aarts (eds.), *How Democracy Works: Political Representation and Policy Congruence in Modern Societies*. Amsterdam: Pallas Publications (pp. 39–52).

Ansell, Christopher K., and Giuseppe Di Palma (eds.) (2004). *Restructuring Territoriality: Europe and the United States Compared*. Cambridge: Cambridge University Press.

Bardi, Luciano (1992). Transnational Party Federations in the European Community. In Katz, Richard S., and Peter Mair (eds.), *Party Organizations: A Handbook on Party Organizations in Western Democracies, 1960–90*. Newbury Park, CA: Sage (pp. 931–73).

(1994). Transnational Party Federations, European Parliamentary Party Groups, and the Building of Europarties. In Katz, Richard S., and Peter Mair (eds.), *How Parties Organize: Change and Adaptation in Party Organizations in Western Democracies.* Thousand Oaks, CA: Sage (pp. 357–72).

(1996). Transnational Trends in European Parties and the 1994 Elections to the European Parliament. *Party Politics* 2: 99–114.

(2002). Parties and Party Systems in the European Union. In Luther, Kurt and Ferdinand Müller-Rommel (eds.), *Political Parties in the New Europe: Political and Analytical Challenges.* Oxford: Oxford University Press (pp. 292–322).

Bartolini, Stefano (1993). On Time and Comparative Research. *Journal of Theoretical Politics* 5: 131–67.

(2000). *The Political Mobilization of the European Left, 1860–1980: The Class Cleavage.* Cambridge: Cambridge University Press.

(2002). Institutional Democratization and Political Structuring in the EU: Lessons from the Nation-State Development. In Cavanna, Henry (ed.), *Governance, Globalization, and the European Union: Which Europe for Tomorrow?* Dublin: Four Courts Press (pp. 129–58).

(2004). Old and New Peripheries in the Processes of European Territorial Interpretation. In Ansell, Christopher K., and Giuseppe Di Palma (eds.), *Restructuring Territoriality: Europe and the United States Compared.* Cambridge: Cambridge University Press (pp. 19–44).

(2005). *Restructuring Europe: Centre Formation, System Building, and Political Structuring between the Nation-State and the European Union.* Oxford: Oxford University Press.

Bartolini, Stefano, and Peter Mair (1990). *Identity, Competition and Electoral Availability: The Stabilization of European Electorates, 1885–1985.* Cambridge: Cambridge University Press.

Bauer, Michael, Knill, Christoph, and Diana Pitschel (2007). Differential Europeanisation in Eastern Europe: The Impact of Diverse EU Regulatory Governance Patterns. *Journal of European Integration* 29: 405–23.

Beetham, David, and Christopher Lord (1998). *Legitimacy and the EU.* London: Longman.

Beisheim, Marianne, Dreher, Sabine, Walter, Gregor, Zangl, Bernhard, and Michael Zürn (1999). *Im Zeitalter der Globalisierung? Thesen und Daten zur gesellschaftlichen und politischen Denationalisierung.* Baden-Baden: Nomos.

Bell, Daniel (1976). *The Coming of Post-Industrial Society: A Venture in Social Forecasting.* New York: Basic Books.

Bell, David S. (2003). French Socialists: Refusing the "Third Way". *The Journal of Policy History* 15: 46–64.

Bendix, Reinhard (1964). *Nation-Building and Citizenship: Studies of Our Changing Social Order.* New York: Wiley.

Bennett, Colin J. (1991). What Is Policy Convergence and What Causes It? *British Journal of Political Science* 21: 215–33.

Benoit, Kenneth, and Michael Laver (2006). *Party Policy in Modern Democracies.* London: Routledge.

(2007). Estimating Party Policy Positions: Comparing Expert Surveys and Hand-Coded Content Analysis. *Electoral Studies* 26: 90–107.

Berejikian, Jeffrey (1992). Revolutionary Collective Action and the Agent–Structure Problem. *American Political Science Review* 86: 647–57.

Berge, Benjamin von dem, and Thomas Poguntke (2013). The Influence of Europarties on Central and Eastern European Partner Parties: A Theoretical and Analytical Model. *European Political Science Review* 5: 311–34.

Berglund, Sten, and Jan Åke Dellenbrant (1994). *The New Democracies in Eastern Europe: Party Systems and Political Cleavages* (second edition). Aldershot: Elgar.

Betz, Hans-Georg (1994). *Radical Right-Wing Populism in Western Europe.* New York: St. Martin's Press.

Beyme, Klaus von (1985). *Political Parties in Western Democracies.* Aldershot: Gower.

Blondel, Jean, and Maurizio Cotta (eds.) (2000). *The Nature of Party Government: A Comparative European Perspective.* Oxford: Oxford University Press.

Blumer, Jay G., and Anthony D. Fox (1982). *The European Voter: Popular Responses to the First European Community Elections.* London: Policy Studies Institute.

Bobbio, Norberto (1996). *Left and Right: The Significance of a Political Distinction.* Cambridge: Polity.

Bochsler, Daniel (2010a). *Territory and Electoral Rules in Post-Communist Democracies.* Houndmills: Palgrave.

(2010b). Measuring Party Nationalisation: A New Gini-Based Indicator that Corrects for the Number of Units. *Electoral Studies* 29: 155–68.

Boix, Carles (1999). Setting the Rules of the Game: The Choice of Electoral Systems in Advanced Democracies. *American Political Science Review* 93: 609–24.

Bordandini, Paola, Di Virgilio, Aldo, and Francesco Raniolo (2008). The Birth of a Party: The Case of the Italian Partito Democratico. *South European Society and Politics* 13: 303–24.

Bornschier, Simon (2010). *Cleavage Politics and the Populist Right: The New Cultural Conflict in Western Europe.* Philadelphia, PA: Temple University Press.

Börzel, Tanja (1999). Towards Convergence in Europe? Institutional Adaptation to Europeanization in Germany and Spain. *Journal of Common Market Studies* 39: 573–96.

Brack, Nathalie (2012). Eurosceptics in the European Parliament: Exit or Voice? *Journal of European Integration* 34(2): 151–68.

Brady, David W., D'Onofrio, Robert, and Morris P. Fiorina (2000). The Nationalization of Electoral Forces Revisited. In Brady David W., Cogan John F., and Morris P. Fiorina (eds.), *Continuity and Change in House Elections.* Stanford, CA: Stanford University Press (pp. 130–48).

Braun, Dietmar, and Fabrizio Gilardi (2006). Taking Galton's Problem Seriously: Towards a Theory of Policy Diffusion. *Journal of Theoretical Politics* 18: 298–322.

Braunias, Karl (1932). *Das parlamentarische Wahlrecht: ein Handbuch über die Bildung der gesetzgebenden Körperschaften in Europa.* Berlin: Walter de Gruyter.

Budge, Ian, Hearl, Derek, and David Robertson (1987). *Ideology, Strategy, and Party Change: Spatial Analyses of Post-War Election Programmes in 19 Democracies.* Cambridge: Cambridge University Press.

Budge, Ian, Klingemann, Hans-Dieter, Volkens, Andrea, Bara, Judith, and Eric Tanenbaum (2001). *Mapping Policy Preferences: Estimates for Parties, Electors, and Governments, 1945–1998.* Oxford: Oxford University Press (supplemented with CD-ROM).

Butler, David, and Donald E. Stokes (1974). *Political Change in Britain: The Evolution of Electoral Choice.* London: Macmillan (second edition).

Camia, Valeria, and Daniele Caramani (2012). Family Meetings: Ideological Convergence within Party Families across Europe, 1945–2009. *Comparative European Politics* 10(1): 48–85.

Campbell, Angus (1960). Surge and Decline: A Study of Electoral Change. *Public Opinion Quarterly* 24: 397–418.

(1966). Surge and Decline: A Study of Electoral Change. In Campbell, Angus, Converse, Philip E., Miller, Warren E., and Donald E. Stokes (eds.), *Elections and the Political Order*. New York: Wiley (pp. 40–62).

Campbell, James E. (1987). The Revised Theory of Surge and Decline. *American Journal of Political Science* 31: 965–79.

Capoccia, Giovanni (2005). *Defending Democracy: Reactions to Extremism in Interwar Europe*. Baltimore, MA: Johns Hopkins University Press.

Capoccia, Giovanni, and Daniel R. Kelemen (2011). The Study of Critical Junctures: Theory, Narrative, and Counterfactuals in Historical Institutionalism. *World Politics* 59: 341–69.

Caporaso, James A., Marks, Gary, Moravcsik, Andrew, and Mark A. Pollack (1997). Does the European Union Represent an N of 1? *ECSA Review* 10: 1–5.

Caramani, Daniele (2000). *Elections in Western Europe since 1815: Electoral Results by Constituencies*. London: Palgrave (supplemented with CD-ROM).

(2003a). The End of Silent Elections: The Birth of Electoral Competition, 1832–1915. *Party Politics* 9: 411–43.

(2003b). State Administration and Regional Construction in Central Europe: A Historical Perspective. In Keating, Michael, and James Hughes (eds.), *The Regional Challenge in Central and Eastern Europe: Territorial Restructuring and European Integration*. Brussels: P.I.E.-Peter Lang (pp. 21–50).

(2004). *The Nationalization of Politics: The Formation of National Electorates and Party Systems in Western Europe*. Cambridge: Cambridge University Press.

(2006). Is There a European Electorate and What Does It Look Like? Evidence from Electoral Volatility Measures, 1976–2004. *West European Politics* 29: 1–27.

(2009). *Introduction to the Comparative Method with Boolean Algebra*. Thousand Oaks, CA: Sage (Quantitative Applications in the Social Sciences).

(2010a). Of Differences and Similarities: Is the Explanation of Variation a Limitation to (or of) Comparative Analysis? *European Political Science* 9: 34–48.

(2010b). Debate on the Future of Comparative Politics: A Rejoinder. *European Political Science* 9: 78–82.

(2011a). Electoral Waves: An Analysis of Trends, Spread and Swings across 20 West European Countries 1970–2008. *Representation* 47: 137–60.

(2011b). Stein Rokkan: The Macro-Sociological Fresco of State, Nation and Democracy in Europe. In Campus, Donatella, Pasquino, Gianfranco, and Martin Bull (eds.), *Maestri of Political Science* (volume 2). Colchester: Routledge/ECPR series (pp. 177–205).

(2012). The Europeanization of Electoral Politics: An Analysis of Converging Voting Distributions in 30 European Party Systems, 1970–2008. *Party Politics* 18: 803–23.

(2014). Introduction to Comparative Politics. In Caramani, Daniele (ed.), *Comparative Politics* (third edition). Oxford: Oxford University Press (pp. 1–17).

Caramani, Daniele, and Simon Hug (1998). The Literature on European Parties and Party Systems since 1945: A Quantitative Analysis. *European Journal of Political Research* 4: 497–524.

Caramani, Daniele, and Yves Mény (eds.) (2005). *Challenges to Consensual Politics: Democracy, Identity, and Populist Protest in the Alpine Region*. Brussels: P.I.E.-Peter Lang.

Carrubba, Cliff, and Richard J. Timpone (2005). Explaining Vote Switching across First- and Second-Order Elections: Evidence from Europe. *Comparative Political Studies* 38: 260–81.

Castles, Francis G., and Peter Mair (1984). Left–Right Political Scales: Some "Expert" Judgments. *European Journal of Political Research* 12: 73–88.

Castles, Francis G., Mair, Peter, and Morgens M. Pedersen (1997). Left–Right Political Scales. *European Journal of Political Research* 31: 147–57.

Cheibub, José Antônio (2007). *Presidentialism, Parliamentarism, and Democracy.* Cambridge: Cambridge University Press.

Chhibber, Pradeep K., and Ken Kollman (1998). Party Aggregation and the Number of Parties in India and the United States. *American Political Science Review* 92: 329–42.

(2004). *The Formation of National Party Systems: Federalism and Party Competition in Canada, Great Britain, India, and the United States.* Princeton, NJ: Princeton University Press.

Claggett, William, Flanigan, William, and Nancy Zingale (1984). Nationalization of the American Electorate. *American Political Science Review* 79: 1171–3.

Cornford, James (1970). Aggregate Election Data and British Alignments, 1885–1910. In Allardt, Erik, and Stein Rokkan (eds.), *Mass Politics: Studies in Political Sociology.* New York: Free Press (pp. 107–16).

Cox, Gary W. (1997). *Making Votes Count: Strategic Coordination in the World's Electoral Systems.* Cambridge: Cambridge University Press.

(1999). Electoral Rules and Electoral Coordination. *Annual Review of Political Science* 2: 145–61.

Crewe, Ivor, and David T. Denver (eds.) (1985). *Electoral Change in Western Democracies: Patterns and Sources of Electoral Volatility.* London: Croom Helm.

Croissant, Aurel, and Teresa Schächter (2008). Die Nationalisierung politischer Parteien und Parteiensysteme in asiatischen Neo-Demokratien. *Politische Vierteljahresschrift* 49: 12–36.

Cusack, Thomas, Iversen, Torben, and David Soskice (2007). Economic Interests and the Origin of Electoral Systems. *American Political Science Review* 101: 373–91.

(2010). Coevolution of Capitalism and Political Representation: The Choice of Electoral Systems. *American Political Science Review* 104: 393–403.

Daalder, Hans (1966). The Netherlands: Opposition in a Segmented Society. In Dahl, Robert A. (ed.), *Political Oppositions in Western Democracies.* New Haven, CT: Yale University Press (pp. 188–236).

Dalton, Russell J., Flanagan, Scott, and Paul A. Beck (eds.) (1984). *Electoral Change in Advanced Industrial Democracies: Realignment or Dealignment?* Princeton, NJ: Princeton University Press.

Dalton, Russell J., and Martin P. Wattenberg (eds.) (2000). *Parties without Partisans: Political Change in Advanced Industrial Democracies.* Oxford: Oxford University Press.

Dahl, Robert A. (ed.) (1966). *Political Oppositions in Western Democracies.* New Haven, CT: Yale University Press.

(1971). *Polyarchy: Participation and Opposition.* New Haven, CT: Yale University Press.

Dahrendorf, Ralf (1959). *Class and Class Conflict in Industrial Society.* London: Routledge and Kegan Paul.

Della Porta, Donatella, and Manuela Caiani (2009). *Social Movements and Europeanization*. Oxford: Oxford University Press.

Deutsch, Karl W. (1953). *Nationalism and Social Communication: An Inquiry into the Foundations of Nationality*. Cambridge, MA: MIT Press.

Diez, Thomas (2001). European Federation of Green Parties. In Johansson, Karl M., and Peter Zervakis (eds.), *European Political Parties between Cooperation and Integration*. Baden-Baden: Nomos (pp. 125–59).

Diez, Thomas, Stetter, Stephan, and Mathias Albert (2006). The European Union and Border Conflicts: The Transformative Power of Integration. *International Organization* 60: 563–93.

Dimitrakopoulos, Dionyssis G. (2011). *Social Democracy and European Integration: The Politics of Preference Formation*. London: Routledge.

Dinas, Elias, and Kostas Gemenis (2010). Measuring Parties' Ideological Positions with Manifesto Data: A Critical Evaluation of the Competing Methods. *Party Politics* 16: 427–50.

Dolowitz, David P., and David Marsh (1996). Who Learns What from Whom: A Review of the Policy Transfer Literature. *Political Studies* 44: 343–57.

(2000). The Role of Policy Transfer in Contemporary Policy-Making. *Governance* 13: 5–24.

Döring, Holger, and Philip Manow (2010). Parliament and Government Composition Database (ParlGov): An Infrastructure for Empirical Information on Political Institutions. Version 10/02 (www.parlgov.org).

Downs, Anthony (1957). *An Economic Theory of Democracy*. New York: Harper Collins.

Duverger, Maurice (1950). *L'Influence des Systèmes Électoraux sur la Vie Politique*. Paris: Presses de la Fondation Nationale des Sciences Politiques.

(1951). The Influence of Electoral Systems on Political Life. *International Social Science Bulletin* 3: 314–52.

(1954). *Political Parties: Their Organization and Activity in the Modern State*. London: Methuen.

Dyson, Kenneth (ed.) (2002). *European States and the Euro: Europeanization, Variation, and Convergence*. Oxford: Oxford University Press.

Eisenstadt, Shmuel N. (ed.) (2002). *Multiple Modernities*. New Brunswick, NJ: Transaction.

(2006). *Comparative Civilizations and Multiple Modernities*. Boston, MA: Brill.

Ennser, Laurenz (2012). The Homogeneity of West European Party Families: The Radical Right in Comparative Perspective. *Party Politics* 18: 151–71.

Enyedi, Zsolt, and Paul G. Lewis (2006). The Impact of the European Union on Party Politics in Central and Eastern Europe. In Lewis, Paul G., and Zdenka Mansfeldova (eds.), *The European Union and Party Politics in Central and Eastern Europe*. London: Palgrave (pp. 231–49).

Epstein, Leon D. (1961). *Political Parties in Western Democracies*. New York: Praeger.

Erikson, Robert S. (1988). The Puzzle of Midterm Loss. *Journal of Politics* 50: 1011–29.

Ersson, Svante O., Janda, Kenneth, and Jan-Erik Lane (1985). Ecology of Party Strength in Western Europe: A Regional Analysis. *Comparative Political Studies* 18: 170–205.

Fabbrini, Sergio (2004). The European Union in American Perspective: The Transformation of Territorial Sovereignty in Europe and the United States. In Ansell, Christopher K., and Giuseppe Di Palma (eds.), *Restructuring Territoriality: Europe and the United States Compared*. Cambridge: Cambridge University Press (pp. 163–87).

(ed.) (2005). *Democracy and Federalism in the European Union and the United States: Exploring Post-National Governance*. London: Routledge.

(2007). *Compound Democracies: Why the United States and Europe Are Becoming Similar*. Oxford: Oxford University Press.

Featherstone, Kevin, and Claudio Radaelli (eds.) (2003). *The Politics of Europeanization*. Oxford: Oxford University Press.

Ferrera, Maurizio (2005). *The Boundaries of Welfare: European Integration and the New Spatial Politics of Social Protection*. Oxford: Oxford University Press.

Flanagan, William G. (1993). The Structural Roots of Action and the Question of Convergence. *Research in Urban Sociology* 3: 233–53.

Flora, Peter (1983). *State, Economy, and Society in Western Europe, 1815–1975: A Data Handbook*. Volume 1: *The Growth of Mass Democracies and Welfare States*. Frankfurt-am-Main: Campus.

(1999). Introduction and Interpretation. In Rokkan, Stein, *State Formation, Nation-Building, and Mass Politics in Europe*, edited by Flora, Peter, Kuhnle, Stein, and Derek W. Urwin. Oxford: Oxford University Press (pp. 1–91).

(2000). Externe Grenzbildung und interne Strukturierung: Eine Rokkanische Forschungsperspektive. *Berliner Journal für Soziologie* 2: 151–65.

Flora, Peter, Kraus Franz, and Winfried Pfenning (1987). *State, Economy, and Society in Western Europe, 1815–1975: A Data Handbook*. Volume 2: *The Growth of Industrial Societies and Capitalist Economies*. Frankfurt-am-Main: Campus.

Franklin, Mark N., Mackie, Thomas T., and Henri Valen (1992). *Electoral Change: Responses to Evolving Social and Attitudinal Structures in Western Europe*. Cambridge: Cambridge University Press.

Gabel, Matthew, and Simon Hix (2002). Defining the EU Political Space: An Empirical Study of the European Elections Manifestos, 1979–1999. *Comparative Political Studies* 35(8): 934–64.

Gaffney, John (ed.) (1996). *Political Parties and the European Union*. London: Routledge.

Gagnon, Jean-Paul (2012). Post-Colonial Public Law: Are Current Legal Establishments Democratically Illegitimate? *African Journal of Legal Studies* 5: 21–43.

Gallagher, Michael (1991). Proportionality, Disproportionality, and Electoral Systems. *Electoral Studies* 10: 32–51.

Gallagher, Michael, and Paul Mitchell (eds.) (2005). *The Politics of Electoral Systems*. Oxford: Oxford University Press.

Gallagher, Michael, Laver, Michael, and Peter Mair (2001). *Representative Government in Modern Europe* (third edition). New York: McGraw-Hill.

Gartzke, Erik (2007). The Capitalist Peace. *American Journal of Political Science* 51: 166–91.

Gellner, Ernest (1983). *Nations and Nationalism*. Oxford: Blackwell.

Green Cowles, Maria, Caporaso, James, and Thomas Risse (eds.) (2001). *Transforming Europe: Europeanization and Domestic Change*. Ithaca, NY: Cornell University Press.

Grofman, Bernard (2004). Downs and Two-Party Convergence. *Annual Review of Political Science* 7: 25–46.

Grunberg, Gérard, Perrineau, Pascal, and Colette Ysmal (2000). *Le Vote des Quinze: Les Elections Européennes du 13 Juin 1999*. Paris: Presses de Science Po.

Haas, Ernst B. (1958). *The Uniting of Europe: Political, Social and Economic Forces, 1950–57*. London: Stevens.

Habermas, Jürgen (1989). *The Structural Transformation of the Public Sphere: An Inquiry into a Category of Bourgeois Society*. Cambridge: Polity.

(2001). Why Europe Needs a Constitution. *New Left Review* 11: 5–26.

Hale, William (2008). Kirchheimer Revisited: Party Polarisation, Party Convergence, or Party Decline in the German Party System. *German Politics* 17: 105–23.

Hall, Peter A., and Rosemary C. Taylor (1996). Political Science and the Three New Institutionalisms. *Political Studies* 44: 936–57.

Harbers, Imke (2010). Decentralization and the Development of Nationalized Party Systems in New Democracies: Evidence from Latin America. *Comparative Political Studies* 43(5): 606–27.

Harmel, Robert, Somer, Zeynep, and Jason Smith (2005). Effects of "Europe" on National Party Issue Profiles: Assessment and Explanation of Convergence within Party Families. Paper presented at International Studies Association, Chicago.

Hearl, Derek J., Budge, Ian, and Bernard Pearson (1996). Distinctiveness of Regional Voting: A Comparative Analysis across the European Community (1979–83). *Electoral Studies* 15: 167–82.

Hicken, Allen (2009). *Building Party Systems in Developing Democracies*. Cambridge: Cambridge University Press.

Hix, Simon (1994). The Study of the European Community: The Challenge to Comparative Politics. *West European Politics* 17: 1–30.

(1996). The Transnational Party Federations. In Gaffney, John (ed.), *Political Parties and the European Union*. London: Routledge (pp. 308–31).

(1999). Dimensions and Alignments in European Union Politics: Cognitive Constraints and Partisan Responses. *European Journal of Political Research* 35: 69–106.

(2001). Legislative Behaviour and Party Competition in the European Parliament: An Application of Nominate to the EU. *Journal of Common Market Studies* 39: 663–88.

(2002). Parties at the European Level. In Webb Paul, Farrell, David, and Ian Holliday (eds.), *Political Parties in Advanced Industrial Democracies*. Oxford: Oxford University Press (pp. 280–309).

(2005). *The Political System of the European Union* (second edition). Basingstoke: Palgrave.

Hix, Simon, and Amie Kreppel (2003). From Grand Coalition to Left–Right Confrontation: Explaining the Shifting Structure of Party Competition in the European Parliament. *Comparative Political Studies* 36: 75–96.

Hix, Simon, Kreppel, Amie, and Abdul G. Noury (2003). The Party System in the European Parliament: Collusive or Competitive? *Journal of Common Market Studies* 41: 309–31.

Hix, Simon, and Christopher Lord (1997). *Political Parties in the European Union*. Basingstoke: Macmillan.

Hix, Simon, and Michael Marsh (2011). Second-Order Effects plus Pan-European Political Swings: An Analysis of European Parliament Elections across Time. *Electoral Studies* 30: 4–15.

Hix, Simon, Noury, Abdul G., and Gérard Roland (2005). Power to the Parties: Cohesion and Competition in the European Parliament. *British Journal of Political Science* 35: 209–34.

(2007). *Democratic Politics in the European Parliament.* Cambridge: Cambridge University Press.

Hirschman, Albert O. (1970). *Exit, Voice, and Loyalty: Responses to Decline in Firms, Organizations, and States.* Cambridge, MA: Harvard University Press.

Hobsbawm, Eric (1973). *The Age of Revolution, 1789–1848.* London: Cardinal.

(1975). *The Age of Capital, 1848–1875.* London: Weidenfeld and Nicolson.

(1987). *The Age of Empire, 1875–1914.* London: Weidenfeld and Nicolson.

(1994). *The Age of Extremes: The Short Twentieth Century, 1914–1991.* London: Viking Penguin.

Holmes, Michael, and Simon Lightfoot (2011). Limited Influence? The Role of the Party of European Socialists in Shaping Social Democracy in Central and Eastern Europe. *Government and Opposition* 46: 32–55.

Hooghe, Liesbet, and Gary Marks (2001). *Multi-level Governance and European Integration.* Lanham, MD: Rowman and Littlefield.

(2008). A Postfunctional Theory of European Integration: From Permissive Consensus to Constraining Dissensus. *British Journal of Political Science* 39: 1–23.

Hooghe, Liesbet, Marks, Gary, and Carole J. Wilson (2002). Does Left/Right Structure Party Positions on European Integration? *Comparative Political Studies* 35: 965–89.

Horowitz, Donald L. (1985). *Ethnic Groups in Conflict.* Berkeley: University of California Press.

Huber, John, and Ronald Inglehart (1995). Expert Interpretations of Party Space and Party Locations in 41 Societies. *Party Politics* 1: 73–111.

Hug, Simon, and Tobias Schulz (2007). Left–Right Positions of Political Parties in Switzerland. *Party Politics* 13: 305–30.

Huntington, Samuel P. (1991). *The Third Wave: Democratization in the Late Twentieth Century.* Norman: University of Oklahoma Press.

(1996). *The Clash of Civilizations and the Remaking of World Order.* New York: Simon & Schuster.

Ignazi, Piero (2003). *Extreme Right Parties in Western Europe.* Oxford: Oxford University Press.

Inglehart, Ronald (1977). *The Silent Revolution: Changing Values and Political Styles among Western Publics.* Princeton, NJ: Princeton University Press.

(1990). *Culture Shift in Advanced Industrial Society*: Princeton, NJ: Princeton University Press.

Inglehart, Ronald, and Christian Welzel (2005). *Modernization, Cultural Change and Democracy: The Human Development Sequence.* Cambridge: Cambridge University Press.

Irving, Ronald E. M. (1979). *The Christian Democratic Parties in Western Europe.* London: Allen & Unwin.

Ishiyama, John T. (2002). Regionalism and the Nationalization of the Legislative Vote in Post-Communist Russian Politics. *Communist and Post-Communist Studies* 35: 155–68.

Jachtenfuchs, Markus, Diez, Thomas, and Sabine Jung (1998). Which Europe? Conflicting Models of a Legitimate European Order. *European Journal of International Relations* 4: 409–45.

Jackson, Robert H., and Georg Sørensen (2007). *Introduction to International Relations: Theories and Approaches* (third edition). Oxford: Oxford University Press.

Jérôme, Bruno, Jérôme, Véronique, and Michael Lewis-Beck (2006). Partisan Dynamics and the European "Nation". Paper presented at the Midwest Political Science Association, Chicago.

Joffé, George H. (2001). The EU and the Mediterranean. In Telò, Mario (ed.), *European Union and New Regionalism*. Aldershot: Ashgate (pp. 207–25).

Johnsson, Karl M., and Peter Zervakis (eds.) (2002). *European Political Parties between Cooperation and Integration*. Baden-Baden: Nomos.

Jones, Mark P., and Scott Mainwaring (2003). The Nationalization of Parties and Party Systems. *Party Politics* 9: 139–66.

Kalyvas, Stathis N. (1996). *The Rise of Christian Democracy in Europe*. Ithaca, NY: Cornell University Press.

Karvonen, Lauri, and Stein Kuhnle (2000). *Party Systems and Voter Alignments Revisited*. London: Routledge.

Kasuya, Yuko, and Johannes Moenius (2008). The Nationalization of Party Systems: Conceptual Issues and Alternative District-Focused Measures. *Electoral Studies* 27: 126–35.

Katz, Richard S. (1973). The Attribution of Variance in Electoral Returns: An Alternative Measurement Technique. *American Political Science Review* 67: 817–28.

Katz, Richard S., and Peter Mair (eds.) (1992). *Party Organizations: A Data Handbook on Party Organizations in Western Democracies, 1960–90*. Newbury Park, CA: Sage.

(eds.) (1994). *How Parties Organize: Change and Adaptation in Party Organizations in Western Democracies*. Thousand Oaks, CA: Sage.

Kawato, Sadafumi (1987). Nationalization and Partisan Realignment in Congressional Elections. *American Political Science Review* 81: 1235–50.

Keating, Michael (1988). *State and Regional Nationalism: Territorial Politics and the European State*. New York: Harvester Wheatsheaf.

(1998). *The New Regionalism in Western Europe: Territorial Restructuring and Political Change*. Cheltenham: Edward Elgar.

(ed.) (2004). *Regions and Regionalism in Europe*. Cheltenham: Edward Elgar.

Keating, Michael, and John Loughlin (eds.) (1997). *The Political Economy of Regionalism*. London: Frank Cass.

Kirchner, Emil J. (ed.) (1988). *Liberal Parties in Western Europe*. Cambridge: Cambridge University Press.

Kitschelt, Herbert (1994). *The Transformation of European Social Democracy*. Cambridge: Cambridge University Press.

(1995). *The Radical Right in Western Europe: A Comparative Analysis*. Ann Arbor: University of Michigan Press.

Klausen, Jytte, and Louise A. Tilly (eds.) (1997). *European Integration in Social and Historical Perspective, 1850 to the Present*. Lanham, MD: Rowman and Littlefield.

Klingemann, Hans-Dieter, Mochmann, Ekkehard, and Kenneth Newton (eds.) (2000). *Elections in Central and Eastern Europe: The First Wave*. Berlin: Sigma.

Klingemann, Hans-Dieter, Volkens, Andrea, Bara, Judith, Budge, Ian, and Michael McDonald (2006). *Mapping Policy Preferences II: Estimates for Parties, Electors, and Governments in Eastern Europe, European Union and OECD, 1990–2003*. Oxford: Oxford University Press (supplemented with CD-ROM).

Knill, Christoph (2001). *The Europeanization of National Administrations: Patterns of Institutional Change and Persistence.* Cambridge: Cambridge University Press.

(ed.) (2005). Cross-National Policy Convergence: Causes, Concepts, and Empirical Findings. *Journal of European Public Policy* 12(5): special issue.

Knill, Christoph, and Andrea Lenschow (2005). Compliance, Competition and Communication: Different Approaches of European Governance and Their Impact on National Institutions. *Journal of Common Market Studies* 43: 583–604.

Knutsen, Oddbjørn (1995). Value Orientations, Political Conflicts and Left–Right Identification: A Comparative Study. *European Journal of Political Research* 28: 63–93.

(1998). Expert Judgements of the Left–Right Location of Political Parties: A Comparative Longitudinal Study. *West European Politics* 21: 63–94.

Kohler-Koch, Beate (1998). La Renaissance de la Dimension Territoriale en Europe. Florence: EUI Working Paper (Robert Schuman Centre, no. 98/38).

Kommisrud, Arne (2009). *Historical Sociology: A Rokkanian Approach to Eastern European Development.* Lanham, MD: Lexington Books.

Koopmans, Ruud (1992). *Democracy from Below: New Social Movements and the Political System in West Germany.* Boulder, CO: Westview.

Kreppel, Amie (2002). *The European Parliament and Supranational Party System: A Study in Institutional Development.* Cambridge: Cambridge University Press.

Kreuzer, Markus (2010). Historical Knowledge and Quantitative Analysis: The Case of the Origins of Proportional Representation. *American Political Science Review* 104: 369–92.

Kriesi, Hanspeter, Grande, Edgar, Dolezal, Martin, Helbling, Marc, Höglinger, Dominic, Hutter, Swen and Bruno Wüest (2012). *Political Conflict in Western Europe.* Cambridge: Cambridge University Press.

Kriesi, Hanspeter, Grande, Edgar, Lachat, Romain, Dolezal, Martin, Bornschier, Simon, and Timotheos Frey (2006). Globalization and the Transformation of the National Political Space: Six European Countries Compared. *European Journal of Political Research* 45: 921–95.

(2008). *West European Politics in the Age of Globalization.* Cambridge: Cambridge University Press.

Kuechler, Manfred (1991). Issues and Voting in the European Elections 1989. *European Journal of Political Research* 19: 81–104.

Kuhnle, Stein (1975). *Patterns of Social and Political Mobilization: A Historical Analysis of the Nordic Countries.* London: Sage.

Kumar, Krishan (2003). The Idea of Europe: Cultural Legacies, Transnational Imaginings, and the Nation-State. In Berezin, Mabel, and Martin Schain (eds.), *Europe without Borders: Remapping Territory, Citizenship, and Identity in a Transnational Age.* Baltimore, MA: Johns Hopkins University Press (pp. 33–50).

Kurzman, Charles (1998). Waves of Democratization. *Studies in Comparative International Development* 33(1): 42–64.

Laasko, Markku, and Rein Taagepera (1979). Effective Number of Parties: A Measure with Application to West Europe. *Comparative Political Studies* 12: 3–27.

Ladrech, Robert (1993). Social Democratic Parties and the EC integration. *European Journal of Political Research.* 24: 195–210.

(2002). The Europeanization of Political Parties: Towards a Framework of Analysis. *Party Politics* 8: 389–403.

(2008). Europeanization and the Variable Influence of the EU: National Parties and Party Systems in Western and Eastern Europe. *Journal of Southern Europe and the Balkans* 10: 139–50.

(2009). Europeanization and Political Parties. *Living Reviews in European Governance* 4: 1–21.

Lago-Peñas, Ignacio, and Santiago Lago-Peñas (2009). Does the Nationalization of Party Systems Affect the Composition of Public Spending? *Economics and Governance* 10: 85–98.

(2011). Decentralization and the Nationalization of Party Systems. *Environment and Planning C: Government and Policy* 29: 244–63.

Landes, David S. (1998). *The Wealth and Poverty of Nations: Why Are Some so Rich and Some so Poor*. New York: Norton.

LaPalombara, Joseph, and Myron Weiner (eds.) (1966). *Political Parties and Political Development*. Princeton, NJ: Princeton University Press.

Lavenex, Sandra (2004). EU External Governance in Wider Europe. *Journal of European Public Policy* 11: 680–700.

Laver, Michael, and Ben W. Hunt (1992). *Policy and Party Competition*. New York: Routledge.

Laver, Michael, and Kenneth A. Schepsle (1990). Coalitions and Cabinet Government. *American Political Science Review* 84: 873–90.

(eds.) (1994). *Cabinet Ministers and Parliamentary Government*. Cambridge: Cambridge University Press.

(1996). *Making and Breaking Governments: Cabinets and Legislatures in Parliamentary Democracies*. Cambridge: Cambridge University Press.

Laver, Michael, and Norman Schofield (1990). *Multiparty Government*. Oxford: Oxford University Press.

Lee, Adrian (1988). The Persistence of Difference: Electoral Change in Cornwall. Paper presented at the Political Studies Association, Plymouth.

Lehmbruch, Gehrhart (1967). *Proporzdemokratie*. Tübingen: Mohr.

Leitner, Christian (1997). Electoral Nationalisation, Dealignment and Realignment: Australia and the U.S., 1900–88. *Australian Journal of Political Science* 32: 205–22.

Lewis, Paul G. (ed.) (1996). *Party Structure and Organization in East-Central Europe*. Cheltenham: Elgar.

Lewis-Beck, Michael S., and Martin Paldam (2000). Economic Voting: An Introduction. *Electoral Studies* 19: 113–21.

Lewis-Beck, Michael S., and Mary Stegmeier (2007). Economic Models of Voting. In Dalton, Russell J., and Hans-Dieter Klingemann (eds.), *The Oxford Handbook of Political Behaviour*. Oxford: Oxford University Press (pp. 518–37).

Lijphart, Arend (1968). *The Politics of Accommodation: Pluralism and Democracy in the Netherlands*. Berkeley: University of California Press.

(1984). *Democracies: Patterns of Majoritarian and Consensus Government in Twenty-One Countries*. New Haven, CT: Yale University Press.

Linz, Juan J. (1976). Patterns of Land Tenure, Division of Labor, and Voting Behavior in Europe. *Comparative Politics* 8: 365–430.

Linz, Juan J., and Alfred Stepan (eds.) (1978). *The Breakdown of Democratic Regimes.* Baltimore, MA: Johns Hopkins University Press.

Lipset, Seymour M., and Stein Rokkan (1967). Cleavage Structures, Party Systems, and Voter Alignments: An Introduction. In Lipset, Seymour M., and Stein Rokkan (eds.), *Party Systems and Voter Alignments: Cross-National Perspectives.* New York: Free Press (pp. 1–64).

Lodge, Juliet (1975). Britain and the EEC: Exit, Voice or Loyalty. *Cooperation and Conflict* 10: 199–216.

(1986). *Direct Elections to the European Parliament 1984.* London: Macmillan.

(1990). *The 1989 Election of the European Parliament.* New York: St. Martin's Press.

(2001). *The 1999 Elections to the European Parliament.* Basingstoke: Palgrave.

Lorwin, Val (1966). Belgium: Religion, Class, and Language in National Politics. In Dahl, Robert A. (ed.), *Political Oppositions in Western Democracies.* New Haven, CT: Yale University Press (pp. 147–87).

Lowe, Will, Benoit, Kenneth, Mikhaylov, Slava, and Michael Laver (2011). Scaling Policy Positions from Coded Units of Political Texts. *Legislative Studies Quarterly* 26: 123–55.

Luebbert, Gregory M. (1991). *Liberalism, Fascism, or Social Democracy: Social Classes and the Political Origins of Regimes in Interwar Europe.* Oxford: Oxford University Press.

Lyons, Pat, and Lukáš Linek (2010). Party System Nationalisation and Non-Uniform Vote Switching: Evidence from the Czech Republic. *Czech Sociological Review* 46: 375–99.

Mackie, Thomas T. (ed.) (1990). *Europe Votes 3: European Parliamentary Election Results 1989.* Aldershot: Darbouth.

Mackie, Thomas T., and Frederick W. S. Craig (eds.) (1985). *Europe Votes 2: European Parliamentary Election Results 1979–84.* Chichester: Parliamentary Research Services.

Mahoney, James, and Richard Snyder (1999). Rethinking Agency and Structure in the Study of Regime Change. *Studies in Comparative International Development* 2: 3–32.

Mair, Peter (1996). Party Systems and Structures of Competition. In LeDuc, Lawrence, Niemi, Richard G., and Pippa Norris (eds.), *Comparing Democracies: Elections and Voting in Global Perspective.* London: Sage (pp. 83–106).

(2000). The Limited Impact of Europe on National Party Systems. *West European Politics* 23: 27–51.

(2007a). Party Systems and Alternation in Government, 1950–2000: Innovation and Institutionalization. In Gloppen, Siri, and Lise Rakner (eds.), *Globalisation and Democratisation: Challenges for Political Parties.* Bergen: Fagbokforlaget (pp. 135–54).

(2007b). Left–Right Orientations. In Dalton, Russell J., and Hans-Dieter Klingemann (eds.), *The Oxford Handbook of Political Behaviour.* Oxford: Oxford University Press (pp. 206–22).

Mair, Peter, and Cas Mudde (1998). The Party Family and Its Study. *Annual Review of Political Science* 1: 211–29.

Mair, Peter, and Jan Zielonka (eds.) (2002). *The Enlarged European Union: Diversity and Adaptation.* London: Frank Cass.

Majone, Giandomenico (ed.) (1996). *Regulating Europe*. London: Routledge.

Manin, Bernard (1997). *The Principles of Representative Government*. Cambridge: Cambridge University Press.

Mann, Michael (1993). *The Sources of Social Power* (two volumes). Cambridge: Cambridge University Press.

Mansbridge, Jane (2003). Rethinking Representation. *American Political Science Review* 97: 515–28.

March, James G., and Johan P. Olsen (1989). *Rediscovering Institutions: The Organizational Basis of Politics*. New York: Free Press.

Marks, Gary (1997). A Third Lens: Comparing European Integration and State Building. In Klausen, Jytte, and Louise A. Tilly (eds.), *European Integration in Social and Historical Perspective, 1850 to the Present*. Lanham, MD: Rowman and Littlefield (pp. 23–43).

(2007). Introduction: Triangulation and the Square-Root Law. *Electoral Studies* 26(1): 1–10.

Marks, Gary, Hooghe, Liesbet, Nelson, Moira, and Erica Edwards (2006). Party Competition and European Integration in East and West: Different Structure, Same Causality. *Comparative Political Studies* 39: 155–75.

Marks, Gary, and Marco R. Steenbergen (2002). Understanding Political Contestation in the European Union. *Comparative Political Studies* 35: 879–92.

Marks, Gary, and Carole J. Wilson (2000). The Past in the Present: A Cleavage Theory of Party Responses to European Integration. *British Journal of Political Science* 30: 433–59.

Marks, Gary, Wilson, Carole J., and Leonard Ray (2002). National Political Parties and European Integration. *American Journal of Political Science* 46: 585–94.

Marquand, David (1978). Toward a Europe of the Parties. *Political Quarterly* 49: 425–45.

Marsh, Michael (1998). Testing the Second-Order Election Theory after Four European Elections. *British Journal of Political Science* 28: 591–607.

Marsh, Michael, and Mark N. Franklin (1996). The Foundations: Unanswered Questions from the Study of European Elections, 1979–94. In Van der Eijk, Cees, and Mark N. Franklin, et al., *Choosing Europe? The European Electorate and National Politics in the Face of Union*. Ann Arbor: University of Michigan Press (pp. 11–32).

Marshall, Thomas H. (1964). *Class, Citizenship, and Social Development (with the 1950 essay Citizenship and Social Class)*. Garden City, NY: Doubleday.

McNeill, William H. (1963). *The Rise of the West: A History of the Human Community*. Chicago, IL: University of Chicago Press.

Mény, Yves, and Yves Surel (eds.) (2002). *Democracies and the Populist Challenge*. Basingstoke: Palgrave.

Michels, Robert (1962 [1911]). *Political Parties: A Sociological Study of the Oligarchical Tendencies of Modern Democracies*. New York: Free Press.

Mikhaylov, Slava, Laver, Michael, and Kenneth Benoit (2008). Coder Reliability and Misclassification in Comparative Manifesto Project Codings. Paper presented at the Midwest Political Science Association, Chicago.

Milward, Alan S. (1992). *The European Rescue of the Nation-State*. London: Routledge.

Mitchell, Brian R. (2007). *International Historical Statistics: Europe 1750–2005* (sixth edition). Basingstoke: Palgrave.

Moenius, Johannes, and Yuko Kasuya (2004). Measuring Linkage across Districts: Some Party System Inflation Indices and Their Properties. *Party Politics* 10: 543–64.

Moore, Barrington Jr. (1966). *Social Origins of Dictatorship and Democracy: Lord and Peasant in the Making of the Modern World.* Boston, MA: Beacon Press.

Moravcsik, Andrew (1998). *The Choice for Europe: Social Purpose and State Power from Messina to Maastricht.* Ithaca, NY: Cornell University Press.

Morgan, Edmund S. (1988). *Inventing the People: The Rise of Popular Sovereignty in England and America.* New York: Norton.

Morgenstern, Scott, and Richard F. Potthoff (2005). The Components of Elections: District Heterogeneity, District-Time Effects, and Volatility. *Electoral Studies* 24: 17–40.

Morgenstern, Scott, and Stephen M. Swindle (2005). Are Politics Local? An Analysis of Voting Patterns in 23 Democracies. *Comparative Political Studies* 38: 143–70.

Morgenstern, Scott, Swindle, Stephen M., and Andrea Castagnola (2009). Party Nationalization and Institutions. *The Journal of Politics* 71: 1322–41.

Morris, Ian (2010). *Why the West Rules – for Now: The Patterns of History and What They Reveal about the Future.* New York: Norton.

Mudde, Cas (2004). The Populist Zeitgeist. *Government and Opposition* 39: 542–63.

Müller, Wolfgang C., and Kaare Strøm (eds.) (2000). *Coalition Governments in Western Europe.* Oxford: Oxford University Press.

Müller-Rommel, Ferdinand (ed.) (1989). *New Politics in Western Europe: The Rise and Success of Green Parties and Alternative Lists.* Boulder, CO: Westview.

Neumann, Sigmund (ed.) (1956). *Modern Political Parties.* Chicago, IL: University of Chicago Press.

Niemi, Richard G., and Herbert F. Weisberg (eds.) (1993). *Controversies in Voting Behavior* (third edition). Washington, DC: Congressional Quarterly Press.

Nikolenyi, Csaba (2009). Party Inflation in India: Why Has a Multiparty Format Prevailed in the National Party System. In Grofman, Bernard, Blais, André, and Shaun Bowler (eds.), *Duverger's Law of Plurality Voting: The Logic of Party Competition in Canada, India, the United Kingdom and the United States.* New York: Springer (pp. 97–114).

Noël, Alain, and Jean-Philippe Thérien (2008). *Left and Right in Global Politics.* Cambridge: Cambridge University Press.

Nohlen, Dieter, and Philip Stöver (eds.) (2010). *Elections in Europe: A Data Handbook.* Baden-Baden: Nomos.

Olsen, Johan (2007). *Europe in Search of Political Order.* Oxford: Oxford University Press.

Ostrogorski, Moisei Y. (1902). *Democracy and the Organization of Political Parties* (two volumes). London: Macmillan.

Palmer, Robert R. (1959). *The Age of Democratic Revolution.* Princeton, NJ: Princeton University Press.

Panebianco, Angelo (1988). *Political Parties: Organization and Power.* Cambridge: Cambridge University Press.

Paterson, William E., and James Sloam (2005). Learning from the West: Policy Transfer and Political Parties. *Journal of Communist Studies and Transition Politics* 21: 33–47.

Pedersen, Morgens N. (1979). The Dynamics of European Party Systems: Changing Patterns of Electoral Volatility. *European Journal of Political Research* 7: 7–26.

(1996). Euro-parties and European Parties: New Arenas, New Challenges and New Strategies. In Andersen, Svein S., and Kjell A. Eliassen (eds.), *The European Union: How Democratic Is It?* London: Sage (pp. 15–40).

Pennings, P. (2006). An Empirical Analysis of the Europeanization of National Party Manifestos, 1960–2003. *European Union Politics* 7: 257–70.

Perrineau, Pascal, and Colette Ysmal (eds.) (1995). *Le Vote des Douze: Les Elections Européennes de Juin 1994*. Paris: Presses de la Fondation Nationale des Sciences Politiques.

Pierce, Roy (1999). Mass–Elite Linkages and the Responsible Party Model of Representation. In Miller, Warren E., et al., *Policy Representation in Western Democracies*. Oxford: Oxford University Press (pp. 9–32).

Pierson, Paul (1994). *Dismantling the Welfare State?* Cambridge: Cambridge University Press.

Pitkin, Hanna F. (1967). *The Concept of Representation*. Berkeley: University of California Press.

Poggi, Gianfranco (1990). *The State: Its Nature, Development, and Prospects*. Cambridge: Polity.

Poguntke, Thomas, Aylott, Nicholas, Carter, Elisabeth, Ladrech, Robert, and Kurt R. Luther (2007). *The Europeanization of National Political Parties: Power and Organizational Adaptation*. London: Routledge.

Pollack, Mark A. (2003). *The Engines of European Integration: Delegation, Agency, and Agenda Setting in the European Union*. Oxford: Oxford University Press.

Pomeranz, Kenneth (2000). *The Great Divergence: China, Europe, and the Making of the Modern World Economy*. Princeton, NJ: Princeton University Press.

Powell, G. Bingham Jr. (2000). *Elections as Instruments of Democracy: Majoritarian and Proportional Visions*. New Haven, CT: Yale University Press.

(2009). The Ideological Congruence Controversy: The Impact of Alternative Measures, Data, and Time Periods on the Effects of Election Rules. *Comparative Political Studies* 42: 1475–97.

Powell, G. Bingham Jr., and Guy Whitten (1993). Cross-National Analysis of Economic Voting: Taking Account of the Political Context. *American Journal of Political Science* 37: 391–414.

Pridham, Geffrey (1996). Transnational Party Links and Transition to Democracy: Eastern Europe in Comparative Perspective. In Lewis, Paul G. (ed.), *Party Structure and Organization in East-Central Europe*. Cheltenham: Elgar (pp. 187–219).

Przeworski, Adam, and John D. Sprague (1986). *Paper Stones: A History of Electoral Socialism*. Chicago, IL: University of Chicago Press.

Przeworski, Adam, Stokes, Susan C., and Bernard Manin (eds.) (1999), *Democracy, Accountability, and Representation*. Cambridge: Cambridge University Press.

Putnam, Robert D. (1971). Studying Elite Political Culture: The Case of "Ideology". *American Political Science Review* 65: 651–81.

Radaelli, Claudio (2000). Whither Europeanization? Concept Stretching and Substantive Change. *European Integration Online Papers* 4 (no. 8): online article.

Rae, Douglas W. (1971). *The Political Consequences of Electoral Laws* (second edition). New Haven, CT: Yale University Press.

Ragin, Charles C. (1987). *The Comparative Method: Moving Beyond Qualitative and Quantitative Strategies*. Berkeley: University of California Press.

Rallings, Colin, and Michael Thrasher (2007). *British Electoral Facts, 1832–2006*. Aldershot: Ashgate.

Raunio, Tapio (2002). Political Interests: The EP's Party Groups. In Peterson, John, and Michael Shackleton (eds.), *The Institutions of the European Union*. Oxford: Oxford University Press (pp. 257–76).

Ray, Leonard (1999). Measuring Party Orientations Towards European Integration: Results from an Expert Survey. *European Journal of Political Research* 36: 283–306.

Reif, Karlheinz (1985a). National Electoral Cycles and European Elections 1979 and 1984. *Electoral Studies* 3: 244–55.

(1985b). Ten Second-Order National Elections. In Reif, Karlheinz (ed.), *Ten European Elections*. Aldershot: Gower (pp. 1–36).

(1997). European Elections as Member State Second-Order Elections Revisited. *European Journal of Political Research* 31: 115–24.

Reif, Karlheinz, and Hermann Schmitt (1980). Nine Second-Order National Elections: A Conceptual Framework for the Analysis of European Election Results. *European Journal of Political Research* 8: 3–44.

Rihoux, Benoît, and Charles C. Ragin (eds.) (2009). *Configurational Comparative Methods: Qualitative Comparative Analysis (QCA) and Related Techniques*. London: Sage.

Rogowski, Ronald (1989). *Commerce and Coalitions: How Trade Affects Domestic Political Alignments*. Princeton, NJ: Princeton University Press.

Rokkan, Stein (1966). Norway: Numerical Democracy and Corporate Pluralism. In Dahl, Robert A. (ed.), *Political Oppositions in Western Democracies*. New Haven, CT: Yale University Press (pp. 70–115).

(1970). *Citizens, Elections, Parties: Approaches to the Comparative Study of the Processes of Development*. Oslo: Universitetsforlaget.

(1974a). Politics between Economy and Culture: An International Seminar on Albert O. Hirschman's Exit, Voice, and Loyalty. *Social Science Information* 13: 27–38.

(1974b). Entries, Voices, Exits: Towards a Possible Generalization of the Hirschman Model. *Social Science Information* 13: 39–53.

(1999). *State Formation, Nation-Building, and Mass Politics in Europe: The Theory of Stein Rokkan*. Oxford: Oxford University Press (edited by Peter Flora with Kuhnle, Stein, and Derek W. Urwin).

Rokkan, Stein, and Jean Meyriat (eds.) (1969). *International Guide to Electoral Statistics. Volume 1: National Elections in Western Europe*. The Hague and Paris: Mouton.

Rose, Richard (1993). *Lesson-Drawing in Public Policy: A Guide to Learning across Time and Space*. Chatham, NJ: Chatham House.

Rose, Richard, and Derek W. Urwin (1975). *Regional Differentiation and Political Unity in Western Nations*. London and Beverly Hills, CA: Sage Professional Papers in Contemporary Political Sociology (no. 06-007).

Russett, Bruce M. (1964). Inequality and Instability: The Relation of Land Tenure to Politics. *World Politics* 16: 442–54.

Sartori, Giovanni (1976). *Parties and Party Systems: A Framework for Analysis*. Cambridge: Cambridge University Press.

(1982). *Teoria dei Partiti e Caso Italiano*. Milan: SugarCo.

(1986). The Influence of Electoral Systems: Faulty Laws or Faulty Methods? In Grofman, Bernard, and Arend Lijphart (eds.), *Electoral Laws and Their Political Consequences*. New York: Agathon Press (pp. 43–68).

Schakel, Arjan H. (2013). Congruence between Regional and National Elections. *Comparative Political Studies* 46: 631–62.

Scharpf, Fritz W. (1999). *Governing in Europe: Effective and Democratic?* Oxford: Oxford University Press.

Schattschneider, Elmer E. (1960). *The Semisovereign People: A Realist's View of Democracy in America*. New York: Holt, Rinehart, and Winston.

Schimmelfennig, Frank (2005). The EU: Promoting Liberal Democracy through Membership Conditionality. In Flockhart, Trine (ed.), *Socializing Democratic Norms: The Role of International Organizations for the Construction of Europe*. Basingstoke: Palgrave (pp. 106–26).

(2007). Europeanization beyond Europe. *Living Reviews in European Governance* 2: online article.

Schimmelfennig, Frank, and Ulrich Sedelmeier (2004). Governance by Conditionality: EU Rule Transfer to the Candidate Countries of Central and Eastern Europe. *Journal of European Public Policy* 11: 661–79.

(eds.) (2005). *The Europeanization of Central and Eastern Europe*. Ithaca, NY: Cornell University Press.

Schmitt, Hermann (1990). Party Attachment and Party Choice in the European Elections of June 1989: A Cross-National Comparative Analysis of the Post Electoral Survey of the European Voters Study 1989. *International Journal of Public Opinion Research* 2: 169–84.

Schmitt, Hermann, and Jacques J. A. Thomassen (2000). Dynamic Representation: The Case of European Integration. *European Union Politics* 1: 318–39.

Schmitter, Philippe (2000). *How to Democratize the European Union ... and Why Bother?* Lanham, MD: Rowman and Littlefield.

Schneider, Carsten, and Claudius Wagemann (2012). *Set-Theoretic Methods for the Social Sciences: A Guide to Qualitative Comparative Analysis (QCA)*. Cambridge: Cambridge University Press.

Schumpeter, Joseph A. (1962). *Capitalism, Socialism and Democracy*. New York: Harper & Row.

Sciarini, Pascal, Fischer Alex, and Sarah Nicolet (2004). How Europe Hits Home: Evidence from the Swiss Case. *Journal of European Public Policy* 11: 353–78.

Sigelman, Lee, and Sing N. Yough (1978). Left–Right Polarization in National Party Systems: A Cross-National Analysis. *Comparative Political Studies* 11: 355–79.

Simmons, Beth A., Dobbin, Frank, and Geoffrey Garrett (eds.) (2008). *The Global Diffusion of Markets and Democracy*. Cambridge: Cambridge University Press.

Skocpol, Theda (1979). *States and Social Revolutions: A Comparative Analysis of France, Russia, and China*. Cambridge: Cambridge University Press.

(1995). Why I Am an Historical Institutionalist. *Polity* 28: 103–6.

Sloam, James (2005a). West European Social Democracy as a Model for Transfer. *Journal of Communist Studies and Transition Politics* (special issue) 21: 67–83.

(2005b). *The European Policy of the German Social Democrats: Interpreting a Changing World*. Basingstoke: Palgrave.

Smith, Anthony D. (1986). *The Ethnic Origins of Nations*. Oxford: Blackwell.

Snow, David A., Soule, Sarah A., and Hanspeter Kriesi (eds.) (2004). *The Blackwell Companion to Social Movements*. Oxford: Blackwell.

Stasavage, Davis (2003). *Public Debt and the Birth of the Democratic State: France and Great Britain, 1688–1789*. Cambridge: Cambridge University Press.

Steenbergen, Marco R., and Gary Marks (2007). Evaluating Expert Judgments. *European Journal of Political Research* 46: 347–66.

Steiner, Jürg (1974). *Amicable Agreement versus Majority Rule: Conflict Resolution in Switzerland*. Chapel Hill: University of North Carolina Press.

Steinmo, Sven, Thelen, Kathleen, and Frank Longstreth (eds.) (1992). *Structuring Politics: Historical Institutionalism in Comparative Analysis*. Cambridge: Cambridge University Press.

Sternberger, Dolf, and Bernhard Vogel (eds.) in collaboration with Dieter Nohlen (1969). *Die Wahl der Parlamente und anderer Staatsorgane: Ein Handbuch* (two half-volumes). Volume 1: *Europa*. Berlin: Walter de Gruyter.

Stokes, Donald E. (1965). A Variance Components Model of Political Effects. In Claunch, John M. (ed.), *Mathematical Applications in Political Science*. Dallas, TX: The Arnold Foundation (pp. 61–85).

(1967). Parties and the Nationalization of Electoral Forces. In Chambers, William N., and Walter D. Burnham (eds.), *The American Party Systems: Stages of Political Development*. Oxford: Oxford University Press (pp. 182–202).

Stonecash, Jeffrey M., Brewer. Mark D., and Mack Mariani (2003). *Diverging Parties: Social Change, Realignment and Party Polarization*. Boulder, CO: Westview.

Strøm, Kaare (1990). *Minority Government and Majority Rule*. Cambridge: Cambridge University Press.

(2000). Delegation and Accountability in Parliamentary Democracies. *European Journal of Political Research* 37: 261–89.

Strøm, Kaare, Müller, Wolfgang C., and Torbjörn Bergman (eds.) (2007). *Cabinets and Coalition Bargaining: The Democratic Life Cycle in Western Europe*. Oxford: Oxford University Press.

Sundquist, James L. (1973). *Dynamics of the Party System: Alignment and Realignment of Political Parties in the United States*. Washington, DC: Brookings Institution.

Taggart, Paul (1998). A Touchstone of Dissent: Euroscepticism in Contemporary Western European Party Systems. *European Journal of Political Research* 33: 363–88.

Tarrow, Sidney (1994). *Power in Movement: Social Movements, Collective Action and Politics*. Cambridge: Cambridge University Press.

Taylor, Charles L., and David A. Jodice (1983). *World Handbook of Political and Social Indicators* (third edition). New Haven, CT: Yale University Press.

Taylor, Michael (1989). Structure, Culture, and Action in the Explanation of Social Change. *Politics and Society* 17: 115–62.

Thelen, Kathleen (1999). Historical Institutionalism in Comparative Politics. *Annual Review of Political Science* 2: 369–404.

Thiem, Alrik, and Adrian Duşa (2013). *Qualitative Comparative Analysis with R: A User's Guide*. New York: Springer.

Thiem, Alrik, and Adrian Duşa (2014). *A Package for Qualitative Comparative Analysis*. R Package Version 1.1-3, 2014.

Thomas, John C. (2006). The Changing Nature of Partisan Divisions in the West: Trends in Democratic Policy Orientations in Ten Party Systems. *European Journal of Political Research*: 397–413.

Thomassen, Jacques J. A., Noury, Abdul G., and Erik Voeten (2004). Political Competition in the European Parliament: Evidence from Roll Call and Survey Analyses. In Marks, Gary, and Marco R. Steenbergen (eds.), *European Integration and Political Conflict*. Cambridge: Cambridge University Press (pp. 141–64).

Thomassen, Jacques J. A., and Hermann Schmitt (1997). Policy Representation. *European Journal of Political Research* 32: 165–84.

Tilly, Charles (ed.) (1975). *The Formation of National States in Western Europe*. Princeton, NJ: Princeton University Press.

(1990). *Coercion, Capital, and European States, AD 990–1990*. Oxford: Blackwell.

Todorov, Antony (2010). Bulgaria. In Nohlen, Dieter, and Philip Stöver (eds.), *Elections in Europe: A Data Handbook*. Baden-Baden: Nomos (pp. 351–98).

Urwin, Derek W. (1980). *From Ploughshare to Ballotbox: The Politics of Agrarian Defence in Europe*. Oslo: Universitetsforlaget.

(1982). Germany: From Geopolitical Expression to Regional Accommodation. In Rokkan, Stein, and Derek W. Urwin (eds.), *The Politics of Territorial Identity: Studies in European Regionalism*. London: Sage (pp. 165–250).

Van der Eijk, Cees, and Mark N. Franklin (1991). European Community Politics and Electoral Representation: Evidence from the 1989 European Elections Study. *European Journal of Political Research* 19: 105–28.

(2004). Potential for Contestation on European Matters at National Elections in Europe. In Marks, Gary, and Marco R. Steenbergen (eds.), *European Integration and Political Conflict*. Cambridge: Cambridge University Press (pp. 32–50).

Van der Eijk, Cees, and Mark N. Franklin, et al. (1996). *Choosing Europe? The European Electorate and National Politics in the Face of Union*. Ann Arbor: University of Michigan Press.

Van der Eijk, Cees, and Erik Oppenhuis (1990). Turnout and Second-Order Effect in the European Elections of June 1989: Evidence from the Netherlands. *Acta Politica* 25: 67–94.

Vanhanen, Tatu (2000). A New Dataset for Measuring Democracy, 1810–1998. *Journal of Peace Research* 37(2): 251–65.

Verz, Laura L., Frendreis, John P., and James L. Gibson (1987). Nationalization of the Electorate in the United States. *American Political Science Review* 81: 961–6.

Volkens, Andrea, and Hans-Dieter Klingemann (2002). Parties, Ideologies and Issues. Stability and Change in Fifteen European Party Systems 1945–1998. In Luther, Kurt, and Ferdinand Müller-Rommel (eds.), *Political Parties in the New Europe: Political and Analytical Challenges*. Oxford: Oxford University Press (pp. 143–67).

Wallerstein, Immanuel M. (1974). *The Modern World-System I: Capitalist Agriculture and the Origins of the European World-Economy in the Sixteenth Century*. New York: Academic Press.

(1980). *The Modern World-System II: Mercantilism and the Consolidation of the European World-Economy, 1600–1750*. New York: Academic Press.

(1989). *The Modern World-System III: The Second Era of Great Expansion of the Capitalist World-Economy, 1730s–1840s*. New York: Academic Press.

(2011). *The Modern World-System IV: Centrist Liberalism Triumphant, 1789–1914*. Berkeley: University of California Press.

Warkotsch, Alexander (2006). The European Union and Democracy Promotion in Bad Neighbourhoods: The Case of Central Asia. *European Foreign Affairs Review* 11: 509–25.

Weber, Max (1978). *Economy and Society: An Outline of Interpretative Sociology* (two volumes). Berkeley: University of California Press.

Weiler, Joseph H. H. (1999). *The Constitution of Europe: "Do the New Clothes Have an Emperor?" and Other Essays on European Integration*. Cambridge: Cambridge University Press.

Welzel, Christian (2013). *Freedom Rising: Human Empowerment and the Quest for Emancipation*. Cambridge: Cambridge University Press.

Wendt, Alexander E. (1987). The Agent–Structure Problem in International Relations Theory. *International Organization* 41: 335–70.

Weyland, Kurt (2014). *Making Waves: Democratic Contention in Europe and Latin America since the Revolutions of 1848*. Cambridge: Cambridge University Press.

Wilensky, Harold L. (2002). *Rich Democracies: Political Economy, Public Policy and Performance*. Berkeley: University of California Press.

Wimmel, Andreas, and Erica E. Edwards (2011). The Return of "Social Europe": Ideas and Positions of German Parties towards the Future of European Integration. *German Politics* 20: 293–314.

Wittenberg, Jason (2013). What do We Mean by Historical Legacy? *Qualitative and Multi-Method Research* 11: 7–9.

Youngs, Richard (2001). *The European Union and the Promotion of Democracy: Europe's Mediterranean and Asian Policies*. Oxford: Oxford University Press.

Zaborowski, Marcin (2005). Westernizing the East: External Influences in the Post-Communist Transformation of Eastern and Central Europe. *Journal of Communist Studies and Transition Politics* (special issue) 21: 16–32.

Zielonka, Jan (ed.) (2002). *Europe Unbound: Enlarging and Reshaping the Boundaries of the European Union*. London: Routledge.

Zürn, Michael (1998). *Regieren jenseits des Nationalstaats: Globalisierung und Denationalisierung als Chance*. Frankfurt: Suhrkamp.

(2001). Politische Fragmentierung als Folge der gesellschaftlichen Denationalisierung? In Loch, Dietmar, and Wilhelm Heitmeyer (eds.), *Schattenseiten der Globalisierung*. Frankfurt-am-Main: Suhrkamp (pp. 111–39).

Zürn, Michael, Beisheim, Marianne, Dreher, Sabine, and Gregor Walter (2000). Postnationale Politik? Über den politischen Umgang mit den Denationalisierungsherausforderungen Internet, Klimawandel und Migration. *Zeitschrift für Internationale Beziehungen* 7: 297–329.

Zürn, Michael, and Gregor Walter (eds.) (2005). *Globalizing Interests: Pressure Groups and Denationalization*. Albany: State University of New York Press.

Index